D0554088

CR-1574

Scenarios

Scenarios

The Art of
Strategic Conversation

2nd Edition

Kees van der Heijden

John Wiley & Sons, Ltd

Other Wiley Editorial Offices

John Wiley & Sons Inc., 111 River Street, Hoboken, NJ 07030, USA

Jossey-Bass, 989 Market Street, San Francisco, CA 94103-1741, USA

Wiley-VCH Verlag GmbH, Boschstr. 12, D-69469 Weinheim, Germany

John Wiley & Sons Australia Ltd, 33 Park Road, Milton, Queensland 4064, Australia

John Wiley & Sons (Asia) Pte Ltd, 2 Clementi Loop #02-01, Jin Xing Distripark, Singapore 129809

John Wiley & Sons Canada Ltd, 22 Worcester Road, Etobicoke, Ontario, Canada M9W 1L1

Wiley also publishes its books in a variety of electronic formats. Some content that appears in print may not be
available in electronic books.

Library of Congress Cataloging-in-Publication Data

Van der Heijden, Kees.
  Scenarios : the art of strategic conversation / Kees van der Heijden.—2nd ed.
    p. cm.
  Includes bibliographical references and index.
  ISBN 0-470-02368-6 (cloth)
  1. Communication in management.   2. Creative thinking.   3. Strategic planning.   I. Title.
  HD30.3.V36 2005
  658.4'52—dc22   2004018710

British Library Cataloguing in Publication Data

A catalogue record for this book is available from the British Library

ISBN 0-470–02368-6

Typeset in 11/12pt Bembo by Dobbie Typesetting Ltd, Tavistock, Devon
Printed and bound in Great Britain by TJ International Ltd, Padstow, Cornwall
This book is printed on acid-free paper responsibly manufactured from sustainable forestry
in which at least two trees are planted for each one used for paper production.

To Anta

Contents

Preface

A CONVERSATION

Between Peter Schwartz, chairman of Global Business Network (and probably the world's best-known scenario planner (Schwartz 1992)), and the author, about scenarios and the art of strategic conversation.

Peter: How did you come to combine scenarios with strategic conversation in the title of your book?

Kees: I wanted to project the power of scenarios as a process tool, in addition to how they are normally seen, as analytical devices. Scenario work always involves a conversational process among people involved. If the process works well the organisation achieves a higher level of strategic skill.

I think there are essentially three ways of looking at how strategy comes about: rationalist, evolutionary and processual. The rationalist assumes there is one truth out there, and the art of the strategist is to get as close to it as possible. First, you work it out in your mind, then when you are close enough to the optimal strategy you decide, and then you implement. Thinking is separate from action. That means the task can be delegated, e.g. to a planning department. You can ask them: "Go and analyse the situation, and come back with a report on how things hang together out there, and what in the light of that is the best line of action to take."

Peter: That approach is common enough. A popular paradigm apparently. And a lot of very good scenario analysis is being done from that perspective. This is where people try to increase their grip on the future by understanding better the pre-determined elements in the situation in which they find themselves.

Kees: Yes, it is the area in which Pierre Wack, the father of scenario-based planning, made his greatest contributions. He was of the opinion that if you looked long and hard enough you would always come to see the situation in a new light. He called this reperceiving. And reframing the situation and gaining a new unique insight is the ultimate source of success.

Peter: No organisation can be successful unless it has something unique to offer to the world. Really good strategy can only be based on being different from anybody else. If everybody follows the same strategy, however good it seemed at the time, it cannot be good for very long. This applies across the board, from the corner shop to the global/multi-national company. It seems so obvious, yet it is nowhere near enough in people's consciousness. Pierre's quest was for that unique insight that would provide the opportunity to create that distinctiveness.

Kees: Pierre recognised that this would always be difficult to do. Imagine that good strategy would be easy, then everyone would do it, and for that reason alone could not lead to success. We need to make the necessary resources available and we must take our time. Formal planning processes with deadlines and preformatted reports are the enemy of thinking.

Peter: Pierre could not be hurried. And he didn't want to work on more than one project at the time. He created the iterative scenario thinking process, in which scenario building alternates with deep thinking and research of the underlying systems that gradually emerge. And this has to continue until the moment of truth, when you suddenly discover: "I can see it now."

Kees: But there is another view, known as the evolutionary paradigm. This is epitomised by Henri Mintzberg's idea of emergent strategy. He argues that most strategy can only be defined in retrospect, as a pattern you recognise in what has already happened. There is not much you can do about it; your power over the future is actually quite small. Almost everything is uncertain and unexpected. The idea of controlling your destiny is an illusion. He talks about the "fall of strategic planning".

Peter: I have often been struck by how the majority of CEOs I have met are very modest in their beliefs about the degree of control they have over their situation.

Kees: Yes, rather different from how this is often portrayed in the media. However, in its extreme form most people find the evolutionary paradigm not intuitive. You cannot give up good thinking in organisations, it must pay out somewhere. This has given rise to the third paradigm, the processual one. This says that in a fast moving situation, where there is a lot of uncertainty, success is more related to having a good process than to having found the "optimal strategy". After all, when things are moving fast what looks optimal today may look like disaster tomorrow. Mental agility is what counts.

Peter: Yes I recognise that paradigm. Microsoft thought that putting all attention on W95 was the best strategy, and they set up MSN as an information provider. Meanwhile they overlooked the internet (for a time). Shell had carefully worked out that dumping the Brent Spar was the best strategy. Suddenly they were facing unexpectedly strong environmental resistance.

I think it is right to call these views on strategy paradigms. People are unconscious of their paradigm, and therefore unaware of the fact that others may work from a different one. I have seen things going wrong between planners and CEOs working from different paradigms without being aware of it.

Which paradigm do you subscribe too?

Kees: I think they are all three valid. I believe that the situation we look at in strategy is so complex that we can use all the help we can get. I suppose I start from process, but very soon I am aware that content enters the picture. Creating a successful organisation is not about improvisation! You can't ignore Pierre's view that there is no success without a unique insight. And all the time you take account of uncertainty and ambiguity that separates the strong from the weak. So all three perspectives are helpful and important. Each tells a part of the story. For example, start from the processual view. As soon as more than one person is involved in the organisation the process involves conversation. For action to occur mental models in the minds of the individuals need to be aligned. And they are coupled through the strategic conversation. The norm for organisational conversation is rationality. We try to argue our case to each other. So you have to rationalise things. My thesis is that, because of the strategic conversation, organisations are more rational than individuals as decision makers. One reason why they continue to exist and thrive.

Peter: Looked at in that way conversation becomes quite central in strategy, both in its process and its content aspects. It is at the heart of good process, and talking about strategy makes it a rational thing.

But the rationalist should not forget the incredibly important role of motivation and emotion in strategy. Being able to mobilise this can make or break a strategy project. You have got to know your organisational psychology. So I would like to view conversation in a wide sense, in the context of people's experiences and actions, on the basis of which they are motivated to engage in the conversation. So not only what they say, but also why they say it and why they don't say something else. Call it their learning loops if you like.

Kees: Yes, the conversation couples together the people with power-to-perceive, those with power-to-think and those with power-to-act. All three are necessary in a good strategic conversation. All three roles have an essential part to play.

Peter: The conversation is the common force through which they align their joint learning. If you then call strategy the pattern in their resulting actions you have closed the loop between the community, their conversation, their alignment, their motivation, their joint thinking and action, back to creating and reinforcing the community.

Why do you think this is of importance to the practitioner?

Kees: I believe that processes can be influenced, even managed to some extent. The strategy process has a formal part, designed by the managers, and an informal part, which consists of the casual spontaneously emerging conversation about the future. The latter is extremely important because it determines where people's attention is focused. Managers cannot control the latter, but they can intervene. The issue here is to find the high leverage points.

Peter: Yes, an imbalance between formal and informal processes can lead to serious problems. I once worked with an energy company where things were too hierarchical and formal. So, when their situation changed in a fundamental way, a new CEO announced that there would be no more top-down strategy. He was going to facilitate the bottom-up generation of ideas. On the other hand we have done work for a construction company, where things were so informal that people talk only about operational issues, without any focus at all on the longer term. A degree of formality is probably required in all organisations, even the fast moving. I have seen examples of companies that have gone too far leaving things to informal conversational processes. They find that they have become very short term and are not any longer focusing enough on the strategic horizon and creating the potential for the future. Such companies have to reinforce the formal system, simply to put strategy back on to the agenda.

Kees: I think there is a link with the rate of change. Fast-moving organisations, or organisations that go through a patch of white water in their business environment, will find that too formal arrangements make the system rigid and not adaptable enough. You find that in companies working in the new technology areas. On the other hand in slow-moving periods there is time to install a proper formal system of strategy. But we should not forget that simultaneously there is always the informal conversation. In fast-moving times this will become relatively more important. In such companies you will need a culture of open communications and success in management will depend more on facilitation than command and control.

Peter: In such cases you require particularly strong processual skills in the planner. First, the planner needs to work on understanding the mind of management. Remember, the object of the exercise must be not just to come up with clever ideas, but also to change the mental models of the management. Second, he needs to be prepared to open channels and create the conversation while subordinating his own opinion to the views emerging from the conversation. We sometimes speak of the "altruistic planner". Third, the process must be ahead of the game. Quite a challenge.

Kees: Yes, companies need to find an optimum here. It is the dilemma that every organisation faces, working simultaneously towards integration and differentiation. Too much differentiation and the organisation fragments, there is no longer any strategic conversation, formal or informal, everyone follows their own agenda, puts up the political barriers and goes their own way. Such organisations stop functioning. Political parties go through periods when internal conflict makes them completely dysfunctional. Voters don't like parties that do not have a clearly defined platform. On the other hand too much integration and you move into the pathology described as "groupthink", with its danger of impoverishment of mental models, leading to poor perception and failure to see early signals. IBM in the late 1980s is the classical example. You have to stay away from these two extremes, and this requires constant attention and active management of the group process.

Peter: Indeed, so we see management trying to intervene, for example by bringing in "new blood" to move away from groupthink (this is what IBM did), or by engaging in "team building", to move away from fragmentation, for example by taking the management team on an outward-bound training project.

These are examples of intervention by management in the strategic conversation.

Kees: Another powerful intervention is by creating more space for the informal conversation, by organising events through which views can be exchanged outside the pressure of immediate decision making. A company I know well introduced "strategic forums" through which all managers participate in a conversation about the future away from the workplace. The effect is dramatic in the way in which a rigid organisation is being loosened up. But this type of intervention needs to be carefully designed to ensure that it works towards the balance between integration and differentiation, and doesn't drive the system into one of the two pathologies.

Peter: This is, I suppose, where scenarios come in. They are the best tool I know to allow the conversation to reflect different perceptions of the situation (differentiation), but in such a way to create room for people to consider these different viewpoints and gradually align on what needs to be done, and what they want to do (integration). After all, the evolutionary paradigm makes us aware of uncertainty and ambiguity in the strategic situation, which means thinking in terms of multiple, different, but equally plausible interpretations of what is happening. Scenarios are a way of doing that.

Kees: Absolutely, scenarios as a process tool in an ambiguous world. But they are also a content tool, a way of gaining a new perspective on the world. Let's not forget Pierre's legacy. Good strategy requires an original invention. And an original invention requires the ability to see the world in a new way, as no one has seen it before.

Peter: Scenarios can be such a reframing tool. By breaking out the uncertainties you gradually get into view what is driving the system and its underlying structural relationships, and what is already "in the pipeline". Once you have arrived there your strategy will be laid out in front of you. It will be clear what needs to be done; there will be no doubt. But this is not a process for the squeamish, only the strong with tenacity and staying power will get there. Whether the new way of seeing is accurate or just a construction created by the management team is a moot point, and basically an unanswerable question. But the crux of the matter is the originality and the clarity of the new vision, the unique insight. The team is ready to move. And while engaging with the world they will quickly find out where adjustments need to be made.

Kees: I want to re-emphasise a point we made earlier: this "eureka" moment of invention cannot be forced, it has to emerge. People who approach scenario-based planning as an algorithmic step-by-step process that has to be finished at a predetermined time are unlikely to reach this point. Only if the team are prepared to stay with it, continue to ask questions and research answers, explore new territory and reiterate the process will they eventually open the door towards this new way of seeing and acting.

Peter: I agree that good strategy can't possibly be easy. It is a contest that you need to win. You have to be different and better than the next guy. It requires both strength and good coaching. A strong management team and a big responsibility for the scenario planner.

OVERVIEW

The above conversation, which I had some time ago with Peter Schwartz in front of an audience of strategic planners, provides in a nutshell an overview of the territory this book covers. Let me reiterate a few crucial points here.

This book is about organisational strategy. The words "scenarios" and "strategic conversation" in the title indicate some aspects of strategy that I judge are underdeveloped in the literature. I see strategising as thinking about how we can intervene in the hustle and bustle of the evolutionary process that organisations are subject to. Strategy is about winning in this process, judged in terms of survival and self-development. I will assume that it takes place against a background of irreducible uncertainty and human/social interpretation, where communication is just as important as individual thinking, and where intuition and creativity are just as important as rational reasoning.

Strategy is a highly dynamic area, full of fads and fashions that come and go. Yet a few texts seem to remain valid over the years. These mostly aim at analysing underlying structures rather than proposing specific strategies. After all, copying ideas that "work" for others is unlikely to be a winning strategy. Success can only be based on being different from (existing or potential) competitors. This will be a fundamental point of the line of argument developed here.

I find it helpful to sift through the rich literature on strategy by distinguishing between three "schools of thought":

- Rationalist (aimed at finding the "optimal strategy", e.g. Michael Porter),
- Evolutionary (assuming that strategy emerges and can only be understood in retrospect, e.g. Henri Mintzberg), and
- Processual.

Managers tend to have a preference for the rationalist school; it assigns to them the power to affect the destiny of their organisation. However, they also realise that it does not always work very well. Things often turn out rather unexpectedly, compared to plan, and there is a lot of uncertainty about implementation, even if the plan turns out to have been just right.

Most managers don't have a lot of sympathy for the evolutionist school. It disempowers them to a large extent and this feels counter-intuitive. Managers need something in between the rationalist and the evolutionary schools of thought. This is where the processual school of strategy comes in.

If things change rapidly and are unpredictable, today's best strategy may be tomorrow's disaster. Managers have to stay with the issues as these change around them until real world action is taken, and then they have to stay with the consequences. The lower the level of predictability the more attention you need to pay to the strategy process.

Uncertainty has the effect of moving the key to organisational success from the "optimal strategy" to the "more skilful strategy process".

The essential medium of any strategy process is the strategic conversation that goes on in any organisation. It has a formal part, designed by the managers, and an informal part, which consists of the casual conversation about the future that spontaneously emerges. The informal conversation affects strongly where people's attention is focused. Managers cannot entirely control this, but they can intervene. It is the most powerful lever they have to affect where the organisation is going. The issue here is to find the high leverage points. That's what this book is about.

The language of the organisational strategic conversation is largely rational. Managers aiming to intervene try to build a solid line of strategic reasoning, around which others in the organisation can gather. This starts with aligning views in the management team. If there is one thing that kills management interventions it is mixed signals from the top. Management needs to keep up this strategic conversation until change champions stand up and go out to "make things happen". A significant part of this book, therefore, is about how management should get its own strategic process in order.

But building solid logic cannot be sufficient. In the end organisational success derives from being different. *Success requires an original strategic invention.* Management can contribute by creating the enabling conditions that make it favourable for inventions to emerge. But there will always be an unfathomable part to this; how else could the invention be truly original? Blending original invention into the logical language of strategy is an art, the art of strategic conversation. Nobody can tell you how to make an original invention. We can learn from studying the great masters who have gone before us, and create appropriate conditions in the organisation, but when the moment comes we are on our own.

The question, of course, is how we can create the conditions for true strategic creativity to emerge. Pierre Wack suggested that if we look long and hard enough the moment of reframing will always come, when we suddenly see the world in a new light, and gain a unique insight in how to find/regain success. An example of management intervention for this purpose is the creation of more "space" for the informal conversation, by creating a process of events through which views can be exchanged outside the pressure of immediate decision making. Taking the strategic conversation away from the pressure of immediate decisions allows people to explore possibilities more freely.

Generally speaking strategic conversation is shaped by the way people in the organisation see their world. Their mental models have been built up over time, and have become coupled through a common language that makes the strategic conversation possible. Over time people influence each other in the way they see their world. The result is a degree of overlap in their mental models, the socially constructed "reality", sometimes called the "Business-As-Usual" model, or the dominant orthodoxy in the organisation. Without such overlap there cannot be a strategic conversation, and therefore no strategy, the organisation fragments into a bunch of separate and unconnected individuals. But danger also looms at the side of too much overlap. If everyone sees the world in the same way the organisation loses the ability to perceive a wide range of weak signals in the environment, based on multiple viewpoints. As a consequence it fails to develop understanding and cannot introduce this into the system and the conversation, and react. Therefore there are two pathologies at both ends of the organisational behaviour continuum from integration to differentiation of mental models, namely "groupthink" in case of an excess of integration and not enough differentiation, and fragmentation in case of an excess of differentiation and not enough integration. Organisations, if left to their own devices, will inevitably drift towards one of these extremes. A healthy balance requires active management involvement and intervention.

Scenarios are the best available language for the strategic conversation, as it allows both differentiation in views, but also brings people together towards a shared understanding of the situation, making decision making possible when the time has arrived to take action.

Managers have always been involved in these tasks. However, through the conceptualisation of the notion of the strategic conversation, as the underpinning "nervous system" of the organisation, it has become visible how these interventions link to the strategy of the organisation, and ultimately to its success or failure. Being aware of the strategic conversation in the organisation and the opportunities it offers helps managers practise more skilfully and intentionally the many aspects of the job that the best managers have always addressed intuitively anyway.

INFLUENTIAL THINKERS

This book represents my experience as a planner and as a manager during my 35 years with Shell. The last 12 years, which I spent as an academic at Strathclyde University, have been a great opportunity to articulate this experience and confirm its validity over a much wider range of organisations. During all this time I have had access to the heritage of thinking about strategy through reading and direct interaction with a number of remarkable people who stick in my memory as pivotal at crucial times in the development of my thinking.

While many people were experimenting with scenarios for organisational decision making in the 1960s and early 1970s Pierre Wack, through his work in Shell since the mid-1960s, is the undisputed intellectual leader in the area of organisational scenario-based strategic thinking. He was the first to set out the essentials of the use of scenarios as instruments for strategy development. Subsequent historical evolution has clearly shown his far-sightedness, as most other, more probabilistic approaches have fallen by the wayside. Crucial elements of this thinking include:

- The need to take existing mental models of the decision makers as the starting point.
- Creating a reframing of the situation, through the introduction of new perspectives. The essential link between successful strategy and "seeing" the world in a new way. The new unique insight.
- The need to understand predictability and uncertainty.
- The aim of changing mental models of decision makers.

From the early days of scenario-based planning in Shell a prominent role was given to what became known as the "remarkable people", who could be helpful in creating such a reframing. The network of remarkable people became a crucial instrument of the scenario activity, first in Group Planning in Shell and subsequently embodied in Global Business Network. Nobody understands the power of such a network better than Napier Collyns, now with GBN, who showed the art and power of networking, and what was required to make it happen. The remarkable person "par excellence" for me is Peter Schwartz. I don't think I know anyone who has his ability to introduce a new perspective into just about any conversation in which he participates (Schwartz 1991).

Interestingly, while Shell as a company did not have any problems seeing the value of scenarios, planners from the early days of scenarios onwards considered it somewhat problematic that they could not always lay a clear trace from the scenario activity to organisational action. In studying the work of Emery and Trist it became clear to me that scenarios become meaningful only in the context of an understanding of the "organisational self" (Emery & Trist 1965). Thoughtful managers have powerful insights, albeit often intuitive, into the characteristics of the organisational self against which the scenarios can be made meaningful. Jay Ogilvy's metaphor of scenarios as test conditions in a wind-tunnel for designing strategic success helps to clarify this. From this it seemed to me that in order to understand the overall notion of scenario-based planning it would be useful to help people articulate the essentials of the organisational self. This would allow them to look at the organisation and its environment in each other's contexts, and in this way make both more meaningful.

Pierre Wack also led the way in thinking about the organisational self. While Pierre is well known for his contribution to the area of scenario-based planning (his *Harvard Business Review* articles are the most frequently cited in scenario related literature, Wack 1985a, Wack, 1985b) few people realise that he was one of the first to articulate a "resource view" of strategy. In the late 1970s Pierre undertook a comprehensive study of strategy making as practised at that time, with the aim of showing the strategic context of scenario-based planning more clearly. In the heyday of the "positioning school of strategy", articulated by Michael Porter in 1980, Pierre intuited (inspired by Richard Normann 1977) that a resource view might lead to a more stable theory of corporate success. At the end of his second HBR article (Wack 1985b) he summarises his conclusions in a simple diagram in which he introduces the notion of "Strategic Vision". He saw Strategic Vision as "the counterpoint of scenarios" for coping with turbulence and uncertainty, a "complexity reducer", a common frame of reference within which information can be organised. It enables executives to know what signals to look for, against the "noisy" background of the business environment.

His basic thinking on this, dating back to the 1970s, has never been published. Internally in Shell he described his concept of Strategic Vision as follows:

- It is a clear and explicit rationale for achieving business success, focusing on building up "profit potential", by developing a reservoir of potentialities.
- It is a system for dominance, expressed as a commitment to excellence in a number of capabilities (more than two, less than 10) perceived as the few critical factors of success, the importance of which tends to override everything else.
- Coalesced into a unique combination it is experienced as a strategic vision of what the company wants to be.

Note his "hard-nosed" emphasis on profit potential, and the systemic view of a limited number of capabilities working together to create uniqueness. At Shell we subsequently developed this concept further in what I call in this book the "Business Idea". But the conceptual underpinning of the thinking in this book, including the insight that scenarios can only acquire meaning against an (tacit or explicit) understanding of the identity of the organisation – the organisational self and its Business Idea – derives from Pierre Wack.

Arie De Geus (1988) introduced me to the theories of William Stern. It made me realise that the search for profit potential may be related to shareholder interests, but is in the final analysis a manifestation of a basic characteristic of any "living system", namely the urge to survive and grow. Another major component, related to this, was the view of organisations as systems of loops. This has a long history, with contributions from Darwin, Maruyama, Bateson, Varela and many others. From that perspective growth means "reinforcing feedback". Michel Bougon used the concept for drawing out the essentials of the organisation's success formula (Bougon & Komocar 1990). It became clear that a "success formula" would always be based on a reinforcing feedback loop. I will argue that uniqueness results from reinforcing feedback. The discussion of uniqueness has a long history in economics. It is usually discussed in terms of scarcities, barriers to entry and competencies. The term Distinctive Competencies goes back at least to Selznick (1957). Today people seem to prefer to talk about "core competencies" (I find this a step backwards, contrary to distinctiveness the notion of "core" is entirely metaphoric and cannot be conceptually tested). Pierre Wack introduced Dick Rumelt to Group Planning in Shell in the late 1970s, and through him I became aware of the economic literature in this area. Shortly afterwards I had the opportunity to work closely with Paul Schoemaker (Schoemaker & van der Heijden 1992), who joined us for an extended sabbatical from the University of Chicago. Together we worked through the literature and experimented with ways to apply these concepts in the real world of Shell. Paul pointed out that distinctiveness could never be forever, it would always depreciate over time, and organisations need to maintain and develop these if they want to stay ahead.

Gradually the specifics of the reinforcing feedback loop we were looking for became clearer, with Distinctive Competencies leading to competitive advantage (Porter 1985), leading to profit potential, leading to resources which can be invested in maintenance and development of the Distinctive Competencies. Richard Normann helped us a great deal in clarifying the relationship between competitive advantage, customer value and Distinctive Competencies. I am most grateful for the many in-depth discussions with Richard and his colleague Rafael Ramirez, as part of the "Business Logics for Innovators" initiative, launched by their company SMG. I believe that their books (Normann & Ramirez 1994, Ramirez & Wallin 2000, Normann 2001) will be some of those lasting contributions to the strategy literature. In this way the concept of the Business Idea took shape. It has proven powerful in bridging the gap between scenario analysis and strategic thinking and conversation. The underlying paradigm emphasises the ongoing process of strategy making. Don Michael made me realise that from the moment of acknowledgement of uncertainty the key to success moves from the idea of one-time development of "best strategy" to the most effective ongoing strategy process (Michael 1973). Under the influence of Colin Eden, at Strathclyde University, I began to understand the overriding importance of the quality of the ongoing strategic conversation in the organisation (Eden 1992, Eden & Ackermann 1998). As said earlier the strategic conversation is partly formally embedded in various mechanisms, including the planning system, mandatory submissions and documentation, meetings and decision-making processes. But a large part of it is informal, and takes place when people meet casually. It is important to understand the role of scenarios and the Business Idea in the context of this total process.

At the time of his involvement in Group Planning Arie De Geus promoted the idea of "Organisational Learning" to encapsulate all of this (De Geus 1988). Our purpose became to conceptualise the notion of Organisational Learning beyond the metaphorical. Colin Eden suggested the crucial interaction between learning and action. The embodiment of this in the learning loop as articulated by David Kolb (Kolb & Rubin 1991) allows a direct connection with the idea of a reinforcing feedback loop, and helped me to develop an overall framework for the argument in this book.

In writing this book it has been my intention to discuss practical tools and techniques. I wish to acknowledge the contributions of many people with whom I have been working over the years in trying things out in a practical setting. I am grateful to have been able to work in a company like Shell that provides room for experimentation. And we experimented a lot. The person I worked with most to make our theories useful in a practical setting is Jaap Leemhuis. Our partnership dates back to 1980, and in the course of the years we have worked on scenarios, strategy development, entrepreneurial innovation and organisational development. Many of the approaches suggested in this book go back to that partnership. I am also grateful to my friends in Group Planning, in particular Graham Galer, Brian Marsh and John Collman, without whom most ideas in this book would have remained stuck in theory. They suggested that the best laboratory to test approaches to strategy are the smaller companies, without complex planning resources obscuring a higher-level overall view. As it turned out the smaller companies have forced us to become very clear about what it is we are trying to do if any practical result is to be achieved. It proved a salutary discipline.

Over the last 20 years I have been privileged to participate in the conversation among the world's top practitioners in this area who are part of the Global Business Network. GBN was one of the early enthusiastic adopters of electronic networking in the early 1980s through which practitioners compared theory and real-life experiences. Much of this conversation has been captured. Going through it one cannot be anything else but impressed with the quality of the thinking developed in those conversations.

I finally acknowledge the contributions of Colin Eden, George Burt and Ron Bradfield who played such a crucial role in extending our work since I joined Strathclyde University.

HOW TO USE THIS BOOK

The book has four parts that cover the subject in the following way. In Part One we will discuss a number of the underlying assumptions on which thinking about strategy is based. Specifically we will discuss the three paradigms, based on views of the world characterised by rationalism, evolution and process. Consideration of uncertainty and ambiguity will allow us to see that all three are valid perspectives on a situation that is too complex to be packaged in only one of these views. We will then argue that a synthesis can be achieved by the introduction of the notion of institutional learning. We will show how all three traditional views on strategy have a logical place in the organisational learning loop. Finally we will argue that scenario-based planning can be seen as a form of such integrative institutional learning. Using that as a basis we discuss what this means in terms of shaping the approach with the objective of creating a practical tool, using all three modes of thinking about strategy.

In Part Two we will discuss the theory of scenario thinking. This is based on articulation of the characteristics of the organisation itself, and consideration of the environment in which it exists. Understanding of the organisational "self" is the starting point of skilful strategy. We will introduce the concept of the "Business Idea" as a way of making explicit those aspects of the organisation that are crucially tied up with the question of survival and development. In the business environment we will be particularly interested in ambiguity and uncertainty, which will lead to a characterisation in the form of multiple, equally plausible futures. We will then bring these two together and address the question of how to judge the robustness of the Business Idea in the future business environment, and reinvent it if necessary. We will distinguish adaptive scenario-based planning, in which incremental change is considered sufficient, from generative processes in which a more fundamental redesign is required for institutional survival. This will lead us towards an understanding of strategic direction.

Part Three introduces the practice of the scenario-based planning process. Specifically we will discuss how a management team can go about engaging in a thinking and discussion process to surface the understanding of the executives in a form which allows rational discussion leading to strategic conclusions and action. We will also discuss how external perspectives need to be introduced into the process, to avoid "institutional myopia". Although there are many ways in which this can be achieved we will suggest specific approaches that can be adopted by the less experienced. Following these, a management team will articulate its shared Business Idea, analyse its business environment in all its uncertainty, analyse its competitive position, and then discuss its strategic fit in the world. On the basis of the conclusions reached the process helps in articulating options available for strategies to either improve the fit, or develop its position by exploiting an already strong situation.

After Part Three has taken the management team through a rational thinking process to articulate its position, Part Four introduces the wider institutional behaviour context. The institutional learning model underpinning this book argues the crucial role of action and experience in strategy development. It therefore cannot happen only within the management team of an organisation but involves all layers of decision making. A management team that tries to develop strategy in isolation will quickly find that there is not much relation with the actual behaviour the organisation as a whole displays in the world. If the ultimate aim is to make the organisation more adaptable in a changing world, strategy processes must pervade the organisation. Therefore we will need to address the formal planning and decision processes, and we will discuss steps that can be taken to move the whole organisation into a more skilful behavioural pattern. We will also reach the conclusion that an organisation that wishes to move from a traditional rationalist approach towards a corporate learning approach will need to work towards changing the culture. The decision by management to introduce scenario-based planning will not be effective unless followed by a cultural process in the organisation. This is a time-consuming process that will require not only a conscious decision, but also persistence and consistency on the part of management over a considerable period of time. They need to realise that they have embarked on a road that will be demanding. On the other hand, we are discussing questions of life and death for the organisation; it would be unrealistic to expect survival to come "cheap and easy".

Supplementary resources can be found at www.wiley.com/go/scenarios

Part One

The Context

OVERVIEW

In this part we introduce scenario-based planning and consider it in the wider general management context. We will base this discussion on the premise that the ultimate purpose of the scenario planner is to create a more adaptable organisation, which first recognises change and uncertainty, and second uses it creatively to its advantage. Traditionally this has been the subject of a discipline known as "strategic management", and we review the various schools of thought that have developed over the years under this heading. We will argue that three main directions can be distinguished which tend to be put forward by protagonists as competing explanations of what happens in real-world organisations.

We will then develop a framework for integrating these schools of thought by means of the concept of organisations as learning organisms. We will move beyond the metaphor and develop a model for organisational learning, based on a general learning model suggested by David Kolb.

This unified theory of strategic management will put us in a position to discuss the contribution that scenario-based planning can make. We will argue that, properly institutionalised, the effect of scenario-based planning can be all-pervasive in an organisation's ability to adapt and be successful in a continuously changing world.

Chapter One

1965 to 1990:
Five Discoveries at Shell

Scenario-based planning has a long history. Its emergence in the organisational world is preceded by its use by the military in war games. It moved into the civil domain through the activities of the RAND Corporation during and after World War Two, and was subsequently developed by the Hudson Institute, created by Herman Kahn after he resigned from RAND. Kahn adopted the term "scenario", with its Hollywood association as a detailed outline of a future movie that was fictional, reinforcing his assertion that he did not make accurate predictions, but stories to explore. The Hollywood link was strengthened when director Stanley Kubrick used Khan as part of the model for his film character Dr Strangelove.

Kahn's most quoted scenario publication was his book *The Year 2000* published in 1967 (Kahn & Wiener 1967). From the late 1960s onwards scenario-based planning took off in the corporate world. Scenario analysis has evolved quite considerably since then. A short history of this evolution will help in understanding the basic principles involved.

Initially scenario analysis was essentially an extension of the traditional "predict-and-control" approach to planning, except that a single line forecast was replaced by a probabilistic assessment of alternative futures, leading to a "most likely" projection. This did not prove a fundamental advance over other forecasting approaches. By the end of the 1960s, the flaws in this approach were widely known. It is important to understand that the scenario-based planning process described in this book has at its core an entirely different central idea. This type of scenario-based planning relies not on probability but on causality. As such it appeals more to the intuitive needs of the typical decision makers in their search for enhanced understanding of the changing structures in society. Shell, one of the pioneers of scenario analysis, can probably claim to be one of the first and most consistent users of the methodology.

In Shell, interest in scenarios at a more conceptual level arose with the increasing failures of planning based on forecasts in the mid-1960s. Scenarios were initially introduced as a way to plan without having to predict things that everyone knew were unpredictable. Through Pierre Wack, who introduced scenarios in Shell, the early attempts were based on the Kahn philosophy. He suggested that planning must be based on the assumption that something is predictable. If the future is 100% uncertain planning is obviously a waste of time. The primary task therefore is to separate what is predictable from what is fundamentally uncertain. The predictable elements became known as the predetermined elements. The idea of the Kahn scenario approach was that predetermineds would be reflected in all scenarios in the same predictable way. Uncertainties, on the other hand, would be reflected through the different ways they play out in various different scenarios.

ROBUST DECISION MAKING

These multiple, but equally plausible, futures served the purpose of a test-bed for policies and plans. In Shell, an engineering dominated company, most big future-related decisions are project related. Each project is evaluated economically against a set of, say, two or three scenarios, so two or three performance outcomes are generated, one for each scenario. And a decision on whether to go ahead with the project is made on the basis of these multiple possible outcomes, instead of one go/no-go number. The aim is to develop projects that are likely to have positive returns under any of the scenarios. The scenarios as such are not the decision calculus indicating whether or not to go ahead with a project, they are a mechanism for producing information that is relevant to the decision. Decisions are never based on one scenario being more likely than another; project developers optimise simultaneously against a number of different futures which are all considered equally plausible, and treated with equal weight. In this way both the value and the downward potential of the project are assessed.

Similarly if a particular strategy or plan needs to be evaluated this is done against each scenario. This produces multiple outcome assessments, which are considered by the decision makers. Instead of one picture they look at, for example, three. After more than 35 years of scenario analysis top management in Shell would not want to make do with anything less. They are fully aware that if the quality of a strategic decision has been whittled down to one single indicator, important knowledge about the fundamental uncertainty in the project has been filtered out. *In this way the first objective of scenario-based planning became the generation of projects and decisions that are more robust under a variety of alternative futures.*

STRETCHING MENTAL MODELS LEADS TO DISCOVERIES

One of the early findings of the scenario planners was that the search for predetermined elements required them to consider driving forces in the business environment in some depth. The need to separate predetermineds from uncertainties requires a considerable degree of analysis of causal relationships.

The earliest examples of scenarios created by Wack's team are a good example. The first item on the scenario agenda in the early 1970s was, not surprisingly, the price of oil. So planners had to consider what was predictable and what was fundamentally uncertain in the price of oil. That meant they had to examine what drives oil price, and, therefore, the whole question of supply and demand.

Interestingly, in those days the outlook for total demand worldwide was hardly problematic. It was regarded as predictable, growing around 6% every year. This had been a consistent pattern since World War Two and was not questioned. So attention turned to supply. To what extent was this predetermined or uncertain? This involved the question of where the supply would be coming from. Of course the Middle East loomed large in this.

Shell's technical people had concluded that supply availability was predetermined, the resource in the ground was plentiful, and the necessary number of wells could be drilled. But Pierre Wack was not satisfied with that answer. He looked behind it, considering the people who have control over the reserves who would be making the actual production decisions. In the late 1960s these were still the major oil companies, but the producing governments had started to establish their sovereign authority. It was one of Pierre's great contributions to the scenario process that he insisted on looking at the people behind decisions, not just at the technical or macro phenomena. The planners started to wonder whether it would make sense, from the point of view of the producing governments, to continue to supply the increasing quantities required by the oil consumers. They had to conclude that this was sufficiently uncertain to make it worth developing a new scenario. This scenario (one out of six initially) became known as the crisis scenario, in which producing countries would refuse to continue to increase production beyond what made sense from the perspective of their own cash needs.

When the oil crisis actually occurred in 1973 it became clear that the scenario analysis had put the company on a thinking track where traditional forecasting would never have taken it. Mental models had been stretched well beyond what traditional forecasting would have achieved. Forecasting produces answers, but scenario-based planning had made people ask the crucial questions. Scenario-based planning allowed the company to override the domination of the credible, popular but very wrong imagined future. As Shell's managing director Andre Benard commented: "Experience has taught us that the scenario technique is much more conducive to forcing people to think about the future than the forecasting techniques we formerly used" (Benard 1980). *Better quality thinking about the future became the second objective of scenario-based planning.*

ENHANCING CORPORATE PERCEPTION

Not much later a third powerful effect was observed resulting from using scenario techniques in an institutional context: people who practised scenario-based planning found themselves interpreting information from the environment differently from others around them.

For example, against the background discussed earlier of a crisis scenario in the oil industry, the actions of a group of Shell executives stand out. This group recognised in developments taking place in the Middle East during 1973 some of the elements of the energy crisis scenario they had been discussing earlier. They interpreted persistent signals from that part of the world as an indication of the unfolding of the crisis scenario, and so they made a number of critical strategic decisions. The most important decision was a change in refining investment policies to allow for the possibility that the crisis scenario was in fact playing out. They interpreted the October 1973 events in the Middle East as the confirmation of the causal model in the scenario, on the basis of which they were able to quickly shift their investments. While most of the refining industry needed years to decide that something really fundamental had happened, Shell moved immediately, switching investments well ahead of their competitors. As a consequence of this industry inertia, refining capacity in the industry ran into considerable oversupply, with disastrous consequences for profitability. However, due to Shell's early adaptation of alternative policies they suffered much less from overcapacity and outperformed the industry by a long margin. This later could be shown to have had a fundamental impact on the way the company as a whole came through the turbulent 1970s and early 1980s.

Other parts of the company, such as the marine transport sector, which had not worked with the scenarios, did not appreciate the depth of the changes taking place and so did not adjust effectively. They continued putting money into more and more tanker capacity until much later, and that part of the business never recovered fully from the losses it incurred as a consequence of the oversupply.

What the scenarios did was to enable Shell's manufacturing people to be more perceptive, appreciate events as part of a pattern they recognised, and so appreciate their implications. As a result of this they were able to respond quickly to events in a way that would have been impossible without the mental preparation of the scenario analysis. This became the third objective of scenario-based planning.

Important in all this is the institutional aspect. Decisions of the type described here are not made by any individual in isolation, but require a considerable degree of institutional consensus or accommodation. The ability to read signals must be institutional: enough people must have jointly acquired the mental model if any action is to result. Only if scenario analysis has become an institutionalised planning tool, embedding the insights in the institutional conversational process, do we see the development of consensus, or at least accommodation, necessary for action. When a company commits to this process, scenarios quickly become part of the institutional language. This is due to the effective way in which a storyline is capable of representing and transferring a complex inter-disciplinary reality to a listener in a simple and effortless way (Allen *et al.* 2002).

ENERGISING MANAGEMENT

A fourth aspect of scenario-based planning emerged later, when top management began using it as a way of influencing decision making down the line through context setting, rather than direct intervention.

Most organisations have formal "rules of the game" concerning how important decisions are made, involving top management's approval for significant outlays. A simple change in the rules made at Shell in the early 1980s required the justification of any proposed major project against the set of the going scenarios. This replaced the usual procedure in which such justification was made against a single line forecast of the environment for the project. The result of this was significant. Since the scenarios now provided the context for making key strategic decisions project champions needed to pay attention.

For example, assume that project developers, matching a project against scenario A, find an attractive payout, but against scenario B they find a poor return. They will be reluctant to submit the proposal, as it may be rejected due to the possibility of this poor outcome. The effect of this will be that people will try to modify the project such that the performance under scenario B is improved, aiming, of course, for maintaining the performance under scenario A. The result of this will be a more robust project, one that is likely to be successful under a wider range of circumstances.

What we see here is that the scenarios will influence project development work even before the project is submitted to top management. The scenarios make an impact when the detailed project decisions are made. *This early influence by top management is not exercised by means of direct instructions, but by using scenarios to set the context within which decisions are made down the line.*

SCENARIOS AS A LEADERSHIP TOOL

A further consequence of this is that the interest of top management in the scenario process is reinforced. They will become more involved in the generation of scenarios when these become a powerful contextual tool for influencing the development of projects down the line.

Interestingly, in the day-to-day practice it quickly became apparent that this could work only if scenario planners are fully conscious of their role as intermediaries. When scenario planners start following their own agendas the resulting scenarios are quickly experienced as less relevant in the organisation. This in turn leads to reduced interest from the top, a signal that is quickly perceived in the organisation, isolating the scenario-based planning effort even more. If this reinforcing loop takes hold a point is reached quickly where the context-setting role of scenarios becomes ineffective.

In Shell, top management use scenarios to provide leadership to the organisation. For example, in 1989 (Kahane 1992a) top management became concerned that the company as a whole needed to renew their approach towards environmental issues. They considered the general attitude too defensive, and felt it was important that the company should rethink this. As a consequence one of the 1989 scenarios described a world in which environmental factors developed in such a way that only companies responding positively could survive. As a consequence this issue was on the agenda whenever a project with significant environmental aspects was considered.

Box 1   The Shell 1990 scenario process – using scenarios to communicate new ideas to the company

By the late 1980s top managers at Shell were particularly concerned with environmental issues. Protecting the environment had become a powerful movement in the whole world. Shell was usually finding themselves on the defensive, based on good scientific evidence and engineering logic but not necessarily in tune with the world. The Shell top management found this unsatisfactory. They would prefer the company out in front, considered progressive, fighting for a better world instead of being seen as defending the old order. However, it was not initially very clear how to project this message in the company. They could not instruct the company to drop good scientific and engineering practice, and become irrational! So they decided to use scenarios as one of the ways to communicate their idea to the company. They asked for a scenario where the world goes "seriously green", which became known as the "Sustainable World" scenario. It was a very interesting and dramatic scenario, but based on intense systemic analysis and fully arguable and plausible. Shell had a policy that every big investment project submitted to top management had to be economically evaluated against all current scenarios. Since the green scenario was one of these every manager who wanted to submit an investment proposal was forced to think through how his or her "pet project" would be able to survive in a green world.

They were successful in significantly influencing several projects in this way. However, the culture was not sufficiently affected, as we saw later, when Shell faced the infamous Brent Spar issue. It later transpired that the decision-making process had been done very carefully, and even had included a scenario with significant pushback by societal pressure groups. Even so, on balance the management team had decided to go for the scientifically preferred solution and accept this risk. The decision having been taken the implementation was handed over to operators and the management's attention turned somewhere else. When difficulties started to develop it took management some time to re-engage with the project. The operators initially wanted to deal with the problems themselves and did not immediately turn to management for further guidance. Unfortunately things were moving very fast and precious time was lost in making a fundamental response to the situation that had arisen.

Scenarios are an important part, but only a part, of transforming an organisational culture. We need to look at scenarios in a broader context that includes the total organisational learning system. Also the operators down the line need to be part of it.

Scenario thinking now underpins the established way of making decisions at Shell. People throughout the company, dealing with significant decisions, normally will think in terms of multiple, but equally plausible futures to provide a context for decision making. This is known as focused scenario thinking. Focused scenarios are not directly related to the global scenarios used by top management to establish the overall strategic framework. They are of a more ad hoc nature, developed by departments to aid in lower-level decision making. The company is satisfied to let scenario analysis take place at different levels in this way without trying to connect these efforts formally. What matters at Shell is the thinking process rather than the bureaucracy of planning.

The distinguishing feature of the scenario culture is that it has invested in assumptions, values and mental models. Tools and techniques are secondary. However sophisticated the tools, if there is no significant effect on assumptions, values and mental models, people will quickly fall back into the old habit of asking "Tell me what will happen." In contrast in a true scenario culture people will understand both deep structure as well as fundamental uncertainty, and deal with the day-to-day issues accordingly. Strategic thinking and strategic tools in Shell have co-evolved in the company. Better tools have created more effective thinking, and enhanced conceptualisation has created room and demand for superior tools.

The account of Shell's experience illustrates the fundamental point that scenario-based planning is vital to the normal day-to-day management task (Kirkland 1987). It is not a new management fad, an episodic special activity, a disruption of the normal flow of activities, but a way of thinking which penetrates the institutional mind and eventually affects all activity. It is based on a number of basic assumptions that in Shell are considered just common sense:

- Possessing sound strategies reduces the complexity of the management task rather than adding to it. Investing time in structuring the strategic debate will pay off many times over in increased efficiency of dealing with the day-to-day issues managers face.
- Discussing strategy is a natural part of any management task, and not the exclusive domain of specialists.

There is nothing unusually difficult in good strategy, even in the context of acknowledging fundamental uncertainty, if based on common sense thinking.

Chapter Two

Introduction to Scenario-based Planning

WHY PLAN?

This is a book for practitioners of strategic management. These are managers who believe in making an investment in thinking about where they want to go. Their aim is to achieve a better result through approaching daily decisions in a structured and efficient way to make the best use of time and resources. Thinking and articulation also meet psychological needs for coherence. Most managers would be reluctant to rely entirely upon a "seat of the pants" approach.

The question of what constitutes a "good" decision is not trivial. Circumstances change after a decision has been taken and one will never know what would have happened if the decision had been different. The quality of the decision cannot be measured by reference to outcome, but only on the basis of how it was arrived at, i.e. how resourceful and vigilant the decision maker was before the decision was taken. Janis (Janis & Mann 1977) suggests that a decision is vigilant if:

- Reasons are rational (i.e. are explicit and intelligible, have logical coherence and are congruent with existing knowledge)
- Reasons stand up to appropriate search for relevant empirical data
- Reasons take account of future indeterminacy (contingency planning).

The intellectual challenge of vigilance is to focus attention on the longer term. This is one side of the management coin. The other side is the day-to-day practice where one operational urgency after another consumes the manager's working day. The manager is fully aware that the urgent drives out the important. When sitting back for a moment, many admit that they are dissatisfied with the level of vigilance they manage to apply in their daily life. It is this need that I hope to address in this book.

The approach discussed here is premised on the assumption that it is both necessary and efficient for organisations to make an investment in thinking through in advance where they want to go, and in developing policies and strategies based on this. The aim is to achieve a better structured and more efficient day-to-day management practice, so that managers at all levels can take account of longer-term aims in their daily decision making. Research suggests that this leads to superior overall results (e.g. Hart & Banbury 1994).

There are other reasons for investing in the creation of a strategic business policy:

- A modest up-front investment in planning avoids the need to think through every crisis situation from scratch. It is efficient in terms of use of time and thinking resources.
- Appropriate planning assists in making the transition from individual insights to institutional action.
- Appropriate planning creates an institutional learning and memory system; it helps an organisation avoid repeating mistakes.

Managers who are experiencing problems in their business cannot help but think about their situation and try to work out how to change things. They normally need little convincing that a bit of strategic thinking would be helpful, if only to better structure their understanding of what they are experiencing. The urge for coherence in organisations is very strong. Coherence is associated with strong action. The problem mostly is to find the time and resources to engage in a strategic thinking process. This book is about scenario-based planning, an efficient approach to strategic business planning, focusing on business ideas in an uncertain world.

The need for efficient strategic thinking is most obvious in times of accelerated change when the reaction time of the organisation becomes crucial to survival and growth. All organisations experience such periods from time to time. The problem is that they alternate with periods of relative stability, when organisations often get stuck into established ways of doing things, making them ill-prepared for when the change comes. Slow reaction to change can be very costly. If we want to know how quickly companies react to change it is useful to study their behaviour when they are subjected to large step-change shocks. As we saw in Chapter One the oil industry was subjected to a major discontinuity in

BT/annum

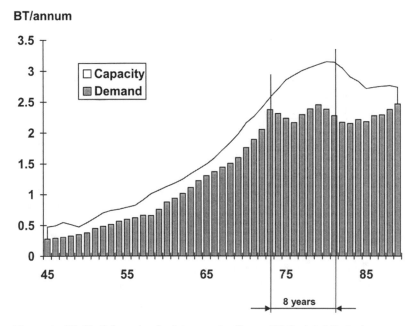

Figure 1. *World oil demand and refining capacity (Source: BP Statistical Review)*

1973 with the first energy crisis and in the following paragraphs we will try to draw lessons from this.

The first behavioural example relates to investment decisions in refining. Figure 1 shows the total industry demand for all oil products as this developed since 1945, through the crisis in 1973 until well into the 1980s. We clearly see the 1973 break in the trend for the demand for products in reaction to the crisis. Consistent exponential growth, experienced until the crisis took place, was replaced with level demand afterwards. Fluctuation in demand levels continued to be experienced from year to year, but the broad demand trend became essentially static from then onwards.

Figure 1 also shows how the oil refining industry reacted to this dramatic change in the business environment. The line representing worldwide refinery capacity in the industry shows very little initial reaction. The industry had become accustomed to an exponential growth of 6 to 7% per year; it seemed difficult to imagine anything else. Planning new capacity in this business had become an established routine. One knew that the business would expand by 6% next year; it was not difficult to figure out how much additional capacity was required. And if you got it wrong in any one year continuous growth would ensure that correction was relatively painless in the following years. Then, suddenly, from 1973 things changed. For our purpose the development of capacity during this time is enlightening. For two years it continues to grow at the rate that the industry has been accustomed to, 6% per year, with no apparent reaction to the crisis. From then onwards we see the growth slowing down somewhat, but continuing. It is not until the early 1980s that the industry adjusts its capacity back to the level of demand as it had actually developed since 1973.

This industry apparently needed *two years* to discover that anything at all had happened, and then required another *five or six years* to work out the real impact of the oil crisis on demand.

Of course there are lead times of considerable length in planning and building refinery capacity, but not as long as eight years. The difference is a significant cognitive gestation time, measured in years. Eventually the oil companies reacted, modified their construction plans, and adjusted to the new situation, but the time needed to come to a conclusion caused losses of billions through the resulting pressure of overcapacity.

The second example concerns new building orders for crude oil tankers. Figure 2 shows new tanker orders by the industry from 1973

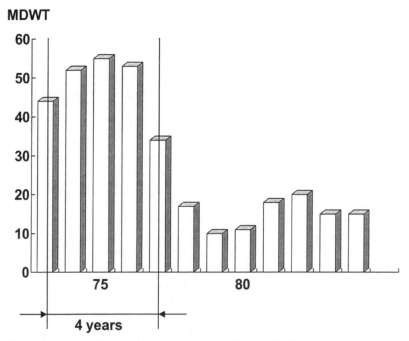

Figure 2. *Demand for new tanker capacity (Source: BP Statistical Review)*

into the 1980s. Even though demand flattened in 1973 it was only in 1977 that new building orders started to drop off. The effect on the industry was dramatic. Huge overcapacity resulted in large numbers of tankers laid up in various anchorages around the world, and freight rates stayed at rock bottom for many years.

The oil crisis example is one of the clearest illustrations of how long it can take for organisations to react to change in the environment. But most of us have similar stories about events in a whole range of other industries (steel, motor cars, IBM etc.) in which response times are clearly measured in years rather than months.

Imagine a company that would have required only one year, rather than three years, to reorient its business. Imagine the competitive advantage resulting from moving two years earlier than one's competitors. Significant competitive advantage does not require perfect and total foresight and prescience. Enhancing the institutional skills of perception and adaptation to produce a more inventive and faster response to environmental change than one's competitors is all that is required. This book aims to help managers to achieve such a superior performance.

SCENARIO-BASED PLANNING IS "LEARNING"

What is it that we are ultimately after in scenario-based planning? In the final analysis the organisation needs a good and unique fit with its ever-changing environment if its aims are to be achieved. The purpose of strategising is to develop policies guiding personal behaviour of individuals in the organisation such that the total system achieves and maintains a good and unique fit. The problem is that this has to be achieved in a situation of uncertainty and ambiguity. If everything is known and predetermined there is no place for strategy. But equally, if everything is totally uncertain and nothing is predictable strategy is impossible. *The idea of strategising for the future is fundamentally based on the unpredictability of the future, of which some aspects, we assume, can be foreseen.* Traditional "common sense" requires good strategy to be based on the following elements:

- Acknowledgement of aims, either through an external mandate, or the organic purpose of survival and self-development.
- Assessment of the organisation's characteristics, including its capability to change.
- Assessment of the environment, current and future.
- Assessment of the fit between the two.

- Invention and development of policies to improve the fit.
- Decisions and action to implement the strategy.

Scenario-based planning is an approach towards dealing with all six steps. It distinguishes itself from other more traditional approaches to strategic planning through its explicit approach towards ambiguity and uncertainty in the strategic question. The most fundamental aspect of introducing uncertainty in the strategic equation is that it turns planning for the future from a once-off episodic design activity into an ongoing learning proposition (Eden 1987). In a situation of uncertainty planning becomes learning, which never stops. We have an in-built urge to try to pin down situations, and to try to reach a point where we have got it sorted out in our mind. If uncertainty is acknowledged it is not any longer possible to take this position of "we have done the planning".

The idea of continuous learning may be less comfortable for some, as it does not give us this feeling of problem closure. However, strategy is about the future, and therefore involves uncertainty. The traditional approach tries to eliminate uncertainty from the strategic equation, by the assumption of the existence of knowledgeable people who have privileged knowledge about "the most likely future", and who can assess the probabilities of specific outcomes. Scenario-based planning, on the other hand, assumes that there is irreducible indeterminacy and ambiguity in any situation faced by the strategist, and that successful strategy can only be developed in an ongoing dynamic response to this.

The study of scenario-based planning is the study of learning and invention. It involves the total system, the people who make up the organisation and influence the outcome, but also institutional cognition and behaviour, which have emergent characteristics rising above the cognitive characteristics of the members making up the institution. The total is different from the sum of the parts:

- Organisations are made up of people who approach their organisational actions in a thinking way.
- The organisation does not simply behave as the sum of the behaviour of individuals. Through their interactions unique institutional behaviour emerges.
- Individual strategies need to take account of the systemic properties of the "institution in its environment" as a whole, if they are to lead to their intended results.

The managers I particularly want to reach are those running successful organisations. They often are less aware of the need for a disciplined approach towards strategic management than their colleagues facing serious problems. There is something pernicious in business success. An observation I have made over many years of practice is that management teams in charge of successful organisations show significantly more consensus on strategy than teams in trouble. They often ascribe their success to this clear and shared vision. In my view the causal relation may well be the other way around, with success leading to focusing in the team. Miller (1993) argues that most successful organisations lapse into decline because they develop too sharp an edge. They narrow the focus of their attention to a reducing set of strengths and functions, while neglecting others. The organisation will become a more and more efficient machine, doing fewer things increasingly well. Initially the organisation may experience considerable success with this focusing strategy. This will lead to strong reinforcement of the "success formula" through cognitive, cultural and structural mechanisms. The problem arises when societal change reduces interest in the business offering. The organisation then finds that it does not have the "requisite variety" (Ashby 1983) to take cognisance of, and adjust to, evolving needs.

Such organisations and their management teams need to take on board a disciplined way of looking outside their daily business, and reflect on their observations. In order to improve their perceptual capabilities they need to become more nuanced in their understanding of the business environment. They need to invest resources and time in perception, reflection and learning until they have gained that new unique insight that will position them for long-term success. What is needed is a complete philosophy mobilising the cognition, culture, structure and process throughout the organisation. Only in this way can the company as a whole acquire the perceptual skills needed to see, understand and act on important changes in the business environment across a wide front. This book approaches strategic management and scenario-based planning with such an integrated focus.

THE PURPOSE OF SCENARIO-BASED PLANNING

In practical scenario projects this general aim tends to be particularised in terms of specific contributory tasks. Some scenario projects are undertaken to address a specific problem or question, some are meant to install a permanent capability. Some are intended to open up minds, some to create closure around a strategy. Some aim to make sense of a puzzling situation; some intend to produce ideas for action. Some aim to develop anticipatory skills; others are intended to turn participants into experiential learners. And so on. Many emphasise creativity, expanding mental maps and thinking the unthinkable with only a vague reference to strategy. For example, a large American car manufacturer specifies as their objective to push the limits of thinking on what is possible in the future. In contrast, others strongly emphasise the need for an integrated approach explicitly linking scenarios to strategy development.

It seems that there isn't one size that fits all. Both the process and the end product need to be designed to maximise the chance that the process is experienced as successful. All this has to start from knowing the client and their aspirational system. We have to "look before we leap".

In fact, when launching into scenarios, people are seldom specific about what they are after. The decision to "use scenario-based planning" more often than not is based on a rather vague and implicit picture in the mind's eye that mixes up many elements into a positive image of "a good thing", based more on feeling than on reasoning. None of these reasons are invalid. The problem is they are insufficiently precise and can mean many things to different people. No wonder that scenarios sometimes disappoint.

There are no general-purpose scenarios or general-purpose scenario approaches that are guaranteed to result in a satisfied client. There isn't a one size fits all scenario project that can be bought off the shelf. The chance that someone else's scenarios have any use for you is small. Each project has to be custom-designed based on the specific objectives and needs of the specific organisation. Only dedicated customised approaches can work, and have the potential to become highly successful.

HOW POPULAR IS SCENARIO-BASED PLANNING?

A question I am frequently asked is how popular is scenario-based planning? Two recent reports from the Corporate Strategy Board deal with this question. The first report is based on a survey of over 200 chief strategy officers at large companies. This report found that scenario-based planning is the single most commonly used conceptual tool by strategists. In fact, there is a large margin between scenario-based planning and the next most commonly used tool. A separate study, also by the Board, on scenario-based planning found that half of all their member companies had used scenario-based planning at some point. On the other hand the consultancy firm Bain and Co. have reported a levelling off.

To be sure, these reports beg the question of what kind of scenario-based planning was done (and how well it was done). On close inspection one should not draw too many conclusions from these statistical observations. They are based on the assumption that scenario-based planning is one well-defined tool among many in the strategist's toolbox. This is a misunderstanding. Rather than "a tool" scenario-based planning is a paradigmatic way of strategic thinking that acknowledges uncertainty with all the consequences this entails.

I will argue later that every human being is a scenario planner by nature. As individuals we think scenarically, and individual thinking about the future cannot be done without it. Scenarios therefore are part of every organisational strategic conversation. Every organisation applies aspects of it, some more, some less. When thinking about strategies for the future every organisation considers uncertainty, sensitivity and multiple plausible futures, at least on an ad hoc conversational level. On the other side of the scale there are those organisations that have created elaborate formal planning structures around scenarios, bringing it from the background strategic conversation into the foreground of strategy development. Somewhere in between are those who plan scenarically more or less formally.

Trying to express the popularity of scenario-based planning in a single measure is meaningless. On the other hand there is no doubt that general acceptance has grown strongly in the past decade.

A related question is the following: "If this is such a great methodology, which are the companies that have seen significant increased profits as a result?" Significant increases in profits can only be established by comparing real outcomes with what would have been the result without the scenario approach. And the latter we will never know. But in a few cases we can make a guess. The Shell example on page 6 is a case in point. The scenario conversation resulted in a specific policy being implemented, which eventually was copied with a significant delay by the whole industry. We can figure out what Shell's results would have been if the company had been as slow as the rest of the industry, and the difference is measured in billions. But such relatively clear-cut cases are rare. Attempts to develop statistical correlations between ROI and interventions tend to be inconclusive, not only for scenario-based planning but generally for strategic interventions. There seem to be four reasons for this:

- ROI-based success measures are misleading on a year-to-year basis over long periods of time (the "value of money" problem).
- Equivocal definitions, e.g. in accounting definitions of profitability and conventions, or in what is meant by "scenario-based planning".
- Time and distance between cause and effect. Much of the research measures immediate relationships, while in reality there is considerable time delay and systemic distance between cause and effect, making it difficult to attribute specific interventions to observed outcomes (see the Shell example quoted).

- Empirical noise. The greater the systemic distance between two variables, in this case scenario-based planning and corporate value, the greater the effect of other unrelated events.

However, there is a more fundamental point to be made. Like anything else in business uncertainty around this issue makes scenario-based planning worth considering. Assume that one could come to one single definition of scenario planning and prove that scenarios lead to profit; then everyone would quickly adopt it. And in a competitive world a recipe followed by everyone cannot possibly be a formula for success (see page 31). It will probably always remain difficult, if not impossible, to prove that scenarios lead to profit. The question seems fundamentally indeterminate.

Chapter Three

Three Competing Paradigms in Strategic Management

Management is a much-studied activity. Academic thinkers have tried for a long time to interpret and understand what is going on. The thinking that evolved over the years can be categorised as schools of thought that gradually developed in this area. It is useful to consider these briefly in order to place scenario-based planning in context.

The theories that developed over the years can be grouped into three schools of thought on how managers and entrepreneurs think about their daily business. We'll call these the rationalist, evolutionary and processual schools, or paradigms. Other taxonomies have been proposed (see, for example, Whittington 1993 or Mintzberg 1990) but it is not difficult to map these on to the three paradigms suggested here.

The rationalist school codifies thought and action separately. The tacit underlying assumption is that there is one best solution, and the job of the strategist is, with the limited resources available, to get as close to this as possible. The strategist thinks on behalf of the entire organisation, and works out an optimal strategy as a process of searching for maximum utility among a number of options. Having decided the optimal way forward, the question of strategy implementation is addressed separately. Mintzberg (1990) lists the assumptions underlying the rationalist school:

- Predictability, no interference from outside
- Clear intentions
- Implementation follows formulation (thought independent of action)
- Full understanding throughout the organisation
- Reasonable people will do reasonable things.

The reader may want to reflect on the plausibility of these assumptions. Even so the rationalist strategy school is alive and well, in fact by far the largest part of the strategy literature and reporting reflects this viewpoint.

The evolutionary school emphasises the complex nature of organisational behaviour, beyond the realms of rationalist thinking (Lindblom 1959, Mintzberg & Waters 1985). It has recently found support in the emergent field of "complexity theory". This holds that when studying any situation involving many independent agents overall system behaviour may become fundamentally indeterminate and emergent. Strategy is nothing more than a perspective on such emergent behaviour. A winning strategy can only be articulated in retrospect, interpreting the behaviour as it proved the fittest in the evolutionary process of the business environment.

In this context evolution refers to the emergent properties of systems that have a discriminating and transmissible memory of successful strategies. Discrimination may be self-applied or it may be imposed from outside, but it ensures that the strategies which survive are those which are best fitted to do so. In this school of thought strategy is a process of random experimentation and filtering out of the unsuccessful.

The problem with this theory is that, in common with most other evolutionary theories, it has rather little predictive power. Most managers believe that they have some power to influence things, and therefore that strategic thinking is useful. Proactive managers do not often subscribe to the evolutionary view, because it relegates them to insignificant pawns, played by circumstances.

The processual school takes a middle position. It suggests that while it is not possible to work out optimal strategies through a rational thinking process alone, managers can create processes in organisations that will make them more flexible and adaptable, and capable of learning from mistakes. It looks for successful evolutionary behaviour of the organisation as the ultimate test of a successful process. But it believes that this can be influenced. The "management of change" literature is a manifestation of this view.

The three schools differ in the way organisations are perceived. Morgan (1986) argues that people understand their organisations metaphorically, by comparing these with well-known analogues in nature (compare also Douglas 1986). For example:

- The rationalist paradigm suggests a machine metaphor for the organisation.
- The evolutionary paradigm suggests an ecology.
- The processual paradigm suggests a living organism.

While much energy has been invested in arguing the relative merits of the three perspectives, strategy making in the real world manifests elements of all three. Rather than preferring one school of thought over another it is more productive for the purpose of creating skilful and adaptive organisations, to see these as three aspects of the same complex phenomenon. The approach to strategy in this book attempts to integrate these three schools of thought in strategy. Before we attempt to do so we need to discuss each in some further detail.

THE RATIONALIST PARADIGM

In the 1950s and 1960s planning for the future was mostly based on a "predict and control" principle, based on the rationalist paradigm (Mintzberg 1990). This works well when the questions for the future are well defined. It requires that we know in principle what we need to do, reducing the question of choice of action to one of degree rather than nature. It requires relatively stable interfaces between actors in society. If the value systems of the players on both sides of an interface are relatively stable both parties can assume that things between them are well defined and get on with optimising their own part of the transaction activities. Businesses will look at the fixed elements in the customer interface to define themselves, for example in terms of the products they produce or trade ("we are in the textile business"). They concentrate on being effective and competitive in putting their well-understood products on the market. The nature of what needs to be done is clear, the problem is to design and optimise the detailed blueprint. This is where predict-and-control planning, based on the rationalist paradigm, works well.

The Rationalist Approach to Strategy

The rationalist perspective starts with the concept that there is one right answer and the strategic task is to find it, or get as close as possible to it. For the rationalist, the starting perspective of the strategist him/herself is not important. If there is only one right answer, then anyone, given the right resources, will ultimately find it. It may be the chief executive, but (s)he may legitimately delegate this job to an intelligent subordinate if this brings more rational thinking power to bear.

Box 2 shows the rationalist approach in terms of a series of steps that translate the purpose of the organisation into strategies pursuing that purpose as effectively as possible.

Rationalist strategy-making starts with the definition of a purpose of the organisation. This is often called a "mission". The outside "owner" of the organisation determines this purpose, or the CEO does this on

---

Box 2   Steps in strategy development

- Defining the mission
     Defining utility
     Defining strategic objectives
- SWOT analysis
     Internal analysis
     Environment prediction
     Identifying strategic options
- Selecting maximum utility option
- Implementation
- Appraisal and control

---

behalf of the real or imagined outside owner. The idea of a mission goes back to the military origin of the concept of "strategy". The military organisation does not decide whether or not a war will be fought. An outside political entity decides their mission and the military organisation develops its strategy on that basis. Similarly, rationalist business strategists work from a given mission statement. Interestingly, few strategy textbooks say anything about where the mission comes from. They provide examples from a variety of statements invented by companies in the past and invite the student to crib from these examples. What seems to happen in reality is that the founders of the firm imprint their personal vision on the activity, and when the company has grown up and operates successfully people feel at home with the business they know and there is no need to question the basic purpose.

The next task for the rationalist business strategist is to derive a set of strategic objectives based on the mission. These link the mission of the organisation with the operational scene, and translate its purpose into a series of operational goals. For example, if the mission is "to maximise return on investments" then an objective might be to achieve an improvement in profitability of x points next year. In order to translate this in operational terms the internal situation must be analysed, including the organisational capabilities and limitations. Then the attention moves to the contextual and transactional environments. Out of this analysis feasible objectives are formulated.

Strategies are designed to achieve the objectives. Normally there are a number of options to be considered and the rationalist strategist needs to select the most effective. In order to do this a forecast must be made of the future business environment against which various strategic options can be evaluated. After deciding what the future will look like, the utility of each option is calculated. The one with the highest utility is the preferred strategy. Having accepted the mission, and chosen the preferred strategic option on the basis of maximum utility, then there is no longer room for argument.

That is the theory. In reality the rationalist planner faces a number of limitations. How to identify the options in the first place? Rationalist strategists always face the nagging problem that their intellectual and computing power is limited and that therefore the best option may still be eluding them. They are never finished searching. There is a constant doubt about how close they are to the "real" optimum.

Then there is the problem of forecasting the environment in which the strategy will play out.

Types of Forecasts

In the rationalist paradigm the strategist, thinking on behalf of the whole organisation, works out an optimal strategy as we described above. In order to do so he needs to predict the future, forecasting a "most likely" picture of the future against which plans can be judged. Everyone is of course aware that there is considerable uncertainty in the future, and that it is not possible to predict things precisely. However, the assumption underlying forecasting is that some people can be more expert than others in predicting what will happen, and the best we can do is ask them for their considered opinion on what might be in store, either as individuals or as a group (e.g. using the Delphi technique). The rationalist's final result describes one future world, specifying his best guess of the conditions in which the organisation will find itself. Although this prediction cannot be exactly correct (in 1971 a "Delphi" conducted among experts within Shell on future oil price did not come up with any number higher than $2 per barrel. In 1974 the price had increased to $12), it is as close as we can get.

All forecasts are based on the assumption that the past can be extended into the future. At the simplest level this means a statistical extrapolation of variables. When radical change occurs, this mode of forecasting fails first. A more sophisticated kind of forecasting involves the development of a simulation model, which allows for the possibility of inter-relationships between variables to be taken into account. Examples range from macro-economic models to war-games. However, simulation models are also based on the assumption of projecting the past into the future, in this case not of variables but of relationships. They are based on the assumption of a stable underlying structure. However, underlying structure shifts from time to time and simulation models often do not deliver when it really matters.

Although it is convenient for the decision maker to consider strategic options against one future only, there is a cost to pay. What will happen if the future turns out differently? Will the organisation still survive? Forecasts do not communicate uncertainty. Their use in strategy is strictly limited.

Sensitivities

One way of dealing with this is to consider sensitivities. The decision maker studies what would happen if an important variable in the environment turns out to be somewhat different from the forecast. For example, we could consider what would happen to profitability if sales were to be lower by 10%. However, this begs the question whether sales could be down by that amount. And if so, whether it is reasonable to assume that this would happen in isolation. Or should we assume that lower sales would be due to increased competition, accompanied by lower prices? Or could the drop in volume be due to higher prices? Sensitivities give us very limited information because they do not deal with all interlinkages of variables in the situation. They are not internally consistent futures, and therefore misleading decision-making tools.

Probabilistic Approach to Scenario-based Planning Belongs in the Rationalist School

In the literature the term scenario planning is sometimes used to indicate a method of traditional decision analysis, involving probabilistic assessment of different futures. The aim is consistent with the rationalist paradigm, to develop a single criterion against which options can be considered and to build a line of reasoning at the end of which the one optimal decision falls out. A typical example of this approach is the development of high and low lines of sales, judged to be possible developments at specific levels of probability. The outcomes of various policy options can then be assessed against the scenarios (typically three: high, low and most likely), and weighted according to the probability of these futures materialising. In this way one overall quality measure is produced for each option, and the one with the best result is selected.

This is not the way in which the term scenario-based planning will be used here. Scenarios are not seen as quasi-forecasts but as perception devices. A high/low line approach does not enhance perception, as it does not add new concepts to the "forecasting" frame of mind. Creating three futures along a single dimension, with subjective probabilities attached, is conceptually the same activity as forecasting. It does not cause us to explore conceptually different ways the future could pan out. In this book, *scenarios are a set of structurally different futures*. These are conceived through a process of causal rather than probabilistic thinking, reflecting different interpretations of the phenomena that drive the underlying structure of the business environment. Scenarios are used as a means of thinking through strategy against a number of structurally quite different, but plausible future models of the world. Once the set of scenarios has been decided upon they will be treated as equally likely, all being given equal weight whenever strategic decisions are being made.

When Predict-and-Control Fails

Risk is inherent in every business. It varies over time. Sometimes things suddenly seem to change direction. Every business encounters periods of accelerated change when old assumptions suddenly become irrelevant. Typically new actors do not play the game according to the understood rules. They start reconfiguring the interfaces between actors in society (often made possible by new-found power, possibly based on a new technology) and the established community feels undermined. Predict-and-control no longer works.

On the other hand, during periods of relative calm things seem more predictable. This doesn't mean "no change". In the oil industry before the 1973 crisis, relative calm meant exponential growth, 6% every year. As this was experienced year in and year out, capacity expansion was planned accordingly. Such a high growth situation is particularly benign for the industry. Competition is less severe and an error in planning expansion is corrected quickly.

But most companies experience times when such periods of relative calm are interrupted by extraordinary turbulence (see Figure 3, derived from Johnson & Scholes 2002). Something fundamental shifts and the basic rules of the game are overthrown. In that situation, the company isn't quite sure where to go; lessons learned from history are no longer a good guide. New ways of doing things need to be found. Experimentation is the new game. Many experiments fail and new ones have to be invented and tried.

IBM went through such a state of flux (Gerstner 2002). Through its dominant position in the mainframe computer market IBM lived in a predictable and well-organised industry where small adjustments in business policy kept the business nicely on track. But at the end of the 1980s fundamental technological change crept up on it, throwing it seriously off course. Once again we see a well-established industry

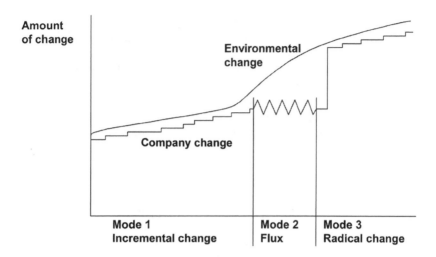

Figure 3. *Periods of turbulence*

needing a considerable period of time to come to realise what is happening to it. IBM spent a number of years in the turbulent zone, doing experiments to find a new way forward (e.g. decentralise, centralise again, single/multiple branding etc.). While these experiments were going on the company did not seem to progress. With the business environment moving on, the gap with the market seemed to widen. The company seemed to be getting into more and more difficulty.

Inevitably the gap between business environment and the organisational understanding of it gets reflected in the bottom line, profitability goes down and the company moves into the red. At that stage, the company is in crisis. Management realises that the experiments aren't working. At this point, one of two things may happen. Many companies collapse. Or, just in time, the company makes a radical step change, something that would have been culturally impossible in an earlier era. Often this is associated with bringing in new people, possibly a new chief executive. The new team institutionalises a new way of doing things. If the diagnosis is right the company may come back from the brink.

Mintzberg (1979) has portrayed this process as cyclical, suggesting that all organisations will periodically run into such major life-or-death situations. Having found the new successful approach the organisation will move out of crisis by building its new business around the new idea. But when the business grows again things will become more and more organised. Under competitive pressure, it will increasingly operate, and think, as an efficient machine. This means that its range of vision will narrow, and developments in the business environment will start to escape its attention. Until the new crisis hits.

The problem is often seen as one of forecasting, but the issue is more fundamental than that. Organisations need to be concerned about their ability to "see". "Predict-and-control" cannot deal with structural change as it does not generate the right questions. It is clear that if we wish to make some headway we need to move on from forecasting to a more flexible way of looking at the future. Scenario analysis, contrary to forecasting, can react flexibly to structural change.

The Problem of Business Success

There are a lot of very successful organisations. Without being aware of it they may be more in need of a strategic management rethink than those who are struggling. Pierre Wack in his well-known *Harvard Business Review* article (1985) on scenario-based planning suggested that in times of rapid change the large well-run companies are in particular danger of suffering from strategic failure, caused by a crisis of perception. He defines this as the inability to see an emergent novel reality by being locked inside obsolete assumptions. As we saw earlier, Miller argues that most outstanding organisations lapse into decline because they have developed too sharp an edge. They narrow the focus of their attention to a reducing set of strengths and functions, while neglecting others. The organisation will become a more and more efficient machine, doing fewer things increasingly well. Considerable initial success with a focusing strategy leads to strong reinforcement of the "success formula" through cognitive, cultural and structural mechanisms.

Large organisations get set in their ways more firmly than small ones. They need to organise things in more detail. Procedures and methods, once in place, become more and more difficult to change. Underlying premises get forgotten, and are impossible to question. Change is not welcome; it is "difficult to argue with success". Often assumptions get embedded in strong cultures, determining also informal and non-verbal ways in which people communicate with each other. The system reinforces the mental models, and these become more and more rooted. Contrary observations in the business environment are explained away or denied. Or signals received are considered "inconsistent" and therefore insufficiently reliable to act on. In times of sudden change the crisis of perception has become almost unavoidable.

The problem comes to the surface when societal change reduces interest in the organisation's main activity. The organisation then finds that it does not have a rich enough mental model to observe and internalise signals of evolving need in the outside environment and invent a new success formula.

If a system cannot account for seemingly contradictory and inconsistent signals, its model of the world is not detailed enough. If an organisation finds inconsistent signals overwhelming, it should consider that its model of reality may be too simplistic. In order to survive organisational systems need a degree of complexity, commensurate with the complexity of the environment with which they interact (Ashby's law of requisite variety, Ashby 1983). Organisations that have come through an extended period of success almost invariably lack this requisite variety.

GM's CEO, when put under considerable pressure by environmentalists during the annual general meeting, suggested that "Detroit would play ball, if only the market would make up its mind." This raises the interesting question whether it is the market that reacts "chaotically" to the environmental challenge, or whether the Detroit mental model is inadequate to make sense of what is going on. And if the latter is the case could it learn to understand pattern and consistency in market signals if its variety were developed to the requisite level? A system that lacks requisite variety will not perceive signals that fall outside its narrow coherence model. Its vision is blinkered.

In those circumstances it is advisable to heed Weick's (1979) advice to organisations to "complicate yourself". In these circumstances it is more than ever important that new perspectives are introduced from the outside.

Crisis of the Rationalist Approach

The rationalist paradigm is based on a number of tacit assumptions, which are fundamental to its capability to deliver. As we saw the basic tenets are the following:

- It is useful to think of the organisation as a unitary actor in its environment.
- There is only one best answer to the strategy question.
- Everyone thinking rationally on behalf of the organisation will arrive at the same conclusion.
- Implementation follows discovery of the strategy.

It can work only if things are clear and predictable, and people understand and act reasonably.

Box 3   Role of invention

A successful competitive strategy must be an original invention. It cannot be otherwise. One should not be misled by "gurus" peddling general-purpose business models or success formulas. Firms live in a competitive environment, and are surrounded by competitors who are ready to copy anything that seems to lead to success. Competitive success requires finding barriers to such emulation. Therefore successful strategies must belong uniquely to the organisation, and are not available to the rest of the world. If there would be a codified way to work out the one right answer, this would be available to all competitors in the market, and would for this reason alone quickly become the wrong answer. In the final analysis this is the overwhelming philosophical problem with the rationalistic paradigm in the context of organisational strategy.

Rationalist strategic management has allowed people over the years to successfully express their strategic situation, helping them to move forward. But there have also been major failures. Observers such as Mintzberg (*The Rise and Fall of Strategic Planning*, 1994) describe the symptoms of many of these. But surfacing the fundamental underlying premises of the rationalist paradigm raises the question whether rationality can ever explain the whole picture of organisational behaviour. This has given rise to alternative views on strategy.

EVOLUTIONARY PARADIGM

The traditional rationalist approach to the discipline of strategic management has gradually become less and less capable of modelling strategic thinking. This is due to logical problems with the notion of sustainable prescriptions for business success in an ever faster moving competitive world, and growing insights in the area of complexity that make us realise better the fundamental limitations to prescience. In reaction the evolutionary school of thinking has emerged.

Doubts about the rationalist school of thought are not new. Researchers studying organisational decision making and analysing what decision makers do on a day-by-day basis observe that decision making is not only a rationalist process. For example, Charles Lindblom studied managers in organisations in the 1950s (Lindblom 1959). He observed that, rather than goal-seeking, "ills-avoiding" better characterises what is happening, aiming at strategies for avoiding pain, harm, or constraints.

Stewart Brand suggests that nature evolves away from constraints, not toward goals (Brand 1999). Lindblom saw the same thing happening in management. Moreover, different people are moving away from different constraints, depending on where they are in the organisation. The organisational decision-making process is polycentric. Mutual adjustments and bargaining between these centres is required before the organisation can do anything coherent at all.

That means high value is placed on consensus-seeking behaviour. Without agreement, an organisation will be paralysed. On the whole, organisations don't like mavericks. People are needed who are prepared to make the effort to come to a common conclusion. When different ideas exist, they are often held back and not articulated clearly, as people fear that it would make the negotiation process more difficult.

As a consequence policy decisions are created in a serial process. There is no grand strategy, only "just one thing after another". Lindblom called this "muddling through".

A more recent analyst in this school is Brian Quinn. Based on his experience in General Electric and other large mainstream corporations, Quinn writes:

> The full strategy is rarely written in any one place. The processes used to arrive at the total strategy are typically fragmented, evolutionary, and largely intuitive. Although one can frequently find embedded in these fragments some very refined pieces of formal strategy analysis, the real strategy tends to evolve as internal decisions and external events flow together, to create a new, widely shared consensus for action among key members of the top management team. (Quinn 1980)

Mintzberg observed that executives going about their job:

- Prefer verbal over numeric information.
- Prefer conversation to reading.
- Gather information on an anecdotal basis.
- Are highly mistrustful of others' general theories.
- Avoid the "grand design" sort of decisions.
- Prefer to make smaller incremental decisions.
- Let the overall strategy emerge.

He coined the term "emergent strategy" to indicate that when people talk about their strategy they will normally talk about something that comes to them from the past, a series of events that have retroactively been interpreted as a pattern, recognised as "our strategy".

Lately complexity theory has impressed on the world the view that many phenomena taking place in nature are unpredictable not just because we lack the requisite analytical knowledge and capacity, but because they are unpredictable in principle. This is related to complexity and non-linear characteristics of systems, which can be shown to result in behaviour, which is intrinsically unknowable in its detail. Terms such as "the butterfly effect" ("the flap of the butterfly's wing in Brazil triggering a tornado in Texas") illustrate this view. The lessons of complexity science for organisations can be summarised by simply noting that human activity that involves the interaction of many participants, such as in organisations, generates the possibility of emergent behaviour. Emergence is defined as the appearance of unpredictable or incalculable behaviour resulting from the interaction of many simple components that cannot be derived from knowledge of what each component of the system does in isolation.

A picture emerges of strategies existing primarily to satisfy the psychological needs of the managers, in particular the need to feel in control. Meanwhile, random mutations take place, and only the fittest survive. Apple survived, while Commodore (how many remember this once well-known computer manufacturer?) did not. But if you look for some mistake in Commodore's argument or reasoning versus Apple's, the evolutionary theorists argue you won't find it. You will merely find that some systems have had a random mutation that helped them, while others were not so lucky and went under.

The evolutionists tell us that the idea that we can change and improve our corporate survival chances by thinking through our situation and trying to develop an adequate strategy is based on an illusion. Mintzberg suggests that people are discovering this and we are witnessing "the fall of strategic planning".

The evolutionary perspective while intellectually appealing cannot be popular with organisational managers. They are not prepared to accept that thinking about the future is done only to satisfy psychological needs to create order in the mind. Managers believe they ought to be able to accomplish something in the real world. The pure evolutionary paradigm has little or no forum in the organisational world.

Yet, in times of unusual turbulence the business environment may seem chaotic. Change seems to accelerate and managers have difficulty in continuously redeveloping theories-in-use which organise observations. There may be a feeling of information overload, and loss of grip on the situation. In such circumstances the view takes hold that there is not a lot of sense in spending time trying to think through strategy, the world is too complex to try to get a handle on it. The best we can do is react as things come at us, and hope that serendipity makes us choose the mutations which will make us into the winning species on the competitive battlefield. Most managers have an acute awareness of a considerable element of randomness in what happens. As Mintzberg observed, most managers do not believe in the one grand "strategic answer" that will solve everything. Lindblom saw a lot of ambivalence among managers about declaring a position. They know that they operate in a system driven by negotiation and compromise, so it is better not to be too "up front", and to keep things fluid, so that there is room for manoeuvre. While the media project the story of the all-powerful and heroic CEO, and consultants and academics try to advise on the best strategy forward, managers maintain a healthy dose of scepticism. They need the reports; they pay considerable fees for them, but the reports have some other function than telling them what to do.

PROCESSUAL PARADIGM

Variance Theories and Process Theories

In discussing what we can and cannot know about our situation it is useful to distinguish two types of theories about the world (Mohr 1982), called variance theories and process theories.

A variance theory states that result Y is associated with a change in variable X. There is a fixed relationship between the two. X is necessary and sufficient to explain Y. More X means more Y (although there may be statistical variation in the prediction). For example, lung cancer is related to smoking. More smoking means more lung cancer. Or more resources into R&D will increase innovation. Or a more self-reliant workforce is more productive. Inflation erodes confidence. And so on. Variance theories are empirical. As soon as we try to explain causally how smoking causes cancer we enter the realm of process theory.

A process theory explains how X causes Y. It specifies how X is necessary for Y to happen. However, it may not be sufficient, there may be other factors to consider. The theory allows us to explain the past but it is not entirely predictive. For example, malaria is passed on by mosquito bites. If I find I am suffering from malaria I can conclude that a mosquito has passed the disease after having been in contact with a malaria sufferer. However, not all mosquito bites result in malaria. Evolution is a process theory. A process theory needs to take account of the temporal order of events – time order and history are important in process theory. As far as the future is concerned the only thing we can say is "if not X then not Y".

Variance theories aim to predict, process theories aim to causally describe or explain. In strategy the PIMS database (Buzzell & Gale 1987) was an attempt to develop a variance theory of organisational success. It aimed to pronounce on how ROI varies with a number of strategic variables, based on a large database of experience. Most managerial experience results in variance theories in the managers' heads. On the other hand organisational evolution is a process theory, it can be brought to bear to explain causally how a specific organisation has emerged over time. But it has limited value in predicting what type of organisations will survive from now on.

Making the distinction between variance and process theory can be generally helpful in clarifying a paradigmatic battle. Blair Gibb (Amnesty International, Schwartz & Gibb 1999) suggested the following example. For years the human rights community has been exercised by debates about "universality" versus "cultural relativism" of human rights standards and norms. The debate seemed somehow sterile and dead-end. Blair Gibb believed that the problem, being expressed in variance terms, was not being posed properly. Thinking about slavery, and the process by which it stopped being an acceptable value, made her theorise that human rights were not "things" out there to be discovered, but were instead the state of a process occurring over time, being formed continually by the ongoing conversations between powers (such as states, armies, employers etc.) and people (subjects, civilians in wartime, employees etc.) and then among the various cultures (Asian, Western etc.) within which these relatively bounded conversations were taking place. The conclusion is that rather than push particular values the movement should understand this process and try to find intervention points where influence can be exercised.

A Process Theory of Strategy

While the rationalist approach to strategy is based on the assumption of ongoing valid variance theory the evolutionist approach limits itself to the use of process theory. But this does not imply that the only thing you can do is sit back and let things come over you. A process theory allows managers to think about how to intervene in the process, in order to improve the chances of success in the future. How to do that is the realm of the processual school of strategy.

The reason for the existence of the different paradigms in strategic management is uncertainty in the business situation. In long-term strategy uncertainty dominates and the evolutionist view comes to the fore. The nearer term one looks the more predictable the future seems to become, and in the very short term most people are inclined to forecast in the rationalist paradigm. How else would one cross the street in the face of oncoming traffic?

However, uncertainty exists not only in the environment but within organisations as well. As Mintzberg points out, the rationalist paradigm is based on the assumption that intentions in the organisation are clear and that reasonable people, having full understanding of the strategy, do reasonable things. No manager can be entirely confident on these scores. The institutional aspects of organisational behaviour are ambiguous. This is the domain of processual thinking.

The processual view starts from the premise that business success cannot be codified in the form of a variance theory, but that we can try to make the strategising process more skilful. As we discussed earlier success can only be based on an original invention. This implies that the organisation needs a process that mobilises the brain power of its people and their networking and observational skills. The process needs to make room for ideas. Any inventive idea directed towards improving the match between the organisational competencies and the business environment needs to be surfaced and considered, wherever these may originate in the organisation.

The strategist looks at evolution not so much in terms of the survival of actual organisations, but the survival of ideas. This makes them interested in what happens inside organisations. Rationalists and evolutionists worry less about how the organisational process works; why bother, if there's only one right answer, or alternatively if there is no answer at all? The processualist on the other hand is keenly interested in internal processes.

Studying the processes taking place inside organisations leads to the fundamental starting point of the processual paradigm, namely the interwovenness of action and thinking. Albert SzentGyorgi tells a story of a group of soldiers lost in the mountains (relayed by Weick 1990):

A small Hungarian detachment was on military manoeuvres in the Alps. Their young lieutenant sent a reconnaissance unit out into the icy wilderness just as it began to snow. It snowed for two days, and the unit did not return. The lieutenant feared that he had dispatched his men to their death, but the third day the unit returned. Where had they been? How had they found their way? "Yes," they said, "we considered ourselves lost and waited for the end, but then one of us found a map in his pocket. That calmed us down. We pitched camp, lasted out the snow storm, and then with the map we found our bearings. And here we are." The lieutenant took a good look at the map and discovered, to his astonishment, that it was a map of the Pyrenees.

Weick suggests: "If you are lost any old map is better than nothing." The map enabled the soldiers to get into action. They had been mentally disabled; but now the map, believed to represent the surroundings, gave them a new feeling of understanding and a reason to act. By taking action the soldiers started to obtain new feedback about their environment, and they entered a new "learning loop" which gradually built up their own understanding and mental map. The map got them out of the paralysed state that they were in. Accuracy did not come into it.

The processualist agrees with the evolutionist that most organisational situations are too complex to analyse in its entirety. Whether the strategic "answer" is right or wrong is initially not the main point.

The processualist holds that we need to get into a loop linking action, perception and thinking towards continual learning. An effective strategy is one that triggers our successful launch into that learning loop.

THE LEARNING LOOP

The "learning loop" is an integrative learning model, suggested by David Kolb, who synthesised it from the theories of Kurt Lewin, John Dewey, Jean Piaget, and others.

Figure 4 shows a diagrammatic representation. Starting at the top:

- We have experiences, some of which are important to us. Of particular interest are experiences that we perceive as related to our previous actions.
- We reflect upon these experiences, looking at what our action has created in relation to other events. The product of this reflection is a growing awareness of new patterns and trends in events we did not perceive before. Reflection is related to our ability to differentiate between our existing mental model and perception of a different reality.
- Through "cues of causality" we develop new theories on how our ideas about the world need to change as a result of these observations and reflections. The old mental model and the new reality are integrated in a new theory.
- Then we use these theories to plan new steps, and continue to turn these plans into action, testing the implications of our theory in new situations.

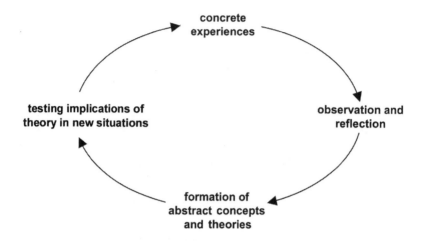

Figure 4. *Kolb's "learning loop"*

- This brings us back to the top. We obtain new experiences related to our actions, which only partly overlap with our expectation. Reason to reflect again.

And so we learn! Our new reflection on the results of our actions shows us that our theory needs developing again. And the process continues. Fundamental in the Kolb model is the role of action in any learning. The importance of the inclusion of action in the learning process was effectively summarised by Weick when he suggested "how do I know what I think until . . . I see how I act?" (Weick 1979).

Applied to strategy development the learning model projects integration of experience, sense-making and action into one holistic phenomenon. It suggests that for things to go right we need to:

- Perceive weak signals,
- Remember lessons from the past, and
- Adapt quickly if these have not prepared us for what actually happens.

The model is based on the idea of continuous development and improvement, rather than "the one right answer". Therefore the process view requires less emphasis on forecasts. Instead uncertainty and ambiguity are faced head on.

The application of the learning loop in an organisational context is discussed further below. However, we first need to consider the basic force, which drives an organisation to act as a learning organism. This is related to the organisation's perception of its purpose in the world.

Organisation as Organism

The processual paradigm sees the organisation as a complex adaptive system. It is open to the outside world, and adjusts its activities according to what it discovers there. However, the behaviour of complex adaptive systems is not simply a direct function of impinging external forces, like the behaviour of a ping-pong ball. Rather, as open systems become more complex, they tend to develop within themselves more and more complex mediating processes that intervene between external forces and behaviour. At higher levels of complexity these mediating processes become more autonomous and more determinative of behaviour. Through these processes the total organisation behaves differently from what would happen if all units in it were independent from each other. This difference, which determines the organisation's identity, manifests itself in the emergent behaviour of the total system. Emergent behaviour is the outside behavioural manifestation of the internal mediating processes. In systems terms the higher hierarchical level guides and constrains the actions of the lower levels. It is the constraints on the lower-level members that create the emergent behaviour of the total system (Checkland 1981). By imposing the appropriate "rules of the game" (either formal or informal) the upper level steers the emergent behaviour in a desirable direction. If such constraints did not exist, lower-level members would carry on as if they were independent, and there would be no emergent behaviour, and therefore no identity for the larger system.

Schein (1992) suggests that in organisations the constraints operate at three levels. At the deepest level are basic assumptions, mostly shared but also imposed by the organisation. This gives rise to the next level, which takes the form of shared values, creating beliefs about what is good, bad or indifferent. At the third (most visible) level we find the artefacts the values give rise to. At each of these levels the behaviour of the members of the organisation is being influenced, they are not any longer free to act.

The purpose of these processes is to perform essentially three functions (Checkland 1981):

- Adjusting the system's behaviour to deal with external contingencies.
- Directing the system towards more favourable environments to improve survival chances.

- Reorganising aspects of the system structure to make it more effective in these two tasks.

The need to perform these functions is driven by the need to survive. Stern discusses "living" systems, which he defines as systems that are continuously directed towards dual objectives of:

- Survival in a hostile environment, and
- Self-development in a benevolent environment (Stern 1906).

There are organisations that do not aim to survive, but that have been created to do a specific limited job, after which everyone involved fully intends to liquidate it. However, most organisations develop a way of acting in the world aimed at their own survival and development. These organisations therefore can be seen as living organisms in "Stern" terms.

Learning as Growth

Many organisations subscribe to a "progress or regress" view, lack of growth being taken as an indication of erosion and as basically unhealthy. The objective of growth, or self-development, however expressed, is a natural characteristic of a living organisation. Growth implies the existence of a reinforcing feedback loop driving the system forward. Later on we will associate this loop with the Business Idea of the organisation.

Organisations with a strong success formula often develop resistance to change. While busy with the business of development it will attempt to keep disturbances outside the system, by operating smaller subsidiary balancing feedback loops (single-loop learning, see below). This systemic behaviour can persist only as long as the environmental disturbances are small.

In turbulent environments the reinforcing feedback growth loop may need to be adapted to the changing situation in the environment (compare Figure 3 Periods of turbulence, page 28). Rather than resist change the organisation will try to create it, in what is sometimes called double-loop learning. In double-loop learning the system does not only attempt to make adjustments such that a predetermined preferred condition can be maintained, but also modifies its preferred condition in line with the fit with the environment (see Argyrus & Schon 1978).

The distinction is illustrated in Figure 5. Once we have developed an idea about a desirable future we will try to steer actions such to reduce the gap with current reality. It requires observation and measurement of

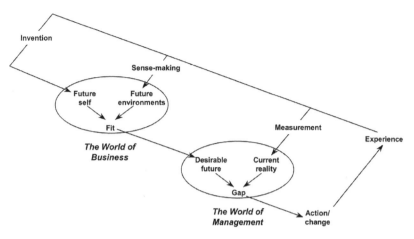

Figure 5. *Elements in strategic management*

the state of affairs and corrective action if required. This is single-loop learning, taking place in what is termed here the "thinking world of management". As long as external fluctuations are within the bounds of the organisation's capability to correct nothing much more is required. However, if things change to move the system outside its scope for corrective action the desired future needs to be reviewed. We are moving to a higher level of strategy-making, in what is called here the "thinking world of business". The task here is to first of all make sense of experience, to allow a new view on how the environment is functioning to emerge. The second part of the task is to reinvent one's success formula, or Business Idea, in order to create a better fit with this new view of the future. The result of this strategic thinking is a reformulation of the desired future to take account of these new insights that from now will steer action in the world of management. Engaging this higher-level strategic loop moves the system into double-loop learning.

GROUP LEARNING

The processual view suggests that organisations, in order to be successful, need to adopt the idea of the learning loop and build up related capabilities for perception, reflection, the development of theories about the environment, and joint action. However, we need to consider these ideas explicitly in an organisational context. Learning in institutions is not the same as learning by individuals. Organisational learning is not only the sum of individual learning by organisation members. People influence each other in their learning behaviour, which has additional specific group aspects that need to be considered.

Kolb suggests selecting individuals in the decision-making team such that all four skills in the loop (see Figure 4) are represented. The assumption is that a combination of people with these diverse aptitudes will improve the learning capability of a group as a whole as all essential capabilities are represented in the team.

We use the model in a different sense. Our interest is in applying the model to the learning of a group of people, or even a whole organisation. This aspect introduces specific questions concerning institutional learning, involving organisational processes that turn individual perceptions into institutional ones.

Institutional Learning

As Lindblom suggested, in the world of organisations it is only when people align their ideas that the organisation starts exhibiting specific institutional behaviour. The learning loop can only work in an institutional sense if people participate together, share ideas about new patterns resulting from reflection on experience, build a common theory, plan and act together. As a result of that they have a joint experience without which organisational learning is impossible. We extend the theory from its base of individual learning to institutional learning by introducing the notion of institutional action. We define this as "a coherent set of individual actions which are supported as a set by a self-sustaining critical mass of opinion in the organisation". We suggest that one can speak of institutional action only if a "critical mass" of sense-making and response planning is shared. Below the critical mass there are only unrelated individual actions, which lead to individual rather than organisational learning. Without consensus or shared meaning individual actions will not cohere, the organisation will fragment and, if left in this stage, ultimately disintegrate. However, if a degree of alignment of mental models has taken place within the organisation, planning becomes effectively a joint activity, and experiences will be common, leading to joint reflection in the group and reinforcement of a shared mental model.

Therefore the institutional version of the learning loop introduces the additional factor of the degree of alignment on theories of meaning in the organisation. With an initial "critical mass" of it, consensus can feed on itself through the learning loop by feedback from joint action and experience. In this context the learning loop works as a reinforcing feedback loop. With alignment above a minimum critical level it spirals towards increasing consensus, and stronger action. For this to function institutional learning requires an effective process of conversation, through which strategic cognitions can be compared, challenged and negotiated. Through this participants learn to understand each other's worldviews and line of argumentation, creating a joint understanding of the situation at hand, so that a collective experience results.

Strategic Conversation

In the world of institutions the processual paradigm revolves around conversation. The learning loop model shows the interwovenness of thinking and action. If action is based on planning on the basis of a mental model, then institutional action must be based on a shared mental model. Only through a process of conversation can elements of personal observation and thought be structured and embedded in the accepted and shared organisational theories-in-use. Similarly new perceptions of opportunities and threats, based on the reflection on experiences of actions playing out in the environment, can only become institutional property through conversation. An effective strategic conversation must incorporate a wide range of initially unstructured thoughts and views, and out of this create shared interpretations of the world in which the majority of the individual insights can find a logical place. And it is only through such embedding that joint action can result leading to new joint experiences and reinforcement of the shared theories-in-use.

What is required to create an effective institutional conversation? Obviously any conversation requires first of all a language in which the objects of our attention can be expressed. Some of the language of strategy is codified in public domain language, and can be learned from strategic management textbooks. In addition most organisations over time build up their own language, based on their own responses to specific breakdown situations they experienced and their own unique success formula. The existence and proliferation of labels and jargon are manifestations of this process of language building, essential for organisational learning to take place. However, language concepts can only be representations of yesterday's problems. They were generated in the past as categorisations of particular historical patterns of events, and used in coping with specific breakdown situations. It is inevitable that any new situation will at first be described in terms of past categorisations. This will almost by definition stop short of completely describing new reality. Yet the search for a new and original response to a new situation is facilitated by the conversational process. Yesterday's concepts lead to tomorrow's unique inventions!

The conversational process needs to lead to increased alignment of ideas in order to activate the organisational learning cycle. The language of organisations is rational. People talk in order to convince each other. "I argue my case trying to convince you, and you do the same to me. Eventually we come to a negotiated solution in which I am convinced by some points you made and you see some arguments my way." This is a process of measuring and comparing the utility of competing ideas by reference to the shared worldview, from which the organisation derives its purpose. This can only be achieved by starting from basic shared principles. This shared worldview (for example, based on the dual purpose of survival and growth of the organisation, as suggested by Stern, see page 40) provides the platform for the strategic conversation in which a line of logical argumentation will be built leading to a preferred outcome. Rationality may not be the way in which strategy emerges but it is an essential shaping force in the strategic conversation process leading to the strategic invention.

Contribution of the Evolutionary View

So far we see the contributions to the institutional learning process from rationality (conversation based on rational argument) and process (the creation of alignment and joint plans and actions). However, the model is not complete without evolution. Learning can take place only if experience deviates from plan in an unexpected way. If everything happens according to expectation there is no learning. This aspect highlights the contribution of the evolutionary perspective, not so much evolution of organisations, as the evolution of theories and ideas inside organisations. If we define evolution as a process that works through (1) a source of variation, (2) a weeding-out mechanism which rejects the less effective ideas and (3) a source of constancy – so that the lesson that has been learned can be retained for the future – then every learning process is a process of evolution of ideas, their generation, testing and embedding.

Members of the team need to know that there is no one right answer. Different views must be legitimate. As a result the institutional "theory of the world" mutates, with a consequent adjustment in action. The group observes the consequences of this in its experiences, and learns the effectiveness of the mutation. Depending on the result it will be retained or filtered out.

Learning Pathologies

There are two potential pathologies in this institutional learning process. The first one manifests itself if the "critical mass" of consensus is not reached. Divergence of view can become a self-enforcing process, with lack of consensus leading to divergent action, divergent experiences, and a further erosion of what is left of the common view. The reinforcing feedback loop spirals towards fragmentation. This may become an out-of-control systemic reaction. The organisation will not overcome the problem without conscious management action to move the team back over the minimum consensus threshold. Management action needs to be directed towards increasing cohesion, recreating the "critical mass" of shared views, such that joint action can resume.

However, at the opposite extreme there is the pathology, which relates to a lack of diversity of thought, sometimes referred to as "groupthink". If consensus is strong enough it starts feeding on itself through the learning loop. The feedback loop spirals towards one view of the world. More cohesion in theories of action leads to an increase in commonality of action, leading to more shared experiences and a reinforcement of the dominant theory about how the world works. The ideas focus and impoverish more and more, and the organisation's stock of reactions to environmental disturbance reduces. An effective learning system requires enough variety in its mental model to interlink signals, received from the outside world, with each other. Without this these signals will be experienced as inconsistent or incoherent, not understood and therefore not relevant for any useful learning and adaptive action.

The two pathologies generate the managerial dilemma between cohesion and innovative divergence. Management of organisational learning involves a continuous attention to the balance between the two.

THE INTEGRATIVE MODEL

Summarising the above the following four crucial points emerge:

- Alignment of ideas and mental models (integration) is crucial to trigger the institutional learning loop through joint action.
- The learning process acts as a reinforcing feedback loop. Without active management it will spiral out of control towards serious dysfunctionality.
- Too much alignment leads to a lack of requisite variety (differentiation), leading to an impoverished ability to appreciate what is going on.

- Too little alignment leads to fragmentation and ultimately dissolution of the organisational logic.

The deviation of emergent strategy from intended strategy is the driving force of the institutional learning loop. Such deviation initially creates differentiation in views in the organisation, with different people interpreting the situation in their own way. The alignment process then needs to bring these views together and arbitrate on the basis of rationality. In this way all three schools of thought in strategy have their role in the organisational learning process, see Figure 6.

The perspective of "organisational learning" provides a viewpoint that allows the three models (rationalist, evolutionary and processual) to be holistically incorporated. This can be illustrated by the application of Kolb's model of learning with its four elements of obtaining experience, reflection, mental model building and action, as shown in Figure 6. The institutional aspect adds the key role of the strategic conversation.

It seems that in a situation of this complexity three perspectives is not a luxury. Organisational learning represents a way in which we can integrate these three perspectives, all three playing a key role in describing reality, and therefore demanding consideration.

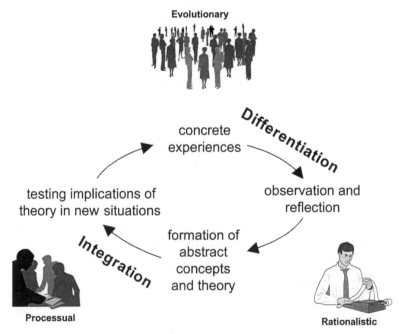

Figure 6. *Integrating the three schools of strategy*

Box 4   How organisational learning links with strategy

Organisational learning	Strategy
Learning loop driving force	Aims
Mental model, theory of the world	Organisational success formula
Perception, differentiation, reflection on experience, seeing new patterns	Analysis of the environment
Integration of reflection into mental model	Assessment of strategic fit
Planning future steps	Development of policy to increase fit
Act	Implement

Traditional strategy is based on the rationalist paradigm. In this book we propose a richer model, based on organisational learning, to cope with the modern fast-moving world. The bridge between traditional strategy and organisational learning is summarised in Box 4.

Speed of Organisational Learning

We emphasised the importance of action for the learning loop to take off. Wherever we find power to act in the organisation a learning loop is at work. Therefore the organisation is not just one loop but many, working through individuals and groups throughout the organisation. The shorter the loop the faster learning takes place. For this reason individuals learn faster than groups, and groups learn faster than whole organisations. Communication in organisations is a time-consuming business, as each level needs to internalise observations, reflect on these and adjust mental models before the message can be transferred to the next level. This is the reason why large hierarchical organisations react so slowly, as illustrated by the oil industry at the time of the energy crisis (see page 14).

De Geus has suggested that speed of organisational learning is the ultimate competitive weapon (De Geus 1988). What can organisations do to increase it? Unblocking communication channels is obviously a first essential condition. If information does not flow up and down the hierarchical ladder the overall learning loop cannot function. But even if communication is effective, delays due to personal information gestation times at the various levels in the loop will limit overall reaction time. The speed with which individuals appreciate new situations can be influenced to a degree (see Box 5). But the time an individual requires to reflect on incoming information sets a limit here.

Box 5   Speeding up decision making

At a major chemicals company strategists plan simultaneously for four different short-term outcomes for each initiative, setting up predetermined "signposts" to indicate when it's time to take another course. This, says the chief scenario strategist, enables the company to abandon a strategy or alter it in hours or days.

Some time ago the company was considering whether to resell another producer's chemical used in computer-chip production. "We thought that because of our expertise, we'd have a wonderful new business opportunity here", recalls the strategic planner. But at the first inklings of a lacklustre market for chip memory, one of the company's predetermined signposts for danger, it abandoned the project in hours. "In the past, we'd have had one goal, to make the business work regardless of what happens in the market-place", the strategist says.

The only alternative left to increase speed of learning is to reduce the length of the loop itself, by reducing the number of individuals in it. *Short learning loops mean delegation of decision making, locating the power-to-act organisationally close to the point of experience and perception.* Organisations in fast changing environments tend to decentralise, with top management acting more as a co-ordinating body than as a setter of strategy. The learning organisation does not have one all-embracing strategy, but many more or less co-ordinated strategies. Such organisations can be highly flexible and adaptive, but there is a price to pay. Breaking up the organisation in small units reduces synergy opportunities, such as economies of scale advantages.

In relatively stable situations, where cost leadership dominates competitiveness, power tends to be centralised with the purpose of creating a finely tuned organisational machine, capable of exploiting economies of scale to the maximum. The price to pay here is reduced adaptability.

The situation is a typical managerial dilemma. Managers need to balance economies of scale with adaptability. Extremes on both sides are dangerous. The finely tuned machine goes under with the product it was designed to produce. The ultimate learning organisation goes under due to its high cost. There is no perfect answer here. The situation is a dynamic one, which needs constant attention from top management.

The Contribution of Scenario-based Planning

Earlier we defined scenario-based planning as a learning approach to planning and strategising. *Scenarios play a role in all important aspects of the learning loop.* Against the background of the integrative model we can now be more specific about the contribution of scenario-based planning. At the individual level:

- As a cognitive device: A set of scenarios is a highly efficient data organisation tool. It creates structures in the events/patterns in the environment and names these. Stories are efficient for giving many different bits of information a mutual context, thereby making the cognitive aspects of any situation more manageable to deal with (see also "Memories of the Future" in Part Two, page 133).
- As a perception device: As individuals people see certain things and overlook others, based on their existing mental models and resulting expectations. The scenario process expands the mental models of participants and increases the range of what they see.
- As a reflection tool: The scenario process helps people think through more effectively ideas generated in the strategic conversation. It brings in new perspectives from the outside world.

At the group level:

- As a ready-made language provider, assisting the strategic conversation across a wide range of (even partly conflicting) views: The process allows diverse views to be considered. It identifies irreducible uncertainty. It provides room for multiple interpretations.
- As a conversational facilitation vehicle: Scenario-based planning provides an organised way of discussing relevant aspects of the business in an organisational context. It taps into knowledge available in the individual members of the organisation.
- As a vehicle for mental model alignment: It puts all the above in a form suitable for corporate strategic conversation and consideration, accommodating coherent joint strategic action.

Scenario-based planning makes sense of the situation by looking at multiple futures, which are treated as equally plausible, reflecting the inherent uncertainty in the situation, but also what is considered predictable. It is non-prescriptive. It recognises that successful competitive strategies must be original inventions made by organisations. It therefore employs processes that enhance the capability of the organisation to mobilise resources towards greater inventiveness and innovation.

Finally, scenario-based planning helps a management team to avoid the worst aspects of the two pathological opposites of groupthink and fragmentation in the organisation. For an inward-looking tightly cohesive group moving along a single mental track scenarios inject an element of caution, asking "what could go wrong?" It raises the important questions that the group is not asking themselves due to their limited vision. For a fragmented confused group on the other hand scenarios open up new possibilities for joint action by defusing tensions caused by differences of interest and creating the strategic conversation that "creates order in chaos" and increases understanding of others' views.

In Part Two we will first organise the discussion of the role of scenario-based planning in organisational learning by reference to its key roles in the learning loop, namely perception, theory building, and creating joint action. In Part Three we will develop this into ideas for the practice of scenario-based planning. Part Four will deal with the organisational dynamics aspects.

Part Two

The Principles of Scenario-based Planning

OVERVIEW

So far we have discussed the principles of the three perspectives on strategy, and the potential for integrating these through the concept of institutional learning. In this part we will turn our attention to developing an organisational learning framework which will make this effective in the strategic conversation of the normal every-day organisational world.

Strategy succeeds when an organisation manages to adapt itself such that it "gains the high ground", i.e. maximises its chances of achieving its purpose. In order to make this happen the organisation needs to understand itself, its purpose, as well as the environmental landscape. These have to be studied in each other's context.

We will develop a definition of the "organisational self", which we call the Business Idea. It expresses the logic of the organisation's ability to survive and develop in terms of organisational characteristics, which can be articulated and tested against environmental assumptions. We will emphasise how each successful Business Idea for the future has at its core an original entrepreneurial invention, underpinned by a new and unique insight about how this organisation can interact with the world.

We will then consider the business environment around the current and future Business Ideas of the organisation. We will find it riddled with uncertainty and ambiguity. We will then introduce scenario-based planning, which does not attempt to predict what is unpredictable, but copes with uncertainty by considering multiple, equally plausible futures.

We will discuss *iterative* scenario-based planning as a means of learning to see the organisation in its environment in a new perspective, and in this way gaining, over time, the unique insight that is at the core of each successful Business Idea. We will consider how this unique Business Idea can be tested, using a set of scenarios as a test bed. Resulting from this the way forward will gradually emerge.

Following this we discuss these topics from an institutional perspective and develop the crucial role of the "strategic conversation" in the organisation. The three fundamental steps of learning – perception, theory building and joint action – are all group activities that depend on the strategic conversation. Scenario-based planning can be seen as an effective way of enhancing the strategic conversation. Sharing multiple stories about the future makes the organisation more perceptive about its environment, and forces reflection on experience and theories-in-use. Institutional reflection on the Business Idea creates options for joint action.

Finally, we repeat, there can be no organisational success without an element of uniqueness in the organisation's approach to the world. The essence of strategy is invention. The process of strategy invention can be helped along with tools and techniques as explained here, but they can only help, not replace the thinking of the manager/entrepreneur and his/her team who have to stay with it until the moment of insight arrives. An original invention cannot be forced.

Chapter Four

Strategising

This chapter provides an overview of scenario-based planning in the wider context of management's strategising task. In later chapters we will develop important aspects in more detail.

STRATEGY AND LEARNING

We base the following discussion on the model of the organisation as a living and learning organism, with its inherent ultimate purpose of survival and self-development. We have seen how strategising of a successful organisation can be interpreted as an integration of perception, thinking and action in one learning loop. And how this allows us to provide a useful place to the lessons of all three strategy paradigms (rationalist, evolutionary, processual). This is the definition of strategising that we will take as the starting point of our discussion. In other words we will consider strategy invention and development as part of a wider integrated mental activity of which perception and real world action are also fundamental parts. Strategising along this definition is portrayed as a loop, i.e. it is never finished. Reality is always different from expectation and behaviour therefore always needs to be adjusted.

Introducing the idea of organisational learning begs the question of what needs to be learned in order to create a successful organisation. Following our "double-loop learning" model discussed in Part One (Figure 5, page 41) we will consider this in two parts, single-loop or adaptive learning and double-loop or generative learning.

Adaptive learning is comparable to the process of navigation. Consider an animal navigating its way through the forest, on its way to access resources needed for survival. What is needed to do this successfully? The first thing it needs to be aware of is its own capabilities for moving around. Birds have very different capabilities from monkeys, which are different from lions. Each has its own strengths and weaknesses and has to optimise its behaviour accordingly. These creatures also need to know the territory and adapt their behaviour to the obstacles they find there. Moving in a straight line can be dangerous; somewhere you are going to hit something. Twisting and turning while moving around requires an ability to perceive the lay of the land. Having the use of an accurate mental map of the territory is as important for survival as knowing your own capabilities. This is the adaptive part of strategising. It involves knowing one's own strengths and weaknesses and mapping out the environment such that strengths can be exploited and the effect of weaknesses minimised. The strategising aspect relates to considering how strengths can be developed further and weaknesses repaired in order to improve the system's navigating performance in the future.

The animals are on their way somewhere. They carry a more or less complex system of goals that motivates them to go on the move. Organisations are human activity systems, and as such can exercise a higher degree of control over their aspirations. As human navigators we are particularly interested in the final destination of our trip and the sense of direction this instils. We can question the current aspirations and invent new ones. In organisational terms this is the area of deciding a vision for the organisation's mission. It is what we call here the generative part of strategising.

Generative strategising often takes a backseat against the immediate needs of adaptive strategising. Most organisations try to consider, express and target how they want to develop in the future, but many get stuck in survival mode, where the need for "finding nutrition" overwhelms the care for "long-term direction".

Navigation management in this metaphor involves matching behavioural routines and recipes to situations. The system must be capable of learning, which means reflect on feedback, and express this as adaptation of behaviour in terms of its routines. The routines are based on past experience and need to be adapted from time to time. The navigation manager needs to know the system itself that has generated these routines. The routines tend to develop a life of their own; they are embedded in the system itself. They need to adapt to what the system finds in its environment. The strategic thinking process becomes addressing a sequence of questions, "what are we doing?", "what could we be doing?" and "what should we be doing?" (Normann 2001). The first question focuses on the "self", the second on the environment and the options it presents and the third on strategic decision making. Whether we are considering generative or adaptive strategising making an accurate distinction between the self and the environment seems a precondition for successful navigation.

The above definition of generative strategising begs the question of the ultimate criteria on which direction is based. In Part One we specified the highest level of the organisational goal system as the dual aim of survival and self-development (Stern 1906). The issues of survival and growth need to be addressed with reference to the specifics of the organisation under consideration. In order to operationalise this we will later (Chapter Five) introduce the concept of the "Business Idea". We will argue that underlying every successful organisation lays an idea acting as the driving force for success. We will see that this idea is specific to the organisation, and no two organisations can have the same Business Idea.

Uniqueness must be the ultimate criterion on whether we have been successful in our strategising; there is no successful strategy, and therefore no survival and self-development, unless it is different from what others are doing. Survival is a race. Your strategy has to be different, better than that of others.

Therefore the ultimate purpose of strategising (and generative strategising in particular) is to gain a new original and unique insight in where the business environment is going in the future, in an area where the strengths of the organisation can be utilised. The Business Environment can be interpreted as a system. Insight means perceiving the connections and finding the sensitive points of maximum leverage. Strategising, thinking and practice, is about perceiving what, behind the apparent uncertainties, is predetermined, as the basis for the unique insight that is needed for a strategic edge.

Being the first to see the new reality allows you to use outside forces to your advantage (like a judo player), rather than avoiding the punches (like a boxer). We'll discuss later how scenario-based planning can assist management in this task.

ORTHODOXY AND REFRAMING

Satisficing

But history has shown that there is a serious danger that we are unable to see the emergent novel reality by being locked inside obsolete assumptions. Making original inventions is not something that managers set themselves as their daily task. As problem-solvers managers, under constant pressure of the day-to-day, are subject to what Perkins (Perkins *et al.* 1983) has called "makes-sense epistemology". We work until we feel a situation makes sense, i.e. that it hangs together and is congruent with prior beliefs. Early closure then protects from the danger of contrary evidence. This does not require a lot of scenario-based planning. A claim that seems self-evident already may be enough. It also means that one story about the situation is enough. When sense is achieved there is no need to continue. It is essentially what Simon (1979) called "satisficing". Managers are overloaded with information. "What information consumes is rather obvious: it consumes the attention of its recipients. Hence a wealth of information creates a poverty of attention, and a need to allocate that attention efficiently among the over-abundance of information sources that might consume it" (Simon 1971). So managers default to the simplest more or less functional thing to do. The "makes-sense" approach seems robust for a number of reasons:

- It is quick
- It is (mostly) adequate
- It filters out bad theories
- It feels natural and comfortable
- It protects cherished beliefs and recipes.

The "makes-sense" explanation of the situation has the tendency to become the dominating thinking orthodoxy. Most organisations spend energy and money on environmental analysis, in order to gain new insights. This analysis takes many forms, from personal conversations by managers to detailed statistical research by expert departments. The problem with any traditional analysis is, however, that underlying it is always this dominating thinking orthodoxy setting the research questions, limiting the search and prejudicing the answer. In scenario-based planning we call this the Business-As-Usual mental model. Strategising only on the basis of Business-As-Usual is fighting yesterday's war and is doomed to fail.

The Big Unarticulated Issue

However, most companies, even those in "makes-sense" thinking mode, have looming somewhere at the edge of their collective consciousness what Peter Martin (1997) calls "the big unarticulated issue". Everybody feels it, it is there, always present, the imminent threat or the unseized opportunity. The challenge that nobody can face. It is so vast, so different from Business-As-Usual, that existing management thinking just can't cope. But all the time there's that nagging worry: what should we be doing about the big issue, the challenge we're not yet ready to tackle? So the organisation looks elsewhere, carrying on with the day-to-day business. Sometimes this is a sensible reaction:

anticipating the future prematurely can be just as costly as reacting too late. And in any case, even if you have identified the challenge correctly this does not mean you will respond to it properly.

Peter Martin suggests some examples. Consider computers, where no one in the industry has yet come to terms with a fundamental change in customers' needs. They don't want to buy computers any more: instead, they want effortless, low-cost, transparent information processing. They want all the rest of the hoo-ha, the standards battles, the product choices, the compatibility issues, the security problems, to go away. Locked in a struggle for market dominance, the industry is not ready to recognise it yet. But eventually, someone will, setting a pattern for the industry for a long time to come.

In cars, the issue is distribution, responsible for nearly half the value added. The old system of small, franchised dealerships is cracking up. There are lots of tentative stabs at a new framework: car sales on the internet, auto superstores, Daewoo's wholly-owned distribution chain in the UK, Ford's possible introduction of direct sales in Indianapolis. But so far, they are just straws in the wind, an indication that everybody in the industry knows about the issue – but that none of the big boys is yet ready to make a wholesale commitment to a new approach.

In financial services, the issue is the potential disappearance of most of the physical manifestations of banking. When customers switch the loyalty in their banking relationship from an institution to a budget program running on their home PCs, the industry will be transformed. So far, most big banks are treating this with extreme caution, confining their experiments to telephone banking or proprietary electronic systems. At some point, though, one of the big players will switch to a standard program like Intuit's Quicken or Microsoft Money. At that moment, retail banking will change forever. Until it does, the industry is pretending the problem doesn't exist.

In healthcare and pharmaceuticals, the unaddressed issue is health economics. At some point, purchasers will start to address the question of which illness is most cheaply addressed by drugs and which by hospital treatment. When healthcare purchasers start doing this sort of calculation, some expensive drugs will suddenly appear enormous bargains; others will clearly not make the grade. Similarly, some types of hospital treatment will clearly come out as economically superior, but others will give way to pharmaceuticals. The drugs pecking order will be transformed; so will the established pattern of hospital treatment. At the moment, both industries nervously know the issue is a big one, but they are keeping it at arm's length.

The list goes on. In fast-moving consumer goods, the issue is product proliferation. In advertising, it is the question of when to start paying consumers for their attention. In accounting and some types of consultancy, it is the prospect of using computers to commoditise much routine work. And in newspapers the issue is how far to move towards selecting news for each reader, to produce a "Daily Me".

There may be barriers to good thinking in the entire industry but history shows that eventually the big issue overwhelms the players and change becomes inevitable.

Gaining Unique Insights in the Adjacent Space

The first company to break ranks is not always the ultimate victor. But as Christensen (1997) points out the company that holds out longest, attempting to ignore the new reality, is always the loser. Every organisation must be involved in strategic renewal, making entrepreneurial inventions for which unique insight is required.

A key role for strategising is to decide when and where we need to go beyond the Business-As-Usual model, in the light of internal and external change. If we want to widen the search we have to remove the strict limits of the underlying orthodoxy and move to what Kauffman (1995) calls "adjacent space", or what Vygotsky calls the "zone of proximal development", where new and unique insights can be found. The problem is the hold the orthodoxy, firmly rooted in the past, exercises over strategic thinking. This does not make the thinking process conducive to moving into adjacent space, to make original inventions and develop worthwhile generative strategy.

The Innovator Attitude

The characteristic outcome of the successful strategising project involves an original invention, based on a unique reframing of the strategic situation of the organisation in its world. It can only be based on a deeper and wider systemic understanding of the interrelations between the driving forces at work, new and unique insights into the deep prevailing structure of the situation and a better and more accurate view of what is already in the pipeline; in short a new and original way of seeing the situation and its opportunities.

The scenario project requires the frame of mind of an innovator:

- Being attuned to the timeless and predetermined, as well as to change
- Understanding what is already changing
- Building a bridge between the future and the present

- Following the chain of consequences
- Searching for the transcendent themes
- Digging deeper, working out the deep dynamic
- Building the big stories around it all
- Working out the potential of what is changing/has changed
- Working out the opportunity in this
- Doing mental prototyping
- Trying, testing, revising
- Learning from failure
- Being active, always searching for new ideas, opportunities, or sources of innovation.

In other words, be a scenario planner (based on Hamel 2000).

STRATEGY DEVELOPMENT

Management's Process Role

Many organisations decide to intervene. They introduce an institutional process, aiming to overcome the danger of myopia, by attempting to provide access to the adjacent space and develop strategy there. Scenario-based planning is such a process.

The process can be facilitated, and in the next sections we will discuss some general principles. But the moment of invention cannot be forced. There are predefined steps one can take to help the thinking along but the moment of insight cannot be legislated in advance. Invention is not a step-by-step algorithm and it does not fit in with any of the business and planning processes that the organisation engages in. The only thing management can do is recognise the need for depth and persistence to arrive at "new seeing". This means proactively select an appropriately skilful group thinking process, keep it going, keep the attention on it and work towards gaining the new insight.

This is the purpose of scenario work. Think in terms of asking the why question, trying to find the causes of the causes of the causes. It therefore needs to be a process that uses all cognitive aspects, experience, existing insights, predetermineds, predictable structures, uncertainty, doubts, expert knowledge, remarkable people and their original ideas, intuition, curiosity, courage (to suspend disbelief), invention, originality, emotion, intellectual sparkle. It takes time and it cannot be forced. There is little or no value in a few isolated workshops. You must spend time hunting for surprises. If you have limited time it is difficult not to come up with the obvious.

The Components of Strategy

Strategy development starts with understanding the organisational "self". The word "self" stands here for the unique formula of capabilities and activities that the organisation believes underpins its success. The description of this in its simplest form, which nevertheless identifies all essential elements, is called the "Business Idea", an expression of the success formula of the organisation. At this point suffice it to say that in a Business Idea we try to understand the nature of three essential components:

- The societal/customer value created by this organisation (i.e. the societal scarcity addressed)
- The Distinctive Resources and Competencies, owned by the organisation, which allow it to create and appropriate value
- The reinforcing feedback loop, which turns the idea into a self-sustaining engine for ongoing survival and growth.

Chapter Five develops the concept of the Business Idea further.

The boundary line between the self and the environment is defined as follows: the "self" is delineated as that part of the total system that can be substantially controlled by the organisation's management. External to that is the business environment, which can only be influenced, to various degrees. Where there is a significant degree of influence we speak of the transactional environment, the part where influence is weak or non-existing we call the contextual environment. We discuss this in more detail in Chapter Seven. Although the organisation has little or no influence over it, the contextual environment determines success or failure of the Business Idea of the organisation. It therefore needs to be watched, studied and understood in terms of its future impact.

The tool employed to characterise the environment needs to be able to address a number of essential requirements:

- It needs to be able to cope with uncertainty, i.e. multiple equally plausible futures (as there is considerable irreducible uncertainty – indeterminacy – in the environment there is not just one future, but several).
- It needs to be able to take account of multiple interpretations of what is going on, representing the different views of the stakeholders in the strategy.
- It needs to be able to integrate elements of knowledge from a wide variety of knowledge disciplines to create coherent holistic characterisations of several futures.

We will use scenarios to characterise the future business environment. Because of uncertainty scenarios always come in sets, representing the various different outcomes that are all plausible.

The Notion of Fit

How can the tools described (Business Idea and scenario characterisation of the business environment) be used to develop strategy? The basic idea is that of fit between the two (van der Heijden 1993). A good fit means that the organisation has (or can develop) distinctive resources and/or competencies in an area where there is a significant perceived scarcity in the world. A poor fit means that the resources and/or competencies of the organisation do not meet any strong needs in society. In the first case the organisation will do well and generate new resources to maintain and develop its Business Idea. In the second case there will be little surplus available for investment in the future, and the organisation may wither and collapse. The big looming issues we looked at earlier (page 56) are all examples of the business environment shifting such that existing distinctiveness in the industry loses its value. Organisations ought to consider these while the going is still good, such that resources can still be generated to make the adjustment to the new world. Organisations suffering from "denial" who wait till the shift actually takes place will find that their resources have dried up such that adjustments to the new situation are so much more difficult.

The way these questions can be addressed is by working out both the existing Business Idea and the set of relevant scenarios, put these two in juxtaposition and consider the degree of fit (see Figure 7). If the fit is poor the process will have to continue, analysing Business Idea and scenarios in each other's context, until a new idea for the future starts taking shape.

It Cannot be Cheap and Easy

Good scenarios are thinking and perception devices. They are not about forecasting highs and lows but about making a new reframed perspective visible. Most people who have participated in scenario workshops come away with a positive feeling caused by having had a look at a situation in a new integrative way. This presumably is the reason for the current popularity of scenario-based planning. However, the question of how the project as a whole contributes to the well-being of the organisation is more difficult to address. Our research into success/failure indicates that

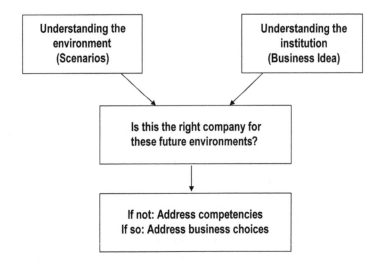

Figure 7. *Fit between the environment and the Business Idea*

projects with real strategic impact are generally significant in scope, with scenario building iterating with deep research and analysis, and plenty of time allowed for ideas to mature. The products of simple scenario building projects on the other hand tend to be forgotten very quickly, confirming the logic that good strategy cannot be simple (if it were everyone would be going down that path and a strategy that everyone is following cannot be a good one).

Scenario-based planning is not a "free lunch".

Chapter Five

The Business Idea
of an Organisation

In this chapter we define the Business Idea, discuss the main underlying principles and work through their implications. As we saw, the Business Idea is the organisation's mental model of the forces behind its current and future success. The scenario planner, aiming to accelerate organisational learning, needs to articulate the Business Idea. Only when articulated can it be studied, discussed, modified and improved.

We are deliberately not using the word business model, which is used in the literature for a range of organisational representations, from a description of a customer interface to complex mathematical models of profitability. The Business Idea is a more tightly defined concept that integrates all major factors for success in an organised way. It depicts what is fundamental for success in specific terms in one holistic representation. As an organisational device, the Business Idea is embedded in the language of the organisation. Organisational language is rational. Therefore, in order to work effectively in the organisation, the articulated Business Idea must be a rational explanation of why the organisation has been successful in the past, and how it will be successful in the future. The Business Idea needs to be built up from first principles.

PROFIT POTENTIAL

Firms are successful if they create value. This can be done in two ways:

- Firms creating a surplus for stakeholders, which the latter can use for their own purposes or (totally or in part) for protecting and developing the strength of the enterprise.

- Firms creating the expectation among stakeholders of a future surplus, which they will be able to use in order to grow.

Strategy relates to success in the future. Its purpose is to feed an expectation, by indicating and making it credible how circumstances will be created in the longer term that are favourable for corporate value generation. Strategy must instil confidence; otherwise it does not represent value. The aim can be defined as creating *credible* profit potential. This is not the same as profit. Management cannot rely on strategy alone for profitability. Strategy facilitates, it sets the scene and creates coherence, but the actual profit is earned in day-to-day hands-on operations. Because of this there cannot be a one-to-one relationship between strategy and profit. Quality of execution is the other part of the profit equation (see Box 6).

The typical business situation involves a high level of complexity, so the time period over which the system is predictable is short – days or weeks rather than months or years. On the other hand many management decisions have long-term repercussions. They affect future profit potential and need to be considered in that light.

To illustrate the concept of profit potential, consider the thought processes of the new entrepreneur. These focus first of all on an idea of a possible activity, believed to create value for a customer group, for which they consequently will be prepared to pay a price. The idea specifies how

---

Box 6 Strategy and profitable change

Strategy has the potential to improve performance, but other things need to happen. The new understanding needs to do the following:

- Become entrenched in the managers' mental models
- Become connected up with their recipes for success
- Become linked to competitive advantage
- Create an awareness of an imperative for change
- Create a critical mass of consensus, or at least accommodation, in the management team towards action
- Be translated into a change project
- People in the change project need to be identified and motivated
- Leadership needs to ensure that the change project stays on the agenda and is not swamped by the day-to-day.

The chain is as strong as its weakest link. Non-performance on each individual point kills the project.
Expectation of profit potential requires confidence that the chain will not be broken.

this value can be created through bringing together a number of factors and competencies in a new distinctive combination that has not been thought of before. Entrepreneurial success results from a combination of three ideas:

- Discovering a new way of creating value for customers.
- Bringing together a new combination of competencies that creates this value.
- Creating uniqueness in this formula in order to appropriate part of the value created.

The "offering" is the vehicle by which the seller and customer systems are linked together to exploit the supplier competencies in the customer value system. The offering includes all aspects of the supplier/customer interface, including the product advertised, but also intangible aspects such as service, risk management, information, trust, etc. As Richard Normann points out, each commercial transaction (including the sale of a product) can be seen as a division of work between the supplier and the customer (Normann 1984). Therefore the creation of a successful product is the result of a process of maximising the effect of the supplier competencies in the total customer value system.

Where does customer value come from? Economists use the word "rent" to indicate profit potential in a transactional situation. Economics equates rent with scarcity. If a product is abundantly available, and

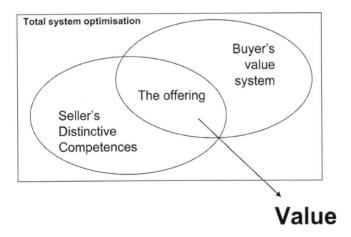

Figure 8. *Overlap between competencies and value creation*

assuming efficient markets, competition will ensure that the price of the product will reflect its (marginal) cost. There will be little profit potential or rent available to the marginal supplier. If a product (at its specific cost level) is scarce this competitive force is absent. In that case the price will not reflect the cost of the product but the cost to the customer of alternatives. Since this can only be above the cost of supply (otherwise there would not be a scarcity), there is profit potential or rent available to be exploited. In the process the supplier incurs costs. The customer derives value from the product as (s)he avoids buying the alternative. The best overall outcome maximises the difference between customer value and supplier cost.

The product that represents this optimum will normally incorporate both tangible and service elements. In some aspects of the product the cost/benefit balance indicates the work is best done by the supplier (e.g. performance guarantees), sometimes the balance shifts to the buyer (e.g. self-service, Normann & Ramirez 1994). The entrepreneur tries to find the best bundle of tangible product and service elements in the overall offering such that supplier competencies are exploited to the maximum effect in the customer value system.

The resulting surplus of value over cost is shared between the two parties. The degree to which it accrues to the customer or to the supplier depends on the relative bargaining power of each party (see below).

We define structural profit potential as an attribute of a supply system capable of creating value for customers in a unique way that others find difficult to emulate. The two aspects of value and uniqueness are closely related. Value is associated with gaining access to a scarce resource, which can only be made available through a system with unique characteristics. A specification of these two elements together (value creation in a situation of scarcity, and making a unique contribution) constitutes what is defined here as the Business Idea of the firm.

DISTINCTIVE COMPETENCIES

Sometimes the entrepreneur finds that others can easily emulate the new combination. In that case cost of entry is relatively modest, new competitors flock in, the resource is not any longer scarce and success is short-lived. Alternatively, there may be something distinctive or unique about the combination of competencies that makes it difficult for others to copy (Grant 1991, Kay 1993).

Scarcity is not always due to lack of the resource as such, but may well be caused by failure in the allocation process. This in turn may be due to lack of information and transparency leading to what is known as market failure. Scarcity may also be due to the exercise of supplier power. If there is only one supplier the company may decide to maintain a degree of scarcity in the market, keeping the resource valuable to buyers. In this way a powerful Business Idea appropriates a larger part of the value created.

The degree to which this can be done depends on the relative power of the firm vis-à-vis the customers in the bargaining process. Customer power is determined by possible alternatives open to them. If there is only one buyer and there are many more or less equally positioned suppliers they will find it difficult to make money. Defence suppliers are an example. They often build only a few special objects, get paid little over cost for doing so (that is how government can squeeze a long-term dependent player) and the product has to work. Unless they can create some unique capability or competence, which is recognised by the customer as unique, they will never become very successful. The way to maintain and appropriate value is to become the only or the dominating supplier. Only coming up with an offering that has an element of uniqueness built in will lead to success.

The Business Idea needs to address the relative position vis-à-vis real or potential competition. But competition here means competition for the value surplus over cost. This obviously includes people who supply the same resource, but they are not the only competitors. There are others in the game, aiming to increase their cut of the pie. These include stakeholders such as (Freeman 1984):

- Suppliers
- Employees
- Money providers
- Government (taxation).

Ultimately the power of the supplying firm to appropriate value relates to the degree of uniqueness of the competencies brought to bear in generating the product. Appropriation requires that the competencies individually, or the system of competencies with their interactions, are difficult to imitate by potential competitors.

The word "distinctive" in the concept Distinctive Competency needs some further elaboration. Company "strengths" are not the same thing as Distinctive Competencies. Many strengths companies believe they have are not very unique and can be easily copied by existing or new competitors. If a strength can be bought, e.g. by acquisition or alliance, it cannot be a source of rent. If a Business Idea consists only of such components long-term profit potential is vulnerable, and therefore the Business Idea weak. A strong Business Idea contains elements that have been created in the organisation over time, and which uniquely belong to that organisation.

Therefore, in considering the Business Idea one needs to ask the devil's advocate question: "What is unique about this particular formula, and why are others unable to emulate it?"

Teece (1986) investigated the reasons why Distinctive Competencies might arise, and why competitors would be restrained from copying some successful formulas. Based on his and Rumelt's work mapping out "Barriers to Entry", we can derive a list of five fundamental sources of distinctiveness in two main categories (Rumelt 1987, Rumelt *et al.* 1991):

- Uncodified institutional knowledge:
  − In networked people
  − In embedded processes
- Sunk costs/irreversible investments:
  − Investments in reputation
  − In legal protection
  − In specialised assets

If the competency is based on tacit uncodified institutional knowledge it cannot be copied. But unique knowledge in itself is not enough; there is an important proviso. The competencies must also belong to the firm as an institution, and not exclusively to its members individually. If the company relies only on an individual expert for its business success profits will eventually be appropriated by him personally (consider, for example, the football star). In those circumstances it is unlikely that the firm will find it possible to translate these strengths into profit potential for the company on a sustainable basis. However, if a Business Idea is based on institutional knowledge profit potential can be sustained. Therefore a distinction needs to be made between Personal Knowledge and Institutional Knowledge. Often the individual can exploit personal strengths only when supported by the strengths of the organisation. This support may be tangible (e.g. in the form of computing facilities) or intangible (e.g. in the complementary knowledge and "sounding board" function provided by colleagues in the organisation). An institution's knowledge base is created through people networking with each other, and through processes embedded in the organisation.

The second source of distinctiveness relates to competitors having to incur costs in order to be able to compete for the profit potential. For example, a new competitor might have to make investments that existing companies have already made. If these cannot recover these costs anymore they essentially have the investment for free. However, the principle of "opportunity cost" has to be applied here. If these investments are in marketable assets, then a cost has to be assigned, based on its market value, and there is no competitive distinction between existing and new players. Existing players have to consider their option of realising their assets in the same way as new players have to consider their acquisition, i.e. not selling the asset creates the same sacrifice and barrier for the existing players as making the investment in the first place for the newcomers. However, many investments are irreversible, at least to some extent, and in relation to that the existing players do not face the hurdle of the economic decision facing the newcomers. Their opportunity cost is lower.

Examples of Distinctive Competencies

The following range of examples of Distinctive Competencies illustrates these principles:

Institutional knowledge

- Institutional R&D capability
- Company know-how
- Functional knowledge pools
- Knowledge of customer value systems
- Shared assumptions and values.

Embedded processes

- Leadership style and commitment
- Access to consumers
- Access to distribution channels
- Institutional relationships with government
- Internal communication, systems/culture
- Staff identification with the firm, staff commitment.

Reputation and trust

- Brand
- Dominant size and presence
- Installed base
- Financial clout.

Legal protection

- Concession agreements
- Patents
- Ownership of prime sites.

Activity specific assets

- Investments in dominant size, market share and image
- Sunk investment in sites, exploration, experimentation, specialised equipment etc.
- Investments in economies of scale, e.g. in distribution (e.g. low stock levels, low unit overheads)
- First mover investments in production capacity.

Uniqueness can derive from Distinctive Competencies individually or from their combination. It may be that some aspects of specific Distinctive Competencies are difficult to emulate. However, the strongest Business Ideas derive from a set of competencies that are unique because of the way they are combined systemically. Strong Business Ideas contain Distinctive Competencies that feed on each other. Synergy between even a handful creates distinctiveness at a wholly superior level of strength. A good example is IKEA. Not only did they create value by reinventing the "division of work" between the furniture industry and furniture buyers, but they made this possible by building a system of unique competencies combining institutional knowledge (design, global manufacturing, shopping behaviour, customer capabilities, supply systems, etc.) with investments in a manufacturing and retail system that dominates this segment of the industry. Many have tried to emulate IKEA, nobody has (so far) been able to copy the complete formula.

The overall Business Idea is particularly strong and difficult to emulate if the sets of underlying Distinctive Competencies reinforce each other, as is the case with IKEA. This is why drawing a causal loop diagram (a way of showing such mutual causal interaction) provides a powerful level of insight into the driving forces for success (see below).

Distinctive Competencies depreciate over time. Business is not static; change is an essential part of organisational life. In an evolving world survival implies continuous updating of the organisation's Business Idea. This is necessary for two reasons:

- Eventually a competitor finds a way to emulate the essence of the competency, or

- The overlap between the competency and the customer value system reduces, because of evolving customer values.

As a consequence a Business Idea is not valid forever. It needs to be kept up to date. Existing Distinctive Competencies need to be strengthened, and new ones created. Although entrepreneurial invention and luck may present the perceptive organisation with potential new Distinctive Competencies, normally new Distinctive Competencies must be created out of the exploitation of already existing ones. The organisation does not have another source of distinctiveness.

Schoemaker (1992) has analysed the nature of Distinctive Competencies. His suggestions for hallmarks of real distinctiveness summarise the points made:

- Investments are largely irreversible.
- Distinctive Competencies cannot be transferred (sold) to other firms.
- There is a limit to which development can be speeded up by ever-increasing investments.
- Development is a process of gradual evolution through collective learning and information sharing.
- Strong Business Ideas exploit multiple Distinctive Competencies reinforcing each other in a synergetic way.
- Distinctive Competencies create competitive advantage in the eyes of customers.

Competitive Advantage

If the Business Idea and its Distinctive Competencies are effective it creates Competitive Advantage. Competitive Advantage can translate into profit potential in two ways (Porter 1985):

- The Distinctive Competencies are used to create a differentiated product, the characteristics of which cannot be matched by the competition and for which the customer is prepared to pay a superior price. Profit potential derives from a premium price.
- The Distinctive Competencies create a unique low-cost way of making the (non-differentiated) product available. This allows the supplier to make available a competitively priced product, with some additional margin left to enhance profits. Profit potential derives from cost leadership.

Product differentiation

A firm that can produce a product that results in additional customer value on an ongoing basis enjoys a competitive advantage. If competitors cannot match the distinctive element the supplier can appropriate part of the additional customer value.

There are two categories of sources of product differentiation (Normann & Ramirez 1994):

- Generative, i.e. a capability to produce offerings with unique attributes, including quality, design, cost, availability and support.
- Relational, i.e. a dynamic capability to keep in touch with, and understand, customers, including aspects such as trust, access, effective communication.

Differentiation requires a deep understanding of what creates value for customers. A Distinctive Competency of the supplier may be based on an ability to "read the customer's mind" better than competitors. Researching customer needs is not enough. Customers cannot articulate their needs if they are not aware of the potential offered by the supplier's competencies. The unique differentiated product can be created only out of the optimisation of the total customer/supplier system. It must be conceptualised as an integrated project. Product research is not enough; the differentiated product company needs to engage in continuous concept research, searching the total supplier/buyer system for new opportunities.

Structural cost leadership

Sometimes customer value is relatively easy to determine. This happens when products have become "commodities", i.e. when open market trading has created standardised and clearly defined products for which there is a continuing market and identifiable market price. In that case the value an individual supplier contributes to the customer is equal to the established market price of the product (as the customer has plenty of alternative opportunities to acquire the product at that price). In a commodity market it may still be possible to create significant long-term profit potential, by means of a uniquely superior cost situation.

An example of structural cost advantage is what is known as mining rents. If a mining company has gained privileged access to uniquely cheap reserves, for example by means of a concession agreement, profit potential is assured. The ultimate example of mining rents is associated with the oil reserves in countries such as Saudi Arabia. Anyone having access to these cannot help but make money. Mining rents are the prime profit generators of all oil and gas companies.

Most businesses believe that it ought to be possible to develop some unique customer value, and companies for this reason try to distinguish themselves by creating a differentiated offering. But some companies accept the commodity market as their strategic starting point and concentrate on creating a uniquely favourable cost position.

SYSTEMIC STRUCTURE OF THE BUSINESS IDEA

Management cannot just select any strategy they can come up with. It must be based on a set of Distinctive Competencies, which through their interaction in a Business Idea create a differentiated product or structural cost leadership. The Business Idea is prime; the Competitive Advantage is its manifestation, and the strategy has to be based on that. The process of articulating the Business Idea usefully starts with identifying the Competitive Advantage that the firm exploits (differentiation, cost leadership, or both). Starting from there the analysis then searches for underlying causes of this Competitive Advantage until characteristics are uncovered that pass the test of "distinctiveness". As we discussed above, Distinctive Competencies depreciate so a firm needs to spend resources in maintaining and renewing its Business Idea. These resources are generated from the exploitation of the Business Idea itself. A Business Idea contains a "Reinforcing Feedback Loop"; competitive advantage generates resources and knowledge, which are used to strengthen the competencies driving the competitive advantage, leading to more resources, and so on. Such a loop can be the source of ongoing success and growth. But a reinforcing feedback loop can also collapse (less competitive advantage leading to fewer resources, leading to weaker competencies, leading to less competitive advantage). The primary concern of management is to keep the loop working in the upward direction. Bateson (1967) suggested that the fundamental nature of organisations could only be understood by conceptualising them as a cybernetic system of loops in a network of relationships, both internal as well as external. Through such networks people influence each other. This influence cascades both up- and downward. Alleged inferiors have influence over alleged superiors. As we saw, suppliers influence clients as much as clients influence suppliers. While hierarchy identifies formal relationships, informal influences can loop around through long pathways that include indirect effects. Social systems tend to be heavily influenced by such influence loops, which often determine behaviour more than hierarchies. Loops tend to create the behaviour, and therefore the identity, of organisations. Bateson suggested that if you focus only on physical or legal representations of organisations you would miss entirely the fundamental shaping forces driving organisations and change!

Firms can be interpreted as systems of balancing feedback loops, designed to maintain favourable conditions for the one dominant reinforcing feedback loop, its Business Idea, to create the growth of the enterprise.

Summarising the above we see that the following four elements need to be specified in order to define a complete Business Idea:

1. The societal/customer value created (i.e. the scarcity addressed).
2. The nature of the Competitive Advantage exploited (differentiation or structural cost advantage).
3. The Distinctive Competencies, which, in their mutually reinforcing interaction, create Competitive Advantage.

Then, these three elements must be configured into the fourth element:

4. A reinforcing feedback loop, in which generated resources drive growth.

Due to its systemic nature a Business Idea is best represented as an influence diagram. Figure 9 shows this in its generic form, containing the elements listed above in context, as well as the role of entrepreneurial invention in creating the idea in the first place.

Figure 9 is an example of an influence diagram, showing the cause/ effect relationships between key variables in the situation under consideration, expressed by arrows. The head of the arrow points towards the effect, caused by the variable indicated by the tail of the arrow. If an arrow is annotated with a plus sign, or if no sign is shown (as in Figure 9) both variables change in the same direction, an increase in the causing variable leading to an increase in the effect, or a decrease in the causing variable leading to a decrease in the effect. If a minus sign is shown the movement is in the opposite direction, an increase in cause leading to a decrease in effect, and the other way around.

In Figure 9 increasing Competitive Advantage (premium price or cost advantage) leads to increasing results, which cause increasing resources to be available to enhance Distinctive Competencies, through investments in assets and/or learning. This strengthens a set of unique activities that

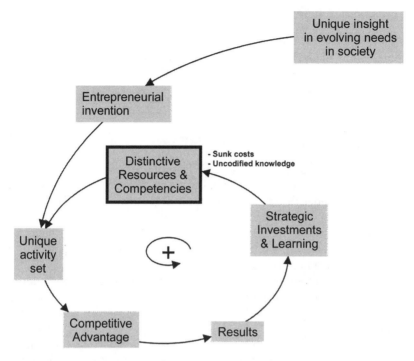

Figure 9. *Elements of the Business Idea*

are the basis of the Competitive Advantage, completing the reinforcing feedback loop discussed.

The generic diagram also shows how the unique activity set was initially created by an entrepreneurial invention, based on a uniquely superior understanding of evolving needs in society. This is the central theme of this book. *Organisational and business survival and success depend on building a unique capability that derives in the final analysis from an original invention.* And an original entrepreneurial invention can only come from gaining a new and unique insight. All our strategising must work towards a discovery through which we see the world in a new way, as it has never been seen before. This also applies to scenario-based strategising. As we have seen there are many reasons why people decide to engage in scenario-based planning. But these are (or should be) all subgoals of the one ultimate objective, to gain a new and unique insight. Success implies uniqueness. Without a new and unique insight at the end of it our strategising efforts are in vain. Creating a unique insight is the ultimate success criteria of all strategy work.

EXAMPLES OF BUSINESS IDEAS

A specific Business Idea diagram contains the elements of the generic diagram, but made specific in its elements and their inter-relationships for the situation under consideration. This can best be explained by means of a few examples.

KinderCare

Our first example is the creation of the Business Idea for KinderCare, the leading private provider of child day care in the US. The analysis is based on the entrepreneur's own account (Smith & Brown 1986, Bougon & Komocar 1990).

KinderCare was started by Perry Mendel who perceived a need for innovative child care. He reasoned that many parents experience a feeling of guilt when they provide their children with simple custodial child care. His entrepreneurial idea was to create centres where children would not only be cared for but would also be provided with a learning environment similar to preschools, thus creating a positive image in the minds of the parents. This is emphasised in the phrase "learning centres" as the schools are called. In an early attempt to franchise the centres Mendel found that the ideal type of individual attracted to a franchise was an ex-schoolteacher. Such a person could instil confidence with the parents that this was not simple custodial care but involved a key educational component. But while having the professional expertise, these individuals did not normally have the management and financial expertise (or interest) required for running a franchise. If the learning centres were to be financially successful they would have to be created and managed by KinderCare management.

The strategy based on these observations created a set of inter-dependencies in a system of loops. Figure 10 is derived from the diagram developed by Bougon from Mendel's report (Bougon & Komocar 1990).

The KinderCare system can be understood by reference to the four elements making up its Business Idea:

1. The societal/customer value created

The creation of customer value starts with the recognition of many parents' unhappiness associated with custodial day care for their children. The ability to overcome this by the provision of a learning environment

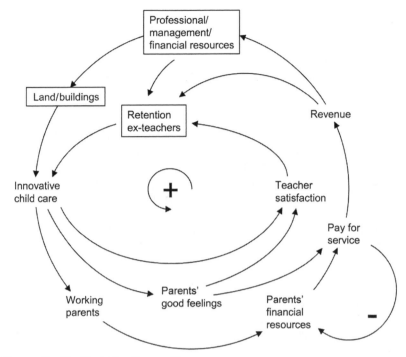

Figure 10. *The KinderCare Business Idea*

makes parents feel better and allows them to send their children to these institutions, freeing them up to seek employment where this was considered inappropriate before. The entrepreneurial invention creates value for customers, through reallocation of resources or generation of additional income.

2. The nature of the competitive advantage exploited

The purpose of the KinderCare operation is to offer a new enhanced product, which creates value for customers through its differentiated nature, largely based on trustworthiness. KinderCare does not aim to be a cost leader.

3. The Distinctive Competencies exploited, in their mutually reinforcing configuration

KinderCare has developed a number of competencies allowing the realisation of the entrepreneurial idea, including:

- Knowledge of key personnel characteristics
- Knowledge of facilities required
- Management system and expertise
- Access to specialised facilities
- Reputation and image as an educational institute, resulting in parents' trust.

These competencies reinforce each other as shown in the diagram. Note that having hired the appropriate personnel (a scarce resource) does not as such create a Distinctive Competency for the firm, as any value resulting from that alone would eventually be appropriated by the individuals with the requisite characteristics and not benefit the company. It is in creating the system in which the teacher can make use of their specific expertise that the company has created the corporate distinctiveness.

4. The reinforcing feedback loop, driving growth

The system contains a number of loops. For example, more innovative child care leads to more teacher satisfaction, which leads to more retention of motivated ex-schoolteachers, which leads to more innovative child care. Or, innovative child care allows a parent to feel better about going to frequent or full-time work, increasing willingness and ability to pay for the use of more innovative child care.

We see that the main strategic loop is a positive feedback loop. This explains the successful growth of KinderCare: innovative child care induces customers to pay for a service which enables investments in increased management and financial capability, which causes an increase in the amount and quality of innovative child care offered. It does not seem very difficult to emulate the individual competencies that KinderCare incorporates in its Business Idea. The reason why the company nevertheless has been successful lies in the idea's dynamic nature, and the relatively slow response of its competitors. By growing fast, well ahead of the ability of the competition to catch up, the company has exploited scale effects to the maximum. It has built up and strengthened both its management system and its reputation, associated with the name KinderCare, well before others could catch up, thus creating barriers to entry for newcomers. The company needs to consider whether these are high enough for sustainable competitive advantage.

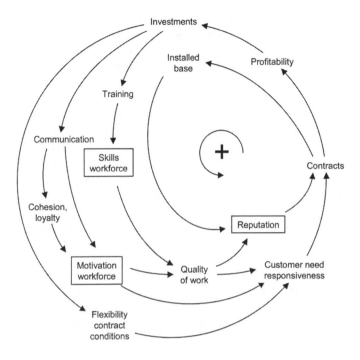

Figure 11. *The Business Idea of a construction company*

The Business Idea of a Construction Company

Figure 11 shows the diagrammatic representation of the Business Idea of a construction company. A building project tends to be a relatively significant investment for most customers, which needs to serve them for a long time to come. As a consequence, customers in this industry tend to be risk averse. As the product cannot be inspected before the sale, the reputation of construction companies for the quality of the work they typically deliver is important. Construction companies need to be able to demonstrate the quality of their products by reference to the "installed base". Therefore existing, well-established companies are protected by the positive feedback loop, from the installed base to reputation for quality work to new contracts, which add to the installed base. This creates a considerable barrier to entry for newcomers, and is a fundamental part of the Business Idea of every established construction company. However, a company cannot entirely rely on this loop for its success. There is potential competition from other established companies in the industry, and from time to time new entrants make the investment to break in. Therefore the Business Idea needs to be strengthened by company specific Distinctive Competencies.

In the example in Figure 11 a construction company responds to the needs of the risk-averse customers. They create an internal culture, which differentiates the company in the eyes of the clients as a flexible collaborative business partner in contrast to the traditional legalistic and sometimes adversarial customer/contractor relationship where the builder tries to make money out of every contract change. Such collaborative customer relationships require:

- An internal culture based on collaborative relationships. The company portrayed in Figure 11 develops and stimulates this culture by organisational measures and investments in people.
- A flexible approach to developing customised contract conditions. The company has invested heavily in an ability to customise every contract to the needs of the individual client.
- Financial strength to deal with the specific financing requirements of every contract.

In this way the company stays ahead in its chosen market niche where clients are prepared to pay a premium price for the security of proven quality as well as non-adversarial collaborative relationships.

The strength of the Business Idea of Figure 11 lies in its cultural embeddedness. Companies setting out to change their corporate culture are embarking on a long-term project that must be measured in years rather than months. Companies that have made such investments in the past are generally well protected, provided that there is a good match between the resulting behavioural characteristics and customer needs.

Limits to Growth

The KinderCare example contains a balancing feedback loop which will eventually limit the growth created by the reinforcing feedback loop as explained. This balancing loop indicates that growth of the activity will level out, caused by saturation in demand. Customer value creation and willingness to pay will reach a limit based on parents' financial resources. Michael Porter's five force competitive framework (Porter 1980) provides a useful model to consider the limits to growth in a Business Idea, which may be due to:

- Demand limits
- Supply limits
- Competition limits
- Limits imposed by the possibility of new entrants
- Limits imposed by possible alternatives and substitutes.

The KinderCare example demonstrates a demand limited Business Idea. Examples of limitations in the other categories include:

- Supply limits. The Business Idea of a mining company may be largely based on "legal protection" through a concession agreement. The company may not be able to extend this, for example if there are no other reserves available. In this case the exploitation of the Business Idea is limited on the supply side, dictated by the potential in the available reserve.
- Competition limits. In an oligopolistic market situation the growing company must expect retaliation from its competitors when the exploitation of its Business Idea leads to unacceptable dominance.
- All Distinctive Competencies depreciate. Eventually all Business Ideas can be emulated at a cost. Any firm working a successful Business Idea will reach a point in the growth curve where it has become attractive for new entrants to incur the emulation cost, and enter the market as alternative suppliers.
- The same applies to substitute products.

In each of these examples we see a mechanism at work that, at some point in the growth process, introduces a balancing feedback loop in the Business Idea, due to which its surplus creation potential will reduce and eventually disappear. At that point growth stops.

If the balancing feedback loop is intrinsic in the Business Idea it will not invalidate it. For example, the limits of the parents' financial resources limit the scope of the KinderCare Business Idea but does not make it invalid. If the compensating balancing feedback emanates from an independent source the situation may be more dangerous, as there is a possibility that it overwhelms the reinforcing loop. For example, balancing feedback loops introduced through existing or new competition are more dangerous than those resulting from supply or demand constraints.

LEVELS OF BUSINESS IDEAS

Wherever a management team pursues an organisational purpose, a Business Idea will emerge. Management teams can be found at various levels in the organisation, at the top of the organisation but also at the level of the business units. Business Ideas can be found at all these levels.

The Business Unit has external customers. Being able to interrogate external customers makes it relatively straightforward to identify the contribution made to customer value. Taking this as a starting point the Business Idea can be articulated by considering what specific Distinctive Competencies in the business unit and in the wider company are brought to bear to create this value.

Having defined the current Business Idea the management has to think about the Business Idea for the future. At the Business Unit level this task revolves in the first place around the question of what will be considered value creation by future customers. Thinking this through is a creative task. Asking existing customers will not provide the answer as they are not aware of how their value systems will evolve in the future under the influence of new potential contributions of suppliers that are unknown to them at this time.

In companies where a corporate management team supervises a number of Business Units the articulation of a corporate Business Idea offers special challenges. This is complicated by the external customer being one step removed. The Corporate Unit does not interact with external customers; this takes place via the Business Units. Business logic at the corporate level is based on developing shared resources, visible or invisible, that exploit synergy between Business Units and the Corporate Units. This can take place in a number of different ways:

- Business Units may include in their Business Idea the Distinctive Competencies of other Business Units. For example, marketing may rely on manufacturing flexibility to approach their customers with customised offerings. Manufacturing flexibility then becomes a Corporate Distinctive Competency.
- More than one Business Unit may pursue the same Distinctive Competencies, which then develop into Corporate Distinctive Competencies, e.g. an open culture through participative management.
- Some features of the company are essentially corporate, and any distinctiveness in those can only be developed at the corporate level e.g. financial strength, risk spreading, corporate reputation etc.
- The corporate parent may develop a Business Idea around value creation in the interaction between the parent and the Business Units ("parenting advantage", Goold, Campbell & Alexander 1994).

The Corporate Business Idea needs to be based on the Business Unit Business Ideas, concentrating on Distinctive Competencies that operate across business boundaries.

Segmentation

This raises the issue of what can be considered a Business Unit for the purpose of articulating a Business Idea. Many schemes have been invented to segment a business for the purpose of analysing its underlying characteristics. For the purpose of developing a Business Idea most of these schemes can be short-circuited. The Business Idea is in the first place a cognitive device. It is a vision that lives in the minds of individuals, managers and others in the unit considered. It is they who determine the identity of their operation, and who develop the vision for its future. Therefore the single criterion whether it is worthwhile to attempt to surface a Business Idea is the question whether people, mostly in a management team, are aware of its separate identity.

Mapping out and comparing the Business Ideas of a number of Business Units, making up a corporation, may lead to reconsideration of the segmentation of the business within the organisation. Putting the lower-level maps next to each other quickly reveals possible ways in which the same business can be reorganised more coherently, leading to more concise Business Ideas with more clear-cut overlap and interdependence, and simplified inter-unit interfaces.

Once the set of Business Ideas existing in the corporation becomes clear the elements of distinctiveness on which success is based come into focus. Activities that are not part of any of the Business Ideas can be (and often are) contracted out to another firm without harming the profit generating potential of the company.

The Holistic Nature of a Business Idea

A Business Idea becomes a powerful driving force in the organisation if it can be held in the mind as one holistic concept. Its essence flows from the way that the elements work together. The reinforcing feedback loop cannot be understood in terms of its elements in isolation. Only the overview makes the important point. If complex systems cannot be understood holistically, the mind will try to break down the system into parts. In the case of a Business Idea this fragmentation destroys the essential meaning of it.

The human mind can consciously retain only a limited number of concepts at the same time. (Miller 1956, suggested a number of seven concepts, plus or minus two.) Our experience has shown that the most effective Business Idea diagrams indeed do not contain many more than (say) 10 elements. A representation much beyond that seems to quickly reduce to a "list of things" in people's minds, a fragmented collection of tasks and activities each looked at in isolation. At that point the power of a holistic direction–indicating device has been lost. Therefore it is advisable to conceptualise and draw up the diagram at a level of detail that summarises the Business Idea in terms of (say) 10 constructs. If further detail is required this can be included as an expansion of individual elements in the Business Idea in separate diagrams. The art of Business Idea articulation lies in conceptualising and defining the major elements of the system at the appropriate resolution level and maintaining consistency of this across the diagram.

This seems in the first place a point of good practice. But it is worth considering other more fundamental aspects of the human inability to overview large systems. Pursuing an entrepreneurial Business Idea requires a high degree of coherence, consistency and persistence across the organisation and over time. Staying on course requires a clear unambiguous compass. A Business Idea can provide that as long as it can be perceived as one thing.

Wherever we find a management team we find a Business Idea. Management teams cannot pursue more than one Business Idea at the same time. This is clearly illustrated by the frequent failures of mergers and acquisitions, proving the difficulty of combining two businesses into one Business Idea. Financial markets are aware of this and tend to discount management's stated aim to pursue more than one Business Idea, as manifest from the frequently observed enhancement in market value resulting from demergers. Markets prefer clear management structures and coherent aims, and discount companies that are perceived to lack clarity of purpose.

The fact that a management team pursues only one Business Idea does not mean that the company is in only one business. For example, the management of a conglomerate company may be pursuing the overarching single corporate Business Idea of providing specific parenting advantages to its subsidiaries, without getting involved in the detail of the subsidiaries' Business Ideas (Goold & Quinn 1990).

The concept of the Business Idea throws a new light on the notion of synergy as a precondition for success in acquisitions. The overarching Business Idea is important not only because of the "shared resources" aspect, but also because of its function as complexity reducer. It creates one holistic gestalt across the businesses, enabling management to manage the set as one.

The issue comes into focus most clearly where companies consider mergers of dissimilar businesses. The above reasoning argues that the prior invention of one overall synergetic Business Idea is a prerequisite for a successful acquisition.

CONSIDERING THE BUSINESS IDEA
IN THE MANAGEMENT TEAM

As discussed, each reinforcing feedback loop can spiral in two opposite directions. Near the switchover point it takes only a small nudge to flip-flop from growth into decline. Company managers are generally intuitively aware of this danger point and try to maintain a margin of safety. The purpose of a company is often defined as maximising profit for the shareholders. But the urge to be profitable is related less to shareholder considerations than to the need for sufficient reserves to keep the reinforcing feedback loop away from the precipice.

Sometimes companies find themselves exploiting a successful Business Idea, based on a strong set of Distinctive Competencies, built up in the past. After a while people get used to it working in the background and there seems little need to articulate it over and over again. Although initially the underlying entrepreneurial idea was clearly understood it often happens in successful organisations that attention moves to the product and the efficiency of its production system, while the underlying driving force is taken for granted. Companies that have been in business for a while often lose sight of the complex reasons why customers buy their particular products or services. While things are going well, many managers get on with the day-to-day business, implicitly relying on the ongoing tacit Business Idea to protect them from competitive onslaught. As time goes on, people in the business often come to take customer value for granted and managers in the company may gradually diverge in their intuitive interpretation of the Business Idea. There are considerable dangers lurking here because, as we saw, Distinctive Competencies depreciate over time.

If the Business Idea is not any longer clearly and jointly understood the danger of the reinforcing feedback loop slipping unnoticed into its decline mode is particularly strong. Considering the long lead times required to build most Distinctive Competencies the company may run into serious difficulties trying to turn things around once profitability has started to decline. There may not be time or resources to adjust the Business Idea to the current market situation.

To avoid this situation the management team needs to jointly articulate and understand the basis of their company's success. Divergent notions of the Business Idea in the management team need to be confronted in open debate. The Business Idea concept assists the team in managing this process more explicitly, through the introduction of a thinking framework and language, allowing joint rational consideration in terms of:

- The current Business Idea
- The strengths/weaknesses of the current Distinctive Competencies in their systemic interaction
- The outlook for the strength of the Distinctive Competencies against the ever-changing values in society.

Once a Business Idea has been articulated, strategic priorities need to be determined to maintain its health. Selection of strategic options for the future needs to be guided by their relevance to maintaining and enhancing the Business Idea. This is "make or break" for the organisation.

VALUE CREATION THROUGH TRUST BUILDING

The Business Idea, and the coherence it brings, injects a sense of strategic direction that helps management as a basis for strategy development. But it also has an important function in value creation through expectation management among stakeholders. Consider, for example, the investors.

Business leaders often complain that financial markets are too short term, i.e. take too short term an attitude vis-à-vis investment opportunities. While management wants to develop the business by making long-term investments the money providers are pressing hard for immediate returns, frustrating management's ability to build for the future. Companies in the Anglo-Saxon world often look enviously at what they perceive to be more long-term relations and attitudes in Germany or Japan. Financial markets are accused of holding back long-term development. How is this possible?

As we saw on page 64 value is created on the basis of an expectation among stakeholders that a surplus will be generated in the future. The current surplus plays an important role in making the assessment. Short-termism is the result of a low expectation of future value generation. If the promise of future profits is convincing enough markets are prepared to wait, as was demonstrated clearly by the availability of easy investment capital to the dotcom companies before the collapse of the sector, even if very few companies were making any current profit at the time. If management complains about short-termism in the markets it means that they have a different perception of the possibility of future value creation from that of the markets. This difference in perception of the level of commercial risk involved can only be explained by an inability on the part of management to communicate and convince the market that they are capable of realising the value perceived.

It seems that management is not getting its message across. The task management faces is twofold. First, to convince the markets that its internal assessment of the risks involved is superior to the assessment by outside analysts. And second, that it has the capability to realise the project. These tasks may be easier in countries where traditionally links between companies and financiers have been closer, which may explain the higher weight given to longer-term considerations in Germany and Japan.

Markets that we frequently accuse of short-termism are often prepared to wait when dealing with young entrepreneurial companies. This may be due to a new Business Idea being clearer and easier to communicate. Older companies often have difficulties projecting their Business Idea with the same degree of clarity, as it often is understood only intuitively. The message from the markets is that the relative level of uncertainty businesses are facing and their consequent valuation can be favourably affected by clarifying and communicating the Business Idea.

BUILDING FOR THE FUTURE

The Business Idea needs to evolve with changes in the business environment. Management needs to develop a view on what new Distinctive Competencies will be called for in the future, and they need to work towards getting these in place. This is best achieved by developing a coherent view of a future Business Idea that will be robust against the various futures the scenarios indicate. How to develop the Business Idea for the future?

Uniqueness as such cannot be bought, it needs to be invented and built. Moving the Business Idea forward requires an entrepreneurial invention that has two elements to it, (1) new customer value potential and/or a new and uniquely efficient way of creating already established customer value, and (2) a way of building on the existing Distinctive Competencies, using old competencies to build new ones, which are better adapted to the new business circumstances envisaged.

A plan to build new Distinctive Competencies for the future of an existing business needs to be based on leveraging of the Distinctive

Competencies the company has at the present time. The task of building the Business Idea for the future has the following characteristics:

- It needs to respond to future customer values.
- It needs to be a new unique combination of competencies, which can be exploited in a reinforcing feedback loop.
- It needs to be created on the basis of the current Business Idea, leveraging existing Distinctive Competencies.

The ability to invent a new combination within these constraints constitutes the entrepreneurial task facing any management team interested in creating long-term profit potential for the company.

Most managers find this intuitive. So why does this go wrong so often? The crux of the matter is the need to consider the *total* Business Idea. Consider, for example, leveraging one's competencies for the future by acquiring another firm with complementary competencies. Acquisition is expected to create synergy resulting from the new combination. However, the list of unsuccessful diversifications is very long. Examples of synergy that never came off include oil companies expecting to use their exploration skills in the metal mining business, or EDS expecting to leverage technology and people's entrepreneurialism by going into management consulting and digital information systems (Lorenz 1993). The oil companies discovered (too late) that exploration was not the "primary game" in metals mining. EDS discovered that distinctiveness in management consulting requires more than technology and entrepreneurship.

The examples show how acquisition goes wrong when people try to leverage just one Distinctive Competency instead of the complete Business Idea. A successful company has one strong overall Business Idea. Success can only be expected from diversification if the complete Business Ideas of the existing business and the new business activity are fully understood and merged into one new Business Idea. Companies who intend to diversify need to be skilful in articulating and understanding Business Ideas.

SUMMARY OF MAIN POINTS OF THE BUSINESS IDEA CONCEPT

We have introduced the concept of the "Business Idea" and suggested that it should drive the strategy of organisations. It is not presented as a new tool that managers are urged to use to increase their chances of success. We believe that the Business Idea already exists in the mental models used by managers to make sense of the world. We are suggesting that managers should try to articulate their implicit Business Idea, to focus the dialogue, which needs to take place in each organisation on the emerging strategic direction. An articulated Business Idea helps management to stay on course under pressure from the many stakeholders vying for a larger piece of the value pie.

Strategy has as its main aim the continuation and growth of the organisation. For this purpose a surplus of resources needs to be created in its day-to-day operations. Before questions of who gets what are addressed the surplus must be created in the first place. It is the primary task. The Business Idea specifies the conditions required for this to happen. The basic motor of the Business Idea is the system of Distinctive Competencies created and exploited by the organisation. Understanding the nature of this leads to an awareness of the scope (and the intrinsic constraints) of their deliberate development.

A successful management team concentrates on one Business Idea only. This is not the same as concentrating on only one business. The same underlying Business Idea with its Distinctive Competencies may drive different businesses. So a Business Idea may encompass more than one business. For clarity's sake, a Business Idea does not relate to what is popularly known as a "core business". Success is in the first place determined by unique competencies, and these may or may not be related to any specific line of business. Rather than jumping to easy conclusions management need to think through carefully what the basis of their success is and take things from there.

A successful Business Idea implies continuous invention and renewal. Strategy is first of all about doing something different from what your competitors are doing. This can only be based on gaining a new and unique insight.

EasyJet and Ryanair did not intend trying to run a better airline than BA. They created a new kind of business. What is more, the formula is impossible for traditional airlines to imitate. Continental Airlines of the US and BA both tried. Continental's attempt was a failure and BA's budget operation was sold off. Management can pursue only one Business Idea. And the Business Idea of the low-cost operation cannot be combined with the Business Idea of a mainstream airline. The budget companies have invented an unexploited niche in the market and developed distinctiveness that protects them from emulation.

IKEA, the Swedish furniture manufacturer, reinvented the furniture business, offering cleanly designed products in vast, brightly lit warehouse stores at rock-bottom prices. They saw that a trade-off could be made. Customers have to collect the furniture from the shelves and transport it home and assemble it themselves.

Direct Line, the UK insurance company, invented cheap insurance over the telephone. Dell invented computers sold over the telephone and the internet. They saw that you don't need a sales force or retailers. And so on.

Invention is the key to a successful Business Idea. Technological developments, such as the internet, and economic, political and economic shocks throw up new possibilities all the time. But companies don't yet know what the new opportunities are. Only being open to the possibilities of the outside world, digging deep into people's thinking and maintaining an ongoing conversation internally and externally about what is, or will be, unique in the company will lead to the new and unique insight that is the basis of the entrepreneurial invention needed for success. The job is not finished until management "sees" the next Business Idea clearly in front of them. This involves rather more than going through a step-by-step process, organising a couple of workshops or running a planning system. These may be useful instruments on the way, but the job is not finished until management can see their new unique future. It requires time and resources, and most of all attention and energy. And management has to stay with it until the job is done. Survival is a difficult and resource-intensive thing to pursue. This is almost definitional. Imagine that good strategy would be easy. Then everyone would pursue it, and something pursued by everybody cannot possibly be a good strategy.

Unique insights and entrepreneurial invention continues to be the precondition for survival and success. The concept of the Business Idea puts entrepreneurial invention firmly on the agenda of every management team.

In entrepreneurship, invention goes together with risk. The entrepreneur needs to think about his Business Idea against an uncertain future. The same applies for organisations. In the next chapter we discuss various ways of thinking about the future business environment, aiming to see its opportunities and its uncertainties. This will lead to a discussion of scenario-based planning in comparison with other ways of describing the future world.

Chapter Six

The Uncertain Environment

The Business Idea identifies the underlying principles on which success of the organisation is based. But how does management know that its ideas are sound and a strong basis for the future? The success or failure of a Business Idea must be related to its business environment. There must be a good fit between the organisation and its surrounding world. Developing a sound and healthy organisation requires understanding of the environment as much as understanding of the organisation.

The business environment is uncertain. Business is about taking risks. Strategic management is about exploiting opportunities within a context of uncertainty about the future. Without uncertainty everyone would be in the same position and there would not be success or failure. Thinking about strategy only makes sense in conditions of uncertainty.

If uncertainty is a precondition for success why is it such a problem? Uncertainty disconfirms the institutional codifications and abstractions. It is an attack on its identity. This threatens coherence. Organisations must find a way to deal with this, if only because lack of coherence is a significant energy drain and leads to paralysis. If coherence is to be preserved, there must be a response to uncertainty, in order to rebuild context. We are now turning to the question whether anything useful can be done in this area, and if so, what and how.

BUSINESS ENVIRONMENT COMPLEXITY

The main problem, but also the main opportunity, in business environment analysis is in dealing with complexity. Lack of understanding of the complex environment is the first important source of uncertainty. But lack of understanding is also the part of uncertainty we can do something about. By analysing the situation and its history we can gradually learn to make sense of what is happening, and become better at anticipating aspects of the future. The idea of strategising implies that there is both uncertainty as well as predictability in the business environment. If everything was predictable there would be no room for strategising. If nothing was predictable strategising would make no sense. Something must be predictable, be predetermined. How do we decide what is predictable, and how do we deal with the remaining irreducible uncertainty? We will need to find a way to decide what is worthwhile spending our limited resources on. Which elements do we wish to consider in planning our business? We have to prioritise.

The area where we concentrate our limited resources is delineated by what would really make a difference for our business. The scenario planner needs to try to answer the question of what would really make a difference by identifying a small number of key uncertainties in the business environment. Scenarios are constructed by combining these and the predetermined elements as illustrated in Figure 12. In this way we consider multiple futures that reflect various different underlying structures of cause and effect, depending on how the key uncertainties will play out.

More Uncertainty Means Fewer Variables to Focus on

Figure 12 illustrates how scenario-based planning operates in a situation that is perceived to manifest both uncertainty and predetermineds. The activity aims at enlarging the perceived predetermined area, by reducing

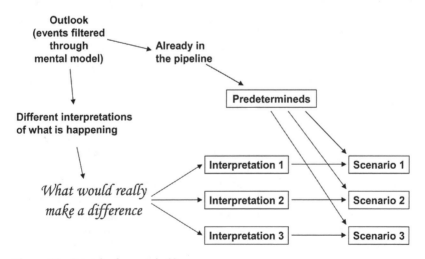

Figure 12. *Principle of scenario building*

complexity and discovering predetermined elements in the uncertain situation.

The remaining level of inherent uncertainty determines the appropriate level of detail in the analysis. More inherent uncertainty means that the analysis can stay more at the surface and the broad brush. Specifically if multiple uncertainties are perceived as moving independently from each other (orthogonality) then only those factors with the largest impact need to be taken into account. Because of the characteristics of orthogonality (quadratic addition of standard deviations) only a handful of factors will normally overwhelm all the others in their impact on the scenario client. And the higher the overall level of uncertainty in the situation the smaller the number of key uncertainties that need to be considered. More uncertainty allows focusing on fewer key uncertainties. Without this principle, scenario work in highly complex situations would be impossible.

In general terms strategic management is the art of the *appropriate* broad brush, and of focusing on what is really important.

FORMS OF UNCERTAINTY

We do not know what will happen in the future, but our ignorance is not total. The degree to which we can make useful statements about the future differs from case to case. In this context we identify three categories of uncertainty:

1. Risks, where there is enough historical precedent, in the form of similar events, to enable us to estimate probabilities (even if only judgementally) for various possible outcomes.
2. Structural uncertainties, where an event is sufficiently unique to deny us a perception of likelihood. The possibility of the event may present itself by means of a cause/effect chain of reasoning, but we have no evidence for judging how likely it could be.
3. Unknowables, where we cannot even imagine the event. Looking back in history we know that there have been many of these, and we must assume that this will continue in the future. But we have no clue what these events could be.

Uncertainty has to be assessed before business decisions can be made. Risk can be calculated on the basis of probabilities. These are derived from historical performance which is assumed to continue into the future. On this basis forecasts can be made as input to decision making.

However, in the strategy domain this is different. Here uncertainty translates into multiple interpretations that can be put on events. Based on these different interpretations different futures will emerge. In such situations of structural interpretation we will find ourselves mostly in entirely new and uncharted territory, without any basis for probability estimates.

Scenario-based planning accepts structural uncertainty with the multiple interpretations and therefore multiple futures it brings. It can help managers to get on top of the situation by developing a better judgement of what the current situation could mean. It does this by working through how each of the possible interpretations would create change in the future business environment. It obviously cannot take away the uncertainty in the situation, but it can reduce it and help managers to come to a reasonable judgement on the degree of robustness of a specific decision across the range of uncertainty. In this way managers can come to a conclusion on whether to move ahead, and in this way remove the paralysis that comes with incoherence.

Finally, in the area of unknowables, we appreciate that prescience is not possible. The only thing we can try to do in relation to unknowables is to become more skilful in reacting to the unexpected. It means that generative thinking towards success is not the whole story; we also need an adaptive part in our strategising. We can do that by developing our perception skills. Scenarios can provide powerful help here. Indeed, many would argue that this is the most important use of scenarios.

We will now discuss these areas of uncertainty in some more detail.

PREDICTABLE RISK

If there was no risk, there would be no business returns and no profitability. Chances have to be taken in the light of irreducible uncertainty if the organisation is to continue to exist. On the other hand, taking unwarranted levels of risk causes major problems. The art of the game is finding the appropriate balance, where risk is acceptable and calculated. Risk assessment, recognising what is going on, thinking about the future, and then being more skilful in adapting in advance to possible future situations is the fundamental business competency.

Not all uncertainty is uncomfortable. Many companies have learned to live in a situation of considerable risk. In oil exploration, for example, companies live with making significant commitments of money in conditions of high risk of failure. This is not problematic for them, as they have developed a readily available conceptual framework and analytical toolbox to deal with this. These allow them to consider individual decisions in the context of an ongoing flow of many similar decisions, which on average will produce positive results. One individual decision that misfires is not seen as "error", requiring managerial intervention. Performance is judged over multiple similar decisions over a longer time period. The same applies in sales. There is acceptance that "you cannot win them all". The approach is basically probabilistic.

There are many ways in which risks can be managed in this way. For example, in the area of business finance the management of risk is a well-developed skill, based on the principles of "predictable uncertainty". Instruments of insurance have been developed to cope with many different situations that may arise. Hedging instruments have the same basic function.

If managers do not feel they have such a ready-made framework for risk assessment decision making and risk taking become conservative. In those circumstances there may be very significant competitive advantage in being able to reconceptualise the environmental conditions to make the current situation part of an ongoing stream of similar or comparable situations, enabling judgement of probabilities and proper risk assessment.

The Need for Forecasting

In the domain where probabilities can be assessed forecasting makes sense. Forecasting is obviously necessary; we cannot live without it. In our personal lives we avoid a lot of trouble by forecasting. For example, if we cross a street we forecast the movements of the approaching cars, before we decide that there is enough time to get to the other side without getting hit. In most cases this is done successfully. We are forecasting all the time; we could not do much without it. When an industry is in a state of relatively slow incremental change forecasting is an effective way of planning. It projects the future on the basis of what was seen in the past. When we enter the supermarket we expect the article we need to be there. If oil demand has been increasing consistently at 6% per year we can plan next year accordingly.

The problem with forecasting is that people settle into a routine implying that the historical situation will continue forever. But there is always a point in time where behaviour changes structurally. Forecasts may work very well for a while, but forecasters need to be aware of the variables that will suddenly break the relationship with the past and create a trend break.

Limits to Forecasting

So why do we so often try to predict the unpredictable? For example, why does the law require the British Treasury to produce a forecast of the British economy, even if their record continues to be so unimpressive?

Albert Olensak of Sun Oil suggested the following metaphor to illustrate the situation. Forecasting can be thought of as analogous to the illumination by the headlights of a car driving through a snowstorm at night. A bit of what lies ahead is revealed, not very clearly. The driver merely tries to avoid danger and pick out enough detail to arrive at his destination intact. He needs to be prepared for sudden major obstacles, be aware of his limited view and try to adjust his speed accordingly. Obstacles will appear suddenly, and then it may be too late to adjust. The obstacles the driver must be prepared for are outside the limited view that he has. The reaction required is an adjustment of speed in response to limits in perception. We have to forecast. We couldn't drive the car with the lights switched off altogether. The important thing is to realise the limits of our view. Making predictions beyond our capability to forecast will inevitably cause a crisis of perception. If we accept the utility of forecasting in the short term, but its diminishing usefulness further into the future, and if we have adjusted our speed accordingly, is there anything else we need to do about the longer term, where our headlights become dim?

Planning Time Frame and Rate of Change

There is a lot in the business environment that exhibits an element of predictability. In slow changing business environments planning can be long term, and policies can involve a high level of commitment.

However, in fast changing business environments planning becomes shorter term, and policies must exhibit a higher degree of flexibility. The detail in the strategy needs to depend on the degree of predictability in the environment. The complexity in the business situation faced by most organisations suggests that the time horizon within which a business system can act as a predictable "machine" is short, often months rather than years. Marketing positioning strategy, concerned with policies aimed at positioning the organisation through interplay with its competitors, is normally seen in a relatively short time frame. That means it must be subject to frequent updating, driven by continuous unanticipated change and opportunity.

Some phenomena exhibit more inertia and momentum than others. For example, energy use shows strong momentum, so oil companies plan a long way out. On the other hand, construction companies seldom plan ahead more than three years. Beyond that they experience little that is predetermined. The time span that business plans for tends to be chosen on the basis of maintaining a reasonable balance between predetermineds and uncertainties.

However, even in the most volatile industries there are issues with long-term implications, such as capital investment, staff training and creating a competent organisational culture. An example would be the construction industry, which is notorious for its volatility and the difficulty to make any reliable plans even a few years out. However, as we saw in the example on page 79, some companies are involved in institutional capability building, aiming for a strong reputation and a client-oriented culture. When dealing with such issues management must consider a longer time horizon, as these capabilities take time to put into place, but bring long-term benefits, even in fast moving industries like construction. The planning horizon depends not only on the nature of the demand, but also on the issue under consideration.

On the other hand seeing further is not always the same as seeing better. An interesting analogy is offered by the game of chess. Contrary to early expectations of computer scientists, neither Deep Thought (the top chess-playing computer program) nor, indeed, human grandmasters need to look very far ahead to play excellent games. Analysis has shown that grandmasters generally first survey the chessboard and forecast all the pieces only one move ahead. Then they select the most plausible few plays and investigate their consequences more deeply. Theoretically at every move ahead the number of possible choices to consider explodes exponentially, yet the masters will concentrate only on a few of the most probable countermoves at each rehearsed turn. Occasionally they search far ahead when they spot familiar situations they know from experience to be valuable or dangerous. But in general, grandmasters (and now Deep Thought) work from rules of thumb, relating to developing generic strengths. Examples include favouring moves that increase options; shying away from moves that end well but require cutting off choices; working from strong positions that have many adjoining strong positions, balancing looking ahead with paying attention to what is happening now on the whole board (Kelly 1994).

Similarly it is the balance between momentum and volatility in the business environment that determines how far a business plans into the future. Figure 13 shows these elements in context. Looking into the future the degree of predictability gradually goes down the further we look, and uncertainty goes up. In the very short term predictability

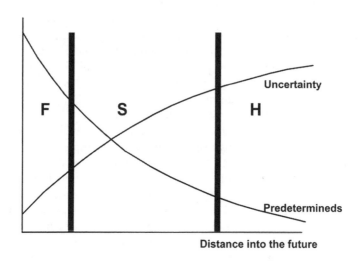

Figure 13. *The balance of predictability and uncertainty in the business environment*

is high and (frequent) forecasting is the preferred planning mode (F – forecasting). In the very long term everything is uncertain and planning demonstrates diminishing returns (H – hope). In the middle zone where there is a level of predictability but also considerable uncertainty scenarios come into their own (S – scenarios).

It is dangerous to plan strategically without being fully aware of the level of uncertainty facing the business. For example, forecasting (instead of scenario-based planning) in the S region of Figure 13 leads to overplanning and false security due to a mismatch between the sense of predictability a forecast suggests and the real level of uncertainty. Similarly scenario-based planning in the F region leads to underplanning.

STRUCTURAL UNCERTAINTY

The second category of uncertainty mentioned above is structural uncertainty. In the middle zone of Figure 13, where organisations are faced with new and uncharted challenges, posed by structural uncertainty, there are no statistics to fall back on. It is not possible to see events as an ongoing stream of comparable events. Each decision is an isolated event, there is no overall coherence. Big strategic questions often fall in this category.

Scenarios operate in this area. Structural uncertainty means that developments in the environment can be explained in more than one way, that there are multiple different cause-and-effect structures that could explain what is going on. This means that the future looks different depending on which structure we adopt. It is not possible to assign probabilities to the different structures on any statistically sound basis; the decision maker will need to confront multiple futures and consider them all equally plausible. An interesting example concerned Lloyd's Names and their insurance underwriters who a few years ago were hit by losses due to a number of large-scale natural disasters coming together, leading to increased insurance claims. The system that operated in Lloyd's put a lot of risk on the Names' shoulders. They were suing the firm of underwriters who they claim had put them in this unenviable position. The court concluded that Names should have figured out that it was inevitable that a disaster of such proportions would happen one day, and that they would not be able to cope financially with the consequences of such an event. The possible events were not hidden from anyone. Probability was not the issue. If Names had considered multiple possible futures, then catastrophes of the magnitude experienced would have been on the agenda. Essentially it was an accident waiting to happen.

Another example of a structural uncertainty is the following. The economic outlook is often of considerable importance for business. We read in the newspapers how commentators try to look into the future. Some may tell us that we are in a recession, and report the first signs of recovery. What is happening is that people are trying to fit observations into a pattern that they know from the past and can extrapolate into the future. The implication of the assumption that "our economic performance is following an economic cycle" is that we can predict that we will be coming out of recession and that growth rates will recover and people will go back to work. The explanation also implies that in five to 10 years' time there will be another recession. Using the model of the economic cycle makes you predict the future in a particular way.

However, other commentators may come up with a different explanation. They may believe that a large contributory factor to the recent economic difficulties of some Western economies is due to new overseas competition. They report that this is caused by the progressive opening up of new skilled low-cost labour markets, one after another, in the newly developing countries. Through increased outsourcing this causes the Western manufacturing sector gradually to disappear to these areas of lower cost. They point towards the rundown of traditional industrial activities in the west, which has been going on for some time. Here we are confronted with a different interpretation of what is going on. If we accept this model, then the manufacturing sector is not going to recover in a few years' time. Based on this model we see a different future on the horizon. Depending on the interpretation we find different ways in which the future will unfold.

An interesting example of alternative interpretations leading to different underlying structures driving events was presented by a set of scenarios of drilling activity in the US oil industry in the 1970s and 1980s, developed by a major oilfield equipment group. While the activity was increasing until 1981, the underlying model in general use related it to demand for oil and oil price. On the basis of this the forecast was for further increases. In retrospect we now know that a much more important driving force was the fiscal law. This made investments in drilling a no-loss proposition, either one found oil, or the government essentially paid for the investment. As soon as this anomaly was rectified the activity fell away. Following the oil price collapse in 1985 the activity fell to an all-time low (Figure 14).

Another example of different interpretations leading to different assumed structures and therefore different outlooks was the boom period of the PC market in the 1980s and 1990s. Depending on whether it

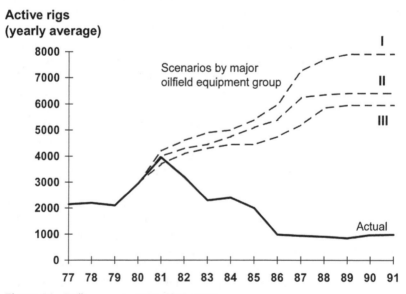

Figure 14. *Drilling scenarios USA 1980–1990*

was assumed to be driven by type of user (business products, consumer products), or by type of information processed (accounting, games) one could come up with very different demand lines.

Predictability

Even if in the area of structural uncertainty quantitative risk assessment and forecasting break down we need to be able to predict something. It is only because some things *can* be predicted that an activity such as strategising makes sense. The fact that we make the effort to strategise means that we recognise that even although there are large uncertainties out there some elements are predictable. These elements are called "predetermined elements".

An example is demography. In the sort of time frames that business planners tend to think (depending on the type of business or issue addressed, two years, five years, 10 years, sometimes even 20 years) population is a predictable phenomenon. It is predictable that the schoolchildren of today will be the parents of tomorrow. However, over the very long term birth rates are just as unpredictable as anything else. The point here is that in the time frame the business planner works the system exhibits enough inertia to allow making predictions. Techno-logical innovation is another example. While invention is probably the most unpredictable phenomenon of all, innovation concerns the application of existing inventions. It is a time-consuming process that therefore exhibits an element of predictability over the planners' time frame. Growth rate of production capacity is another example of a predetermined element. People can build and expand capacity at various rates but there is a maximum beyond which even the most energetic company would find it difficult to move. In some very large engineering construction projects the lead times can be very long, and decision makers have to assume predetermined elements. There is inertia in softer domains as well. For example, political power shifts take time and exhibit momentum allowing an element of prediction. Cultural shifts are even slower. And some human characteristics are permanent, such as the human need to survive, develop and "be connected" (Vickers 1965).

The more precisely we try to pin things down the more difficult prediction becomes. While the overall direction of movement may be predetermined the specific outcomes may be highly uncertain. Culture is often predetermined to a considerable extent. Basic beliefs and values that people develop in communities are slow to change, but predicting the attitude of a small group of people is more problematic. Similarly economic development moves within fairly narrow bands, but economists continue to have problems making detailed macroeconomic growth predictions. Looking at the same phenomenon we may conclude that while the overall structure has a high level of predictability, the details of the possible outcome may be highly uncertain. We may decide that a particular event is predetermined, but its timing may be unpredictable. For example, we may be resigned to the fact that a policy will lead to confrontation with the trade union. But we cannot predict the timing of the strike. Or the overall political trend may be predetermined, but who will win the next election is still undetermined. While the climate may be predetermined the weather remains uncertain. The agriculturist finds climate more interesting than the weather, while the holidaymaker may think the other way around.

If elements of the future are to some extent "predetermined", scenario-based planning needs to be able to deal with both predetermined elements and uncertainty. This is schematically shown in Figure 12 (page 92). The job of scenario design is about finding structure in the events in the environment. Some of these events will be considered predetermined and will be reflected in the same way in all scenarios. But the scenarios will differ in aspects that can be explained by different alternative structures. In this way the set of scenarios will express both what is considered a reasonably firm planning assumption, as well as what is structurally uncertain.

THEORIES OF STRUCTURE

In scenario-based planning understanding structure is the "building of theory" part of the learning loop (page 37). Structure plays a crucial role in all scenario design. This is often expressed as the need for internal consistency in scenarios. Internally consistent scenarios contain all the theory we can develop from our observations, and therefore become the institutional basis for the next step in the loop, the planning of new actions.

Where possible future events are unique in nature, lacking any basis for a probability assessment, but where the possibility of the event presents itself through logical cause/effect thinking we are in the domain of "process theory", page 34. We will now turn to the question of how these logic structures can be understood and developed.

Prediction and Uncertainty

As we discussed, the concept of strategy, while fundamentally dependent on uncertainty, logically assumes that aspects of the contextual environment are to some extent predictable. The purpose of analysis is to reveal something of the underlying meaning of events in the business environment. Analysis starts with perception, and perception starts with observation of events. Events are the raw material we work from to build up our understanding. While considering multiple events we have observed we start seeing trends and patterns. The human mind is particularly good at pattern recognition. Once we perceive a pattern and a degree of order, we wonder where this order comes from. This is the origin of causal thinking. It leads to implying an underlying structure *behind* the events we are observing. The cause/effect structure we build up in our mind becomes our process theory or "mental map" of reality.

Once we have developed this theory of the fundamental driving forces we are in a better position to consider our responses to the challenges presented by the observed events. By thinking through the implications of our new understanding in the context of our Business Idea we start seeing our opportunities in a new way. Environmental analysis then makes it possible to test strategic visions, Business Ideas, strategies and plans.

Assumption of Stable Structure

The power of the scenario methodology lies in its ability to logically (causally) organise a large range of relevant but seemingly disparate data and information. This is done on the basis of the assumption of both predetermined elements as well as uncertainty in the future.

The phenomenon of predeterminism is based on the assumption of a deep stable structure pertaining over the planning time frame. We recognise stable physical structures (climate, geography) as well as social structures (belief systems, culture). On the other hand elements of the future are seen as uncertain if we can explain events in different ways, see more than one possible structure driving events, and if there is no way to decide which structure will dominate in the future. Depending on which structure is considered different futures will be projected in different scenarios.

We will first consider the elements of the future where we feel we can imply a deep stable structure on the basis of which we are prepared to plan. Later we will discuss the other elements of the future, where different interpretations are possible, and uncertainty enters the picture.

Cues for Causality

Scenario planners train themselves to find structure in a multitude of events. One useful way of thinking about data is through the

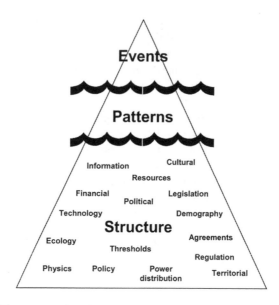

Figure 15. *The perceptional "iceberg"*

categorisation of knowledge known as the "iceberg" (Figure 15), which breaks down knowledge into three categories: events, pattern and structure (see Senge 1990). At the top of the iceberg "above the waterline" are the visible events around us, for example developments in the market, customers' actions, or government legislation. Events can be observed. One sees the world through the events that present themselves and that we perceive. It is the visible part of the iceberg. Initially we describe the world in these terms.

But as soon as important events present themselves we look for underlying patterns and structure, in order to "understand" the situation. Consider, for example, the development of the interpretation of the 9/11 terrorist attack on the World Trade Center in New York. Initially no reason was obvious, the first plane hitting the building seemed an accident to many. But with an attack on the Pentagon and a second hit on the WTC following quickly in succession it became evident quickly that there was a pattern here that indicated a linked causal structure rather than an isolated freak event. This was strengthened with the news of the crash further inland. This is one of the so-called "hallmarks" of Al Qaeda; attacks do not come in isolation but in clusters, sufficient to suggest that these are causally related, and in this way impressing on the consciousness of the world the power of an apparently unitary organisation. The pattern is the message.

Scenario planners start from the premise that there is much more to be said than just reporting events. Some events may be entirely unexpected and isolated, but many seem to display some sort of organised behaviour. The assumption is that events do not just happen at random, but they are related to each other through a structure where causes drive effects and one event leads to another. As a result a variable may be going up with some consistency, or a growth path may be checked and starts turning down. Another variable may be cycling up and down with some regularity. In order to get at the underlying structure behind these patterns we look for inter-relatedness between multiple trends, and ideas for structure present themselves. If variable x is going up and variable y is going up simultaneously we wonder whether they are in some way related.

Structure is the result of our assumption of causality. This is based on patterns we think we recognise in the events around us. We use such patterns as cues for causality (Einhorn & Hogarth 1982). These can take the form of:

- Temporal order, events organised on a time line, for example trends over time in events
- Co-variance, where we see different variables following similar patterns over time.
- Spatial/temporal closeness, if one thing always follows another, we assume a link.
- Similarity in form or pattern.

By discovering multiple cues for causality we infer elements of the underlying overall structure which we assume ultimately drives the visible events. The assumed structure becomes a "process theory" (as distinct from "variance theory", see page 34), which explains cause and effect while recognising indeterminacy. It is an explanation of *why* things might happen, not just the story of what happened.

In this way we compose our mental model of the world. For example, we know that in African countries where the population has tripled and quadrupled in 40 years the present system of production and management is no longer viable. We can therefore expect to see an increase in emergencies and crises, but also experimentation. This is predetermined because it is already in the pipeline, it is "inescapable". What we do not know is what system will be created out of this turning point.

This is an example of a framing based on our ideas about causality in the situation. Other examples of such frames that structure the future include:

- Time delays, developments that are "in the pipeline" and will emerge, e.g. demographics.
- System constraints, e.g. limits to growth.
- Generic behaviour of structural feedback loops in a system, e.g. the arms race.
- Actor logic and motivation, e.g. Labour or Tory politics in the UK, or Democrat or Republican politics in the US.
- The inertia of the system (including societal inertia), e.g. economic development, culture.
- Laws of nature.

There is a lot of room for interpretation. Different people will come to different conclusions because they have different histories. These frame what they see and therefore their causal mental model. What is terrorism for one is a fight for freedom for another. It is the decision maker's task to uncover those frames. It can be done, but only if we respect these differences and the complexity of the world. If we do that then scenarios can penetrate the deep structure of the situation and bring this to the surface in the form of stories, making it actionable.

Finally a lot depends on the level at which we conceptualise the situation. The granularity at which we look at events determines the causal structure we come up with. Complexity pioneer Stuart Kauffman (1995) once explained it as follows: "I once listened with considerable interest to an interior decorator. I learned a useful phrase: 'it's that kind of thing'. Now here's a phrase that has quite cosmic usefulness for even in our incapacity to predict details we can still think about kinds of things." Causal structure may be more evident and clearer at the "kinds of things" level than at the level of the detail of the situation. The question of deciding the appropriate level of granularity of the analysis should always be on the agenda of the decision maker. For example, what is the best level to think about the new global threat, should it be suicide bombers, Al Qaeda or global terrorism. The scenario approach is particularly strong in analysing such questions, based on its underlying assumption of multiple interpretations, and its storytelling nature.

The Structure Analysis

We use these assumed causal structures to link history with the future. The process in principle involves the following steps:

- Specify important events, things we can see happening.

- Discover trends, time behaviour we observe in events, leading to the conceptualisation of variables.
- Infer causal patterns, based on cues for causality applied to behaviour of variables.
- Develop the structure, which connects the system together through causal links (multiple structures may result from different possible interpretations of causal patterns).
- Use the structure(s) to project future behaviour (with multiple structures leading to multiple scenarios).

Out of this we discover that some developments have already been set in motion, and are bound to come out at the other end. Our understanding of predictable outcomes, based on elements of systemic structure, such as inertia or lock-in caused by feedback loops, provides a basis on which we can plan our activities.

Following a process of this type we develop an understanding on predetermined elements, as the basis for future planning.

FORECASTING VS. SCENARIOS

Leaving Uncertainty on the Agenda

Having discussed the principles of scenario design let us now compare this with forecasting (van der Heijden 1994). Forecasting assumes that it is possible to predict the future, on the basis of what we have called a "variance theory", i.e. consistent and ongoing correlations between variables in the business environment persisting over time. It is closely related to the rationalist assumption that there is one right answer to the strategy question and the art of strategising is to get as close as possible to it. The task of forecasting must therefore be given to the people with the requisite intelligence and computing power, as this will ensure that the answer will be as close as possible.

Scenario-based planning has a fundamentally different starting point. The future is not predictable, it contains irreducible uncertainty. However, there is underlying causal structure in events, and it is possible to develop a "process theory" of why things happen as they do. Therefore there is no one best answer, but causal structure implies predetermined elements that can be surfaced and articulated. Scenario-based planning leads to new and original insights in the underlying structure driving events on the basis of which strategising is possible. However, there is a point beyond which accuracy cannot be improved. This means that it is important that decision makers face up to irreducible uncertainty. Making a forecast in an area where there is fundamental uncertainty is dangerous, as it takes away from the decision maker important information needed to come to a responsible decision.

Forecasters sometimes try to reflect predictable uncertainty. For example, forecasts may be a statistical summary of expert opinion, which does not necessarily lead to just one number. Sometimes a range is specified, putting statistical variance around the forecast. The forecaster will specify that demand for automobiles will be within a range of 80 to 100. There may be a high line and a low line with a probability attached. Management will learn that the most likely outcome is 90 but it could be 100 and it could be 80, as the best forecast the experts can come up with. This is a reflection of expert opinion based on probability assessment.

Forecasting is done by experts, away from where the decisions are being made. Sources of uncertainty are generally not made specific, it is considered too technical. They become obscured in the analysis. That means that the decision maker who receives the result of the forecasting activity does not know the underlying thinking process and the margin of error in the correlations that have been used to produce the prediction. The danger to the decision makers derives from this disconnection. If they decide to use the forecast they do not know what risk assumptions enter their decision process. They are no longer in a position to see the different possibilities as they could unfold. They have shifted responsibility on to the expert. Uncertainty falls between two stools. The linear forecasting process runs out to an algorithmically inevitable outcome and thinking tends to stop. The decision process is essentially a chance event.

Compare that with scenarios. In scenarios we specifically address key uncertainties through chains of cause and effect. Because they differ on these key logics scenarios put these on the management agenda. Scenarios let the decision maker look not just at outcomes, but also at the driving forces that could move the business one way or the other.

Forecasters Box in the Future, Scenarios Open up Area of Thinking

Forecasting requires that we first decide what we want to forecast. In the automobile industry people forecast the demand for automobiles. Statisticians and experts go to work and, via macro-analysis of GNP, purchasing power, spending patterns etc. they come up with a prediction of the total demand for automobiles over time in various categories. The decision what to forecast is prime, the analysis follows. *Forecasting is inside-out thinking*. This is important, as unexpected influences that may come at the business sideways are not part of the analysis. The unforeseen variables that do not feature in the expert's model of the business and its environment are not on the agenda. As soon as we are in forecasting mode we have boxed in our mental models and the unexpected has been shut out. Organisations need to be aware of the perceptual limitations caused by this sort of analysis.

Imagine a 1980 strategy meeting at IBM called to develop a PC strategy. The meeting is told that the market forecast for 1990 is 275 000. The conclusion is clear, this is a sideshow; we may as well outsource the operating system and microprocessor. Now imagine that someone walks in saying: "Yes, but imagine that the market is 60 million, think about what you would be giving away to Microsoft and Intel." He would probably have been thrown out.

Something else is required that will make the organisation look outside the framework of Business-As-Usual. What is needed is a processual approach that mobilises knowledgeable individuals throughout the organisation as well as outsiders. Next, the organisation as a whole needs to acquire the perceptual skill of seeing and acting on signals of change in the business environment across a wide front. This is where the scenarios come in. The scenario planner is not in the forecasting strait jacket. (S)he does not start from the notion of the product (e.g. automobiles), but takes a wider canvas. The starting point is "the main uncertainties facing this organisation". Perceptions of areas of concern in the management team are the agenda setting questions for the scenario planner. Demand levels for the product may be included in this, but questions will quickly move beyond that into more fundamental driving forces. For example, in the automobile industry the question of the future of terrorism in its effect on transportation in general may come up with its many driving forces. The scenario planner takes a broader view about the business environment than the forecaster does. The range of vision of the planning activity has been widened. *Scenarios are about outside-in thinking*.

Haeckel (1999) has called this the transition from a "build/sell" to a "sense/respond" mindset. The issue here is one of balance, not choice. Companies have to do all four, but as traditional analysis starts with defining upfront what we will forecast it reduces the space for "sense/ response" thinking. Scenario analysis can restore the balance.

Forecasts, Efficient and Impoverished

A forecast is a very efficient way of describing the future. Its efficiency derives from simple decision-making algorithms. Forecasting is efficient in reducing rich information into a simple form in which it can be passed on easily for operational purposes. For example, the size of the automobile manufacturing unit to be built is relatively easily derived from it. It is a summary. But it is also, because of that, impoverished.

Scenarios have much more information; they are richer because they give the whole cause–and–effect story, leading to an understanding of why things happen. But for this reason they are also less efficient as input to yes/no type decision making, which is now more complex. It is less straightforward to make a decision on the basis of a set of scenarios than a forecast. Scenarios require further judgements. A yes/no decision does not automatically fall out from a scenario analysis. Scenarios do not normally produce conclusions in a mechanistic way. The decision whether the new factory has to be built at all, let alone what its capacity should be, is less obvious. More work, thinking and analysis will be required before an action conclusion emerges. This thinking process involves deepening out levels of understanding of the business environment, until a new way of understanding and thinking emerges pointing to the Business Idea of the future, as the basis for new strategy. It is ultimately about the entrepreneurial invention that we discussed earlier.

Testing Forecasts and Scenarios

Forecasts can be tested after the event. You can compare an outcome with what was predicted. As we saw earlier, sometimes it works and sometimes it doesn't. And unfortunately, it works least where it is needed most, in periods of rapid change. Scenarios, of course, cannot be proved or disproved. First of all the methodology does not claim that they will materialise as such, and they are not supposed to be used on that basis. In fact, as one point on a continuum, the probability that one particular scenario will unfold in all its details is near to zero. But as a set they represent our current understanding of the "sort of thing that could happen" and the range of uncertainty. If we draw the range of scenarios wide enough the chance that reality (less unknowables) will emerge somewhere in between them can be made high. Therefore they are not meant to be tested against what actually will happen. When scenarios are needed and used what will happen is unknown, and therefore can have no bearing on conclusions about effectiveness. The test is whether they represent our current best knowledge of the situation and outlook, our current process theories, and thereby lead to better strategies.

Different Purposes

Summarising, forecasting and scenario-based planning have very different purposes. The strategic question has its origin in uncertainty, both in the environment and within the organisation. Uncertainty increases the further out we look. Forecasting is useful in the short term, where things are reasonably predictable and uncertainty is relatively small compared to our ability to predict. In this range rationalistic "predict and control" planning makes sense and is necessary. In the very long term where very little is predictable planning is not a useful activity. It is in the intermediate future where uncertainty and predictability are both significant that scenario-based planning makes its contribution. This is also the area of strategy. Therefore strategic management and scenario-based planning are closely linked.

Scenarios can help in dealing with uncertainty in three specific ways:

1. They help the organisation in understanding the environment better, allowing many decisions to be seen not as isolated events but as part of a process of "swings and roundabouts". In this way scenario-based planning helps managers to avoid undue conservatism, by allowing "calculated" risk taking.
2. Scenarios put structural uncertainty on the agenda, driving home to the organisation what sort of "accidents are waiting to happen". In this way scenario-based planning helps managers to avoid taking undue chances.
3. Scenarios help the organisation to become more adaptable by expanding their mental models of the business environment and thereby enhancing the perceptual capabilities needed to recognise unexpected events and take proactive action.

Chapter Seven

Scenario Analysis

At this point we need to discuss in a little more depth what we mean by scenarios and scenario analysis. In this chapter we will first develop further the principles of scenario analysis, as an approach towards learning about the business environment. In Chapter Eight we will look at this from an action perspective.

DEFINITION

Scenarios are popular and used in many different contexts and meanings. The reader should be aware that "scenario planning" does not mean the same thing for everyone using the term. The word scenario is not very well defined in the strategy literature. It is used for many different approaches and tools. It is therefore important that we define how we will use it here. We position scenario-based planning within a strategic framework that we have set up in earlier chapters as follows:

- Organisational survival/self-development are the essential and prime driving forces of strategy.
- Strategising is creating a new and unique policy framework for future action, based on deepening understanding of the fit between ourselves and our environment in which we need to survive and develop.
- The Business Idea is a strategic perspective on ourselves as an organisation.
- The scenarios are the strategic perspectives on the environment of this Business Idea.

We make a distinction between what we will call scenarios of the external world and strategic narratives in which the organisation itself plays a part.

Strategic narratives belong to a person or an organisation and relate to their anticipation of future states of the interactional world in which the person or the organisation plays an important role. A strategic narrative takes the form of a causal story, linking an action option with a goal ("if I do this then this will happen which will lead to that and so on until I achieve my objective of A"). It can be seen as one pathway through the web of a person's options map.

For the individual it is quite natural to play a role in his/her own internal story – this is part of our everyday-life thinking process and sense of identity. Internal stories tend to be normative, with some outcomes preferred over others, reflecting our aspirational system. This is the world of good and bad futures. They involve us.

External scenarios are derived from shared and agreed upon mental models of how the external world works. This is the part of the environment where we have little or no influence, but which impacts on us in a major way. The scenarios are expressed as internally consistent and challenging narrative descriptions of possible futures in this external world. They come in sets, representing the fact that there is considerable uncertainty in the future. The set is intended to be representative of the range of possible future developments and outcomes in the external world. They describe circumstances in the environment that could have a major impact on our business, but are essentially outside our own control.

The strategic conversation in the organisation is greatly helped by making a clear distinction between internal narratives and external scenarios, the distinction between what is sometimes called the "world of desire" and "the world of fate". In order to keep this clearly in front us we will use the word *scenarios only for the external business environment* story. Internal stories will be called "strategic narratives".

As scenarios only deal with the external world over which we don't have much control or influence it is important that they should be conceived as value-neutral. Herman Kahn (see page 3) saw as the great value of the scenario approach that it allows the observer to engage in value-free exploration. It helps executives to see the world through different lenses, stretching beyond their conventional mental map. Value-free scenarios can help them see crucial aspects in the situation they were not looking for. We should retain this power of the scenarios by projecting them clearly in the part of the business environment that we have called contextual (see below), outside our own control, and keeping them away from the daily "playing field", where the organisation is one of the players. (Some will argue that a scenario can never be entirely value free. But even so, as Kahn suggested, there is considerable benefit in reducing its emotional charge, considering that each scenario is only one of "multiple possible futures", none of which we can influence.)

It is helpful to distinguish the organisation itself, where the strategist has control, from its *transactional* environment, where the organisation interacts with others, exercising influence but not control. This is the "playing field" where the organisation competes with others for resources. This playing field world is in turn embedded in the *contextual* environment, over which the strategist has little or no influence but which (s)he needs to appreciate in its impact on the playing field and the organisational self. Identifying the boundaries between these three areas is a crucial part of the strategic task.

Following Emery and Trist (1965), we define the two environment categories as follows:

- The contextual environment is that part of the environment which has important repercussions for the organisation but in which it has little or no influence. Actors in the contextual environment are known as "referees", i.e. those who set the rules for what we do, without being subject to our influence. While the organisation does not have power to influence the contextual environment its major task is to arrange its own affairs, such that it remains an effective player whatever may happen there.

- The transactional environment is that part of the environment in which the organisation is a significant player, influencing outcomes as much as being influenced by them. This is the playing field for which the organisation develops its strategy in order to turn the game to its advantage.

External scenarios play in the contextual environment. An (implicit or explicit) aim of the scenario-based planning exercise is to help managers in identifying possible strategies and to consider these against the "test conditions" of the external scenarios in order to assess their strength and robustness. This objective requires the clear distinction between contextual and transactional environments. The test conditions need to be descriptions of the contextual environment, against which characteristics of the behaviour of the organisation, in interaction with its transactional environment, can be judged.

Scenarios defined as descriptions of possible developments in the contextual environment will not be good or bad; they are worlds that may plausibly develop independent from what we do, and in which the organisation may need to be a skilful operator. As individuals we may have a value judgement about these futures, but the organisation as a whole cannot think in those terms. It can only take the position that, being unable to significantly change the contextual world, it will try to be successful in whatever contextual future comes around. This theme will be developed below under the heading "Framing of Scenarios", page 128. Before we do that we first need to consider how the scenarios come into being and what role they play in the strategising process.

THE STRATEGISING PURPOSE

The organisation arrives at the present time with all its historical baggage. An important manifestation of its history is its Business Idea. Through careful observation, experimentation and thinking the organisation arrived at an entrepreneurial idea that is the basis of its past and current success. But time moves on. The business environment is always changing. Adaptations will have to be made. Sometimes changes are so large that the Business Idea itself needs to be reinvented. From time to time each organisation needs to think seriously about strategy development.

The prime question to be addressed is whether the organisation is well equipped to see and understand the futures that are coming. The task is in the first place to study what is going on around it, searching for new developments that might offer pointers towards future sources of value, rent and profitability. By looking long and hard enough such possibilities will emerge affecting one or more of the elements of the Business Idea loop, including customer value, demand, activity set, competitive advantage (cost/differentiation) and Distinctive Competencies. The search is on for an original invention in any of these elements that will allow the organisation to build a new position of strength, where value is created and appropriated in the future. It is on the interface between the organisational "self" and the environment that sources of value creation have to be discovered. We need to understand both. The environment needs to be studied against the background of the Business Idea, and the latter cannot be developed without a deep insight into where the business environment is taking us.

Earlier we introduced the concepts of "generative" and "adaptive" scenario-based planning (see page 53). In the generative mode we study the scenarios against the current Business Idea, to raise the important questions for the future and advance our understanding until a new and unique insight has been gained on the basis of which the Business Idea can be reinvented. In the adaptive approach we study the Business Idea against a range of scenarios to determine, and if possible incrementally improve, the degree of fit.

Studying the Environment in the Context of the Business Idea (the Generative Mode)

The overriding strategic task concerns the response to the big looming issue, the new entrepreneurial invention needed for the future, based on gaining a new and unique insight in where the business environment is going. This is the realm of generative strategising. Scenario-based planning can make a major contribution here.

For this unique insight to occur we need to be able to believe something about the future. The starting point of generative strategy is the idea that by looking in the right way, the future can be "seen". This does not mean clairvoyance or mystical perceptions beyond the capability of the average strategic planner. We need to look for forces and relationships that, by already existing, constrain or determine the future in important ways. In this first more fundamental phase of the strategy task we need to go into the depth of the causal texture of the business environment to discover where the situation is structurally predetermined. In this way one can learn to see not just the generally known well-established facts but also emergent novel reality.

The approach is schematically shown in Figure 16. The scenario activity is essentially iterative. It can be compared to a process of action learning in which the scenarios play the important role of question raisers. The key aspect of the task is to discover what has not as yet been articulated about the situation. As every researcher has experienced, once

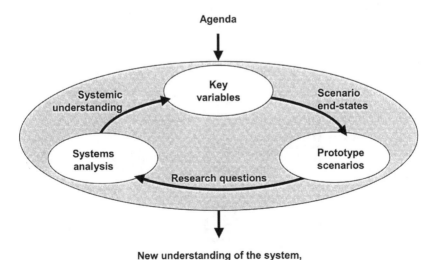

Figure 16. *Principle of iterative scenario building*

the question has been articulated doing the analysis and finding the answer is relatively easy. The art of strategising is in surfacing and formulating the important questions. The iterative scenario method can make a major contribution in this. Because of its systematic approach towards formulating and analysing the future it points towards "white space" in our understanding that is worth analysing.

The scenarios are an important tool in a larger learning process. They change with each iteration. Scenarios of earlier iterations have lost their usefulness in later iterations. The main products of the project are not the scenarios but the systemic understanding and the new perspective on the business that the complete learning loop has created. It is this understanding that will lead us to the new and unique insight as the basis for a new future Business Idea.

Studying the Business Idea in the Context of Scenarios of the Business Environment (the Adaptive Mode)

Once a successful Business Idea is in place it needs to be considered and adapted against the outlook for the environment on an ongoing basis. How can scenario thinking contribute to this process? Figure 17 gives a schematic overview. The scenarios, as they evolve over time, can be seen as test conditions for the Business Idea. They are powerful thinking tools, organising a large amount of disparate, but relevant, data about the multi-dimensional business environment into manageable wholes. They are put together reflecting our knowledge of underlying structures as well as irreducible uncertainty. They are rich "laboratories" in which

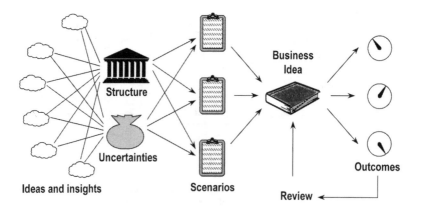

Figure 17. *Scenarios test the Business Idea*

different models of future policy can be tested. And by using more than one, robustness is tested specifically.

The scenario activity is now linear instead of iterative as discussed earlier in Figure 16 for generative strategising. An effective strategy laboratory requires understanding of the key environmental variables and their interlinkages. The business environment is infinitely large, and the organisation selects what is worth considering by reference to its Business Idea. In practical terms, scenario development requires understanding of the nature of the Business Idea in order to decide what are suitable "test conditions". By using the scenarios as a strategy test bed the managers are forced to articulate what they consider really important in the environment.

Adaptive scenario-based planning is a customised activity. The process can be compared with using a wind-tunnel to test the model of an aircraft. A supersonic fighter design requires different conditions in the wind-tunnel than a hang-glider. Generic scenarios are not very helpful.

Sometimes the purpose of the scenario activity may be to make a final decision, but more normally the manager uses the scenarios to test strategy proposals in order to find ways to improve them, i.e. make them more appropriate and robust against the futures which might arise (Figure 17). Scenarios are policy development tools. Rather than a clear-cut yes/no situation they present the organisation with the means to iteratively build/ develop better policy. They need to stretch the range of the organisation's vision beyond what is traditionally seen as relevant, the Business-As-Usual world. The scenario planner will need to widen the area of relevance. So scenarios can also be seen as perception tools, which can be used to develop "peripheral vision" beyond the current focus of attention in the organisation, moving the thinking into the "adjacent space".

The Business Idea in most organisations is tacit, and taken for granted while people get on with the day-to-day tasks. For this reason a strategy project needs to start with bringing the Business Idea to the surface. In Part Three we will discuss processes for doing this and expressing the result of this activity in a manageable form. The purpose is twofold:

- To generate a basis from which the scenario agenda can be formulated.
- To generate an agreed understanding of the basic success drivers of the organisation, which can subsequently be assessed against the scenarios to discuss organisational implications.

Adaptive scenario-based planning can lead to powerful results in terms of confirming the validity of the current Business Idea, or indicating areas where incremental improvements are called for.

THE PROCESS

The scenario planner starts with a set of unrelated concerns of his/her client, including possibly a feeling of insecurity around one or more unarticulated "big issues" (page 56). At this stage ideas are not very well linked into existing cognitive structures. The first step is to develop a preliminary scenario agenda, which sets the process on its way. This needs to be a good starting point for the search for structure around the areas of puzzlement of the client.

Some relevant predetermined elements may present themselves for inclusion in the first analysis phase. One can think of the obvious inertias in the world, for example demographics, economic development, cultural beliefs, and so on. But it is likely that these will produce a very incomplete picture of the driving forces in the specific situation considered. The reason is that most predetermined elements are emergent properties of the slow-changing causal structures of the systems studied. In order to map these out the scenario process needs to identify as many causal links as possible. This will have to come from a search through the history of the system's behaviour for "cues for causality" (see page 37).

The scenario planner will initially search widely for such relationships. In the early stages any idea is considered as a potential building block. In the process of this the area of analysis will be continuously redefined, depending on factors that enter the causal equation, while elements may be removed which have become secondary in any relevant causal explanation.

It is the ultimate aspiration of the scenario planner to develop the process into an ongoing learning experience in the organisation. In Chapter Three we presented scenario-based planning as a cyclical action learning process, operating according to the principles of the learning loop (see page 37). We saw how it alternates between exploring adjacent space (scenario building) and analysis of the questions raised. Both phases are necessary. In this chapter we will discuss how this is realised at the level of both management and the organisation. Generative scenario processes are always iterative, continuing until the strategic situation has been successfully reframed. Adaptive processes are different only in that the scenario-building phase is more linear and predetermined with the resulting scenarios used subsequently in a "wind-tunnelling" phase.

Generative Scenario-based Planning

The exploratory phase of the analysis is sometimes called the "breathing-in" phase. While the situation is being opened up the search for relevant insights is highly dynamic and ever changing, while more and more findings of possible relevance are "put on the table" for consideration. In this seemingly chaotic situation the scenario planner uses scenarios as a way to create some order in the developing knowledge of the situation. The scenarios are a number of stories created in a way that projects this knowledge base into the future in an internally consistent way.

The outcome of the first iteration of the process is a clearer and better-articulated understanding of what one does and does not know about the system, and indicates questions that need to be researched. The questions arise mostly through trying to tell the story coherently in some detail. In doing so one discovers where understanding of the underlying structure in the situation is lacking. Scenario building is about raising these important questions.

The first scenario building phase produces the "first generation" scenarios. This is not the "final product", further work is required. This consists of an analysis phase where the scenario planners engage with any relevant source of knowledge to find out what is known about the questions raised, and what other questions need to be addressed. This is equivalent to the action phase of the learning loop.

There is no limit to the amount of energy that can be invested in this research phase. But somewhere diminishing returns will set in. At this stage the scenario planner once again needs to take stock, organise all new findings in a new scenario framework, which in turn may indicate new lines of productive analytical attack.

Why is the process of research and analysis not enough, why is it necessary from time to time to stop the analysis per se and build scenarios around the findings of the analysis? Initially the problematic situation is ill-defined. Through open-ended interviewing the scenario planner will have obtained some idea of the nature of the concerns of the client, but this will be poorly structured and only vaguely outlined. Uncertainty in the perception of the scenario planner will be due more to lack of knowledge of the system than genuine indeterminates. At the end of the project this needs to be transformed in a clear understanding of what is predetermined and what is indeterminate in the situation. And the more predetermineds that can be discovered the more the client will have been helped in getting on top of the situation. Basically the process is a search for as many predetermineds as we can find.

This process has to be "bootstrapped". In the early stages of a scenario project there is no easy way of distinguishing between predetermineds and indeterminates. Structure will not automatically jump out of the situation description embodied in the scenario themes. Initially the situation facing the scenario planner is extremely ill-defined; there are no obvious points to start analysing. Where to begin?

In this situation a scenario framework can be a powerful organising and focusing device. Developing scenario logics from driving forces and critical uncertainties, the scenario planner implicitly uses systems thinking concepts, finding causes, and the causes of the causes, looking behind events for patterns of behaviour and system structure that might explain how this scenario might come about.

The process of creating a scenario framework should be seen as a way of organising insights, in order:

- To indicate the direction of further analytical enquiry, and/or
- To communicate the results of the analysis.

It points the scenario planner in a direction where analytical work would be useful. The research is now guided by well-defined questions that ensure relevance and usefulness. The scenario planner returns from this active research phase with many new insights and ideas, scattered over many subjects. The process iterates back to the scenario building phase, which is repeated, but now with the input of many new and relevant ideas. The scenario building phase once again serves the purpose of fitting these fragments of knowledge into the bigger framework of the scenario set, developing coherence and internal consistency.

The scenario framework phase forces the scenario planner to reflect on the findings of the analysis so far by fitting these into a number of stories about the future, which express the discoveries made. The stories will overlap where predetermineds (established and predictable causal structures) have been found, but differ in terms of how the uncertainties will be assumed to pan out. At the early stages of the process the uncertainties will indicate both areas of lack of understanding as well as indeterminates. At the later stages one hopes that uncertainties are reduced to only genuine indeterminates.

The principle involved is similar to that of action research (Lewin 1935), carried out on a system that is too complex to understand by reductionist methods. Action research is based on observing the behaviour of an only partially known system after a perturbation has been applied. The system may behave as was expected, in which case not much is learned. But if the behaviour deviates from expectations research into the reason for the deviation from expectation will create new understanding of the system's underlying structure. The activity of scenario building carries out a similar process on one's mental model of the situation under consideration. A good scenario framework process challenges the existing mental models of the scenario planners. This can

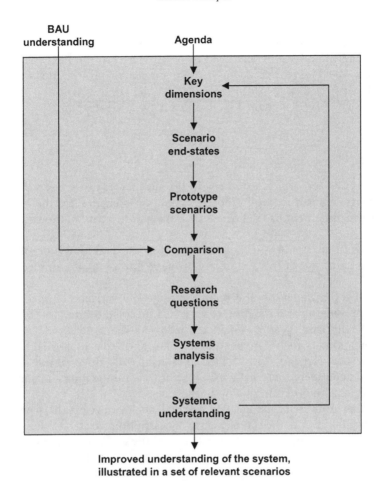

Figure 18. *The iterative scenario analysis process*

be done, for example, by the discipline of designing a number of significantly different scenario end-states in a future "horizon year". Attempting to tell the logical story of how we arrived there starting from the "Business-As-Usual" world of the recent past and present will bring out the areas where understanding is lacking, and research needs to be done. The process is worked out in steps in Figure 18.

The scenarios as such are instruments in the learning loop (page 37). They allow us to take stock of what we know and don't know, and formulate the questions that need to be answered in the next round of analysis (see Figure 18). As in any other research project most of the intellectual challenge is in formulating the right questions to be researched. A well-designed scenario exercise facilitates this.

An example

A few years ago a group of scenario planners set out to work with the management of a major European airport on scenarios for the future. Earlier management had defined as their main dimensions of the situation:

- Political constraints on movements (noise and pollution control)
- Degree of use of the airport as European hub by major airlines.

They had bracketed the uncertainty in these key variables by specifying two opposing polar outcomes for each in a specified future year (known as the "horizon year"). This then allowed them to produce four combinations, which can be worked into the basis of four different scenarios. In fact they had decided to develop only three, as one of the four was considered internally inconsistent (accommodating a major hub operation within existing constraints).

At that time management had decided not to develop the scenarios further, and just use the three end-states descriptions related to these two dimensions as strategic test conditions. However, that project was perceived as somewhat less than successful as it did not seem to lead to new strategic insights. It had organised existing knowledge, but had not added very much. It is clear that management at that time looked at first generation scenarios only.

The scenario team then decided to develop the stories over time. While doing that they discovered two major areas where more information was needed to complete the story. The variables that seemed quite crucial in being able to tell these stories were:

- How far will concentration in the airline industry in Europe go?
- To what extent will airlines continue to operate hub and spoke systems?

Such questions come up while trying to construct a coherent story that connects the situation today with that specified in the end-state. The simple process of going through this asking "how could this happen" for every event, looking for the causes, or the causes of the causes, automatically brings these questions to the surface. Having raised these questions the participants then took time off to research these matters, making use of their contacts in the industry.

As a result the second generation scenarios were very different, more complete, expressing a deeper understanding of these phenomena and the underlying system. But as they visited new territory they threw up further questions that did not come up in the first generation. The whole process typically takes multiple iterations.

Strategic insight

So the approach iterates, alternating scenario building with in-depth systems analysis, answering the questions thrown up by the scenario building. And in the process the team learns about the relevant world. They deepen their understanding of the deep steady structure as well as the volatile surface phenomena. They start seeing the driving forces and reinforcing feedback loops behind it all. They start to understand potential feedback that may create instability. Reinforcing feedback loops are important because they lock in the system and create predetermined behaviour. By concentrating on such phenomena quite a simple model can capture a lot of the essential detail. The scenarios are powerful in pointing the way to such simple models.

On the basis of this type of understanding the team starts to see the inevitabilities as well as discontinuities that can be envisaged. And as understanding grows the team starts to see threats and opportunities for the Business Idea, raising important strategic questions. It is in this process that one looks for that final key connection to be made, the one unique strategic opportunity to emerge.

It is a mental journey of discovery in which storytelling alternates with accessing the world's knowledge in relevant areas and bringing it together for a deeper understanding of structural relationships. The moment of discovery, when our understanding of the world suddenly shifts and is reframed, when we suddenly "see it", cannot be forced. The process will mature in its own time. But if successful the resulting scenarios communicate powerful insights about likely changes or potential discontinuities and their impacts, positive or negative, on business opportunities. We will understand events in a new way and see new possibilities to reposition the organisation advantageously. We will have reached the unique insight.

It is the systemic understanding of the strategic environment that is ultimately more important than the stories that display the tendencies of the system. You are not going to help someone who does not know whether to take his umbrella or not by telling him that there are two scenarios, rain or shine. This is "first generation", it is reasonable and effective up to a point, but it has weaknesses as input into strategic choice. It seems that almost anything could happen, so what do you do? Trying to decide strategy against multiple possible conditions leads more readily to hedging and caution than it does to powerful entrepreneurial initiatives. For strategy you need actually to believe something about the future. This can only be achieved by thinking through the detailed scenarios of how the weather might develop from where we are now to rain or shine tomorrow, causing you to look at isobars, wind directions, temperature charts, weather fronts etc., which will lead to interesting insights that may, with a bit of luck, actually help in answering the question whether to take the umbrella. The scenarios did not tell you that, but the analysis based on the questions raised by the scenarios did.

Adaptive Scenario-based Planning

In adaptive scenario-based planning the process of building the scenarios is not fundamentally different from the generative approach as explained above. However, the process will not be open-ended as in the generative mode. In most cases, the first or second generation scenarios will be considered the final set against which the Business Idea will be evaluated. This involves essentially considering the existing Business Idea against what scenarios tell us about the characteristics of the future business environment, to establish the degree of fit. We compared this earlier to a wind-tunnel where a model is subjected to tests to assess its strengths and weaknesses. The purpose is not so much to accept or reject the current model but to engage in a process of design, adjustment and improvement, until a model has been developed that exploits the new insights we have gained on the futures and that fits comfortably in a range of related possible environments that might develop.

This leads to a fundamental rule of adaptive scenario-based planning: once we have decided on the set of scenarios of the future which are considered relevant to our situation, each scenario must be treated as equally plausible. There is no point in working with conditions that are not going to be taken seriously.

Considering strategic fit

The analytical task is to "walk" the Business Idea mentally through the various scenarios, to study how it would stand up if any of these futures were to materialise. While going through the scenarios one after the other the analysis addresses the following questions:

- Will the customer value system overlap sufficiently with the supplier's competence system envisaged to create significant new and surplus value?
- Will its distinctiveness allow the supplier to appropriate enough of the surplus for its own development?
- Will the competence system be capable of being defended against competitive emulation?

While going through the scenarios events unfold, and for each of these the same questions are addressed: how would this influence (1) customer value creation, (2) supplier's ability to appropriate some of this value and (3) the uniqueness of the competence system (see Figure 17)?

Having gone through all scenarios in this thinking mode, a judgement has to be made on whether the answers are positive enough to instil confidence in the future strength of the existing Business Idea formula. There are two possibilities:

First, having looked at the business environment we conclude that the Business Idea is strong and strategy is more about effective exploitation of the proven success formula. But how do you know it is strong? There is first of all managerial intuition. But often there are doubts and confirmation is needed. This is where an adaptive in-depth scenario exercise can be helpful, always asking the questions: "Could anything go wrong with this Business Idea? Are we overlooking important new driving forces? Is there another way of looking at this situation?"

If the fit is confirmed as strong the organisation will want to continue and expand exploiting the Business Idea. In this case the strategic questions concentrate on finding new areas where the competence system can be exploited. This can take three forms:

- New markets or market segments where the existing offering can be exploited.
- Development of the offering to extend or create new customer value.
- Developing new applications for the structural cost advantage.

In all cases the competence system stands as the basis of the strategy. Thinking then concentrates on options in the portfolio of businesses. Strategy development revolves around "Portfolio Options".

Second, we conclude that the Business Idea is weak, has no great future and needs reinvention. This is when an original entrepreneurial invention needs to be made. This is where there is a need for a new unique insight, and discovering this becomes the basic purpose of a scenario analysis. The analysis reverts to the generative mode. The strategic attention moves to the question of how to change and improve the competence system. In this case strategic thinking focuses on the development of new "Capability Options".

FRAMING OF SCENARIOS

Under the heading of "Definition" earlier in this chapter we suggested that scenarios should be as value free as possible. However, strategists often develop a value judgement for individual scenarios in the set. This is mostly related to the degree of change that a scenario indicates as required. If little change is required the scenario is considered a "good future", in which growth is possible on the basis of exploitation of existing strengths. If the traditional business does not do so well, the particular scenario is seen as less friendly. Strong value judgements in this area find their origin in an aversion to change and the need to stay in control.

The meaning of any scenario depends upon the "frame" in which we perceive it. This is illustrated in a story told by Bandler and Grinder (1982). This old Chinese Taoist story is about a farmer in a poor country village. He was considered very well-to-do, because he owned a horse that he used for ploughing and for transportation. One day his horse ran away. All his neighbours exclaimed how terrible this was, but the farmer simply said "Maybe." A few days later the horse returned and brought two wild horses with it. The neighbours all rejoiced at his good fortune, but the farmer just said "Maybe." The next day the farmer's son tried to ride one of the wild horses; the horse threw him and broke his leg. The neighbours all offered their sympathy for his misfortune, but the farmer again said "Maybe." The next week conscription officers came to the village to take young men for the army. They rejected the farmer's son because of his broken leg. When the neighbours told him how lucky he was, the farmer replied "Maybe".

Changing the frame changes the perspective on the scenario, and the perception of good and bad. The frame most frequently used in organisational scenario planning is the existing business definition. However, this is always a limiting frame that is put over a multi-dimensional force field. The narrower the business definition the more likely it is that scenarios fall outside and are seen as uncomfortable. Companies who tend to define themselves in terms of a specific product often suffer from this. By reframing the judgement can be changed.

Take, for example, the meaning of a global warming scenario for an oil company:

- If the company is in the business of producing oil a global warming scenario is bad, as it will reduce the scope for this product.
- If the business is producing energy a global warming scenario is less worrying as it means new business opportunities outside oil.
- If the business is providing a service to host governments of oil-producing countries there is a thriving business in dealing with the consequences of global warming.

The good/bad scenario arises from a rigid and narrow self-definition that belongs more in the world of forecasts than scenarios. In scenarios you start from the outside. If that leads to scenarios in which oil is not the fuel of the future you will also address the question of what will take its place. Scenarios make you think about possible alternative businesses in which you could flourish. Scenarists who manifest strong value judgements are missing the point of multiple perspectives and outside-in thinking that underlies scenario-based planning.

In scenario-based planning life is not good or bad, only more of the same or different. This rather more positive mindset towards the future opens up the strategic conversation for other things that we could do. Widening your self-definition will provide space for strategic development and renewal. How can it be done?

Identifying the company with its product severely limits possibilities for upframing. The problem is that the product isn't really the success formula; it is the organisation's interface with the outside world. A rigid assumption limits severely the chunks of the outside world you are prepared to think about. It is essentially the forecasting mindset. In that respect replacing oil with energy does not make a fundamental difference, energy still is a product, albeit a wider category. On the other hand competence thinking opens up a much bigger part of the world for potentially interesting exploration. In such a frame the scenario mindset is about finding new combinations, entrepreneurship, adventure. There are no downside scenarios there.

Underlying these good/bad value judgements is inside-out thinking and resistance to change. Change tends to be seen as things being taken away, rather than being added. Once change is not judged negatively, but rather seen as the raw material of business success, then there are no good or bad futures. As we saw earlier, the world of business success is a relative world, in which competitors will copy every successful idea. It is a dynamic situation, a race, in which everyone who slows down will be overtaken. The winners are those who develop new business concepts,

---

Box 7   Self-definition in the public sector

A wider definition of the "organisational self" will make the scenarios appear more neutral. Companies find this easier to do than public sector organisations. These have normally been set up to perform a specific task, and changing "the product" is often not seen as an option. On the other hand the mission can normally be defined at various different levels of conceptualisation, and by moving to higher levels (upframing) flexibility of purpose can be regained. A Business Idea exercise is often highly enlightening in this regard, also in the public sector, as it refocuses on competencies in addition to the product.

---

new Business Ideas. Companies who see themselves in the business of change will not find any scenarios good or bad, but will judge them in terms of the degree of opportunity and challenge they offer.

In Part Three we will discuss how the scenario planner can help the company to avoid the good/bad syndrome in futures reconnaissance.

Chapter Eight

Scenarios and the Strategic Conversation

ORGANISATIONAL ASPECTS

Developing the Business Idea for the future is a prime managerial responsibility. This concerns gaining new and unique insights, entrepreneurial invention, wind-tunnelling and developing distinctiveness. But this is not the whole story. The loop is not complete without action. Apart from the entrepreneurial invention success also requires organisational action and feedback from the real world. Action requires coherence in the organisation. The Business Idea for the future needs to be shared in the organisation, by all partners with the power (formal or informal) to act (De Geus 1988). The thinking process must be institutional.

With this in mind scenario-based planning pursues a dual objective with a content and a process component. *The content issue is gaining the new unique insight that underpins every entrepreneurial invention; the process issue is creating coherence in the organisation through the strategic conversation, leading to action that transforms the invention into reality and feedback.* We will now turn to considering this process aspect.

How does scenario-based planning lead to strategic management in an organisational sense? This can be understood using the model of organisational learning discussed in Part One. As we saw organisations cope with uncertainty through learning. We have modelled this as an institutional learning loop, where the organisation takes action, experiences deviations from expectation, reflects on differences and synthesises these into a new shared theory of the world, which is subsequently used for renewed action.

How can scenario planners intervene in these processes, and how can they help the organisation as a whole become a more skilful learner? The most important aspects of this are twofold:

- Scenario-based planning affects and broadens perception, thereby providing the requisite variety in mental models necessary to see and perceive the outside world beyond the traditional business models.
- It provides a language through which the resulting issues can be discussed in the organisation, new theories of action can be jointly developed and shared, and alignment of mental models leads to institutional action.

We will discuss the principles involved under the following headings:

- Personal and institutional perception
- How scenarios institutionalise mental models
- Action.

INDIVIDUAL PERCEPTION

Human beings act in response to an internally constructed version of reality. This is not the same as reality itself. We will need to pay particular attention to the relationship between the two.

Relevance Filters

Consider how signals from the outside world are filtered in the cognitive system. The most obvious filters are the senses, which allow us to perceive only a small part of reality. In addition signals are cognitively filtered through limited attention span and sense of relevance. Only events that catch the attention and are considered relevant will enter awareness, and become the raw material from which mental models are constructed, on the basis of which action is decided.

Relevance filters have various dimensions. One is time: the threat of immediate impact holds our attention more strongly than if the threat is more long term. This is a problem that many managers struggle with, often expressed as "the urgent crowding out the important". Another relevance filter is proximity to system boundaries. We tend to be more interested in what is happening to those whose welfare is important for our welfare than in events far away that do not seem to touch us. In addition strength of signal will make a difference, weak signals are more easily overlooked.

In addition relevance filters are shaped by aspirations. As Bateson (1972) pointed out, a stronger sense of conscious purpose reduces an organism's reactiveness, because it reduces the area of relevance through which events are filtered. An organisation focused single-mindedly on a struggle for survival will pay less attention to the longer term and wider boundaries than an organisation that can afford to experiment. (For an overview of perception flaws see van der Heijden *et al.*, 2002, *The Sixth Sense.*)

But overriding all that is the importance of cognitive pattern. Most of what happens passes us by, as it does not relate to any structures we have available in our mind for sense-making. In addition there must be an upper limit to the amount of change that we can still make sense of. Vygotsky (see page 147) proposes that you can only understand something new based on a structure that is already available to you from the past, a process he calls scaffolding. We can only express the new in the language of the old. In the extreme if everything is new the resulting "noise" cannot be understood or interpreted. It means that your history determines what you can make sense of.

Consider the events of September 11th 2001 when the twin towers of the World Trade Center in New York were attacked and destroyed. As the Congressional 9/11 committee pointed out there were numerous warning signals that could have been interpreted as signposts of impending danger. However, each of these signals in isolation was too small to notice seriously. Only the huge New York event where everything came together focused attention on the underlying structural situation. Had the earlier signals been perceived as a pattern they might have been seen as significant, triggering action to prevent the attack. However, it is logically impossible to deduct valid patterns in developments that are unprecedented.

Memories of the Future

What individuals see in the outside world is determined by the schemas they can bring to bear. If you want to be more observant you have to expand these. The expression "one-track mind" encapsulates the idea that if someone can see only one future, thinking will focus on that, and perception will increasingly ignore outlying unrelated areas. You overcome a one-track mindset by rehearsing alternative pathways into the future, as a way to expanding the area of vision. By considering future implications of what is observed we create a contextual framework in our mind in which these observations can be organised. The device used is a storyline, in which events unfold over time through a progression of cause and effect. There is strong evidence that the human mind retains most of its concepts by relating these to other elements in temporally organised schemas (Ingvar 1985, Rumelhart 1980). These are stored in memory as, what Ingvar calls, "memories of the future".

Going through life, people spin stories about the future in their mind. For instance if a difficult interview is anticipated, thoughts continue to spring up in the mind: "If she says this I would react in this way". This mental preparation builds up a set of temporally organised concepts and schemas through which events are subsequently interpreted. This allows active perception of developments, which would otherwise pass by unnoticed. Even if the specific rehearsed scenario never plays out in reality, the mind has nevertheless built up a readily available set of schemas that allows recognition and judgement of what is going on, causing more skilful observation and interaction in real time. In this way we are all "natural scenario planners".

Stories are efficient vehicles for organising things in our mind, relating data across a wide range of subjects, disciplines, and compartments. Making sense involves relating events causally, with one thing leading to another. Once we have decided what led to the occurrence of an event it has become more plausible, and therefore manageable. The human mind naturally arranges past events in this way. Why have human beings evolved this fictive capacity? Why would telling and understanding stories help us to survive? Harris (2000) suggests that the answer involves language. Children begin to pretend at about the same time they begin to speak. Harris points out that in order to make use of linguistic information from others we need to take their narrative perspective, especially if the story they tell is far removed from our immediate experience. The causal framework this builds up provides natural "slots" for a multitude of events, which no longer require our attention in isolation.

Scenarios make sense of future events in the same way as historical accounts make sense of the past. Memories of (stories about) the future are in a way historical accounts seen from a future perspective. They explain how the world has ended up in a future end-state, by a causal train of events, linking back to the well-known present. While the present is always a blur history that comes out of it is well ordered. Scenario building is a natural activity for the human mind. By putting yourself in the future, the present blur clears up; storytelling creates historical order out of chaos.

Your history determines what you can make sense of. If this is true for individuals would it not also apply to groups and their critical mass of alignment underpinning their joint action?

ORGANISATIONS AS COGNITIVE SYSTEMS

Consider for a moment organisations as similar cognitive systems. One could argue they have ways of seeing and interpreting the world around them, and they have values that they pursue. The knowledge on which this is based is embedded in the people in the organisation, in its systems and in its artefacts. Institutions tend to select recruits in their own image. Once living together individual members affect each other's views through more or less intensive interaction. They come to interpret developments similarly. Through a process of selection and mutual influence the organisational culture is created.

Institutional Knowledge

Even in the most authoritarian environment very few corporate actions are the result of the thinking of one individual only. These views will have been influenced and formed by the interaction with others in the organisation. When we are looking at corporate behaviour we are not dealing with one individual, but with something that is bigger than the sum of the parts, the "corporate opinion". When the world changes, managers must share some common view of the new world if a suitable and effective response is to be created. Groups of people must verbalise the decision-making process in their strategic conversation.

Institutional knowledge, defined here as that pool of knowledge on the basis of which the organisation can act, is not simply the sum of the knowledge of its members. As we saw (page 42) coherence across the organisation is also crucial in the learning loop. It leads to the organisation's ability to act, and act efficiently. People must understand the meaning of what is happening to the total system to ensure their actions fit in. The whole process can be seen as a cognitive system that has ways of seeing, understanding and sharing ideas among its members.

Knowledge has to be verbalised and shared around if it is to be kept alive and relevant. This coherence process relies heavily on stories of two types, (1) ceremonial stories, about who "we" are, and (2) operational stories, about what created success. Many stories people tell each other in organisations have the character of myths; truth-value is only one factor in what makes particular stories popular. But the learning loop heavily depends on them. An example of the importance of this surfaced in a young company we recently worked with. The people in it declared themselves "mythically deprived". Because there was very little to modify (stories, rules etc.) they found they were repeating their mistakes.

It is interesting to note how many operational and ceremonial stories are about management flaws. This may be one of the reasons why networks are often thought to be inherently in opposition to, and destructive of, hierarchies. An important test of overall coherence is the degree to which organisational narratives are being formed by the

---

Box 8   Wider learning systems

A formal organisation is a special case of the more general category "human networks", groups of people who share the same stories. For example, people belong to professional networks, even if they work for competing organisations, because they have all been acculturated to the same stories by their professional training institutions. So someone who works in Silicon Valley has stories that cause him to share ideas even with competitors, because his myths tell him that it's more important to create an innovative product than to be loyal to the specific company he's with.

---

interaction between the explicit views of the management and the implicit, relational experiences of the staff. The rot sets in when management is telling itself stories about what the organisation does that no longer has any relationship to the staff's experience of what the organisation is.

Institutional Problems

Successful organisations in particular are prone to simplify the institutional mental model through the way they interpret the world; "it is difficult to argue with success" (Miller 1993). Managers have got where they are through their "good judgement" and they will not readily suspend that. When things remain stable it will serve them well. Meanwhile fringe stories impoverish and with them the range of vision of the organisation.

However, from time to time organisations experience turbulence in their environment. Explaining what is happening in alternative ways becomes increasingly difficult. There are many examples of failures to perceive a new reality by organisations. Even organisations that are intended to be the eyes and ears of the nation, such as the CIA, suffer from this. Consider Admiral Jeremiah's report on the CIA's failure to anticipate India's nuclear tests, as reported in the *New York Times*: Jeremiah, a former commander of all U.S. forces in the Pacific, described a kind of intellectual laziness at the intelligence services. "Senior U.S. policy-makers and intelligence officials had an 'underlying mind-set' that India would not test its nuclear weapons", he said. That fixed idea was unaffected by the fact that India's newly elected Hindu nationalist leaders openly and repeatedly vowed to deploy the bomb. The United States never understood that they were driven by " 'national pride and psyche' to go nuclear", Jeremiah said. As a result, he said, its $27 billion-a-year intelligence eyes and ears were blind and deaf to the test, which ignited nuclear tensions and an arms race between India and its regional rival, Pakistan. "You fall into a pattern; you start to expect things to happen", he said. "You need to have a contrarian view."

A more recent example is the CIA's conviction that Iraq was stockpiling weapons of mass destruction and their inability to seriously consider that these might have been removed following the Kuwait war. Also Saddam Hussein's reported inability to believe that the US leadership would actually decide to invade, and his unwillingness to consider the possibility that he might be wrong.

There are many examples in the private sector that illustrate limits in perception. Celebrated examples include IBM's inability to see the potential of the personal computer when they launched the IBM PC, Motorola's failure to see how the cellular handset business was shifting from analogue to digital technology, Microsoft's failure to see the potential of the internet in its early days, Shell's inability to anticipate the strength of feeling against the idea of using the ocean as a dumping ground for obsolete large structures, and so on.

There are many well-known examples of companies misjudging their environment against the view of some of its most senior members. Peter Schwartz, working at Shell at the time, understood in the early 1980s that the Soviet Union might collapse under the burden of the cold war and produced a scenario called "The Greening of Russia" to make that case. Although the scenario had been developed within their own organisation "Shell" as a whole didn't have this knowledge among its "theories-in-use", until the Berlin wall came down.

Above we saw how the refining industry and the oil shipping industry misjudged the 1973 oil crisis. On this occasion, as we saw, Shell acquired this knowledge in its theories-in-use before the event and gained significant competitive advantage from that. Another example is the problem experienced by the American automobile industry interpreting pressures from the public concerning the environment, "Detroit would play ball if there were really consistent signals" (see page 30). The trouble is that there never are consistent signals, until interpretation creates consistency as an essential part of organisational perception.

One of the most striking examples include the misjudgement by the established computer industry of the personal computer phenomenon in the early 1980s. Even in the late 1980s, after personal computers were in existence and had been growing exponentially for 10 years or more, IBM as a whole still was largely disconnecting from the fact that computing power was increasingly being distributed away from mainframes (Gerstner 2002). The company was used to developing scenarios but these were examples of what we have called the "probability approach to scenario planning" (see page 26), essentially a forecasting activity. The scenarios were summarised in a number of future demand lines, expressed in terms of worldwide computer capacity required. The question of the form in which demand would shape up was a secondary issue that did not play a role in the scenarios. It was a prime example of how forecasting focuses on specific preselected variables and closes the mind to wider exploration of the environment (see page 109). A lot of effort had gone into analysing possible future demand for computing power, but the resulting scenarios were created from the tacit assumption that computing capacity would continue to be needed in the traditional form. Some individuals saw the fact that new players were redefining the game but these could not make themselves heard against the conventional view. New developments in the market simply were not an issue at the organisational level.

How can institutions overcome these problems?

SCENARIOS AS INSTITUTIONAL PERCEPTION DEVICES

Institutional Perception

Individual people facing this array of failure would be advised by people such as Ingvar, Weick and Vygotsky to enrich their arsenal of readily available stories about the future. But what about organisations?

While perception is in the first place individual, groups of people share and internalise individual perceptions through interaction and discussion. In dealing with groups of people the question arises of how some commonality in individual schemas and language is developed in the group in order for them as a whole to become skilful observers of the business environment, and therefore skilful actors in it. It is not enough for one person to see "it", more likely than not (s)he will be overruled by the conventional wisdom, based on the established orthodoxy. The skill of observing the environment must become a group skill, such that the organisation is able to act on it. This requires that the knowledge be shared by a critical mass of people, who together are able to create action on the basis of their "consensus" view.

The experience of not being able to make one's view heard in an organisation is common to most of us at one time or another. When things have gone wrong it is almost always possible afterwards to find someone who saw weak negative signals at the time the decision was made but who could not make his/her view register. However, the unheard view has no value for the organisation, what counts in terms of institutional decision making is the institutional knowledge embedded in its consensus view. If the Detroit executive above (page 30) complained of inconsistent signals from the market, he in fact indicated that their shared mental model did not allow them to link these signals in a coherent account, which would have allowed them to act coherently on what was observed. As a consequence they did not act.

How can an organisation "complicate itself" (Weick 1979) so that they can develop a sufficiently varied account of the outside world that will make signals meaningful and that can be shared among the members?

Scenarios as Institutional Memories of the Future

If properly developed and institutionalised a set of scenarios can be the institutional "memories of the future" to help organisations perceive their environment. They are an efficient vehicle for making sense out of a large amount of data and information. Scenarios structure data about the future in multiple stories. The concept of using multiple storylines to encapsulate learning is powerful for the following reasons:

- It reflects the uncertainty inherent in the future.
- It allows coherence to be created across knowledge from many separate disciplines in new and unique multi-disciplinary theories about the world.
- It presents findings in a tangible real-world context, illustrating theory rather than espousing it.
- It uses a causal mode of thinking, which is intuitively comfortable.

The language of scenarios is about the future, but they should make a difference in what is happening now. If the scenarios are successful in embedding different models of the business environment in the consciousness of the organisation it will make the organisation more aware of environmental change. Through early conceptualisation and effective internal communication scenario-based planning can make the organisation a more skilful observer of its business environment. By seeing change earlier the organisation has the potential to become more responsive. Its decisions will also become more robust; there will be less "I should have known that". Generally the result should be an organisation more flexible and capable of adapting.

The following examples illustrate how the active availability of scenarios and scenario-based thinking in the organisation can lead to overcoming the perception problems mentioned.

Shell's Experience

The following example of how structuring of a messy situation leads to action should be considered against the industry background, discussed earlier (page 12). We saw how Shell became aware of the possibility of an oil crisis through the use of the scenario methodology. But the criterion for success of such scenario-based planning activity is not the insight alone but whether this was internalised sufficiently in the organisation through an appropriate scenario process, such that it led to action in response to the new perception. Shell's managers saw, very quickly, the results of two different responses to the scenario process.

. . . awareness . . .

One was due mainly to Jan Choufoer, the co-ordinator of Shell's manufacturing activity. With his research background, he was used to questioning practices that others took for granted. Even before becoming co-ordinator he had questioned one of the basic tenets of the oil business: that the purpose of the organisation is to meet all customer demand for oil and related products.

To understand what Choufoer was suggesting, it is important to realise that crude oil, as it is pumped out of the ground, is a mixture of many products, from light fuels (propane, butane) to medium (gasoline, kerosene, gas oil) to heavy (fuel oil, bitumen). The lighter products have more unique value; there is no easy substitute for gasoline in engines. But underboiler fuel oil can be substituted, e.g. by coal, nuclear or alternative forms of energy. Therefore fuel oil must be sold at a competitive price, while gasoline can command a premium. There is, however, a limit to this differential. Refiners can make light products out of heavy ones through secondary processes called "cracking". This is an expensive business, but if the differential is big enough there will be a payout for the investments. Normal practice was to configure the refineries to meet market demand. If this included a relatively high percentage of light products investments would be made in crackers to balance supply and demand. So in the US market, where demand for gasoline was always relatively strong, cracking was done a lot more than in Europe, which had a stronger fuel oil demand. Choufoer suggested that it might be more profitable to build additional cracking capacity also in Europe and elsewhere around the world, reduce fuel oil sales and make the same light product yield with less crude oil intake. This became known as the "upgrading policy". It implied advising the Shell marketers that they would not be supplied their full fuel oil requirement, handing potential customers over to the competition or alternative fuels, a shocking idea that struck at the very foundations of the supply function.

In the early 1970s, calculations of projected oil prices showed, not surprisingly, that building additional upgrading capacity, while offering some opportunities for payout, would be mostly a break-even proposition. Although some Shell managers were intrigued by the prospect of questioning old established practice, and engineers liked the idea of building more upgrading capacity to get the best out of the barrel, the institution as a whole rejected Choufoer's proposal. It was at variance with the established mindset of serving market demand and, anyway, no convincing economic case could be made. But then Pierre Wack came with scenarios showing the possibility of a crisis in crude oil supply, and a resulting explosion in oil prices. From our perspective today, it is difficult to understand the revolutionary nature of Wack's suggestion. The oil price had remained one of the most stable features of the global economic scene for as long as anybody could remember. An earlier Delphi forecasting exercise in Shell, involving the real experts, had come up with no price higher than $2 per barrel. People might be persuaded to consider that oil price might vary between $2 and $3 per barrel, but here was Wack suggesting a jump to $12!

Credibility was stretched to the limit, except with Choufoer, who suddenly saw support for his upgrading idea. When crude oil prices jump, there is an even greater jump in differential between the price of heavy components (which cannot rise too much, because they compete with coal or other alternatives) and that of light components, for which there is no easy substitute. Motor gasoline, in particular, would become disproportionately more expensive. The scenarios implied that upgrading the heavy end of the barrel into light products, hitherto a break-even proposition, would (in the event of a price jump) become extremely profitable. Considering that without a price jump it would anyway break even, implementing the upgrading policy seemed an attractive proposition. As Jan Choufoer moved to head manufacturing, he continued to promote this policy. As a result, when the oil price crisis did actually occur, Shell manufacturing was prepared to act.

. . . and lack of awareness . . .

By contrast, Shell veterans could look at the example of marine, the division responsible for transporting oil overseas. This organisation paid very little attention to an oil crisis scenario, it did not seem relevant to them. According to the conventional wisdom, a price jump would not really affect demand, not when people still needed energy and heat. People would pay the price, and marine would still have to move the oil.

Then came the actual crisis of 1973. However, the shipping industry (not only in Shell, but across the industry) did not consider this a reason to change their policies drastically. As we saw (page 14) investments in shipping capacity continued. When demand started to level off during 1974 and 1975 this was interpreted as a temporary aberration. Demand increased again in 1976, prompting marine to assume the crisis was over. When demand fell away again, the following year, that was interpreted as the consequence of the economic recession, another temporary blip that would work itself out. Only near 1978 or 1979 did it start to dawn on oil shippers that, possibly, demand might be elastic after all. By then, they had built up such a massive overcapacity in the world's fleet, that profitability was destroyed for many years.

Action Triggered by Institutional Perception

While in marine, people continuously looked for signs (and found them) of reversion to the old pre-crisis situation, people in manufacturing saw the trend break as a fundamental change, as explained in the well-rehearsed and shared crisis/upgrading scenario. They acted accordingly. While it took marine years to realise what had happened to them, manufacturing had a shared mental model of the changed situation to hand. Consequently they recognised the events as the crisis scenario starting to unfold. They were ready to move. Shell refineries adopted the upgrading policy with remarkable speed. In the industry, while primary refining capacity ran into a disastrous surplus situation (like the tanker capacity), upgrading capacity became extremely scarce. Shell's early implementation of the upgrading policy provided the Group with a major competitive advantage, which lasted well into the mid-1980s. This proved one of the major factors in Shell's climb up the rank order of major international oil companies, known as the seven sisters, from a position near the bottom to the top of the league.

Scenarios in a Scotch Whisky Company

We once helped the strategic conversation process in one of the larger Scottish whisky companies. We found that the structure of the whisky industry has something in common with the oil industry, with an upstream (distillers), a midstream (processing, bottling) and a downstream (distribution, retailing). The client was a management team in charge of a midstream manufacturing plant, equipped with sophisticated machinery to do processing, ageing, blending, bottling and warehousing. This was a unit in a larger company that covered both the upstream and the downstream. The management of this unit had a degree of independence and wanted to think about their strategy. It was a very conventional scenario project but the scenarios were of high quality, helped by remarkable people recruited from the outside (page 222).

The participating managers came to the conclusion that the way they were structured in the company would become highly problematic in some of the scenarios. Even though they could take certain actions in-house to ameliorate those situations, their life could become much more difficult due to the way the company was organised and responsibilities were shared. They came to the conclusion that a more robust strategy would be for them to become the supply division for the whole company, taking full responsibility for all operational activities, including purchasing and supplying, shipping in and out, delivery etc.

This was by no means a new issue in the company. They had tried to convince top management of this logic before, but so far unsuccessfully. Now, with the scenarios, they found they could better articulate these ideas, in a way they were not able before, being more explicit of why the change was needed. An important aspect of this was that they could now argue the case on the basis of potential outside forces, defusing the usual suspicion that they were engaged in an empire building exercise. So they prepared a new presentation as a result of which the strategy was approved. This resulted in significant expansion of the activity and a management team more in control of their destiny.

It is a nice example of how scenarios can improve the quality of a strategic conversation. The idea for this strategy existed before, but not enough consensus could be built to turn it into action. Proponents were accused of being involved in a battle for power, a typical internal battle for control that goes on in so many organisations. With the scenarios, the enemy was moved to the outside. It became a battle of everyone against one common external enemy, leading to a more rational and logical conversation, and significant results. Scenarios do not always have to produce new strategy, it may be enough to use them to articulate an existing idea so much more effectively that it can be turned into action, rather than remaining a subject of internal debate.

Experience of a Microchip Equipment Manufacturer

The following example illustrates how a company can overcome embedded perceptual limitations. This concerns a scenario exercise in a company making equipment used in microchips manufacturing. We spent a great deal of time analysing the main uncertainties. The state of the general economy in the world affects demand significantly. Some time into the project one senior manager suggested that he was worried about a possible recession. At this time, a recession was just starting, and the conventional wisdom was that it would be short, shallow, and not affect high technology too much. This manager said, "That seems our assumption, but what if it turns out not to be true? What if we're entering a deep, 1981-style recession? What would happen to microprocessors, and then to our machines?"

Discussion turned to how these assumptions were reflected in the plans in the first place – who decided what and how did this get worked into the cash projections. Initially no one in the management team could throw much light on this. The finance man looked at the sales man, they both looked at the marketing manager, no answer, they just did not know how it was done. The finance manager volunteered to find out.

The following week he reported back. "Well", he said, "the way we do this projection really makes good sense. As a small company, we cannot afford to invest a lot of money in environmental analysis, so we buy projections from DataQuest, the top-rated high-tech market and economic research company. We don't think we can ever hope to improve on their research capability." "What's their assumption about the recession?" asked the manager who had raised the question. It appeared that DataQuest were assuming a shallow, short recession.

Now the room erupted in discussion. The company apparently did not know much about what would be the consequences if it wouldn't be shallow and short. The scenario exercise had shown them the value of questioning all such "inevitabilities". The CEO suggested that the finance manager ask the planners to produce a new set of projections. But this time, they would substitute a deeper, longer recession for the DataQuest prediction.

At the next meeting, the finance manager came back with some slides of spreadsheet numbers. "We have never done this before", he said, "but we made a few assumptions, and here's what it looks like." The results were dramatic. In case of a deep recession, the company would be in serious trouble. They were about to commit themselves to major research investments, and they could easily fall into insolvency if they were to lose the cash influx they had assumed would come. The conclusion was inevitable, management was betting the company on DataQuest's prediction coming true. As a result, over the next few weeks, they drastically cut back their research investment commitments. Today they are not doing as well as they had hoped several years ago, but they have weathered the recession. They know that if they had committed those funds, they might now be out of business.

They were fortunate to make the jump from an individual mental model to an institutional one. It is not a leap that can be taken for granted. The planner in the finance department from his perspective did the sensible thing to rely on DataQuest's numbers. They were the best numbers available; it did not make sense to try to double-guess them. But nobody else in the organisation seemed to be aware of the underlying assumptions driving the cash projection. A question such as "I wonder about the recession" did not find an institutional response, nobody would know what to do with such a remark, and there was no channel to deal with it.

All organisations have compartmentalisation problems. It is a fundamental part of the efficiency/adaptation dilemma. And a minor lapse in communication can cause a major dislocation. Compartmentalisation means that people down the line may make quite sensible individual decisions, which in aggregate can drive the company as a whole into serious problems. The strategic learning process needs to hit at the appropriate points in the organisational system where an impact can be created. This "node of effective intervention" may well be outside the management team, somewhere deep in the organisation. Finding these points requires processes that are part of the corporate culture, penetrating throughout the organisation.

EFFECTIVE SCENARIOS

What sorts of stories are effective in an organisational setting to achieve this perceptual goal? Like any other storyteller the scenario planner needs to balance carefully the known and the novel:

- Effective scenarios should have enough hooks into the current organisational mental models to make them plausible to a "critical mass" in the organisation.
- But they should also contain an element of novelty and surprise in directions where the vision of the organisation needs to be stretched.

Hooks Into Mental Models

Experience has shown that scenarios that do not link in to current and ongoing concerns and anxieties in the minds of the decision makers are ineffective. They will be interpreted as irrelevant to the operational reality and be rejected. A scenario writer may find a story interesting, but a decision maker who has no mental connection to it will experience it as either boring or "science fiction" and it will end up on the bookshelf without creating much effect. If on the other hand the scenario planner sets out to write a story that addresses the immediate concerns of the management, their worries, the thoughts that keep them awake, then the product will be experienced as interesting and important. Experience shows that top management will listen very carefully to a scenario planner who produces a significant scenario exercise giving a new perspective on events or trends with which they are grappling. Over time it has become very clear that if the scenario planner sets his own agenda and does not relate to the concerns of the client hardly any attention will be paid to the result. The biggest mistake that scenario planners can make is to fail to take enough account of the needs of their clients. The number one rule of scenario-based planning is "know your client". For this reason *scenario-based planning is a customised activity*, generic scenarios have little relevance for organisational behaviour.

Another essential condition for success is plausibility of the scenarios. Only plausible scenarios can be a platform from which to develop the organisation's knowledge and understanding of the situation they may be facing. On the other hand, just feeding back to the managers the views they already share is not a useful thing to do, a new perspective needs to be added. The aim is to create a context within which the issue is seen afresh by the organisation. It requires new knowledge and insights that often only an outside source can provide.

The scenarios that would have allowed correct interpretation of the 9/11 early signals would have had to include elements such as suicidal militancy, passengers being able to fly commercial aircraft and tower blocks crumbling as the result of a kerosene fire. Pre 9/11 a scenario planner might have had some difficulty convincing his audience of the credibility of such stories. Even if he had been right about all this he would still have been ineffective, as people would have considered the story as incredible. Creating such a new perspective is especially difficult for people who have been grappling with an issue, possibly for a long time. The criterion for success is not whether the scenarios are right or wrong, but whether they lead to better decisions.

It is easy to lose the link with the consensus view, which can only result in the message not being heard. The project has to start from where the people in the organisation are now, but they need to move on from there. Scenarios become a bridge between the existing understanding and new alternative views or frameworks that can be used to interpret what is happening in the outside world (Figure 19). That

Scenarios need to connect:

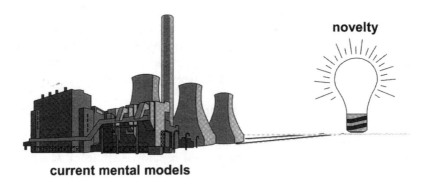

novelty

current mental models

Figure 19. *Scenarios provide a new perspective*

basically constitutes the most significant challenge of any scenario exercise.

Producing an effective set of scenarios is often considered an art form. A writer who wants to get through to his audience starts from where they are now and then adds something new. The crux of the matter is finding the right balance between the known and the new. Erring on the side of the known doesn't make an impact through lack of interest. Erring on the side of the new makes the project lacking in meaning. Somewhere between the two the right answer has to be found.

The process is described by Vygotsky (1986). In his language, the scenarios "scaffold" the thought processes of the client. The scaffolds need to be erected around the existing knowledge structure to allow the client to relate new experiences to existing knowledge. Vygotsky refers to the "zone of proximal development", which is the place where the client's newly acquired but as yet disorganised concepts "meet" the logic of experienced reasoning. The learning capacity of the client is limited to this zone of proximal development. It is what Kauffman (1995) calls the adjacent space.

Introducing Novelty

The "scaffolding" idea illustrates how scenarios need to move the thinking on. They need to throw a novel light on the existing thinking about the future of the business. Where do we find this novel insight? As we saw above, organisational knowledge is less than the totality of the knowledge embedded in its members. Therefore resources are available in house in the range of insights among the individual members of the organisation. The alternative views required are often available from individuals who, without scenario-based planning, find it difficult to make their views legitimate. This resource must be tapped in the first place. This requires a process through which people can make themselves heard. The process must trigger participants to:

- Develop their knowledge through communication with the outside world,
- Articulate their knowledge, and
- Contribute this to the common pool of knowledge from which the shared view emerges.

Through conversation the process must enable structuring of elements of thought or observation, and of resulting perceptions of opportunities and threats. The process must be capable of taking in a wide range of initially unstructured thoughts and views, and create out of this a number of coherent, internally consistent interpretations of the world in which the majority of the individual insights can find a logical place.

However, in most cases, external views must be brought in to enrich the new perspective. One of the most important objectives of scenario-based planning is to make the organisation a better observer of the environment. Its mental model needs to be stretched. This can often only be done from the outside. Therefore scenario planners need to go further than just tapping internal views; they need to incorporate a wide range of outside opinions in the scenarios. A set of scenario stories is an effective means of capturing and organising a wide range of external ideas and making them stick. With this preparation the quality of the scenario process may be significantly enhanced.

Linking the Old with the New

Consequently the scenario analysis needs to adhere to the following principles:

- Start from the platform of the existing "consensus view" in the organisation.
- Recognise the uncertainty and complexity in the business situation.
- Stretch by the introduction of new knowledge from inside and outside the organisation.

● Provide a common structure to seemingly unrelated environmental insights.

In this way scenario-based planning adds new "memories of the future", enlarging the area of vision in which the organisation will recognise weak signals of change. Less will pass the organisation by. It has become a more skilful observer, more flexible and more capable of adapting.

Institutionalisation

Only scenarios that make a difference are worthwhile doing. In the institutional context, scenario-based planning is not only about developing the unique insight and most effective set of futures, it is also about transferring these effectively into the organisation, such that actions are affected through the new insights gained.

Above we defined institutional knowledge as that pool of knowledge on the basis of which the organisation can act. The scenario-based planning project needs to engage the organisation in a process through which the scenarios become the scaffolding of new institutional knowledge. They should be discussed enough to become "memories of the future" for a sufficient number of people so that they lead to common perceptions. The test of this is whether the scenarios become part of the institutional language. If people start using the names of the scenarios as a short-cut to conveying to each other the underlying world picture it is likely that institutionalisation has been achieved.

The institutional context is important in deciding the ultimate quality and value of a scenario project: the test of whether the team has found a good structure for the scenario set and storylines is the degree to which these prove helpful to the people with the power to act in conceptualising a previously unstructured area of concern, leading to new action that ultimately proves beneficial.

The crucial element in this is bringing people together, creating coherence in thinking and accommodation in action. One of the most powerful aspects of the scenario approach is the fact that it works from the outside in. As a consequence it projects the "enemy" outside, moving the conversation from the advocative debate to a substantive sharing of views. Action in organisations has to come from accommodation of different views. Even after the most effective strategic conversation there will be remaining differences in worldview. The important contribution of scenarios is that it recognises the legitimacy of multiple views, in the face of irreducible uncertainty. It moves the moment of accommodation from the point where we interpret the world to the point of action. It is a lot easier to find accommodation at the level of specific actions to be taken than at the level of perspective, worldview and the meaning of it all. We do not need to agree about how things work to nevertheless be able to come to joint negotiated action.

Use of scenarios for this purpose requires the discussion of strategic implications. This discussion starts within the scenario team and the commissioning client team, but needs to be spread around to become part of the general strategic conversation, as part of the process of institutionalisation. Scenario planners need to study carefully how strategic decisions are made, and infiltrate the high leverage points in that process. Not only do formal decision processes need to be considered, the informal conversations are often at least as, if not more, important.

BECOMING AWARE OF EARLY SIGNALS

The learning loop model shows us how scenario-based planning is intrinsically interwoven with action. Only through action does the organisation have joint experiences, which will enable it to develop its mental model of the environment, and in this way become a more skilful actor, and only through more skilful action can the organisation benefit from its investment in scenario-based planning.

For this reason the scenario planner has to focus his thinking on the people with the power to act. They are the ultimate clients of the exercise, and they need to set the agenda. More is required than just an intellectual thinking process. People need to get involved throughout the organisation, and mental models need to be aligned. What is needed is not just another technique, but a complete approach to strategising and strategic management that scenario-based planning offers.

Once scenarios have become part of the institutional mental model they powerfully affect what is seen in the business environment. Scenario planners often comment after a scenario project on how they find themselves noticing and reading articles in newspapers that before the project they were not even aware of. The same applies to the organisation. The scenarios have increased the variety of views on the external world available to the organisation. As perception is determined by the available mental model enriching it means seeing more, broadening the range of view.

This feature of scenario-based planning can be used to advantage through the institutionalisation of the concept of "early warning". If the scenarios have been done properly the team should have articulated a clear model of underlying structure to which the events in the scenarios are related. The same structure can be used to identify developments in the environment, which could be the early signals of the world moving into one of the various directions indicated by the scenarios. After the scenario project the team is able to identify such patterns of key variables and make these the subject of conscious periodic monitoring. The most effective early warning system monitors variables that are central in the underlying structure. By identifying such variables the institutional attention can be directed to where manifestations of structural differences become evident first.

Part Three

The Practice of Scenario-based Planning

OVERVIEW

In Part Two we have presented scenario-based planning as a comprehensive approach to institutional strategic management, based on an integrated philosophy of organisational learning. This has allowed us to integrate the three traditional paradigms of strategic management into one holistic approach to strategising. We have seen how scenario-based planning is the natural implementation of organisational learning, and we have discussed the benefits. We saw how it is used for generative strategising (exploring the environment, leading to new and unique strategic insights) and adaptive strategising (evaluating and adapting the organisational Business Idea), and how this leads to strategic conclusions on the need for change.

Having discussed the principles of scenario-based planning, and how it relates to making organisations more resilient, adaptable and generative, we now turn to translating theory into practice. In Part Three we discuss how a management team can go about introducing scenario-based planning into its institutional strategic thinking.

Some organisations may be able to make larger steps than others, but all start with an existing understanding of their business. The scenario process starts with articulating the organisation's understanding of its business in the form of a Business Idea. Within this context the scenarist then helps the organisation recognise, articulate and understand the relevant driving forces and their inter-relationships in its business environment. This information is a launching platform from which multiple scenarios of the future business environment are developed. Scenario building iterates with in-depth research and analysis of the structural underpinnings of the systems driving the business situation, increasing understanding step by step. Given time to mature the new perspective developing on the business situation leads to new and unique insights on the evolving basis of success.

This part of the book takes as a model a management team wishing to broaden its views and to think more strategically about the future of the organisation. Various exercises and workshops are discussed which will help the team get under way.

Scenario-based planning embeds strategising in organisational processes; it prepares people for action through the strategic conversation. Its effects spread across a wide area of organisational processes, including:

1. In the organisation:

    - Creating new concepts and language in the organisation.
    - Enhancing the quality of the strategic conversation.
    - Managing the focus of attention of the organisation.
    - Making the organisation more perceptive of its environment and therefore more adaptive.
    - Motivating action and change.
    - Making people think.

2. In decision-making:

    - Considering the strength of the organisation and its characteristics in its Business Idea.
    - Developing new and original perspectives on the business situation.
    - Developing unique strategic inventions.
    - Developing adaptive and generative capability.
    - Making a judgement on a strategic proposal.
    - Making strategic decisions.

Chapter Nine

The Practitioner's Art

Scenario-based planning is a practitioner's art. Its origins are in the real world of management, it is therefore more a craft than a science. Over the years a number of general principles have emerged but most of the rules of implementation evolve from day-to-day practice. It has in common with any other craft that there is not just one way of practising it. Students of scenario-based planning initially learn their craft from other practitioners. Practitioners then have to learn from their own mistakes. This means that while new practitioners need enough input from their predecessors to make a start, each must still develop his/her own unique way of producing results.

Scenario-based planning always ultimately aims for the invention of strategy. This includes testing of relevant organisational characteristics against multiple representations of the future business environment and making original inventions on the basis of what is found. Even if scenario development is undertaken as an exercise in trying to understand ambiguous developments in the outside world there will always be a point where we will want to consider the repercussions for our thinking on organisational strategy. Scenarios are always a testbed for something. It is important to keep this in mind, because it means that scenarios must always be focused on a strategically relevant area if they are to be productive. Therefore logically we can distinguish a number of basic components in any scenario project:

- There will be a need to articulate and characterise the strategic situation, where the project needs to provide new illumination.
- A set of scenarios will describe the multiple possible futures of the external business environment around this.
- Scenarios become productive in their juxtaposition with our understanding of the organisational "self", through which a new perspective on the business needs emerges.

- Scenarios are the testbed through which an area of policy is considered and judged.

Scenario-based planning can be used in a focused way, as a testbed for specific strategies, plans or projects. Setting the agenda in focused scenario projects is relatively straightforward. However, in most scenario projects there is not a specific strategic issue on the agenda. Most scenario exercises are inspired by a general desire to do a more skilful job of monitoring and understanding what is happening out there in the business environment and finding an appropriate response. They originate in the management's wish to improve the institutional learning skills. Most scenarios are introduced as an organisational discussion device, to enhance thinking and perception of the changing environment, without any preconceived idea of any specific policy issues that may be affected. This is the most challenging part of strategy development, addressing the question whether the organisation as a whole is capable of seeing and perceiving in time any crucial trend-breaking developments in the business environment, outside the blinkers that every organisation develops over time. Managers generally feel quite capable of dealing with the strategic issues as they arise and mostly do not feel the need for another analytical approach to help them in that area. On the other hand many managers feel they could do with more help in becoming a little better at observing the environment, understanding what goes on out there and in that way anticipating better. In those applications of scenario-based planning the intention is to let the policy repercussions of the exercise emerge naturally from the new insights developed. However, even in this case the scenario process in principle brings together a view of the environment and a view of the characteristics of the organisation, and tries to come to a considered view of what needs to be done internally in the light of the possible developments facing the organisation.

We will argue that it is useful to try to articulate the purpose of the exercise early on. It is of course possible to leave this embedded in the intuitive organisational knowledge, letting conclusions on organisational repercussions emerge naturally as a result of the thinking process and conversation. This is a legitimate approach, preferred by many experienced scenario planners and managers. It requires that all involved are insiders with excellent knowledge of the organisation and its situation, and have tolerance for ambiguity and unpredictable outcomes. However, in many cases where experience with scenario-based planning is limited it will be preferable to be as precise as possible about purpose up front, such that the most appropriate methodology can be selected for the job. There is a potential danger lurking here that needs to be recognised. A crucial aspect of the exercise will always be to surface possible trend-breaking developments in the business environment. One has to face up to the question whether the organisation itself has the requisite variety in its mental model to pick up the weak signals that may indicate a possible major trend break in the future. As we saw in Part Two, what we see is determined to a large extent by what is already in our mental model, and this filtering is even stronger for the organisational conversation than for individuals. In particular the well-run successful organisation almost inevitably suffers from institutional myopia. There is only one way of overcoming a narrow myopic organisational mental model and to create more differentiation, and this is by bringing in fresh outside understanding. Most successful scenario projects involve both internal and external people who together interact on the issues involved.

A device is needed in the process to articulate the organisational characteristics that matter, serving as an agenda for the strategic conversation that the organisation needs to have with new outside conversation partners. This device should not be an already conceived strategy, as this would introduce "old world" blinkers in the strategic conversation. In Part Two we have introduced the concept of the Business Idea to play this agenda-setting role. In the most general scenario-based planning project the scenarios describe the external business environment in which the Business Idea of the organisation will have to live, survive and develop.

The world is very large, and much of it is of secondary importance to the organisation and its strategy. To provide focus scenario planners ideally articulate a Business Idea as part of the scenario project, even if in some cases a more intuitive approach is considered feasible. In any case the essence of the scenario project is the interplay between the two sides of the strategic-fit analysis, the self and the environment. Therefore scenarios need to be:

- Idea generators, relating to future business success, and
- A suitable testbed for the strategic characteristics of the organisation.

The conditions in the wind-tunnel must fit the model to be tested. Therefore, even in the intuitive approach towards scenario-based planning, there needs to be some prior understanding of the sort of issues to be considered before the scenarios can be conceptualised.

We are in a dilemma here. On the one hand we wish to concentrate on issues that are relevant and important for the client. On the other hand too much prespecification of the issues facing the organisation creates the danger of focusing down to the known and traditional, thereby missing important new/weak signals. If the intuitive approach is preferred, and the Business Idea is not articulated in advance, a scenario agenda needs to be drawn up early on. This should be general enough to include study of adjacent territory, which could be of unanticipated importance to the organisation.

PURPOSE

As we suggested in the introduction, the first task of the scenario planner is to pin down the purpose of the scenario project. There are many ways of developing and using scenarios, some of which will be developed later in this book. An informed choice between these can only be made by reference to the purpose of the exercise.

In mapping out the various categories of purpose, it is useful to distinguish first of all four areas of scenario practice which have over time developed their own approaches to scenario planning, namely:

• Crisis management, aiming at improved design of systems and behavioural training.
• The scientific community, aiming at better communication of scientific theories and models.
• Public policymakers, aiming at increased accommodation among stakeholders in a policy decision.
• Organisations, aiming for survival and self-development.

Examples of use of scenarios in the crisis management sphere include pilot training in flight simulators, civil defence exercises and war-games. The common factor here is the design and testing of the suitability of systems, consisting of people interacting with equipment, to deal with unspecified future crises. In order to ensure that equipment is fit for the job and individuals know what to do simulations of possible crises are carried out in which the performance of the system is tested and people are trained to act skilfully. Each simulation is based on a scenario specifying crucial external events when the system needs to perform. As it is impossible to predict all possible events the art of scenario selection is to maximise preparedness. This type of highly specialised scenario design will not be further developed here.

Typical examples of the use of scenarios by scientists are scenarios for the development of climate change, based on environmental computer models, and scenarios for economic development and growth, based on econometric models. The common factor is the increasing degree of complexity of scientific theory and models that makes it difficult to communicate other than in an "if-then" mode. These models can be used as forecasting devices. However, it is difficult to impress on the audience the limits imposed by the underlying assumptions that underpin any forecast. The overwhelming impression is that "forecasts are mostly wrong", affecting the credibility of the underlying scientific work. As a result scientists find it convenient to report on their work in the form of scenarios, illustrating more clearly the limits of the underlying scientific theories. In addition scenarios trigger reactions, especially from people who have their own view on the projections shown. Creating this feedback often is the main purpose of producing the scenarios, as a knowledge elicitation device. The use of scenarios in this domain will not be developed further here.

Scenarios have now become very popular in the public policy development area. The projects seem to take two forms:

- To tackle a particularly intractable problem, where any progress seems to require a degree of multi-disciplinary joined-up analysis by multiple agencies that is so difficult to bring about in ordinary day-to-day business.
- To involve stakeholders in policy decisions and create an accommodation platform that will assist policy implementation. These broad societal discussions are often massive intervention projects involving a large number of people.

The nature of the scenarios is often less important than the analysis and conversation among the stakeholders, to ensure that issues come to the surface and participants develop understanding of alternative perspectives.

There are no objective criteria for what is good policy outside the common will of the stakeholders. Promoting democracy is often part of the goal of scenario work for policymaking in the public sector. Two crucial elements of this are the development of sound and shared policy, and the development of platforms for these policies to be carried out. In most projects a first step is making sense of developments in a specific policy environment and obtaining feedback from stakeholders. While we will not discuss the large-scale public sector intervention processes the comments made here in relation to sense-making and the strategic conversation are all directly relevant.

Organisational Purpose

This book deals with scenario-based planning in the organisational world. This does not in itself pin down the purpose of the exercise.

To illustrate the point here is a typical story about engaging with scenario-based planning. Initially the strategy manager engages with scenario-based planning because it seems "the thing to do". They launch a scenario project, often assisted by external consultants, without having a clear picture of where they want to end up. The logical place to start seems to be to build a number of scenarios. Building a set of scenarios tends to be an interesting fun sort of thing to do for the people directly involved. The scenario builders emerge from the activity with the feeling that they understand things a little better. They have had new insights. The exercise is declared a success. The problem then is to transfer some of this learning to the rest of the organisation. A set of scenarios is produced, written up and published in a good-looking booklet. The scenarios are also verbally presented. Surprisingly the audience is less than excited. They listen politely to what is being said and find it all rather boring. The "eureka" experience that the scenario team had is not repeated. The audience finds some scenarios rather unsurprising, some others way out in the realm of science fiction. In general they cannot link the scenarios with what they are doing in their job and find the whole thing lacking in relevance. If one returns six months later the scenarios are forgotten. The scenario booklet has been put on the bookshelf, often unopened, and people are getting on with something else. The planners who originally promoted the project now tell you that they have tried scenario-based planning but are now using other tools.

The problem is that the activity often is not sufficiently purposeful. Scenario-based planning does not arrive with a purpose attached. So here is the first, and probably most important, question to address by the scenario planner: why do we want to do this in the first place? Reasons commonly specified include: changing the mental map of senior executives, overcoming groupthink, fostering "out of the box" thinking, helping planners expand the horizon of their thinking, anticipating unconventional risks and changes in rules of the game, helping to align views and create a common language among a team, discussing unconventional ideas in a safe setting, giving new impetus to an ongoing strategic conversation, involving both line and staff in the planning process, wind-tunnelling strategic options, triggering invention of new strategic options, networking with new "sparring partners" and many others.

A number of projects we have been involved in recently were undertaken with the purpose to launch government agencies in e-government, to help companies to reconnect with the needs and values of their fast changing customers, to figure out the meaning of the anti-global movement for large multi-nationals, to think in a government organisation about the possibility and meaning of privatisation. The common factor in all cases seemed to be the intention to help people overcome a feeling of paralysis in a puzzling world.

All this seems a bewildering array of reasons why to "do scenarios". How to bring some order in this? At this point we need to remember that the first reason why we need to be clear about purpose is in order to be able to select the most appropriate methodology.

The first methodological issue on the agenda is whether the scenario activity is a one-time project or is part of an ongoing scenario-based planning process in the organisation. A one-time project tackles a particular issue, installing an ongoing process is designed to build a general-purpose capability or competence in the organisation. It would not be wise to launch into scenario-based planning without clarity on what we are aiming for in this regard.

The second design parameter divides the aim of scenario work in "opening up" projects versus projects aiming for closure. In other words, is the primary value of the exercise seen in raising questions, or in answering them and helping decision making.

Let's look at the four possible combinations this produces.

- A one-time exploratory question-raising scenario project. This would be indicated for an organisation that has entered choppy waters, and finds it difficult to articulate what the business environment requires. Let's call this the *sense-making* purpose.
- A one-time decision-making scenario project. This is indicated for an organisation that is facing a major decision of a strategic nature, where uncertainty muddles the decision-making process. Let's call this the *strategising* purpose.
- An ongoing exploratory scenario activity. This is indicated for an organisation that has been caught out too often misjudging what is going to happen in its environment, and needs to sharpen up. The primary job here is to find the important questions we need to consider in an ongoing strategic conversation with the market. Let's call this the *anticipation building* purpose.
- An ongoing decision-making activity. This is indicated for the organisation living in a fast-moving environment, or where strategy comes in the form of relatively big chunks of resource commitment. The task here is to see and understand and, on the basis of that, get the organisation to move and gain the high ground. Let's call this contributing to *organisational learning*.

These four purposes represent four levels of contribution to strategic success. The overarching broad organisational skill called here "organisational learning" gets closest to the ultimate aim of ongoing strategic success. But organisational learning cannot work without anticipation and decision-making skills. And nothing much happens at all if we are unable to make sense of the world around us. What we see here is a hierarchy of aims, serving each other and serving the ultimate goal of "strategic success" at different levels. Going through the list of reasons people give for wanting to engage in scenario-based planning it seems that few aim directly for the ultimate purpose of "ongoing strategic success". Most projects are undertaken to serve a more specific subgoal that will make a contribution towards the overall aim of organisational success in an area that is being felt as particularly weak.

This more limited purpose can be to enhance an element of the thinking process:

- sense-making,
- exploration,
- strategy testing,
- anticipation and reading weak signals,
- generating a unique insight,

or they can be processual:

- knowledge elicitation,
- delivering a message,
- accommodation building,
- consensus building,
- team building,
- morale building,
- strategic conversation enabler.

This seems an entirely sensible and legitimate way of going about it. But in this step-by-step approach towards organisational success the scenario planner needs to understand clearly what the subgoal is. Otherwise the wrong tools are selected from the "scenario tool box", the project will steer in the wrong direction, and client expectations will be disappointed at this early stage, without scenario-based planning having been able to demonstrate its value at the overall strategic level.

This is the main reason why scenario projects fail. Clear upfront purpose definition with the client is a critical success factor in the early stages of the application of scenario-based planning in an organisation. If scenario planners then keep their eyes on the higher level goal of making the client organisation more successful, while pursuing the lower-level defined goals as a means to that end, they will have created the necessary conditions for success.

Roles and Activities

We will discuss the various issues involved from the perspectives of two main actors in the project, the scenario planner and the client. The scenario planner is the person (or the group of people) involved in promoting and facilitating the learning process. This could be anyone in the organisation, a dedicated staff person, a member of the management team or the CEO him/herself. Or it could be an outside consultant brought in for the occasion. We will call this person the facilitator. When we consider the issues from the perspective of the facilitator we primarily consider the process issues involved.

The Client

The other main actor we call the client. This is the individual or group of people struggling with the situation and who will benefit from the thinking as it develops. Typically it could be a management team who are interested in understanding better the developments in the outside world, with the aim of reviewing the general strategic thrust of the organisation. Or it could be a team trying to develop a specific project of strategic importance. Another possibility might be a management team drawing up a strategic plan for discussion with other stakeholders, such as shareholders and finance providers. It is useful for our further discussion to separate the roles of conducting and facilitating the organisational process, and determining the content agenda of the thinking process.

While the facilitator has a major impact on success or failure of the project it is the client who will ultimately decide on whether the project was successful. It is important for the facilitator to understand the mindset of the client. Clients bring their own mental models to the project. It is useful for the project facilitator to understand where his/her client comes from. Some questions worth considering:

- Are they analytically and quantitatively oriented? Do they come from an engineering culture? Or are they intuitive and qualitative, with a background possibly in history, philosophy or psychology?
- Are they optimists or anxiety ridden?

- Are they linear or systems thinkers? Do they think in terms of events following each other in a sequence, or do they look for causal interlinkages?
- Do they have a political position and/or prejudice?
- Are they elitist or populist?
- Are they prone to conspiracy theories, or can they accept the logic of accidents in the past?
- Are they mesmerised by own ambitions and prejudices or will they be capable of learning new things?
- Are they subject to a herd instinct?

It will also be useful for the facilitator to carry out a situation analysis in advance by mapping out the action space of the client. Mapping this space involves surfacing the clients' action perspective, based on desirabilities, plausibilities and uncertainties. For example, the situation analysis will include establishing the regulatory framework within which the project will be carried out. The action space of the client may be constrained by mandatory rules and regulations that need to be adhered to. But it may also be limited by assumptions of freedom or willingness to act by the clients themselves. At this stage the issue of feasible scale needs to be addressed. Having clarity on these points from the beginning will ensure that the results of the project will speak to the client's perceived ability to take action. Conclusions that fall outside this space will be experienced as irrelevant, leading to disappointment. Success or failure will stand or fall with aiming the outcome of the project within this action space from the beginning.

The Contract

The next step will be for the client and the facilitator to come together to negotiate a contract that defines the framing of the project within these boundaries. Aspects that may later lead to differences between the parties should be agreed in advance as much as possible. These include:

- Limitations to exercise of power by each party
- Willingness to be open to new and unexpected information
- Degree to which there is tolerance for unexpected outcomes
- Nature of participation, self-selection or membership, voluntary or mandatory.

Having established the framing of the project the next step is to negotiate its objectives. The previous paragraph discussed categories of purpose that may be of use at this stage. Facilitators must insist on the maximum of clarity. In this type of work the payoff from the project cannot be forced. A real strategic insight and/or strategic renewal will not be generated from a two-day workshop and will require more effort. But few clients are comfortable with an open-ended approach. On the other hand smaller and closely defined projects are not necessarily wasted. But they have a more limited outcome. The important point is that expectations must be realistic if we want to avoid an unhappy client and another attempt at scenario-based planning unnecessarily scuttled at an early stage. It is important that the client thinks realistically on what is possible.

A useful tool for these initial project definition discussions between facilitators and clients is a VOCATE analysis, developed in Soft Systems Methodology, or SSM (Checkland 1981). SSM in general aims to understand purposeful human activity systems. It offers tools and techniques that can assist the facilitator to articulate the needs of the client and on the basis of that design a purposeful scenario project. VOCATE is a mnemonic that identifies the six key categories that have to be described and agreed between client and facilitator, namely Values, Owners, Clients, Actors, Transformation aimed for, and Environment taken as given.

The categories aim to answer a series of questions, preferably in the following order:

T: What transformation will the project achieve, i.e. what is the description of the pre-project relevant situation and what are we aiming for post-project?

C: Who are the people at the receiving end of this activity, and how will they be affected? How will they be reached?

O: Who are the owners of the project, who is the client and who decides afterwards whether the project is a success or a failure?

V: Why do the owners consider the specified transformation a good idea, what value system drives them to want to achieve this?

A: Who are the actors who will bring the transformation about? Who are the facilitators and the other participants?

E. What are the limits of this activity? What will be taken as given?

The VOCATE approach helps the client and the facilitator to arrive at a clear understanding of what is to be achieved, the context of this goal and the role in this of both parties. Having this clearly defined will help the facilitator later in providing legitimacy for actions deemed necessary.

Finally, the most important question to resolve is whether the client aims for an adaptive or a generative scenario project. Can we assume at this stage that a sequential approach towards scenario building, followed by testing and adaptation of the current Business Idea, looks adequate, or is the organisation searching for a new entrepreneurial invention to reposition its business, requiring an iterative approach until a new and unique insight starts to emerge. If things are going well for the organisation an adaptive project may be all that is needed. But projects aiming at making sense of a puzzling situation, including "intractable" problems and fundamental repositioning issues, require a generative approach. The facilitator needs to remind the client that the generative approach is a lot more demanding and less predictable in terms of resources and time required, and this should be factored in when the contract is made.

Direction Setting

The facilitator and the client now need to work together to get the show on the road by setting the scenario agenda. This can be done on the basis of the intuitive knowledge of the client, brought to the surface by the facilitator through the application of elicitation techniques. This approach may well be adequate for groups with considerable experience with scenario-based planning. The Business Idea provides the facilitator with a tool to structure the data collected in the elicitation process, in interaction with the client. In this way a joint conversational device can be created which will help to organise the relevant scenarios, suitable for the discussion of strategic implications for the organisation.

We will first discuss practical ways of eliciting strategic insights and intuitions from the client. We will then move on to the use of the Business Idea concept for structuring understanding of the fundamental success drivers of the organisation. We will see how this can be generated by a management team in a programmed way, and used as a focusing device in their strategic discussion. We will then move on to the scenario activity itself. We will consider the issues involved and practical ways of moving forward on each of these. We will then discuss the use of the scenario process to gain new and unique insights in the business situation (generative scenario-based planning). To conclude we will discuss how the scenarios can be used in conjunction with the Business Idea to come to useful strategic conclusions, and we will consider how these can be expressed in terms of strategic options open to the organisation (adaptive scenario-based planning).

In Part Four we will discuss how all this can be incorporated in an institutional process that involves all those with the power-to-act to make the scenario process part of the institutional learning experience of the organisation as a whole, and link it to action.

SETTING THE AGENDA

The business environment is very large. How to select where to look? This is the first crucial decision to be addressed in the scenario project. The most important stipulation here is the imperative that the work remains relevant to the client. Under no condition must the facilitator "lose" the client on the way. This means that a very clear picture must be obtained of what is strategically important to the client, as the starting point of the project. Any new idea must address these basic needs of the decision makers, if they are to make any impact.

How to surface and articulate the current strategic agenda? The assumption here is that each successful organisation is a manifestation of a formula for success, which we have called a "Business Idea". Sometimes managers may be able to articulate this in some degree of detail, more often it remains tacit in the background while people go about their daily activities, confident in the experience that what they are doing seems to "work". Even in situations where the Business Idea remains in the background managers use it intuitively to prioritise actions. Their thoughts, worries and anxieties are manifestations of a discrepancy between such a tacit Business Idea and perceived reality. By discussing these concerns elements of the manager's Business Idea will emerge. Therefore an agenda for the scenario-based planning exercise can be developed by asking business leaders to express concerns and anxieties about the future. Through a process of discussion an agenda may be developed of issues that managers intuitively feel to be important to the future success of the organisation, on which the scenarios are to throw new light.

As suggested earlier, it is advisable for facilitators to develop an explicit representation of the underlying Business Idea of the organisation, based on the views expressed by the managers. If the process of scenario-based planning is to lead towards reasoned rather than intuitive conclusions concerning the future health of the organisation this step becomes essential.

Elicitation of Views and Insights

Scenario planners need to start from the client's insights, intuitive or otherwise, of what drives (or should drive) the success of their organisation. They need to get access to these insights by engaging the business leaders in a process of elicitation. This can be done through either group brainstorming or individual interview and feedback. The interview process is more elaborate, but more productive in terms of detail generated. However, the time and resources are not always available for the complete job, in which case the group brainstorming approach can make a contribution.

We will discuss two models of team elicitation of strategic insights. The most basic approach is called a SWOT (strengths, weaknesses, opportunities, threats) analysis. An exercise of this type can be conducted in half a day, and provides the scenario planner with a useful insight into the strategic agenda of the management team. The more in-depth approach uses individual interviews, followed by team feedback. Either of these approaches can serve to trigger the managers into articulating what seems important for the future.

After this first step in the elicitation process further work with the team of client-managers is required to structure the insights obtained, until a workable agenda of issues results, which is suitable to set the scene for a scenario-based planning exercise.

The elicitation process in itself can be an important contributor towards enhanced understanding of the business situation. By providing a sounding board the scenario process facilitator at this stage helps managers to express and structure their thoughts. The process of articulating tacit understanding in itself often makes the situation seem more manageable.

The process needs to elicit from the mind of the client what they believe is important in the strategic situation. Not all aspects of the business situation draw the attention of the client to the same extent. Some elements seem further away, some are close in. The task is to build an understanding of this and map out a representation of this thinking.

Figure 20 shows an outline of the elicitation cycle. We get into the cycle by asking trigger questions in a SWOT workshop or in individual interviews. The most effective triggering takes place in an open atmosphere, conducive to creating a free-flowing discussion. Responses need to be carefully recorded in a response database.

Following a SWOT workshop or a series of individual interviews, for example covering the management team, the response database is analysed and interpreted. The result of this is fed back to the client team in a joint session, showing how their insights, as the analyst has heard these, have been mapped out. The presentation highlights clusters, and how these are interconnected. The client normally recognises much of what is fed back, but the new element introduced at this stage is the interpretation and ordering of the various views in a coherent

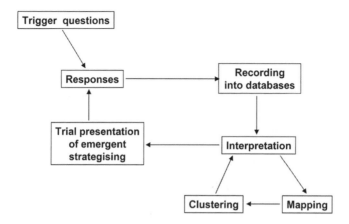

Figure 20. *The elicitation cycle*

framework. Interestingly, there are also surprises. Individual managers often have different perspectives on the business, depending on their area of responsibility. Therefore participants are confronted with views on the business, emerged from interviews, that are different in some places from their own perception of the situation. Managers often do not realise the diversity of thinking in their own management teams. They are often surprised at what their colleagues have to say on strategy and the long term. It seems that most management teams concentrate on discussing operational day-to-day questions and problems, and issues of a longer-term strategic nature are not often on the agenda. Through individual interviews differences can be surfaced and presented back to the team in one or more feedback meetings.

Managers will be triggered to articulate their own views by being confronted with a representation of affairs by their colleagues that does not coincide with their own understanding of the situation. In this way further responses are generated. This new data can then be included in the response database to make it more complete. A further feedback session can be held, in an iterative process, until no further progress is made. The complete cycle of individual interviews and joint feedback is generally experienced as a highly positive experience in most management teams. Reasons for this include:

- Managers are forced to articulate their assumptions and opinions about strategy, helping them in their thinking.

- The ordered database provides an overview of the main strategic issues in a framework, which makes the situation cognitively more manageable.
- Managers become aware of the diversity of thinking available in the team.
- Successful interviews create a feeling of a "common experience" among the group of interviewees, helping to improve the dynamics of their strategic conversation.

THE SWOT WORKSHOP

The SWOT process makes one cycle through the elicitation loop of Figure 20. A SWOT analysis is a way of recording important assumptions about the business situation. It provides a database for a scenario exercise and further discussion on strategy. The four letters SWOT stand for Strengths, Weaknesses, Opportunities and Threats.

The SWOT is developed in a workshop with the client, typically a management team, facilitated by the scenario planner. It consists of:

- An introduction in which the purpose of the exercise is explained,
- A brainstorming session, during which contributions are invited from all participants, without critique, and
- An analysis of the recorded results of the brainstorming.

Idea Generation

After the opening and introduction the participants are invited to write down individually any aspect of the company or its business environment that seems to them either good or bad. The facilitator should try not to be specific at this stage, people should follow their intuition in deciding what good or bad means. These lists do not need to be exhaustive, they only serve to get the ball rolling in the group. While participants think about this the facilitator prepares four flipcharts, which he identifies with an S, W, O or T.

After (say) 10 minutes the facilitator invites participants one by one, going around the circle, to call out one of the points they have written down. Before recording this he invites the team to identify the item as S, W, O or T. Only questions of clarification are allowed. When everyone understands what is meant the facilitator writes the indicated point in a few words on the appropriate flipchart. The facilitator ensures that everyone agrees with the choice of words. The convention for deciding where particular features need to be noted down is as follows:

- A favourable feature of the company is noted under Strengths.
- An unfavourable feature of the company is noted under Weaknesses.
- A favourable feature of the business environment is noted under Opportunities.
- An unfavourable feature of the business environment is noted under Threats.

It is important to be somewhat relaxed with where items end up. Many views of the business cannot be neatly put into one of the categories. If this problem arises it is often useful to discuss the various aspects, and enter contributions in more than one flipchart.

This ideally should become a true brainstorming session in which ideas trigger new ideas. When this happens the facilitator should make room for the discussion of these new ideas and they should be incorporated on the flipcharts in the same way. When ideas dry up the facilitator continues with the next person, going around the group, and so on until no further new ideas come forward.

As a next step, participants are invited to overview the whole table as assembled on the flipcharts, and to ask themselves the question whether this characterises the company in all its important aspects. A holistic overview of this type often triggers further ideas on aspects that have been overlooked so far.

To finish the generation of the SWOT table, participants are now invited to critique the result so far. Participants need to discuss the features that feel uncomfortable. This may lead to a reformulation of what is written down, or the challenged point may have to be annotated, or even removed, as the case may be.

Analysis of the SWOT

The four categories of data collected are now analysed further. This is often initially carried out by the facilitator alone for subsequent presentation to the client team.

Step 1

It is important to identify which Strengths can be considered distinctive, distinguishing the company from its competitors. If a strength is annotated as distinctive the meeting should be capable of providing a suitable answer to the devil's advocate question: "Why would others be unable to emulate it" (refer to Part Two, page 68).

Step 2

Weaknesses should be broken down into three categories:

- Symptoms
- Hygiene weaknesses
- Structural weaknesses.

Some features on the list of weaknesses will be symptoms of weaknesses in the company. They cannot be repaired directly, but will come right when the underlying causes are tackled. Examples might be high debt, poor profits and low share value.

A second category of weakness is known as "hygiene factors". These are deficiencies in the essential basics for running any organisation or business enterprise. They represent current codified knowledge about sound management. No professional manager can be ignorant of this knowledge. It can be picked up by studying the practice of well-managed companies as codified in textbooks on management. Examples are adequate accounting systems, personnel policies, information systems and internal communications, sales and marketing, succession plans, cash planning, inventory and working capital management etc. Looking after hygiene factors puts the company on the starting line. It doesn't as such give a company any competitive advantage, but their absence will make surviving very difficult indeed.

The third category of weakness concerns structural weaknesses, and indicates areas in which the company would like to have, but lacks, a Distinctive Competency, at least for the time being. Examples would include relative size vis-à-vis main competitors, lack of brand awareness etc. When specifying the Business Idea the management team needs to keep these elements in mind, and test whether the Business Idea that emerges can stand up in the light of these weaknesses.

Structural weaknesses often indicate the direction in which the Business Idea for the future needs to be developed. Most of the structural weaknesses can be interpreted as a lack of a strength, which the management intuitively feels the company should have. It is therefore likely that these indicate areas of desirable development.

Step 3

The team identifies opportunity areas. It is likely that so far opportunities will be expressed as options for the company and the facilitator now asks the group to rephrase these in terms of "opportunity areas open to us". Opportunity areas can be of two types:

- Business portfolio areas
- Capability areas.

Portfolio opportunities are areas of potential business where the distinctive nature of the company's Business Idea might be capable of developing a profitable business. In general a portfolio opportunity involves exploiting one (or more) of the company's distinctive strengths. Capability opportunities are areas where the company might develop new capabilities, which are felt relevant to future success. Capability options indicate potential development towards the Business Idea of the future.

Step 4

Threats are features in the business environment, which could undermine the strength of the company. They should be carefully scrutinised by management for signs that the current Business Idea is becoming obsolete and in need of major overhaul. They are the warning signals.

Step 5

The SWOT data can be used as a quick way of coming to a scenario agenda. Overviewing the complete SWOT analysis the team addresses the question of what this indicates for the areas in the business environment that need to be looked at. A new flipchart is used by the facilitator to write down ideas that are highlighted. This can often add up to a considerable list of items of very different levels of potential importance.

Therefore this step is completed by clustering the items recorded in areas of potential impact on the organisation. The facilitator needs to end up with a list of not more than (say) five broad areas of concern to the client management team about the business environment, as the basis to be used by the scenario design team.

The SWOT data have wider use. They can be of importance in subsequent steps of the strategy thinking process. Apart from the scenario agenda they give important indications about the current Business Idea, and where this needs to be developed. In conjunction with an explicit Business Idea SWOT data can also be used to trigger a discussion on options open to the company. Generally the SWOT analysis provides a database, which can be used by the team during various stages of the strategy discussions.

Following a SWOT workshop it is advisable to feed the results back to the client team to allow them to validate and modify.

INDIVIDUAL INTERVIEWS

Normally in scenario projects one works under a time constraint, and the number of iterations through the elicitation cycle will be strictly limited. It is therefore important that the best possible starting point is obtained. The most effective way of developing this is by means of a series of individual interviews.

There are a few general rules that should be followed by the interviewer to create a successful interview. Interviews are as much as possible of an open-ended nature. This means that the interviewer does not arrive with a ready set of specific questions concerning the business. Instead questions are general, and intended to trigger a free-flowing conversation, in which the interviewee sets the agenda.

Interview Introduction

Each interview is opened by explaining the purpose of the exercise. Points to cover include:

- This is the introductory stage of a scenario project, about the future of XYZ. At this stage we would like the interviewee to think generally about the situation as widely as (s)he likes.
- We will be doing X interviews (indicate who is involved). The results of this will be used to set the agenda of the whole project. For this reason we will be asking open-ended questions and we would encourage the interviewee to roam freely over the territory as they see fit. We are interested in particular in what they see as the areas of uncertainty and concern, and in what seems puzzling about the future.
- We will be making notes during the interview. After the interview we will cut up the notes in separate statements about specific aspects

of the future, which we will then merge with statements of other interviews in the same subject area. We will report on the results of the interview round by subject area. All statements will be reported anonymously. In the report readers will see their own views juxtaposed with what others have said about the same subject, but without attribution.

- In addition to the written report (to be sent to all interviewees) we will also report verbally in a feedback meeting, when we will agree the agenda for the rest of the project.

Some personal trust needs to be established as quickly as possible. This is important to enable interviewees to express what they care about, in their relation to the business theme of the interview. It is important that the interviewer explains what will happen to the data collected. It should be clear to the interviewee that any data will be stored anonymously. Data items will be sorted by subject, such that for each topic an overview is obtained of the range of views in the client team. In this way total anonymity is assured. This understanding will help the interviewee to talk more freely.

The challenge for the interviewer is to establish him/herself as a genuine listener. Genuine listening involves paying attention to what arises in the mind of the listener during the conversation (active listening), and feeding this back to the interviewee. In this way listeners signal that they "care". Some degree of interaction of this type is required to establish a trust relationship between the parties in the conversation, a precondition for a successful interview. On the other hand, if it is overdone the interviewer risks dominating the content of what is said in the interview, reducing its elicitation value. A careful balance has to be found. This will be different in each case, depending on the individuals involved and their relationship.

The start of the interview sets the tone for the rest in terms of trust and relationship. A useful way in is to ask the interviewee to briefly relate how (s)he came to be in their present position. This introductory question allows the interviewee to express a personal viewpoint relating to the subject under discussion, and helps to involve him/her in the exercise. This question immediately follows the preamble, explaining the purpose of the exercise.

Interview Questions

After this introduction the interview proper starts. The interviewer must refrain as much as possible from setting the agenda of the discussion. This means that questions must be designed so that they trigger a conversation, but influence the agenda as little as possible. One example of a set of trigger questions that have been found to be effective is known as the "seven questions". The core of these originates from the work at the Institute of the Future (Amara & Lipinsky 1983), but the scenario planners in Shell added further questions later.

The first three questions form a set, the purpose of which is to elicit a list of the main concerns and uncertainties about the business and its environment. It is an intuitive point to start, as uncertainties and concerns overlap in people's minds. The interviewees could be asked straight out to list their concerns and uncertainties. But priorities can be surfaced as well by setting constraints, for example by suggesting a situation in which the client could pose only three questions to a clairvoyant, somebody who could actually foretell the future. How would the interviewee use these three opportunities? In this way one introduces the issue of relative impact. There is much uncertainty in the business environment and it is useful to encourage the interviewee to reflect on what is really going to make a difference.

There is an advantage in posing the first question in a "lighter" way. It takes the weight off the interview and makes the atmosphere more comfortable. It signals "feel free to explore various unusual avenues". Asking trigger questions in a somewhat playful mode is helpful in opening up the interviewee.

When the conversation starts to slow down the next question is introduced. The situation is turned around, and it is suggested that the interviewee might take the role of clairvoyant, answering his/her own questions. However, as we are dealing with an uncertain world, which could turn out in various different ways, the interviewee is asked to concentrate on a future that turns out favourable. "Imagine that the future is a good one, rolling out as you would like it to be, how would you, as the clairvoyant, answer your own three questions?" In response the interviewee produces a "good" story, revisiting all uncertainties, and working out how they develop out in a story that is considered "good".

This question is followed by a similar one in which the world develops in an undesirable direction, representing the interviewee's worst fears.

Earlier (page 128) we saw how a "good" scenario indicates a world in which the existing Business Idea continues to be valid and powerful, while a "bad" scenario addresses possible developments that would invalidate it. This dual question therefore provides information on how the interviewee perceives the current formula for success, and what could threaten it. "Good" and "bad" stories have a role to play in elicitation. However, we reiterate what we said on page 115, scenario planners should in general steer away from good and bad worlds, instead focusing on what is plausible and internally consistent.

These tend to be productive questions. It often happens that one does not get much further than these three questions, and that time runs out before the interviewee runs out of steam. People find it easy to spin stories in this way, particularly after the uncertainties have already been articulated. The good or bad future questions must follow the clairvoyant question if they are to work well. The major uncertainties must already be on the table. The questions do not only surface the interviewee's ideas of how things hang together in the world, but what is considered good and bad will also emerge, and in this way value systems start surfacing. The interviewer must watch not to specify good or bad, the interviewee fills this in.

Sometimes interviewers need to have more open-ended questions up their sleeve. A useful technique is to alternate questions about the past with questions about the future. Ideas about the future are anchored in the past. Therefore questions about the past make the interviewee realise where some of the ideas come from.

Follow-up questions that have proven useful include:

- *Inheritances from the past:* "What pivotal events can you identify in the past of this organisation, good or bad, that should remain in our memories as important lessons for the future?" This question acknowledges that mental models are representations of patterns we have seen in past events. These can be powerful elicitation entry points, leading into territory that has not yet been explored. The interviewer should listen carefully for organisational "myths", stories known to all members of the organisation. Groups of people tend to use myths to codify and remember some of the most basic assumptions underpinning their culture. Surfacing these can be particularly productive in mapping the organisational mental model.
- *Important decisions ahead:* "What major decisions with long-term implications does the organisation face at the moment, decisions that need to be tackled in the next few months?" The time period indicated may vary and should be appropriate for the major decisions that will have to be faced. This question aims to get at the sort of issues that are currently exercising the client's mind, and where help from a scenario project could be particularly welcome.
- *Constraints in the system:* "What major constraints are you experiencing inside or outside of your organisation that limit you in what you can achieve in your business situation?" Many constraints are strongly felt and prove a powerful trigger for elicitation. Internal constraints often are the subject of political battles, and some interviewees may require

some encouragement to bring these out. The interviewer may want to follow up with: "Please do not forget to include cultural constraints in your own organisation."

- *The epitaph question:* "Please consider the situation in the future when you will have moved on from your current position, to the next job or to retirement. What do you hope to leave behind that people will associate with your period in office; what do you want to be remembered for?" This is well suited as a final question to bring the interview to an end. It is aimed directly at the interviewee's value system. Following an initial response, and to help the interviewee to get as close as possible to personal values, the interviewer may want to follow up with the suggestion that the interviewee should try in his/her mind to remove all constraints; imagine (s)he is in total control, and only personal values will shape the response.

Facilitating the Conversation

The contribution of the interviewers during the conversation needs careful consideration. The objective of the interviewer is to engage in a conversation with the client without influencing the agenda of what the client says. This is not a simple matter. In principle, by participating in the conversation the interviewer affects what is being said. On the other hand one cannot expect the client to engage in a monologue of two hours or more. The interviewer must participate, preferably only in a reactive mode. You can do a lot of that by gesture, nodding, and smiling, in general showing interest. But from time to time you may consider it necessary to make a contribution to the conversation.

Doing that in the least obtrusive way possible, such that the effect on the client's line is minimised, requires a bit of skill. It is done by means of questions of clarification or feeding back what has just been heard. Never lead the interviewee or interpret what (s)he has said. Don't say: "Do you mean that . . .", instead say: "What do you mean by . . .".

Box 9   The seven questions

Clairvoyant
Good scenario
Bad scenario
Lessons from the past
Important decisions ahead
Constraints in the system
Epitaph, free hand

General "journalist" questions can be used at any time to keep the conversation going:

- Anything to add. For example: "Is there anything more you could say under this heading, any more uncertainties, anything more happening in your scenario etc. anything you have not yet touched upon in your reply that might prove to be important."
- The "why" question. For example: "Why do you think that is important, what would be the positive or negative result of that, why is that a good/bad idea?"
- The "how" question. For example: "How could this happen, what must be in place for that, how do you think that could be achieved?"

These are the danger points in the interview. It is so easy to lock the conversation into a specific area, and in that way completely miss what the interviewee really believes is important. Interviewers must be aware of what they are doing while they are engaged in this conversation. They need to continuously judge the extent to which they are capable of keeping the conversation natural and normal without steering. This is a matter of practice, if you feel unsure about this find someone to practice on. You'll find it is easier than it looks, once you are in the listening frame of mind.

Remember all the time: this is not recording facts; this is about articulating what is in his/her mind. The challenge is to participate in the conversation while standing apart from it at the same time.

Conducting the Interview

During the interview two activities need to be carried out at the same time; the conversation has to be kept going in a natural but non-directive way and what is being said needs to be recorded. Maintaining a natural conversation without influencing the agenda requires significant mental effort. The interviewer needs to think carefully about what (s)he is going to say so that the conversation is not steered too much. On the other hand the conversation needs to be natural and relaxed, to keep the interviewee at ease. It cannot be combined well with notetaking.

Should interviewers record the interviews on tape? A lot depends on the culture in the organisation. The most important objective of the interview is that it feels to the interviewee like an informal natural conversation, encouraging airing of personal opinions rather than espoused theory or the "party line". The interviewee must be convinced of complete confidentiality if this is to be achieved. Most business managers are not used to their conversation being taped and have "Watergate"-type visions when confronted with such a device. They wonder what might happen with the tapes and cannot help being put on their guard. Pragmatically it must be assumed that in most cases tape-recording is counterproductive. It is preferable to miss a few observations in hand-written notes, if the rest gains in substantive significance. In most interviews notes need to be taken by hand, requiring a second person in the team.

A team of two people often works well, particularly if they can switch roles (engaging in the conversation and notetaking) during the interview. This requires some practice in the team, but after a few interviews the style and approach of one's partner becomes clear. Switching roles during the interview gives it a feel of a natural and comfortable conversation. Experienced interviewers learn to switch roles frequently during the interview.

Adding more people to the team tends to reduce the quality of the interview very quickly. There is a risk that a team of three interviewers entering the interviewee's office is perceived as an event, requiring a "performance". More than three progressively reduces the value of the interview further, due to the increased stress created.

Interviews can be conducted by people belonging to the organisation or by outsiders. Internal people have the advantage that they know the language and much of the background of what is being said. On the other hand this may sometimes turn into a disadvantage. The external person is not expected to know much of what is going on. This may lead the interviewee away from the usual "party-line" formulation of business issues, into aspects of the world taken for granted which are normally not verbalised. This often proves particularly productive in surfacing theories about the world that the person actually uses to guide his/her actions, rather than espoused theories through which people traditionally articulate the situation to each other. The other advantage of the external interviewer is the absence of prior history of interaction with the interviewee, which often inhibits free expression.

Doing a genuine open-ended interview is difficult for a novice. Internal people tend to be inexperienced in open-ended interviewing. They are also part of the political power play, and they often are emotionally involved in the subject matter. The interviewee grants them power over the conversation and it is difficult not to misuse this. Even if they claim they get the idea, as soon as they are off on their own they lead the conversation. In most cases they are not even aware of what they are doing. So the conversation focuses on what interests the interviewer, not the priorities of the interviewee. These interviews tend to be heavily skewed towards the internal, and particularly the internal problems. On the whole that makes internal people poor interviewers.

On balance the external interviewers have the advantage, provided that they have acquired some of the language of the organisation in advance.

Interviews of this type seldom take less than an hour and a half or more than two and a half hours. Realistically one can do three, or at most four, interviews in a day, more would be difficult to handle. This is a quite consistent finding, allowing reliable planning of an interview project over time.

Whom to Interview

In a normal organisational situation focused on a management team it seldom proves necessary to interview more than 15 or so people. Early interviews generally add a lot of additional information. But after say 10 interviews a lot has already surfaced and interviews become repetitive. A typical management team works together, communicates on a daily basis and meets regularly in business meetings and in corridors. For this reason, the fifteenth interview does not surface much new. (The interviewer can use the later interviews to test emerging theses, moving beyond the agenda setting framework. But only after having tested the trigger questions first.) The fact that in most cases the number of interviews can be limited to between 10 and 15 is another important data point enabling the planning of the scope of the exercise. (Some strategy projects require many more interviews, for reasons other than agenda setting, for example to create ownership across the organisation by allowing a wider cross-section to be heard.)

Note Taking

Good listening and note taking is absolutely crucial, it is *the* big challenge of this part of the project.

While the conversation is going on you just have to write down what is being said. Don't try to decide during the interview whether something is or is not worth noting down. You don't know where the conversation may lead, and what seems insignificant at this moment may become a major issue later in the interview or in other interviews. So there is no alternative to writing down everything.

Novices are bad in recording the conversation. Fortunately it is also something one can learn to do better. It takes quite a bit of training to be able to listen and write at the same time. Gaining experience helps people in being able to push back their own preconceived idea filters and to give increasing space to the ideas of the interviewee. Comments need to be captured as completely as possible. Judgement on what is important and what will prove interesting comes later.

It is useful for the two interviewers to compare notes immediately after the interview. Invariably one finds that overlap between the two is not total: one just does not hear all that is being said. Even the best recorders lose at least 15% of what is being said. This is a well-researched fact. But while memory is still fresh a lot can still be recovered. At this stage it is useful to identify and agree on the important ideas.

Only after the interview is finished can you make a judgement on what was important or not. Sit down with your notebook and consider in the cold post-interview light what statements now stand out as really important viewpoints. Underline these. This is a judgemental process, where again the two-person team has the advantage over the single interviewer. The interviewers go through their notes and consider the important observations to be processed further. The test for inclusion is whether the view expressed is relevant and significant in the context of the organisation's position and behaviour in its business environment. This includes internal issues if these are relevant to the way the organisation will react to the outside world. Any views on where the environment might be going are obviously important.

It is important that we exercise a degree of judgement here. We are normally dealing with a significant number of interviews that have to be processed in a very short time. Typically one interview may produce between 40 and 60 important insights that need to be taken forward (ignore this number if it would exclude important material). The interviewers will write these down as short bullet-style statements, each expressing one significant thought.

Analysing the Set of Interviews

Any strategy project ultimately is about considering the fit between the organisation and its environment. For this reason these two domains need to be separated as early as possible in the project.

Interviewees will not have made this distinction, and the interview notes will be a mixture of interwoven external and internal points. The first step in the analysis is to separate statements into these two categories. The analysts need to create two data files, one including the statements about the external business environment, and one containing all other points relating to internal characteristics and phenomena in the organisation. The allocation criterion is whether the company has control over the issue.

One must be aware of language traps that lure here. Very often a statement ostensibly about an internal policy issue is really about the environment. For example, the statement "we may soon have to double our capacity if we want to remain a key player" includes a statement about the rate of growth in demand. Similarly "we should adopt a more customised approach in our product design" may imply the insight that the market may be moving towards giving higher value to customisation. These implied business environment assumptions should be included as separate statements in the business environment file. Before the separation is made all statements seemingly addressing internal issues should be tested for any embedded content on the contextual environment.

Once the statements have been divided between these two files, the data in each file need to be sorted and clustered. Initially the statements are unconnected, a set of random thoughts. The subsequent analysis of these statements involves a process of clustering and linking. It is important that no clustering rules are laid down in advance. It is better to let cluster categories emerge naturally out of the material collected. If categories are predetermined and imposed on the clustering the value of the exercise is significantly reduced. One categorisation scheme popular with novices is the STEP or STEEP categorisation often used in strategic management textbooks. This categorises the environment into societal development, technological developments, economic developments and political developments. Another E is sometimes added (STEEP), standing for ecological environment developments.

The advice here is not to cluster according to such predetermined schemes, as they do not reflect systemic relationships in the specific business environment of the client. If the interview data are forced into an existing framework like this much of the interconnecting richness of what is in the statements is lost. Intuitive clustering, on the other hand, will make the analyst pay attention to conceptual meaning, for example through cause-and-effect reasoning, and if this is reflected in the clustering something new has been learned. The human mind is particularly strong in seeing or inferring patterns.

As a result clusters will start emerging which combine statements together in context. By overviewing the total set of insights produced the analyst will start to see patterns, similarities and natural couplings. The material now needs to be arranged into these emerging categories. At this stage the purpose of the analysis is to cluster ideas and arrive at a smaller number of higher-level concepts, which can be related to each other. Total overview is required in the early stages until the first-level categories have emerged.

Technically there are various ways of doing the clustering, dependent on the number of statements to be considered. Visual methods, allowing for trial and error, tend to be more comfortable in view of the large amount of material the analyst has to overview.

Statements can be written on slips of paper, Post-its or magnetic hexagons, moved around on a display surface or wall-mounted area. If the team has been disciplined in notetaking this should be a relatively simple step. As the purpose of the exercise is to acquire an overview, it is important that text on each Post-it is limited to not more than a few words. These should be written in large heavy characters, so that they can be read from a distance. By scanning the whole display ideas for clustering present themselves.

For small projects this approach suffices. However, if one is dealing with a 10-interview project some 500 Post-its may be generated, more or less equally divided between internal and external issues. This stretches the visual approach to the limit. In this case it is preferable to use a computerised database in the analysis. Sorting and clustering then become an exercise in hierarchical outlining. However, the analyst will still want to use a parallel visual approach using only main statement categories. The reason is that creating an overall overview, required for the first-level of clustering, is difficult in a computer database. Once the first-level categories are established in this way, subcategories can be developed using the computer database.

Initially there will be statements that do not seem to link up anywhere naturally. These may be put aside temporarily while progress is being made on the rest. Following completion of this stage further iterations are needed to try to integrate the odd statements that have been left out so far. The first clustering will be somewhat random, depending on what caught the eye first, but it may not be the most effective way of incorporating as many of the insights as possible. If there are unconnected ideas left, the analyst needs to try to find a home for these by reclustering. They should consider whether any other higher-level criteria can be found, on the basis of which the data can be reclustered, which accommodates the so-far-unconnected ideas. It is worthwhile iterating a couple of times, until there is no further progress.

The exercise is basically iterative. The decision whether clustering has been satisfactorily completed depends on whether clustering principles have become clear, and whether clusters are reasonably independent, with each idea falling naturally in one cluster only. The analyst should try to get as close as possible to this state of affairs. One way of testing this is through naming of the clusters. A cluster name should be a short and unambiguous indication of the principle that keeps the ideas within the cluster together, while distinguishing them clearly from any of the other clusters identified.

From then onwards the analysis moves into each of the main clusters to develop a second level of categorisation. The process of moving and clustering the Post-its on a display area is now the same as moving data in a computer database, using principles of hierarchical outlining. The detail required in the categorisation depends on the quantity of the material collected. If the number of statements runs into many hundreds, a three- or four-level outline may suggest itself. The ultimate aim is to arrive at a level of hierarchical categorisation where each of the lowest subcategories contains not more than some 15 statements. On the other hand the number of statements in a category may be as low as one or two, if statements are self-standing and cannot be grouped with any others. The final step in the clustering process is to move the statements within each subcategory in an order that suggests a logical progression or storyline from one statement to the next, and to identify in each of the clusters common and divergent views and assumptions. These need to be highlighted as powerful triggers for the feedback meeting. In this way the analyst gradually creates a picture of the management team's mental models, including overlap and divergence within the team. The many suggestions made in this chapter all serve the purpose of making the result reflect theories-in-use rather than espoused theories about the situation.

With the initial material divided into internal and external points, the analysis results in two sets of cluster hierarchies. Two products will emerge from the data structuring stage, the scenario agenda and the internal agenda.

INTERNAL AND CONTEXTUAL DATA

The interviewees will have talked widely, dealing with external and internal issues, during the interviews. Many of them will have been concerned with areas where the client organisation has a great deal of control, but where the interviewee is unsure about how to exercise this. These are strategic option issues, including internal client policies, their business policies, actions by other players that can be influenced, and "games" that are being played in the marketplace or with other stakeholders. Outside the areas where the client has a degree of control, which we have called the transactional environment, is the contextual environment where the control of the client organisation is insignificant or non-existing, but where developments may be of the greatest importance to its success or failure (see Figure 21).

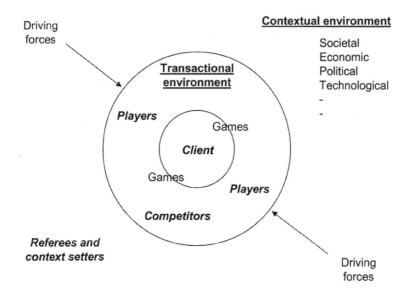

Figure 21. *The business in its environment*

As discussed (page 115) we reserve the word scenarios for stories about driving forces and their effects in the contextual environment, outside the control of the organisation itself, but determining what it needs to do. For strategic exploration to work it is important that external developments are expressed (in scenarios) separately from internal issues (belonging in strategising). Recall that scenarios are a testbed for strategy testing. The test conditions must not include prior choices about aspects of the strategies to be tested, if bias is to be avoided and objectivity maintained. Testbed conditions must be independent of the strategies and plans to be tested. Therefore it is important that clients do not play a role in their own scenarios.

In addition to looking at generic factors, such as represented by the STEEP categories (page 183), organisations need to make a detailed analysis of the structure of the industry and markets they operate in. Industry structure is the result of power structures among the generic categories of competitive forces, which all try to appropriate as much of the overall profit potential as possible. At the contextual scenario level these competing forces include (Porter 1980):

- Generic competitive forces among the existing competitors in the industry.
- Relative power of suppliers.
- Relative power of buyers.

- Relative power of potential new entrants.
- Potential influence of substitute products.

It is useful for the interviewer to make a check that each of these categories has been consciously addressed.

The definition of the boundary line between contextual and transactional is important here. An organisation cannot change its context, because that is how context is defined. But the boundary between the context and the transactional environment is fuzzy. Defining what goes where can be difficult, more so in the public sector than in private business. How far does one's influence reach? While this is often underestimated in the private sector, the public sector tends to overestimate ("we are the government, we set the rules of the game"). The team needs to remain flexible, and be prepared to change the separating line between the internal and the contextual as new insights develop. Role playing can often clarify the issue, along the lines of "in a certain context, if they do this, what are my options to react and what will be their reactions to my actions?" An appropriate metaphor is playing chess, which requires knowing that after each move, you need to re-evaluate and take into account the developments in the transactional environment (the moves of the others) and in the contextual environment (are we still playing chess, or has the world changed to poker?).

At the level of the contextual scenario we are not considering the behaviour of the individual players in the game whose power and stake depend on the strategies adopted by the client organisation. Scenario planners need to be careful with putting specific actors in either one or the other. For example, some competitors have aspects that are transactional, where they can be influenced, but other aspects are contextual. Porter's five forces of competition above are conceptualised as "industry" forces, i.e. mostly outside the influence of any one individual player. They belong in the contextual arena, and should be considered in the scenarios for a client focusing on the competitive situation. Except if there are only a few players, when the notion of "the laws of the marketplace" becomes less useful. In an oligopolistic market, with only a small number of competitors, individual players may have control over the forces of competition, and the game moves into the transactional environment.

The Scenario Agenda

The first product of the elicitation exercise is known as a scenario agenda. This is a list of typically up to four or five broad themes or areas of interest in the business environment where it has become clear that the project has the potential of helping the client. These are areas of major uncertainty that the client is significantly concerned about. Following the clustering exercise a larger number of agenda issues will tend to emerge. There will be much more than can be properly handled in one scenario project. A balance has to be struck between breadth and depth. A good in-depth scenario exercise cannot handle more than five broad themes simultaneously. More than that would make the outcome cognitively difficult to handle. In fact few customised scenario exercises need to go beyond that if the agenda themes have been chosen without significant overlap (orthogonally). In this respect uncertainty actually helps the scenario planner, in that more uncertainty tends to reduce the number of key uncertainty dimensions that dominate the outcome (page 93).

By clustering and reclustering the analyst tries to make the categories as independent as possible, such that uncertainty in one affects uncertainty in the others as little as possible. It often happens that this will reduce the number of clusters to manageable proportions. If this does not prove possible the analyst will have to take the final result back to the client and suggest a ranking exercise to decide the top five themes. The ranking should be conducted using the level of concern and anxiety in the client team as the criterion. The outcome of this ranking exercise is often very interesting to the scenario group. Some issues that are headline news in the world at the time are removed from the agenda, as of secondary importance or relatively unproblematic in the organisation's context. Themes that score lower this time may be ranked higher on another occasion in the future. The analyst needs to clarify that the current ranking does not mean that the lower ranking themes are not important. These areas may have their turn of being included in a scenario project on another future occasion.

Some scenario practitioners define, with the client, an "organising question" at the conclusion of the elicitation exercise. This has pitfalls and needs to be carefully considered, as this will have a significant influence on the further shape of the project.

An organising question turns a scenario project into a "case study". There is a fundamental difference between seeing the project as a case study or as responding to a client need. A case study project starts from a definition of "the problem" and proceeds to attempt to "solve" it. An example is a project with a sense-making purpose, where there is clear focus on a particular puzzling situation. "Intractable problem" projects also fall in this category. These projects belong firmly in the realm of rational strategy. The outcome expected is clear, we want the problem solved.

The alternative is starting with trying to understand the "client", rather than the "issue". The client approach to the project emphasises the importance of process, strategising rather than strategy. Scenarios then become a language for strategising. The strategy emerges in a process, it is not just a "decision". Every project is different, because every client is different.

An organising question helps in giving a strong focus to the project, and ensures that any outcome has strong relevance to the client. It may be particularly helpful to those client teams who lack common understanding of the business environment, and who find it difficult to move forward due to this confusion. On the other hand, strongly cohesive teams, who have little problem moving forward on the basis of their one-track view of the future, need to consider alternative and new interpretations of the world which are not currently part of their shared mental model. We have called this generative scenario-based planning, where the main purpose is to stretch existing understanding and to develop new and unique insights as the basis for a future success formula. In such a case an organising question will constrain space for exploratory trips into the contextual environment and miss those areas where these novel insights need to emerge.

The alternative to selecting an organising question is to spend time with the client discussing the situation in an open-ended way, and reporting back with the interviews properly analysed. A concept around which this feedback discussion can be built without violating the open-ended nature of the discussion at this early stage is the Business Idea, used as a device to bring strands together into a manageable whole. Clients invariably appreciate an organised interview feedback along this line. It is an eye-opener in its own right. It also sets an agenda but leaves the possibility of a genuine surprise.

Whether one adopts the case study (organising question) or the client (scenario agenda) approach, crucial for success is the facilitators' ability to listen to the client, without an agenda of his own. Research has shown that scenario work most remembered in the organisation is produced in response to questions alive in the organisation at the time, i.e. where the scenarios are evidence of an ability of the planners to listen to their audience. If this is done well people many years later often still remember not only the scenarios, but also the underlying systemic structure of the scenarios, particularly if these have been named by the team. On the other hand scenarios that are not clearly related to what people need, however strongly felt by the scenario planners, are quickly forgotten (page 8).

The Internal Agenda

The second product of the elicitation exercise is a first cut at mapping the fundamentals of the organisation itself, the organisational "self".

Scenarios play out in the contextual environment. But the client has not only been talking about the contextual business environment during the interviews. A lot has been said about the organisation itself, in terms of problems and concerns, what is wrong and what is good, problems with other people, why the culture is not right and so on. Typically, more than half of the interview material contains data not about the contextual business environment, but about the organisation itself. This part of the data is important as a starting point for mapping the strategic fundamentals of the organisation, ultimately to be expressed as its Business Idea for the future.

FEEDBACK

Having analysed the data these now have to be reported back to the client, and the interviewees. This may not be the same group. If not, the facilitator may want to circulate a summary of the outcome of the interview analysis to all who have participated in the interviews. Keeping this group in the loop may prove valuable later in the project.

The choice of feedback material depends on a number of parameters that the facilitators may want to review:

- Who is the client, what are his/her needs
- What is the espoused purpose of the project
- What was the espoused purpose of the interview project
- What was promised to the interviewees
- How open is the system
- How professional (non-directed) was the interviewing
- How accurate was the notetaking, how skilful was the listening
- How much care went into formulating the statements
- What is the attitude of the client towards the negative internal stuff.

The client needs to be informed in more detail about the outcome of the exercise as a number of important decisions are now to be taken. As we saw it is preferable to separate feedback on the external business environment from comments on the internal situation. A possible structure for interview feedback might look as follows:

- Historic perspective (how has the situation evolved over time to where it is now)
- External perspective (what is happening in our "business" environment, both contextual and transactional)

- Internal perspective (comments about the "self", culture, behaviour, management, personnel, strengths, weaknesses, business logics etc.)
- Future perspective (options for improvement, notions about desired practices, vision, strategic considerations etc.).

From there the scenario planners report on the result of their analysis of the data. This may include:

- First-cut current Business Idea
- Distinctive Competencies for the future supporting the current success formula
- Possible threats (outside) and weaknesses (inside)
- Purpose of the project
- Proposed scenario agenda
- Possible internal constraints to a successful project.

This may be an opportune point to explain to the client group the difference between adaptive and generative scenario projects. This is particularly important if the client contract provides for the possibility that the project may develop in the latter category. In that case it is particularly important that the client group understands the open-ended nature of the project and the high level of contributions and commitment that is expected from them.

We would recommend that scenario planners only deal with internal issues if these are of obvious significance to the scenario project. If there are clear indications of organisational constraints to a successful outcome these have to be put up for discussion. The facilitators need to be particularly interested in signals for either excessive fragmentation (conflict, hidden agendas, politicking, inability to deal with issues) or excessive groupthink (similarity of views, lack of requisite variety in theories-in-use). Facilitators may also want to look at the difference in quality and quantity of the inside and the outside perspectives as it is indicative of what really occupies people's minds. It may highlight how internally focused people are, and how difficult they find it to look outside.

In circumstances where strong internal issues and emotions move inevitably to the heart of the exercise it may be worth considering to develop a short questionnaire with a series of statements that capture as clearly as possible the relevant controversial themes from the interviews. These can be circulated for quick completion (using a 1–5 strongly agree/strongly disagree ranking) across the group. You can measure surprisingly little, but you can quantify quite a lot. The results of the questionnaires are generally clear, they don't expose particular individuals, and often demonstrate more objectively the areas where there is a wide spread of views, and the red herrings.

Facilitators need to be watchful that this remains a scenario project, dealing with strategy, based on "external" aspects and the Business Idea. It will make use of the already existing strategic conversation in the group. There will be a significant contribution to team building through the new way in which the group will talk about joint visions/missions, Business Idea and business environment.

Written feedback of the analysis should wait until it has been delivered orally in a meeting first. There needs to be a follow-up in writing reflecting the discussion. Try to pick wording that maximises impact, e.g. soften up inflammatory phraseology, while leaving as much of the subject matter intact. Don't include comments that apply to any one person as the point of the exercise is to get people thinking about the business environment first, not to deal with specific internal management issues that relate to individuals.

THE HORIZON YEAR

One of the early decisions by the team is how far the scenarios will look forward into the future. This is known as the "horizon year" of the project. This decision will be made by reference to the issues on the identified scenario agenda and the nature of the Business Idea. The horizon year needs to be selected on the basis of the future impacts of today's decisions and strategies. Major capital investments require consideration of a period up to 20 years. Decisions relating to developing the Business Idea, often of a cultural nature, may also have long-term implications. On the other hand organisations with a robust Business Idea may be involved with business portfolio strategy with shorter-term repercussions. Similarly companies in survival mode may not be able to afford the luxury of looking too long term. The horizon year decision has a considerable impact on the outcome of the scenario-based planning exercise. The guess made at the beginning of the project may later prove to be inappropriate in which case the team needs to decide whether another iteration needs to be made for a different horizon year.

Chapter Ten

Articulation of the Business Idea

The concept of the Business Idea involves a system of Distinctive Competencies creating value and sustaining itself in a reinforcing feedback loop. It constitutes the fundamental formula for success of the organisation. In-depth discussion in the management team of the current and future Business Ideas is greatly assisted by a simple graphical representation that will be developed here.

SURFACING A BUSINESS IDEA IN A MANAGEMENT TEAM

Managers generally know the elements of their Business Idea. This knowledge tends to remain tacit in the day-to-day management practice. The process described here is intended to articulate these views, for subsequent reflection, discussion, adjustment and agreement in a management team. The process described is an iterative one, in which a prototype representation is quickly developed. The managers then react to this model, expressing their understanding of what drives success. Through a number of iterations the prototype representation is gradually brought into line with the views of the managers. By employing this process in the management team the managers debate their differences of view, such that when a stage is reached where not much more progress can be made, the result represents a shared view of the business owned by the team as a whole.

The process needs to be facilitated. The facilitator's role is to remind the management team of the concepts involved, to introduce and lead the process, to take the team through the various steps and to record the views expressed, all the time guarding adherence to solid theoretical underpinning. Choice of the facilitator is important, and will normally be limited to team members or well-trusted outsiders.

In this chapter we describe a process of articulating and discussing the Business Idea in a management team. The process is presented as a series of three management workshops, separated by days or hours, as is most convenient. If necessary the process can be completed in one full-day session.

ELEMENTS OF THE BUSINESS IDEA

As discussed in Part Two the essential elements of a Business Idea describe the following drivers of business success:

- The customer value created and the
- Unique activity set, through which this is done.
- The Distinctive Competencies that enable the activity set, in their mutually reinforcing interaction.
- The nature of the Competitive Advantage exploited.
- All this configured in a positive feedback loop, in which resources generated drive growth.

A word representation of the Business Idea cannot bring out adequately the systemic features of the mutually reinforcing Distinctive Competencies working in a positive feedback loop. The purpose of this exercise is to show the causal relationships between these elements in a cause-and-effect influence diagram that can be perceived as one "gestalt", rather than a list of elements.

INITIAL DATA REQUIREMENT

If companies are dominated by one or a few major business sectors, customer value, Competitive Advantage and Distinctive Competencies may be easier to define at business unit level. It may be useful for the top management team to prepare the ground for their corporate Business Idea review by arranging one or more sessions with the business sector managers, in order to develop joint understanding of the Business Unit Business Ideas. A possible way of approaching this is by means of one or more Strategic Evaluation Sessions, in which top management discusses the strategic aspects of the business in a "for information only" exchange with the business manager. A possible model is discussed in Part Four, page 338.

The discussion of the Business Idea in the management team requires a shared database, which ideally should be generated through an interview/feedback round, to be undertaken by the facilitator as discussed. Alternatively the facilitator develops with the client a SWOT analysis on flipcharts. This is done, if possible, in a separate team session, such that the results can be suitably worked up and presented. If this is not practical the management team may start the Business Idea workshop with a one-hour SWOT analysis.

The critical part of the process of developing a joint Business Idea is getting to the first prototype diagram. The facilitator needs to do some preparatory work in order to be able to help the team along if they have difficulty negotiating this first step. From preparatory work the facilitator needs to develop some initial understanding of the key elements that may end up in the Business Idea diagram, and to prepare these as a checklist of triggers, to be used during the meeting if required.

THE PROCESS

Step 1. Deciding on the Business Fundamentals

The SWOT analysis, developed from individual interviews or as a team exercise, are displayed on the walls of the meeting room.

The group now needs to prepare the ground by articulating a few business fundamentals. What is the business, who is the customer, how is value created? This means that in many cases the business has to be segmented first. The quick way to start here is to follow the organisation chart, and identify the business segments that are reflected there. There may be one segment that dominates the profitability picture of the company, in which case the exercise can focus there. If there are multiple segments that seem equally important it is advisable to carry out the analysis for the business segments separately, and then follow up finding the common factors that create the success formula of the total system. Whatever approach is chosen the segmentation needs to be revisited after completion of the first round Business Idea development as the result may throw a different light on the validity of the segmentation scheme.

Assuming that the business segment under consideration has now been defined the team needs to identify their current ideas about the following:

- Who is the typical customer? What are their cares and worries that concern us?

- What is the product/service bought? What is the total proposition we put to the customer?
- What value does the customer derive from this. What is the scarcity that we help alleviate?
- What value does the customer derive from buying from us instead of sourcing in another way?
- If we consider the activity set on the interface between the customer and us what are the unique elements that bring customers to "our shop"?
- How difficult is it for competitors to copy/emulate this?
- Do our competitors have distinctive activities that we find difficult to copy?

Answers to these questions are written on flipcharts. Use separate flipcharts for each question. Consensus is not required at this stage, if there are different opinions capture them all. If there are conflicting views annotate as such.

Step 2. Deciding on the Company's Competitive Advantage

The process of drawing up the first prototype diagram starts with addressing the question of Competitive Advantage. The main question to answer here is whether we put a differentiated offering to the customer, one that commands a price premium in the market, or whether success derives from a structurally advantageous cost position to produce an otherwise undifferentiated product. A useful way to think about this is to articulate how to explain to potential new customers why they should prefer this organisation as supplier/business partner to any other competitor. If this can be identified the Competitive Advantage derives from differentiated products, otherwise the team should try to identify the cost structure that gives this company a clear advantage.

The purpose of the Competitive Advantage question is to come to an understanding of the basics of the organisation's success. This can be based on either doing better things than others or on doing the same things but better, i.e. at a structurally lower cost. The final answer to the Competitive Advantage question should be specifics in one, or a combination, of the following two categories:

- Product/service differentiation
- Structural cost advantage

A company produces a differentiated product if the market allows a price premium to be charged over what the competition can achieve.

This shows that the product meets a scarcity, representing value to the customer (in terms of unique features, in design, quality, support, availability and so on) and that this supplier has a system of Distinctive Competencies allowing it to put it on the market.

A company has a structural cost advantage if it has a system of Distinctive Competencies or resources, which allows it to make a product/service available at a cost consistently below any competitor (cost leadership should not be confused with cost management as part of any "good housekeeping" principle).

The follow-up question – "What does this organisation have to do well in order to deliver on this promise?" – turns the focus on the activity set and its underlying competencies. It is surprising how much time many teams need to articulate an answer to these seemingly obvious questions. As we saw earlier many teams take the basic strengths of the organisation for granted, and do not think a lot about the underlying driving forces while they carry on with the day-to-day tasks.

When agreement has been reached the facilitator records the answer to this question on a flipchart.

Step 3. Addressing the Devil's Advocate Question

Having done this the facilitator poses the devil's advocate question: "What are the unique factors that allow this company to exploit this Competitive Advantage, and why are others unable to emulate it?" The managers need to burrow deeper into their mental model to search for evidence of the underlying system, not stopping at superficial symptoms at the event level. A company can be a differentiator in the market only if it has competencies that nobody else has. How could this be otherwise? Why would other competitors not simply copy what this organisation is doing when they see the success of the formula? The same applies to a consistent cost performance. Competitors have always tried to copy each other's successes. The popularity of benchmarking is all-pervasive. To stand out, and be successful, companies need something that is distinctive and difficult to emulate.

Initial ideas on elements of uniqueness are recorded on a flipchart as well, as preparation for the following stages of the process.

Step 4. Developing a Cause-and-Effect Diagram

The facilitator now starts the development of the first prototype Business Idea diagram. This consists of short bits of text, indicating variables

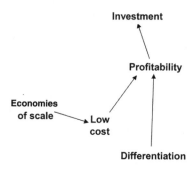

Figure 22. *Start of a Business Idea diagram*

relevant to the success formula, here called elements, connected by arrows, indicating causality. The first element written down is the agreed Competitive Advantage. From there an arrow is drawn to an element called "profitability", and from there another arrow goes to an element called "investment". *An arrow from A to B means: A is a (part) cause of B.*

Following on from the earlier discussion of the sources of the agreed Competitive Advantage (the devil's advocate question) the facilitator now formalises this part by inviting the group to specify succinctly the characteristics of the company that causes the Competitive Advantage. These are recorded, and arrows are drawn from the sources to the Competitive Advantage recorded (for an example see Figure 22).

The attention now moves to the sources identified. The facilitator raises the question: "What causes these sources to exist and how are they being sustained?" In this way new elements enter the picture, connected up with what is already there through cause/effect arrows. This line of questioning is continued until no further progress can be made.

Step 5. Completion of the Diagram

When the group runs out of steam the diagram will contain a number of loose ends, elements for which no sources are shown. This may be due to a number of reasons:

- The element may be sustained by investments, either in capital expenditure or operating expenditure. All expenditure made to buy a hard or soft asset creating long-term value is considered an investment. For example, an R&D capability may be maintained by expenditure, personnel loyalty may require investments in generous rewards, or customer loyalty may be bought by a "low everyday price" policy. In such cases the facilitator will complete the loop by drawing an arrow from the element "investments" already in the diagram to the element under consideration.
- The element may be due to investments, sunk or otherwise, made in the past, the fruits of which are enjoyed by the current organisation. In relation to these elements no further entries on the diagram are required, as the explanation resides in the past only.
- In some cases the organisational success may be related to the leadership by an individual. If the organisation is strongly identified with this individual, e.g. in the case of an owner/manager, then similarly no further explanatory entries are required.

In all other cases questioning should continue until all elements in the diagram are explained, i.e. are supported by explanatory arrows.

Step 6. Identifying the Distinctive Competencies

When loose ends have been tied up, the facilitator needs to complete one more task in this team session. This is to identify the elements in the diagram that are truly distinctive. Referring to the devil's advocate question again the facilitator asks the managers to identify the elements in the diagram that are:

- Unique to the company, and in which it distinguishes itself from its competitors.
- Impossible or difficult to emulate by existing or new competitors.

As explained in Part Two, five broad categories of Distinctive Competencies can be distinguished, and the facilitator needs to take the team through this list, making sure that suggestions by the team fit in one of these:

- Based on sunk costs:
  - Activity specific assets
  - Legal protection
  - Reputation and trust

Box 10   Recording media

Drawing up an influence diagram "on the fly" during a workshop is greatly facilitated by the most flexible recording medium available. A number of possible approaches are listed here in order of reducing ease of manipulation:

- For facilitators with a developed computer aptitude the ideal medium is the computerised systems diagram, using auto-connecting flow diagram software, and made visible to the team by means of an LCD projector.
- The systems diagram can be built up using movable adhesive or magnetic stickers on a white board, each showing one element in the diagram. These are interconnected through arrows drawn on the board, to be wiped out and redrawn whenever a change is made.
- Instead of using movable devices the elements can be written on the board itself. This makes the process of making changes rather more difficult.
- The use of flipcharts is least attractive. The resulting "spaghetti" makes the process unwieldy.

The choice must be left to the individual doing the facilitation as the first requirement is that (s)he feels totally comfortable with it.

- Based on uncodified knowledge:
  - Embedded processes
  - Networked team knowledge.

Elements in the diagram that are agreed on this basis to be distinctive are suitably annotated.

Step 7. Cleaning Up

The first part of the team session is now completed. The flipcharts with the SWOT analysis will be displayed again during the next session. The Business Idea diagram will be in need of cleaning up, and needs to be redrawn in an orderly way, with minimal cross-overs etc. The facilitator undertakes this as preparation for the next part of the meeting. The result at this stage may look typically as shown in Figure 23, which is an example of a first-stage Business Idea diagram. This diagram shows the usual convention with boxed items indicating Distinctive Competencies.

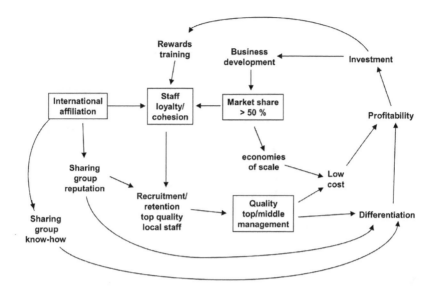

Figure 23. *First stage Business Idea diagram*

Step 8. Review of the Business Idea

After reconvening the management team needs to consider the results obtained so far. To allow members of the management team to prepare for this part of the discussion the facilitator may want to circulate the cleaned-up version of the Business Idea diagram in advance of the meeting. Normally the rearranged picture indicates areas for reconsideration, and the facilitator should be prepared to make numerous changes as requested by the team. During the meeting these are discussed and incorporated.

Having made the necessary changes the management team needs to test the results obtained. The first test is against the strengths and weaknesses developed in the SWOT analysis. This gives rise to the following questions:

- Have all significant strengths been reflected in the diagram, if not why not?
- Can the Business Idea overcome any structural weaknesses identified?

A useful trigger question to open the next part of the discussion is the following: "If we, as a management team, swapped places with that of our best competitor, what would we do to eliminate the Competitive Advantage of the company we now belong to?"

In the final analysis it is the distinctiveness that determines the quality of the Business Idea. We already discussed the "devil's advocate" question. A more fine-grained final test – called the 3E test (Marsh & van der Heijden 1993) – is now made:

- *Emulation:* How easily could the competition emulate our Distinctive Competencies? Not only must a company have more than one Distinctive Competency, it should have competencies in more than one category of distinctiveness. If this is not the case the Business Idea is weak and easily subject to competitive onslaught.
- *Emigration:* Will customers move on elsewhere and seek new satisfaction from other products having properties our offerings do not possess in adequate measure? What do our scenarios teach us on the possible evolution of societal scarcities in the future and the consequences for customer behaviour?
- *Erosion:* Can our Distinctive Competencies be eroded by neglect, by the passage of time, by the normal course of business?

Step 9. Drawing Out the Essentials

This completes the second team session. The facilitator has another task before the Business Idea articulation exercise is completed. In most cases the resulting Business Idea at this stage has become too complex. The systemic nature of the concept is fundamental and it is crucial that the Business Idea is understood as one whole, rather than as a collection of many elements. The human mind cannot simultaneously retain more than some seven concepts (Miller 1956), and the number of elements in a workable Business Idea diagram should, if at all possible, be reduced to this order of magnitude. There are ways of reducing the number of elements. Very often a rather more complex idea can be reduced by combining elements, or replacing them with other concepts, which look at the situation from a higher perspective.

This tends to prove rather difficult to do in a plenary session, and it is recommended that the facilitator drafts a proposal in advance for subsequent scrutiny and approval by the management team. For example, the above diagram might be simplified without losing anything essential as shown in Figure 24.

In this example the essence of the strategic thrust has now been condensed to three elements:

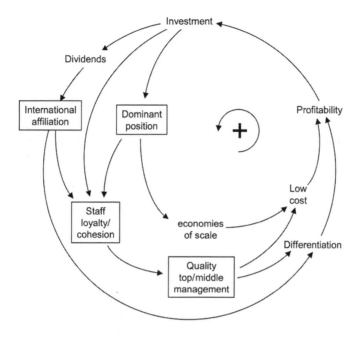

Figure 24. *Reducing the Business Idea to its essentials*

- Investment in people to retain status of most attractive employer and to achieve "best in class" management.
- Maintaining a dominant market position by continuous investment, as the basis of retaining a cost leadership position (economies of scale) and to support status as most attractive employer.
- Using international affiliation as a source of differentiation in the market (brand) and to support status as most attractive employer.

Step 10. Strategic Repercussions

Having reached this stage the facilitator brings the result back to the management team in their next strategy meeting for discussion and final agreement. The analysis so far looked at the Business Idea against the situation in the past and the present. Can the result serve as a powerful leading principle for the future as well?

In order to consider this the management team confronts the Business Idea developed so far with the opportunities and threats identified in the SWOT analysis:

● Does it constitute a strong basis from which to exploit the opportunities?
● What would happen if the threats identified were to become reality?

Ideally, this part of the discussion requires the scenarios as testbed (see Figure 25). If the Business Idea exercise is undertaken as an isolated project, without further scenario-based planning, the question has to be dealt with intuitively. Even so, the team must be prepared to think in terms of multiple equally plausible futures. What do multiple scenarios teach us about possible evolution of societal values and consequent customer values and behaviour? Will the distinctiveness portrayed in the Business Idea be relevant and functional under these possible future circumstances?

The outcome of this deliberation may be to indicate that the Business Idea stands firm as the basis for future business, allowing the discussion to move on to the question of how it can be exploited to best advantage.

Alternatively a Business Idea, even one which has proved to be successful in the past, may not stand up to these questions, and the management team may decide that it needs to be developed to create a better fit with the future business environment. This may be because

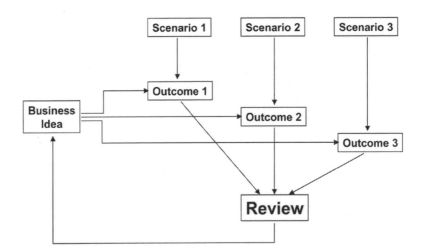

Figure 25. *The Business Idea considered against scenarios*

structural weaknesses or threats will undermine it, or because there are not enough opportunity areas to exploit it. (In the example above, possible new and well-funded competitors may threaten market dominance. Or the company may have reached a relative size where further development is no longer possible etc.)

If the fit is less than ideal the management team need to address the question of how the Business Idea can develop in a direction to make it more robust. In case of a significant misfit the foregoing steps need to be repeated. But this time rather than looking at the past the team will want to look at the *desired* Distinctive Competencies and Competitive Advantage to create a better fit. For example, has a long-standing Distinctive Competency inadvertently been allowed to decline and must it be reinvigorated? Or can fit be improved by careful nurturing of a dormant Distinctive Competency whose time has now come? Or can an existing Distinctive Competency be used to create a new more relevant one?

During this part of the discussion the facilitator needs to remind the management team frequently that the only foundation the company has to build new distinctiveness is its existing Distinctive Competencies. The following important point from Part Two needs to be projected frequently in the management team: "Future corporate success is based on future distinctive strengths, but these can only develop from existing Distinctiveness. Development of Distinctive Competencies comes from internal renewal, nothing else. Specifically it cannot be bought (except possibly for a price that negates all future rent)."

In our example there are a number of important Distinctive Competencies, which can be leveraged, namely group affiliation, staff loyalty, quality of management and dominant position in the market-place. What new Distinctive Competencies can be developed by exploiting these, which are more robust in the future? For example, can the affiliation and staff resources be used to branch out in a new direction? Or can the size-based economies of scale be used to create synergy in a possible merger or takeover deal? And so on.

When a conclusion has been reached it is useful to express the results of the discussion in terms of qualitative strategic objectives. These can take two forms:

- If the existing Business Idea is seen as a good basis for future business development, objectives will be formulated in terms of existing business areas to be further developed or new business areas to be entered where the Business Idea can be exploited. The direction will be towards doing more with what the company has got.

- If the existing Business Idea needs development, objectives will be formulated in terms of the development of new unique capabilities and competencies, to be created in the company by the leveraging of existing Distinctive Competencies.

The facilitator will ensure that the conclusions are recorded on a flipchart and that the wording is agreed all round.

With agreement in the management team the current strategic thrust has become clear. It has been comprehensively discussed and documented, and can serve as a source of coherent management action.

Reinvention of the Business Idea will require more than a few workshops with the management team. It is the domain of generative scenario-based planning, aiming for new and unique insights in what is happening in the business environment, on which a new Business Idea for the future can be based. An isolated Business Idea exercise as described here is useful if it leads to the conclusion that the result forms a firm basis for future development. If the result is weak, requiring a significant revamp, the Business Idea exercise must be part of a bigger generative scenario–planning project, as the basis of the entrepreneurial invention process required.

THE FACILITATOR

Facilitators need to prepare themselves carefully, and approach the project as a programme of action learning. Many aspects of the job have to be learned through participation and experience. Examples of these include:

- Being sufficiently clear about the concepts used and the schemas of the conversation
- Being ready with mini-lectures or explanations as the need arises
- Working iteratively, going deeper at each step. Using fast prototyping
- Having confidence in the process and a successful outcome
- Having sufficient "weight" with the team to be able to steer the discussion as required
- Being able to keep the conversation going, and not getting stuck in detail.

This type of process is often foggy and messy at the start. Having the confidence that this type of process will always lead to a result that is experienced as valuable by the client team is a key success factor.

SUMMARY OF THE BUSINESS IDEA SURFACING PROCESS

Following preparation of a database, by means of a round of interviews or a SWOT analysis, the process of articulating and analysing a Business Idea in a management team consists of the following steps:

1. Articulation of business fundamentals.
2. Identification of Competitive Advantage.
3. Addressing the devil's advocate question.
4. Mapping of causes of Competitive Advantage.
5. Closing the circle of the prototype Business Idea.
6. Identifying the Distinctive Competencies.
7. Finalising the prototype diagram.
8. Vulnerability analysis, testing and reworking of the Business Idea (3E test, SWOT).
9. Drawing out the essentials.
10. Considering strategic implications.

This process is the sort of entrepreneurial thinking that a management team can only do for itself. This job cannot be delegated or farmed out. What has been achieved at the end of it is that the team's current success formula has become clarified, and can now be challenged against scenarios of the future business environment. The model to be tested has been designed, the next job is to design the test conditions.

Once the Business Idea has been tested and found robust against a range of possible futures it articulates what is really important, forming the basis of the strategic direction, which will be taken. The rest of the strategic management process can now be focused. Priorities have become clear. Strategy is the art of making choices. There is no better tool for this than the robust Business Idea. It is holistic, shared and focused on the essentials.

Chapter Eleven

Competitive Positioning

A STRUCTURED DISCUSSION IN THE MANAGEMENT TEAM

Having developed its Business Idea, management needs to consider its distinctiveness against competitors in more detail. Here we move on to the "playing field" (the transactional environment) where the organisation can influence what is going to happen. It is a true "game" situation with all players having interest in and power over the outcome. All are trying to figure out what competitors are going to do, in the full knowledge that competitors are doing the same in the opposite direction!

In competitive positioning, as in most other things in management, knowing what is strategic is the key question. The focus must remain on the fundamental driving forces of success as expressed in the Business Idea.

Top management will normally want to approach competitive positioning at a generic level, approaching it from a top-down perspective in the following six areas:

- Identifying the customers we are competing for.
- Testing business definitions.
- Identifying the competitors.
- Competitive cost driver analysis.
- Competitor response profiles.
- Summarising the most important competitors.

One member of the team needs to take responsibility for organising the discussion. In many cases a facilitator can be useful. The most senior report to the marketing manager is one possible choice. Data and some analysis will be required, mostly from marketing, but also from other areas of activity. In each of these areas the main conclusions should be summarised on a few flipcharts. These are the basis of the discussion in the management team. Findings are presented by the facilitator or by the analysts who can provide back-up information.

The issues worth exploring must not be interpreted as a series of logical steps, which, following one after the other, automatically lead to specific results. Achieving a favourable competitive position cannot be the result of a mechanistic methodology. It requires creative insights, generated during discussion of important aspects of the competitive situation. The six issue areas indicated should be seen as six perspectives on the competitive situation, the discussion of each being capable of triggering new and innovative ideas anywhere. Once again notetaking during such discussions is one aspect that needs careful attention, to ensure that ideas do not evaporate as quickly as they come. The availability of data is a perennial issue. Data may be a particular problem where a management team are analysing a new entry. However, even in such a case a format such as suggested here will help to meaningfully structure a discussion in this important area.

Issue 1. Identifying the Customers We are Competing for

Every competitive positioning exercise starts with identifying customers who are the subject of the competition being analysed. Their views, values and scarcities must be articulated before it is possible to make a judgement on the relative position of those competing for their favour. This issue has been addressed conceptually in terms of the competitive advantage driving the company's Business Idea. This now needs to be analysed a bit further.

Identification of customers is mostly relatively straightforward, by considering who are "the people who pay our invoices, and make the buying decisions". In most organisations it is not possible to review every individual customer. Therefore customers need to be categorised in groups that bring together those who respond in similar ways, and who require similar attention and treatment from the company. Appropriate segmentation of the business is a critical first step. This involves grouping customers on the basis of who they are, their value system, their needs and how they are served.

This is a perennial issue as many business units serving customer segments have grown incrementally over time to exploit potential synergies between existing businesses and new activities. In this interlinked organisation structure segmentation may be justified on the basis of the geographical area of operation, features of the customer groups served, types of (augmented) products, or the technology used to produce products. The question to be addressed here is the following: Does the segment clearly represent a specific customer choice, which drives profit potential and competitive focus? Addressing this question requires consideration of the issues listed under step 1, page 195, but now in more detail. The ability to step into the shoes of the customer and feel the pressures on them is a key skill here.

Normally, management has a good intuitive grasp of the commercial situation. Therefore the job is best tackled using a common-sense approach.

Issue 2. Testing Business Definitions

However, there are markets where customers are distant and ill-defined and where it is difficult to differentiate the offering. These are known as commodity markets. When the company operates in such a market taking the buying decision as the primary driving force can focus attention away from the key stakeholders in the success formula. For example, in a mining company the ability to make a profit may depend more on concessions and the powers of concession/franchise holders than on the favours of the buyers of the product (e.g. oil companies defining themselves in the business of providing a service to host governments, page 129).

A helpful notion is the "competitive moment of truth" when the die is cast concerning the allocation of future business, margins, profitability and competitive success. Normally this occurs when the consumer of the product decides to buy from the company rather than from someone else. In that case competition is for the favours of the consumer. However, in the mining example above the buying decision is effectively made for the consumer. The moment of truth is the supplier obtaining exclusivity of access. In that case competition is for the favours of the concession giver, who becomes the prime customer.

The management team needs to identify the customers being served in these broad categories. This needs to follow the exploration of the "moment of truth" question, in order to identify those categories of customers, which are less than immediately obvious, though crucial for an appropriate business definition.

All along, a powerful instrument for choice is the current Business Idea. This identifies the most important elements of uniqueness on the basis of which the company intends to compete. Segmentation needs to be done such that real or potential competition in the areas of Distinctive Competencies is clearly identified.

Issue 3. Identifying the Competitors

Having identified the main groups of customers, many managers will consider identifying the competitors a straightforward question. They will argue that if you are not aware of your competitors they are not really competing. However, the question can be cast a bit wider than those competitors who are out there in the market trying to take customers away from you. First of all the management team need to think about *potential* competitors, who can come from two directions:

- New entrants into the existing market.
- Substitute products, existing or new.

Most companies know how to deal skilfully with existing competitors. But potential competitors are not so visible, their competition may not yet be felt, and it is easier to overlook them. This is why they are doubly dangerous, and require awareness and preparedness on the part of the company (Christensen 1997). The first need is for their identification, and this should be attempted here.

Having included potential competition the management has not yet delineated the complete playing field. Its margin may be competed for by other players, which would normally not be classified as competitors, but who have potentially the power to affect the outcome of the competitive game. These include:

- Suppliers of goods and services.
- Buyers of goods and services.

Companies buy in part of their requirements. It is interesting to consider the position of the company vis-à-vis their suppliers in competitive terms. Sometimes suppliers are not very powerful, and if the company is unhappy with the service it may switch over to another supplier. On other occasions there is only one supplier and the company has to deal with them. In that case it will be much more difficult to strike an attractive deal and a larger part of the potential margin of the company ends up with the supplier. It shows that suppliers compete with the company for the overall margin obtainable, and it depends on the relative power of each player where the balance will fall.

The same situation applies between the company and its customers. If there are many buyers, and not too many suppliers, the company is in a strong negotiating position, and buyers will have to accept the deal on offer. If the company depends on a very small number of buyers, the latter are in a much better position to get a better deal. Therefore, as with suppliers, buyers and the company compete for the overall margin and the outcome will depend on the relative power of both players.

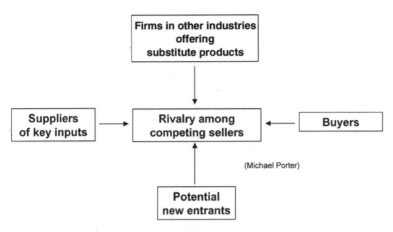

Figure 26. *The five-forces model of competition*

From the above we can identify five categories of competitive forces, known as "Porter's five forces" (after the originator of the concept, Figure 26). In summary they are:

- Rivalry among existing competitors.
- Potential inroads from new entrants.
- Potential competition from substitute products.
- Relative power of suppliers.
- Relative power of buyers.

It is useful to assess the relative importance of each of these forces and identify a few to focus on. Once again, the discussion needs to be framed by the Business Idea. The question to be discussed relates to the way customer value creation and Distinctive Competencies could be threatened or otherwise affected by competitors, new entrants, substitute products, suppliers and buyers.

The discussion in the management team focuses on the ideas generated. But while discussing the five forces the participants will consider specific examples of players in each category. These examples should be carefully recorded on a flipchart as they come up. At the end of this exercise the team should end up with a list of important players and have a good feel for the relative importance of each competitor.

They should now divide these into two categories, "immediately important" and "to be dealt with later". For practical reasons not too many should end up in the first category. A degree of prioritisation is required here, and everyone in the team needs to understand that not everything can be resolved in one fell swoop. After some negotiation a shortlist should be prepared which is the basis for the further analysis.

Issue 4. Cost Driver Analysis

Relative costs vis-à-vis those of competitors is always a major issue in competitive analysis. Cost analysis is particularly important in the more mature stages of a business when products are perceived in the market as commodities. In such markets price competition often dominates and lower-cost companies have the upper hand. In a commodity business the Business Idea is likely to be based primarily on a cost-related competitive position.

Relative costs cannot be discussed usefully in the management team until some analysis provides the basis for it. In the following paragraphs we discuss a few of the most important analytical approaches to be commissioned by management to provide the necessary input to the management review.

Some cost categories are more important than others and a good way to develop a picture of relative levels is by developing a company cost chain (sometimes called a value chain, see e.g. Porter 1985). The purpose of this is to identify the main cost elements to focus on in the discussion.

The principle of the overview is that costs are allocated only if they can be argued to be directly incurred by the activity (i.e. not incurred if the activity does not take place). No arbitrary allocation should take place. If costs are incurred to benefit more than one activity it should become an overhead item. However the task is approached, a compromise needs to be struck between interesting, but paralysing detail, and undue simplification which renders the analysis uninformative.

The next step is to compare one's cost position with that of the main competitors identified. An estimate is made (and presented in the same format) of the cost chain of important competitors and any significant deviations from one's own position are worthy of consideration.

Focusing on the main cost items, cost drivers need to be defined and analysed. Improving the relative cost position is based on finding an advantageous position for the cost drivers. Examples of some of the most important drivers worthy of consideration include:

- Price paid for raw materials.
- Differences in age and efficiency of plant and equipment.
- Productivity.
- Economies of scale.
- Economies of scope (shared activities, cost synergies).
- Learning effects (e.g. the "experience curve").

- Differential wage levels.
- Logistics differences, geography, productivity, working capital.
- Differences in marketing costs.
- Mark-up differences.

Cost analysis is often too extensive a task to discuss exhaustively during one management team meeting. In that case the discussions serve the purpose of highlighting areas of importance, and the task of completing the analysis will have to be commissioned for presentation during the next management meeting.

Issue 5. Competitor Response Profiles

The next part of the competitive positioning discussion relates to behavioural characteristics in the competitive market. Behavioural competitor profiles are closely related to their organisational culture, and these are worth studying carefully. This can often be mapped simply by listing the main behavioural features, e.g. see Box 11.

The analysis is driven by considering the following questions:

1. Offensive

- Do they take the initiative for strategic change?
- What are their probable moves?

Box 11   Competitive behaviour comparison

	Company A	**Company B**
Nature of competitive thrust	Based on few major investment decisions	Based on day-to-day control of investment mix
Decision-making process	Slow committee analysis	Frequent individual decisions based on intuition
Organisational structure	Complex	Simple
Personnel	Matrix Consensus Long-term career Generalists Risk aversion High quality	Functional Authoritarian Short-term career Profit orientated Entrepreneurial Specific experience

---

- How serious are their intentions?
- What are they likely to gain?

2. Defensive

- How vulnerable are they to offensive moves, or to environmental change in general?
- What offensive moves would induce retaliation?
- How effective would retaliation be?

3. The battleground

What are the market segments or strategic dimensions where competitors are:

- Ill-prepared (in skills and competencies)?
- Least enthusiastic (in goals, in emotional attachment)?
- Frozen out, by committed position?

Issue 6. Summarising the Most Important Competitors

The essence of successful strategy is in being different from others. Unique features of a company are expressed in its Business Idea.

Therefore, the final step involves relating the findings of the competitive positioning analysis to the Business Idea. Having specified the behavioural profiles the following questions are addressed for each main competitor, and/or the market in general:

- Who are our competitors now?
- How are they competing with us?
- What does this tell us about our Business Idea?
- How can we change this to be more effective?
- If we change who will be our new competitors?
- How can we be effective in relation to these new competitors?
- Where will our competition be coming from in five years' time, 10 years, 20 years?
- What does this tell us about our Business Idea?
- What new Distinctive Competencies will we need to develop?

After having analysed each of the important competitors in the context of the Business Idea the discussion may be summarised by creating a table with competitors listed vertically and Distinctive Competencies laid out horizontally. Each of the boxes should be considered and where it is felt that a real threat exists this should be annotated, e.g. with a "W" for weak; a "SS" for strong, short term; "SL" for strong, long term. In this way the company team analyses the really crucial competitive questions around their basic formula for success at a holistic level. In the final analysis the debate is about:

- Are our Distinctive Competencies really unique?
- Do competitors pursue the same or different ones?
- Could our Distinctive Competencies be under threat from existing or new competitors?
- If so, what do we do about that?

Viewing the competition in such broad terms encourages rethinking of the nature of one's business and the strategies being pursued.

SUMMARY OF MAIN POINTS OF COMPETITIVE POSITIONING

At the end of the competitive positioning discussion the management team will have considered some or all of the following:

- Identification of main customers, and reframing of the business definition based on the "competitive moment of truth" question.
- Identification of main competitors, not only existing but also potential competitors and others competing for the overall margin and profit potential.
- Analysis of the main cost drivers and the position of the main competitors along this dimension.
- Competitor response profiles.
- Competitive overview indicating the main areas of threat to the company's Business Idea.
- Learning from best practice, both in and outside the industry.

The result of this analysis should improve understanding of the strength of the company's Business Idea. This is based on a system of Distinctive Competencies, and the question of distinctiveness can only be tested vis-à-vis the existing and potential competition. It is likely that following this analysis, the management team may want to revisit the Business Idea to incorporate the lessons learned from the competitive analysis.

Chapter Twelve

Scenario Development

As we saw in Part Two scenario projects can be categorised as either adaptive or generative. In adaptive projects scenarios are used to evaluate the existing Business Idea of the organisation, and to adapt it for the future. In this case building scenarios and using scenarios are somewhat separate activities. In generative scenario work the two are intertwined in an iterative approach in which structuring of scenarios alternates with in-depth research of the questions raised, until a new and unique entrepreneurial insight about the business starts to take shape. Adaptive scenario-based planning is a linear process, generative scenario-based planning is iterative. In terms of scenario development the two types of projects tend to follow a similar path in the early stages. The difference is that the adaptive project comes to a programmed conclusion point, while a generative project may require an unknown number of further iterations. We will discuss the steps in their initial sequence and come back on generative iteration at the end of this.

In this chapter we assume that the facilitator has developed the scenario agenda – areas in the outside world that need to be looked at in the scenario project – preferably based on a series of in-depth open-ended interviews and anchored in an articulated and carefully tested Business Idea representing the organisation's success formula. The attention now turns to the outside world in which this Business Idea will have to perform.

We have argued that a productive scenario-based planning project must under all circumstances remain relevant to the client. The specific scenario agenda will ensure that this is the case. On the other hand not much is gained if the process does not change the client's thinking. Scenario-based planning is the methodical thinking of the unthinkable. Rather than trying the impossible task of guessing exactly what is going to happen, people building scenarios head in precisely the opposite direction. They look for uncertainties. This means that clients need to find in the scenario project an element of novel thinking in areas where they are concerned and anxious.

Having set the scenario agenda the next task facing the scenario planners is to facilitate the development of new insights in the indicated areas where new thinking needs to be developed.

SCENARIO TEAM

Developing new knowledge on the basis of the identified scenario agenda requires active involvement of a "scenario team". The selection of the team members is important. Scenarios will focus on business issues, which are multi-disciplinary, and this needs to be reflected in the composition of the scenario team.

Before the team is selected it is useful to identify the stakeholders in the project. Not all stakeholders are necessarily represented in the scenario team, but they are all potential candidates. In particular the stakeholders with considerable power over the situation are strong candidates. In addition it may be useful to consider participation by experts with subject knowledge that will be relevant and other individuals who can help in opening up the discussion and introduce new perspectives. Before inviting participants it may be useful to remind oneself why people might want to participate. Possible reasons include obligation, fashion, wish to influence, gain support, get access to data and learning, promote an "ideology". The selection process must also consider how the choice of specific candidates might damage the project, through overcomplication, manipulation for own ends, bringing the project into disrepute, or creating feelings of rejection in those who are not invited.

It is increasingly popular to spread participation wider than just members from the organisation involved. Large-scale multi-stakeholder national scenarios are examples. We also see an increasing number of projects with client/vendor participation.

Creating the optimal participation is one of the crucial project design tasks, following the situation analysis and task mapping, mentioned earlier (page 164). Other decisions need to be taken on many subsidiary aspects of the project, including:

- Timing of participation events
- Briefing required
- Appropriate "language" to be used to ensure effective communication
- Selection of suitable facilitator personnel
- Access to specific methodological literacy, in three areas:

- Driving force analysis and scenario development
- Research on systemic analysis and understanding
- Interaction with participants
- The desired level of formality in the modelling of underlying understanding
- Creating an atmosphere akin to a "methodological culture" around the project.

The decision on who should participate cannot be finalised until the project design is completed. On the other hand the project design depends on the question of who is to participate. For this reason the facilitators responsible for the project design may need to iterate a few times through the above steps, until there is a good fit between participation and design. Until this point has been reached the designers need to keep an open mind on who is to participate.

The scenario team's task, once selected, is to look for rich data about the external environment that might illuminate the agenda, and subsequently structure this for further use. The job for the team is to introduce novel thinking. Members need to be able to suspend disbelief, think the unthinkable, and let intuition flow freely. This requires tolerance for ambiguity. The collection and development of outside knowledge needs to be approached with an open mind. During the entire project team members must take what they observe at face value, refraining as much as possible from putting a structure and judgement around observations, until the structuring phase has been reached. They must remain open for surprises.

Once the team has been selected, and before the scenario work proper starts, the facilitators should encourage a discussion on team dynamics. An important umbrella theme is the degree to which the team members share values around the project. A degree of "shared values" in the team is an important condition for success for the project. If we can't pin that down we know we are fighting an uphill battle in keeping the project together. It is worth the team spending some time considering this. Assuming that some shared understanding can be developed on "the common cause why we are all in it" four subsidiary questions about the team are raised:

- What sovereignty do the team members have in the project domain – what levers can they pull?
- How does the team define its agency – what responsibility are the members prepared to take on?
- How would the team define its identity, and how would they want to be seen by the outside world?

- What does the team need from the outside world and how can it reciprocate?

Even if this discussion does not lead to sharp definitions at this stage it can be very helpful in making people aware of the larger context in which the scenario project has to be placed.

A successful team will develop novelty in their thinking. But this needs to be meaningful in relation to the set agenda. The most important challenge in this work facing the scenario planners is to find the optimal balance between:

- Relevance to the client, and
- Novelty.

INTRODUCING NOVELTY

The client interviewees will be the first to provide ideas and insights. Obviously the client will have thought a lot about the business situation and there will be rich information to get. However, as we saw, scenario builders use the client's agenda as a starting platform only, from which they need to take things further in a process that tests, reframes and generates ideas. The scenario planner needs to try to find new ways of conceptualising the agenda area. Although the "maverick" internal view in the client team is helpful here, normally much of the search for innovative thinking needs to take place outside the organisation.

How does a scenario team go about creating novelty in their scenario work in areas relevant to the client? Where does one start? In principle there are various ways of going about attempting to discover new insights, including reading and carrying out original literature research. But experience has shown that the practical way of producing a "eureka" experience in the minds of the client is through interaction with people who can reframe the situation. They are known in the scenario world as "remarkable people", normally abbreviated to RPs. They tend to have studied areas related to the scenario agenda, but are also capable of thinking in the "adjacent space" (see page 58) to come up with new insights. RPs are distinguished from "experts". They are not so much authorities of the official wisdom in a given field. Instead, they need to be people who are very good "throwers of curve balls"; people who can look at the same old dots and connect them in new ways. They are selected on the basis of their power to reframe the discussion at the crucial point in time. That requires some knowledge of the domain, but even more important is a free-thinking style, and intelligence to use it productively. As they are not part of the organisation's existing network they can contribute new insights.

How to look for people from whom such an original contribution may be expected. Typical traits the team are looking for:

- Standing out from others by the resourcefulness of their minds
- Masters of their fields
- Keen, unending curiosity
- Idea generators
- Accessible
- Constant attention to the way the world works
- Acute observation
- Unique insight
- Pushing the edges
- Already living in the future.

They may be academics, commercial researchers, writers, artists, consultants, or perceptive business people. They can come from anywhere.

Literature search and asking around are ways to start. An organisation that has institutionalised its scenario-based planning will maintain a dynamic list of potentially useful RPs. Whenever a scenario project is undertaken and the client's scenario agenda is identified, the list is consulted for possible candidates for the RP role. Normally at this stage the scenario team splits up in subgroups, each dealing with one scenario agenda theme. The job to be done entails:

- Finding the RP and introducing him/her to the issue.
- Eliciting a first contribution, possibly in the form of a written paper of what the RP believes (s)he can contribute.
- Followed by a workshop in which the RP engages in a conversation with members of the scenario team and the client organisation.

Participants to these workshops should prepare themselves by studying the issue area, doing their own reading and internalise all this. On the basis of this a discussion is held in which the new and unexpected views of the RP are elicited, challenged and developed. Capturing of the conversation is once again crucial to retain views as they emerge (and otherwise quickly evaporate) in the give and take of the discussion.

Typical questions for discussion include:

- What is happening that matters/could matter?
- What is the relevant system to study?

- What is the appropriate level of "granularity" (detail) of observation?
- What are other ways of looking at this?

The purpose of the team is to source as many new and relevant ideas as possible.

The scenario team needs to refrain from structuring the information obtained while this search is going on, to avoid closing the mind to further new and unexpected promising lines of thought that might present themselves. This is not an easy thing to do as it often leads to a feeling of information overload. However, scenario planners need to remember that creativity at the time of scenario development requires a degree of overload. They need to develop a tolerance for this. It is helpful if scenario planners set themselves in advance a clear date on the calendar when search stops and structuring of findings will start. Before that date the discipline should be maintained that everything will be considered as potentially worthwhile.

All this makes it all the more important that members of the scenario team train themselves to record any findings, however seemingly small and insignificant. All members should carry a field notebook with them at all times, in which observations are noted down. It has proven useful for scenario planners to regularly take time off to annotate what has been written down to ensure that the crux of the observation is understandable later on. Instilling a notetaking discipline in a scenario team is one of the most difficult things to manage. People find this very difficult to do. Scenario planners beware!

DEVELOPING THE SCENARIOS

Overview of the Scenario Building Process

The scenario team should set themselves a date on the calendar when the team switches from collecting/developing knowledge to making sense of and structuring/integrating the new knowledge acquired by means of scenario construction. This date is important if a delivery date has been promised to the client. But the awareness that this will be done at a predetermined time also helps the team to tolerate the uncontrolled accumulation of disparate ideas and insights before that time.

When the cut-off date arrives the scenario team has developed a considerable amount of data pertaining to the future. They have surfaced the perspective of the client interviewees, and explored novel ways of looking at it, through the eyes of the remarkable people (RPs) consulted. They will now feel a degree of overload, with many ideas concerning the scenario agenda competing for attention, without any significant structure so far.

The next challenge is to find a suitable structure in which all this seemingly unrelated data can be expressed, contextualised and thereby made operationally useful to the user, for the purpose of idea generation and testing of strategy. This is akin to an artistic task. McLuhan once suggested that "for the artist, information overload becomes pattern recognition. What the average person sees as increasingly unmanageable complexity, the artist sees as a new figure/ground relationship, and tries to get that into a form the average person can cope with." This task is not far from what the scenario planner needs to achieve at this stage. Ted Newland describes it as follows: "If you want to get answers frustrate very intelligent people and they will find them. In scenario-based planning, if you frustrate people for a few days the subconscious takes over and you awake to find the scenarios are there. The subconscious is more powerful than the conscious mind at this task. However, it will not intervene until it has been frustrated." Tolerance for overload will help in dealing creatively with the task of scenario conceptualisation.

How to create the necessary structures around the data collected? The principle of the scenario method is to interconnect this data in various ways in a number of causally organised "stories". The main decisions to be made are which data will be packaged in which story, and how the data will be connected up causally within each. This means that we have to decide on how many stories we will tell, and what will be the organising principle of each story. We have to cluster the data down to a point where such a structure becomes visible. At that point the irreducible categories become the organising principles of the scenarios.

How can this category clustering be done? There are a number of principles we can bring to bear on this process:

- The number of scenarios in the set will be 2, 3 or 4. At least two scenarios are needed to reflect uncertainty. More than four has proven to be counterproductive and organisationally impractical.
- Each of the scenarios must be plausible. That means that they must grow logically (in a cause/effect way) from the past and the present and reflect current knowledge.
- They must be internally consistent. That means that events within a scenario must be related through cause/effect lines of argument, which cannot be flawed.
- They must be relevant to the issues of concern to the client. They must provide useful, comprehensive and challenging idea generators and test conditions, against which the client can consider future business plans, strategies, and direction.

- The scenarios must produce a new and original perspective on the client's issues.

Except for these general rules the scenario planner has flexibility in deciding how the stories will be built, what ends up in what story, and what organising principles will be applied to cut up the territory into individual storylines.

We will discuss various ways of processing a large collection of unrelated data and ideas into such scenarios. Some are more formal than others. But in any scenario project the tools are there to help, they should never stand in the way of intuitive leaps of imagination in the scenario team. Our process suggestions should be taken as a handrail, which has shown its worth in practice, for the less experienced to hold on to. Use them while they feel useful, but if you have another and better idea feel free to follow that.

Scenario structuring mostly takes place in workshops, which ideally should take place away from the daily workplace. A typical workshop requires the scenario team to work together for a period of two to three days as a first step. This may be followed with further more focused workshops of shorter duration later, as required. At this stage no outsiders are involved, only permanent members of the scenario team. If possible the team may want to arrange for a permanent central recording workroom, with plenty of display wall space where progress in thinking is recorded and displayed for all team members to inspect and reflect on. This should be available to them until the end of the structuring phase.

A FEW USEFUL DEFINITIONS

In the rest of this chapter we will be using a few terms frequently, which are listed and defined here.

Business factors (or business variables) describe those relatively obvious, relatively close-in issues that shape organisational success or failure. They include, for example, elements as we have discussed in the context of the Business Idea.

Environmental aspects are the broad categories of knowledge about the business environment that need to be considered. Examples include the STEEP categories, politics, demography, economics, technology etc.
Environmental factors (or variables, or forces) are contextual variables related to environmental aspects driving business factors. If business factors are the causes of success or failure, environmental factors are the

causes of the causes. They are less obvious, and often remain off the radar of planners. Examples include role of middle class, work ethic, investment climate etc. Observable changes in society, politics, technology, art etc. are the symptoms of underlying forces. Surfacing them is achieved by asking "why?" repeatedly. For instance, high unemployment is the result of such factors as the rate of productivity improvement. Where to stop asking "why?" is a pragmatic matter to be decided by common sense. Instead of clear chains of causality what will emerge is a "web" of inter-related environmental factors. This web will not be static, but evolve. Over time new factors will be added, existing ones combined and/or replaced etc.

Megatrends are the observable results of several environmental forces. For instance, globalisation and outsourcing are megatrends in the business environment. These result from a number of environmental forces, such as increased complexity and improved communications. The main characteristic of a megatrend is that it is not a "primitive" of analysis, but rather the result of several forces, which might change in their relative importance or even direction.

Critical uncertainty is a "place holder", or a role, for an environmental factor, labelling a dimension of the situation that emerges from a prioritising process as most important and most uncertain. If they are used in a framework (such as a 2×2 matrix) to distinguish scenarios in the scenario set from each other they are called *scenario dimensions*.

Driving force is a "place holder" for an environmental force, driving a possible outcome of a critical uncertainty. A driving force has a relatively high level of explanatory power in relation to the situation being looked at.

Scoping outcomes are a set of (preferably not more than two) specific outcomes in the horizon year of driving forces, which together bracket the range of uncertainty in the driving force. For example, "taxation" could reach anywhere from x to y%.

Horizon year is the chosen cut-off time of the scenario stories, and can be used as a point on the time axis from which the scenarios look back to tell the "history of the future".

Identifying megatrends, environmental factors and driving forces is an iterative process. Some megatrends are already observable today. Uncovering and analysing their driving forces is the basis for identifying new megatrends. For instance, combining driving forces in new ways and alternating their direction may give rise to new megatrends. Identifying the potential for such new megatrends early on or even prior to their emergence is of course of the greatest value.

The megatrends serve several purposes. First, by relating driving forces to observable changes, they help to gauge the relevance of driving forces. Second, they can be used more readily in communicating scenario work. Driving forces can appear very abstract, whereas megatrends are more tangible. They can thus more readily inspire product ideas and in general help managers in discovering new business opportunities. Third, they help to bundle driving forces in an important step towards scenarios.

FIRST DATA ANALYSIS

Initially collected ideas tend to be highly unstructured across a large spectrum of levels of conceptualisation, the result of a typical brainstorming situation. In the structuring phase the first task is to create some degree of overview of what initially seems chaotic.

For this it is necessary to perceive the connections between business and environmental factors in the total system (surprises often arise from seeing a new interconnectedness in the system). This will lead to understanding of the driving forces in the system. Soft data will prove as, if not more, important than hard data.

Once again graphical techniques can be of considerable help here. A simple approach based on the use of Post-it displays was discussed in the context of interview analysis under the heading "Setting the Agenda" in Chapter Nine, The Practitioner's Art, page 184. At this stage the purpose of this technique is to cluster ideas and arrive at a smaller number of higher-level concepts, which can be related to each other.

A good point to start is for the team members to write down, in bullet form, points of learning and discovery obtained during the knowledge development phase, and express these as variables or factors that are uncertain in the situation under review. If the team has been disciplined in notetaking this should be a simple, albeit laborious step, which each of the team members undertakes individually before arriving at the workshop. Once again text on each Post-it is limited to only a few words, which should be legible from a distance. In addition the team members are asked to specify two "scoping outcomes" for each of the factors expressed on a Post-it. This is an important step providing clarification of what is meant and forcing people to express their ideas about environmental aspects as factors. For example, "the economy" is an environmental aspect, but when scoping outcomes are specified as "between 1 and 3%" the economy is pinned down to "GDP growth rate". At that point you have got hold of the underlying factor.

The scoping outcomes provide an important insight into how people interpret the situation. For example, a critical uncertainty might be specified as "the possibility of a strike". The obvious scoping outcomes might be "there will/will not be a strike in the next 10 years". But the outcomes could be different, for example "there will be a strike, but the uncertainty is when; it might happen next year or the conflict may drag on for another three years". In the second set the fact of the strike is predetermined, and should therefore feature in all scenarios. The environmental factor should be changed to "the speed with which unrest escalates".

During the workshop each of the team members puts up the Post-its they have developed, in no particular order, while explaining the short labels and the scoping outcomes to the other members of the team. The scoping outcomes are displayed in a separate area, away from the uncertain environmental factors.

When all team members have done so the job is to try to find logical clusters in the uncertain environmental factors. This is done by moving the Post-its around. Once again there are no rules on what constitute suitable clustering criteria. Intuition should be given free reign. Clustering may be based on patterns, cause and effect, association etc. However, at the end the team should have created a limited number of clusters, which logically contain the elements put into it, while being clearly distinguished from the other clusters. A good test whether a suitable result has been achieved is if the clusters can be given clear short names, indicating that the clustering criteria that have emerged can be articulated. Causal loop diagramming, using influence diagrams (see below under "Driving Forces"), is an effective approach to having a conversation about how the variables inside a cluster hang together. Of course, more than one map may be made showing different perspectives on the world.

Each cluster in turn should now be studied in some depth. The purpose of this step is to identify driving forces. Recall: a driving force is a variable with a relatively high level of explanatory power in relation to the data displayed in the cluster.

Historical Study

Part of the work at this stage should include analysis of the historical behaviour of important variables that the knowledge development stage has thrown up as potentially interesting. It is useful to look back as far as the scenarios will look forward, to ensure that these will constitute a seamless continuation of history and present trends.

This continuation depends on the interpretation put on historical developments. For this reason a set of different scenarios can be seen as a set of different interpretations of what is happening in the present (see also Figure 12 Principle of scenario building). Earlier (page 99) we discussed the example of the interpretation of economic downturn. If this is seen as an economic recession the scenarios will show a recovery in a few years. On the other hand, if economic problems are attributed to decline of the indigenous manufacturing industry, for example due to low wage competition from newly developing countries, activity will stay at a low level in the medium-term future. Historical research needs to find such possible interpretations, which are the basis of the continuity in the scenarios. Therefore the analysis needs to be in some depth, and should consider such factors as typical rate of change, major driving forces, elements already "in the pipeline" and cause-and-effect relationships. Typical questions raised at this time include what are the key driving forces and causal relationships in the system, which forces can be predicted to be there in the future, and what are the important uncertainties about the future. From time to time the question needs to be raised: "What are other ways of looking at this?"

Activities the team might engage in during this stage:

- Listing the key patterns and trends.
- Mapping of causal relationships in influence diagrams.
- Listing of the underlying driving forces.
- Ranking of driving forces by unpredictability and by impact on the strategic agenda.
- Listing of the candidate branching questions based on critical uncertainties.

As a result clear and deep understanding needs to be developed of how the system works and has worked in the past. This will include understanding of predetermined elements and critical uncertainties in the system.

Driving Forces

The team now needs to study the underlying factors in each of the clusters developed above in "First Data Analysis" in more depth, using systems concepts. We are inclined to believe in the continuity of trends rather than in their reversal. We need to overcome this tendency by studying underlying driving forces. Discontinuities can be discovered by systematically asking what would happen to a trend if one or several of its driving forces would suddenly change. For instance, the removal of trade barriers is a driving force for the globalisation of business. Political changes may result in a sudden reversal of trade policies. Considering the driving forces in this way facilitates an exploration of sources for discontinuities, which might otherwise be ignored. There are, of course, other potential reasons for discontinuities. New driving forces may suddenly emerge, for instance, as the result of technological innovation. By creating an evolving "web" of interacting driving forces, it helps us to find gaps, or to think of new forces by association.

In Part Two we described the "iceberg" analysis, a metaphor for understanding the underlying structure of the situation by inferring patterns and trends in the events that are observed. By documenting such a discussion in the form of an influence diagram this underlying structure can be surfaced and used later.

This starts with the articulation of a number of key variables, considered important for the situation being considered. The next step is the development of simple influence diagrams around these variables. Kemeny, Goodman and Karash (1994) suggest that this step can be facilitated by first drawing simple graphs illustrative of the variable's behaviour over time. There should be no attempt at this stage to quantify, only the type of movement should be shown (up, down, stable, cycling etc.). While addressing the question why these movements might occur the influence diagram is drawn up. Initially this will bring new variables into the discussion. This may trigger further ideas about what might be important. Therefore the list of key variables is revisited, and the process repeated.

For example, assume that political instability is an important issue in connection with the situation at hand. The scenario team will be interested in discovering some underlying structure in what is going on. The first task is to surface and list observed events. Following that the task is to try to establish trends over time in some of the underlying variables.

For example, the team might be considering the outlook for violence. They may decide that they can see a trend that can be expressed in a graph of how violence has been changing over time. Let us assume that it is increasing. The next question would be "What other events do we see that might be related?" Ideas come to mind, the state of the economy plays a role, media coverage may seem important, and so on. What would be the relation with media coverage? Someone might argue "More cameras mean more violence." What would be the relation with the economy? How do we express economy? Someone might suggest "level of personal income". Another idea may be unemployment. More unemployment leads to more violence.

Other ideas for related variables might include government control, with government interference in the economy seen to be on the increase. These could also be expressed in simple graphs against time.

In this way trends emerge and while the team are discussing these they start identifying elements of structure. For example, the idea that media coverage means more violence is an element of structure, a cause/effect relationship. They now could start drawing an influence diagram in which media coverage contributes to violence, indicated by an arrow from one to the other. Another variable identified was the economy. Someone might suggest that performance seems to deteriorate and the suggestion presents itself that this might be related to violence. Low incomes and high unemployment might increase violence. Another suggestion was government interference. This raises the question whether this is a cause or an effect. Someone might suggest that violence leads to polarisation in society, which leads to state repression. Meanwhile it might be suggested that foreign investments might suffer, which drags down the economic performance. If violence increases this may well lead to a flight of capital, causing further economic deterioration. What emerges here is known as a reinforcing feedback loop, which underlies all growth phenomena. At this point an interesting influence diagram starts emerging (see Figure 27) representing an upshot of the discussion so far.

Later we will discuss the question of the granularity of the analysis. In this type of preliminary analysis the level of detail is important. Too much detail and the explanatory model becomes too unwieldy, too little detail and it may become impossible to find any explanatory variables. For example, assume that someone suggests that historically people resort to violence because groups become threatened by sudden change: but this might imply that the problem may move from one group to another over time. The conversation might continue: "It's group A who are now creating the violence, whereas previously it was a different type of violence, triggered by a different opposition to the then status quo. There's a difficulty there with one straight line indicating violence, while we are looking at two violent groups following each other in time. They are not one phenomenon. You cannot explain all violence in terms of the causes presented so far, whether it is media coverage or unemployment. The earlier deaths occurred when there was less media coverage, they have to be explained by a different group being violent for different reasons. It is more complex than you have it so far."

And so the diagram grows and insights develop.

The example illustrates the three levels at which we can look at the world. At the event level we talk about the occurrence of violence. By plotting the number of deaths we defined a variable and we looked at a

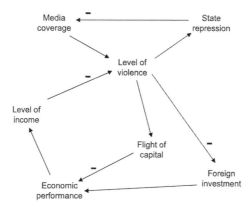

Figure 27. *Starting an influence diagram*

trend. Every trend implies a variable. While we were doing that we started to map out the underlying structure by seeing patterns. By looking for patterns we discovered that looking at violence just as one statistic was too simplistic, we needed to look at different groups at different times. This is what is meant by identification of driving forces. It involves moving from events down to the level of trends and patterns, and from there into the structure, to identify the forces that fundamentally affect the situation. While going down into the iceberg the quality of the discussion improves significantly.

The above example illustrates the use of an influence diagram, see Figure 27, in which variables are linked by arrows indicating the influence they exercise on each other. The example above shows how, in order to develop such an influence diagram from a cluster, the analyst distinguishes events from variables. Variables should be capable of going up and down over time. Check whether putting "an increase in" in front of it makes sense. It makes sense to speak of an increase in violence, but in front of "the fall of the Berlin Wall" "an increase in" does not make sense.

The analyst tries to identify trends over time and expresses this as variable behaviour over time. An explanation is then sought for this behaviour. Why would variable X be going up, and Y be going down? Such explanations provide insight in what is driving what. Once this has been established another link in the diagram has been uncovered. The activity is continued until everything in the cluster has been accounted for.

Variables that play a central role in such a system are likely to be critical uncertainties. For example, a scenario team was discussing whether demand was an appropriate critical uncertainty. One of the members suggested that demand might itself be driven by technological development, which would therefore be a more basic driving force. In order to consider this suggestion the team drew up a simple influence diagram as shown in Figure 28. Having considered the structure of the influences identified the team decided that it needed to consider both technological development and deregulation as independent driving forces in the analysis.

In summary, systemic analysis of the surrounding world looks at the situation in the following steps:

- Break down the database in events, trends, patterns and structure.
- Specify the important events, the phenomena we can see.
- Discover trends, time behaviour we observe in the events, leading to the conceptualisation of variables.
- Infer patterns, based on cues for causality applied to variable behaviour.
- Develop the theories, which connect the system together through causal links (multiple structures will be required, resulting from different possible interpretations of causal patterns).
- Use the theories to project future behaviour (with multiple structures leading to multiple scenarios).

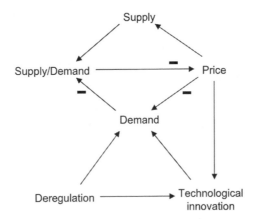

Figure 28. *Example of a driving force analysis*

Driving forces are an important ingredient for scenario development. Both Daimler-Benz and Siemens Nixdorf have turned the identification and description of driving forces into an art in itself. Daimler-Benz prints booklets about driving forces. Siemens Nixdorf has experimented with a special framework to describe driving forces. It includes a description of what the driving forces are, what is happening as a result, what enables or inhibits them, what paradigm they represent, how predictable they are, the degree to which they can be influenced by the organisation and the appropriate time-scale.

Granularity of the Analysis

In the previous section we touched upon the question of the level of detail of the analysis. A significant challenge in this work is hitting the optimal level of granularity. The team are looking for a general pattern, which can be developed into an explanatory theory (or one out of a number of alternative possible theories) of driving forces explaining how things work in general. The key to finding the appropriate level of granularity/amalgamation is to establish the highest level of generalisability.

"Overfitting" the pattern on specific data must be avoided. It's easy to fit the data perfectly, but that makes it difficult to generalise, and the key is to generalise. One must lean towards a fuzzy fit of a somewhat imprecise generalisation, with enough validity to be useful in understanding underlying structure. On the other hand, if events are amalgamated at too high a level the structural relationships between patterns of behaviour may prove too ephemeral.

For example, a scenario team may conclude that explaining the pattern of worldwide demand for gold pitches the analysis at too high a level, providing little evidence of causal relationships with other known variables. On the other hand explaining the demand for gold at the level of every individual gold buyer will not develop a theory general enough to be useful for scenario building. The analysis has to be pitched somewhere between these two extremes. For example, the scenario analyst may decide to break down the worldwide demand into a few categories, including use for technical purposes, adornment, investment and monetary purposes. At this level it may become possible to start seeing some fuzzy relations with other variables, which can be extrapolated.

The process is essentially one of trial and error, around how the world normally explains the phenomena. Experts may be able to provide a starting point, based on the going orthodoxy. From there trying various levels of conceptualisation continues until you start seeing relationships which seem to be sufficiently firm to indicate underlying driving forces. The hard part is keeping it simple. And as we have seen, the more complex and uncertain the problem, the simpler the causal models that prove most useful.

SCENARIO STRUCTURING

So far the scenario team has collected the basic data from which the new scenarios will be constructed, and structure has been put into these by clustering and categorising and by a search for trends and underlying causal structure. The next step is to create a limited number of scenarios in which the insights gained can be reflected. As we discussed in Part Two, storylines are an efficient medium through which ideas across many disciplines can be linked in context. The process we have described so far has ensured that the totality of the data available at this stage is highly relevant to the client and also contains an appropriate level of novelty. The purpose of the next step is to develop a number of internally consistent storylines, which project as much as possible of the learning obtained in the project so far. There are a number of ways in which this can be achieved, which we will subdivide into inductive, deductive and incremental methods. In the inductive method the approach builds step by step on the data available and allows the structure of the scenarios to emerge by itself. The overall framework is not imposed, the storylines grow out of the step-by-step combining of the data. In the deductive method the analyst attempts to infer an overall framework to start with, after which pieces of data are fitted into the framework, wherever they fit most naturally. The difference between the inductive and deductive methods is between letting the framework emerge in the process of building stories from the data upwards, or deducing a framework from the data as a first step.

A third way of developing scenarios is called the incremental method. This approach aims lower and is useful if the client team still needs to be convinced that the scenario approach offers an opportunity to generally enhance the strategic conversation. In situations where scenario-based planning is not yet embedded in the thinking style of the organisation the client team may still be strongly attached to an "official future", a shared forecast that is implicitly the basis of all thinking about strategy. For such a client the first steps on a scenario-based planning road are facilitated by using the official Business-As-Usual future as the starting point, from which the scenarios make excursions into surrounding territory, related to issues defined by the client.

The degree to which the three methods produce similar or different scenarios depends on the clarity with which the team has come to see the main uncertainty bifurcations in the future. If there are only a few major overwhelming uncertainties the three approaches tend to produce similar results. Pierre Wack put it like this: "Good scenarios emerge from an intensely experienced polarity." If the team does not have this clear understanding of the main uncertainties facing the client it may be advisable to spend more time discussing the findings and the underlying structure to try to develop a better insight in the crucial driving forces in the future.

Inductive Scenario Structuring

Induction is a process of reasoning by which a general conclusion is drawn from experience or experimental evidence. Reasoning from the specific to the general. The inductive method has been called that because it is based on scenario building from experiential building blocks to scenarios, from the more particular to the more general.

Inductive scenario structuring can be done at the level of events or at the level of structure. Event structuring starts with team members turning the understanding and new insights gained by the scenario team into illustrative events which are recorded on an event card, with annotations for possible timing and actors involved (see Quinn & Mason 1994). Cards also show clearly whether the event is seen as predetermined or as one pole of an uncertainty (scoping outcome, see page 227). Predetermined events need to end up in all scenarios, while uncertain events are included in only one. If events contain predetermined elements as well as uncertainties this is reflected by representing them in multiple event cards. For example, if it is considered predetermined that OPEC will set a production ceiling, but it is uncertain at what level that will be, then more than one card is generated, for example one with the ceiling set at 30 million barrels per day and one at 25 million barrels per day. The team then needs to make sure that one of these cards is part of each scenario.

The next step is for the team to start building scenarios from the events generated by putting them in time order. Some cards are bound to form a natural cluster while others seem unconnected. In that case the team will start different scenarios, so that both can be accommodated. The jigsaw puzzle is finished only when all cards have found a natural place in one of three or four scenarios. The team invents new events and generates new event cards while it is allocating events to scenarios in order to create connections and complete the overall logic. This is necessary to ensure that the final scenarios all meet the requirement of internal consistency, i.e. events should causally follow from each other. The team will test this by drawing causal arrows between event cards on the display board. In this process the events come first, the logic follows from putting them in time order, and implying causal relationship. After a number of iterations this tends to produce satisfactory scenarios that reflect team learning during the earlier scenario process. When the team members are satisfied that no further progress can be made the scenarios are named and an overall framework is inferred from the storylines as generated. This is often easier said than done. A problem with the inductive method is that the scenarios that emerge rarely have a clear or elegant relationship to one another as they come out. Identifying the overall framework normally requires a lot of additional thinking and reshuffling. Early on it is not easy to tell the weeds from the useful plants. It takes strong facilitation, and a group that is patient enough to deal with the ambiguity and uncertainty of not knowing how to distinguish the weeds from the plants until the very end of the exercise.

The inductive method can be applied at the level of logic. In this approach understanding gained during the preparatory phase is expressed in bits of logical relationship. The vehicle used is a short part of a story, connecting up a few events through a cause-and-effect relationship. These logic fragments have become known as "snippets". They are often generated by interpreting influence diagrams developed by the team.

A typical snippet might indicate that increasing inflation affects the level of business confidence, which in turn affects the level of investments. Or a level of cash generation beyond absorptive requirements would lead oil producers to reduce production levels, which would increase the price. Or prosperity accelerates change, especially in real estate. If the current boom continues another decade, it will put enormous pressure on building turnover. The activity of generating snippets usefully alternates with alternative expression of the situation in influence diagrams, in an iterative process. This type of approach requires sufficient time to be spent on the prior analysis of data, and the articulation of driving forces.

Once diminishing returns are reached in this the snippets developed are written on cards. The next step is for the scenario team to allocate these cards to three or four piles, on the basis of intuitive clustering. Once this has been achieved each of the piles is sorted and turned into an overall story logic. This is achieved in the same way as in the event method, by implying a time dimension and sorting the cards accordingly. In the process of doing so new events or snippets are generated to make the story hang together better. For example, someone might suggest linking the OPEC with the inflation snippets. If demand goes down then production goes down, cash generation falls below requirements, and the pressure is on to produce. This has the interesting effect of lowering prices, reducing cash generation further. In the longer term lower energy cost will lead to reduced inflation, and recovery in the consuming countries. In this way snippets are chained together into storylines. The approach differs from the event-driven process, in this case causal logic generates events, rather than the other way around.

While the inductive method is capable of producing powerful scenarios the team needs to be on guard for the in-built danger that the scenarios end up in a "good/bad mode". There seems to be a natural tendency for developments considered favourable for the client to cluster in one scenario and the unfavourable events in another. This is highly undesirable and significantly reduces the value of the scenario exercise. A basic tenet of the scenario-based planning methodology is that all scenarios are equally plausible. The best set of scenarios contains only futures that the client will find worth preparing for. If some scenarios are experienced as too unpalatable for the client to contemplate, or too rosy to be credible, the team needs to make another iteration with this requirement in mind. As a general rule the team should avoid thinking in terms of good or bad futures, see page 128. Only plausibility and internal consistency should be the yardstick for an effective outcome.

Following is an example of inductive scenario construction. In it Adam Kahane describes a project with a group of political leaders in South Africa (Kahane 1992b).

> Some South African political leaders had been struggling to find a common language with which they could talk about the future. In *1991*, an economist at the University of the Western Cape named Pieter le Roux wondered if scenarios would help, and he invited me to facilitate a project. Scenarios were well-known in South Africa because during the *1980s* a scenario exercise led by Clem Sunter, a senior executive at the Anglo-American Mining Corporation, with important help from Pierre Wack, had played an influential role in building public discussion about the future of the country. This project would be different. The scenario team was to include 22 members from across the spectrum of South Africa's diverse constituencies. The multi-racial group included left-wing political activists, officials of the African National Congress, trade unionists, mainstream economists, and senior corporate executives. Our purpose was to investigate, and hopefully develop, common mental models about the future of the country. When we started, many people in the group were pessimistic; they expected to spend the meetings in endless dispute, unable to agree on anything.

Because of the charged political atmosphere, a "visioning" exercise might not have worked here. In fact, at the first meeting I said, "We're not going to discuss what you would like to happen. We're going to discuss what might happen." This turned out to be a liberating choice of words. If I had asked what future they wanted, each participant would have pulled out their party platform. In the end, the process did produce a scenario they all preferred, but they would never have got there if we had started by looking for it. Instead, we were looking for a common understanding.

We started with an exercise that made people realise that they couldn't predict what would happen. Dividing them into sub-groups, we asked them to come up with stories of what might happen to South Africa, seen from the vantage point of 20 years in the future. When we reconvened in plenary, we had 30 scenarios to consider. During the presentations, no one was allowed to say, "That's a stupid story," or, "You shouldn't be saying that." I allowed only two types of interruptions: "Why does that happen?" and "What happens next?" If the presenter couldn't answer those questions then they had to sit down; the story was no good.

It turns out that this is a great exercise. People came up with all kinds of wild stories, including stories inimical to their own interests. For example, one left-wing sub-group proposed a story called "Growth through repression," suggesting that South Africa might have a tough authoritarian left-wing government. Another story suggested that the Chinese government would provide arms and support for a Communist liberation movement, which would overthrow the government. I don't know whether it was originally proposed seriously, but when people asked, "Why does that happen?" there was no way to substantiate it. So it fell by the wayside.

The rest of the whole exercise was a narrowing process – pruning our scenarios from 30 down to three or four "useful" stories. To be useful, they had to be logically consistent and plausible, which are difficult criteria to meet. But the discussion of plausibility and consistency was very good for this politically charged, diverse group.

Then we asked, "Which of these stories are useful to tell to an audience?" In other words, what did participants believe our audience needed to think about? In our plenary group, after much discussion, we narrowed our selection down to four distinct stories, all focused on the nature of the political transition (perhaps the most important single uncertainty in the country), and all named after winged creatures.

The first was called "Ostrich". The De Klerk government "sticks its head in the sand". Some path other than a free election occurs.

White segregationists gain in influence, as do extremist black groups; they stop communicating, and polarise the country. "Eventually, the various parties are probably forced back to the negotiation table," said the group's report, " but under worse social, political, and economic conditions than before." This doesn't work very well: it might lead, for instance, to civil war.

The second scenario, called "Lame Duck", envisaged a prolonged transition with a constitutionally weakened transitional government. Because the government "purports to respond to all, but satisfies none", investors hold back, and growth and development languish amidst the mood of long, slow uncertainty. This was an important scenario because many people expected a coalition government to form, and now they could see the potential dangers.

The third, called "Icarus," ended up being the most influential. Originally proposed by some of the black left-wing members of the team, it suggested that a black government would come to power on a wave of public support and try to satisfy all the promises it made during the campaign. It would embark on a huge, unsustainable public spending programme, and consequently crash the economy. For government and business observers, the existence of the Icarus scenario was a reassuring phenomenon, as it influenced the policy debate on the left. For the first time, a team, which included prominent left-wing economists, discussed the possibility of government trying to do too much. This was hopeful, because only by discussing a potential catastrophe can you prevent it.

"Flamingos" was the most positive of the four. Like Lame Duck, it concerned a coalition government, but this was a good coalition. The name was chosen because flamingos rise slowly, but fly together. In this scenario the economy gets no kick-start. There is a long, gradual, and − most importantly − participatory improvement, with all the diverse groups in the country "flying together". Because the scenario process keeps asking what would have to happen for each future to take place, the group emerged with a sense that this optimistic future, in which economic growth and political equality reinforced each other, was possible.

By the standards of Shell, these were not very deep scenarios; they had little research or quantification behind them. But their significance came from the fact that they were arrived at collaboratively by a very broad group. All members of the team endorsed all of them − not as desired futures, but as valid mental models for how the future might unfold. When they presented the scenarios to other groups and forums, they all stuck exactly to the basic points, even in cases where they disagreed with the formulation.

This has made the presentation of the scenarios enormously effective. When the scenarios were presented to an ANC audience, for instance (nearly always by presenters who include an ANC-affiliated member of the team), it provided a non threatening way to bring up the unpalatable message of "Icarus" – that a crash public-spending programme might not work. The Lame Duck scenario gave the National Party audiences a way to confront the dangers in their inclination to encumber the transition process with safeguards, and the Ostrich had a similar message for the conservatives.

When the team came together, they had no common view on the difficulties of transition. By arguing over the distinctions between Lame Duck and Flamingos, what distinguished Lame Duck from Flamingos, they came to a common view, on a moderately detailed level, about some of the problems around limiting the power of the transitional government. I'm sure that very few of them, before the meeting, had considered the question of macro-economic constraints on a newly elected government. Now, through the Icarus scenario, they were deeply familiar with it.

You may wonder what keeps people, in these highly charged meetings, from walking out. Conservatives and radicals kept coming back because they felt they were learning a great deal – and enjoying themselves. The advantage of scenarios is that, unlike in a negotiation, people don't have to commit their constituents, but they can see a common language – a common way of understanding the world – emerging fairly early in the process. Once the scenario process is over, that common language should make subsequent negotiations easier to conclude successfully.

This exercise shows the potential of scenarios as a foundation for collaborative action, especially among people who are enmeshed in conflict. As writer Betty Sue Flowers puts it, "In a scenario team, you develop two or three different pairs of glasses to see the world through. You can put them on and off, and by doing that, it gets easier for you to see the fourth and fifth way."

Deductive Scenario Structuring

Deduction is a process of reasoning by which a specific conclusion logically and necessarily follows from a set of general premises. Reasoning from the general to the specific. The deductive method has been called that because it is based on scenario building from a general framework to specific scenarios, from the more general to the more particular.

The deductive method aims first to discover an overall structure in the data, to be used as a framework for deciding the set of scenarios to be developed, rather than let the scenarios emerge step by step, building up from the data as in the inductive methods. The deductive framework specifies the scenarios in the set in terms of scoping outcomes of a few (two or three) critical uncertainties, selected as scenario dimensions. These specifications are sometimes called "end-states" (states-of-affairs in the horizon year, described in terms of the scenario dimensions). Having established the basic nature of each scenario in this way they are then filled in from the data available, supplemented with new data as required. Trying to name the scenarios at this stage with one or a few words expressing the basic nature of the storyline is an effective way to test that the team has reached consensus on what this basic structure is.

The framework is developed by study and manipulation of the data in a few stages:

- Grouping of data in a hierarchical structure.
- Identification of high-level mutually independent dimensions at the event, trend or structural level.
- Ranking these on the basis of predictability and impact on the client.
- Selection of the most important as structuring dimensions.

The process starts with grouping the data hierarchically, in a similar way as the interview data are processed (see interview analysis, page 183). Each insight gained during the research period is summarised in a few words on cards or Post-its. The next step is clustering of these notes. The process alternates intuitive clustering with testing of clusters on mutual independence and internal consistency, iterating until every insight has found a natural place in the context of all other notes.

From this point onwards the structuring process can be conducted on the basis of events, trends or structure. Most scenario teams will want to try all three approaches to see which one produces the most insightful framework.

If the event approach is followed the team now needs to decide on a limited number of key events which will have overriding influence on the future. It is often helpful to express these in an event tree, if decisions logically follow from each other. An example is the Mont Fleur scenarios discussed above, where the group agreed that three events seemed to be of overriding importance:

- Will a power-sharing agreement be reached between the parties?
- Will the transition of power take place quickly or will the process of transition get bogged down?

- Will the new government follow sound economic policies, or will it be more populist?

As shown in Figure 29 the resulting four scenarios can be structured in an "event tree":

- If no agreement were reached the "Ostrich" scenario would unfold.
- If the transition got bogged down the scenario was called "Lame Duck".
- If the policies were populist the "Icarus" scenario showed quick development followed by collapse.
- If all these hurdles could be taken the future would develop in the "Flight of the Flamingos" scenario.

In this way a coherent scenario framework can be derived from key events, depending on how these play out one way or the other.

However, it may not always be possible to find a limited number of key events, which have such overriding influence on the future. In that case the team may wish to look somewhat deeper in the "iceberg" for key trends. If the structured data show a few key trends which may compete for dominance in the future the scenario framework may be based on these.

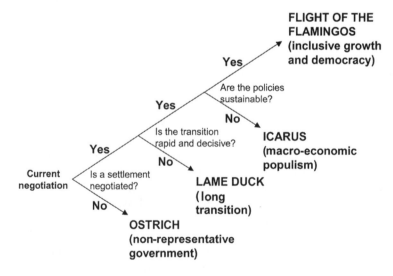

Figure 29. *The "Mont Fleur" scenario structure*

An example of this approach is the 1989 Shell scenario set (Kahane 1992b). Having clustered the data as discussed above the team concluded that developments seemed to fall into two natural clusters, centred on economy and ecology. Analysis seemed to indicate that developments in both of these areas could hit serious constraints, which would have major repercussions on the way the future would play out.

- Parts of the new global economy were clearly developing outside the control of the traditional national control mechanisms; as a consequence overheating could develop out of control, and the world might end up in a depression, following a collapse in confidence.
- On the other hand society was becoming more and more aware of ecological limits, and this might lead to priority being given to restructuring activity, with the possible effect of diverting the economic crisis.

The team concluded that if the ecological awareness trend dominated, attention would move to restructuring of global governance systems, creating significant new investment levels, and leading to the economic confidence being maintained, or restored. But if the economic system hits its limits first, a serious recession would push ecological considerations to the background. One of these trends would come to dominate the other. As a consequence a framework results (see Figure 30) in which two scenarios are indicated, depending on which trend dominates perception in society. The dominant trend would create the scenario driving force, pushing the other into the background to become relatively insignificant.

The third deductive approach is based on identifying two or three key structural variables or driving forces, on the basis of which the scenarios will be distinguished from each other. Expressing each of these driving forces in terms of their dual scoping outcomes will then create a 2×2 (or $2 \times 2 \times 2$ in the case of three driving forces) matrix, indicating four (or eight) scenario end-states as candidates for the scenario set. This approach is only practical if two or three overwhelming driving forces can be identified, as with any more the number of candidate scenarios multiplies exponentially. This means that the team needs to delve deeply into the structural "iceberg" of the data to define those elements that really matter for the future in terms of only two or three driving forces. One of the first examples of this approach was developed by Wack (Wack 1985a) for the French energy business in 1965, where every future uncertainty seemed to be dominated by the two crucial dimensions:

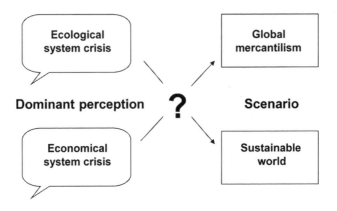

Figure 30. *Scenario structure, based on dominant trends*

- The future of the government regime vis-à-vis the industry ("dirigiste" or "laissez-faire")
- The possibility that nationally significant indigenous natural gas reserves would be found (since then answered in the negative).

The 2×2 matrix is shown in Figure 31.

In another example the environmental factors of "outsourcing" and "flattening of organisations" were causally combined with "scale" to define one dimension with the following scoping outcomes:

- On one end: "dominance of markets by a few global players who directly or indirectly control all smaller companies".
- On the other end: "myriads of small companies stealing away the business from slowly fading giants".

A second dimension combined systemically the factors "economic inequality", "social unrest", and "consumer tastes". This resulted at one end in "a harmonious global segmentation of consumers" and on the other "a violent regional particularisation".

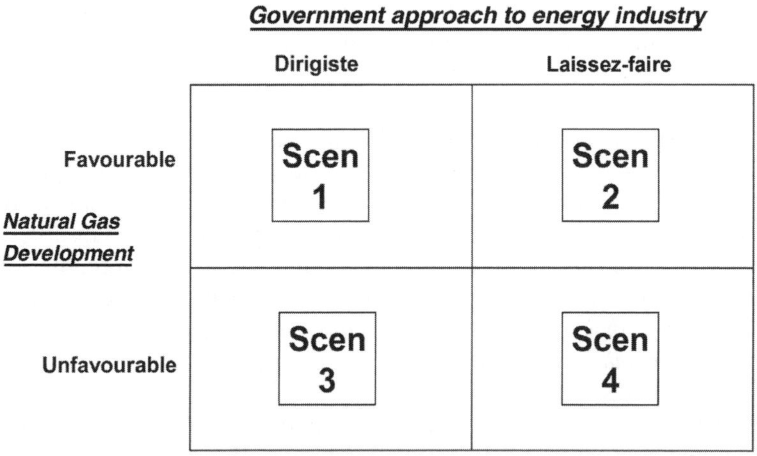

Government approach to energy industry

Figure 31. *Example of a scenario matrix*

The Matrix Approach

Most scenario projects use this "Matrix Approach". It is particularly appropriate in situations of considerable uncertainty, where a few dimensions delineate much of what we know about the situation in the future. This is due to the way that orthogonal uncertainties "add up" (see page 93). We have called these Critical Uncertainties the Scenario Dimensions (see page 227). These are selected on their effectiveness in specifying scoping outcomes that are significantly spread out and different from each other. The scenarios then tell the stories of how the world moved on from history and the current reality to arrive at these very different situations as specified in terms of the scoping outcomes of the scenario dimensions in the horizon year.

Clients find it very useful to see and understand the scenarios in a logical relationship that the matrix provides. But this is not its main purpose. The method ensures that we end up with three or four stories that are as different from each other as possible within the limits of credibility to the scenario user. As a result it makes clients explore more of their business environment space than they would otherwise do. Expanding mental models can only be done within the limits of plausibility. Recall that plausibility is different from probability, it is a subjective notion in one's head, not a mathematical piece of datum. It is based on causality, not on frequency. If a good causal story can be told on how we got there the outcome will be plausible. The matrix method is designed to *maximise the spread of the scenarios in the set within this plausible space.* The team is challenged to think widely, and to produce storylines, with a beginning, a middle and an end, which in its dynamics illustrate the plausible workings and structural inter-relationships of the driving forces.

To maximise scenario spread within the plausible space the choice of the critical uncertainties is made on the basis of their potential impact on the client's situation as well as their relative level of uncertainty. If a dominant driving force is predetermined it cannot be used to distinguish the scenarios in the set. The greater the range of scoping outcomes of a critical uncertainty the more useful it is in a scenario framework.

The natural choice for scenario dimensions are driving forces with high impact and high uncertainty (i.e. large range of possible impact).

Therefore discussion on which variables should be used as scenario dimensions takes account of both impact and level of uncertainty (range of scoping outcomes), and we are looking for those with most impact and least predictability. A useful way to structure this part of the discussion is by using an impact/predictability chart, in which potential candidate dimensions are positioned depending on how the team ranks these on the two characteristics of impact and predictability. The chart is a simple rectangular space running from less impact at the left to more impact on the right, and less predictable in the bottom to more predictable in the top. As we are looking at relative notions here (everything is important, but some things have more impact than others, everything is unpredictable, but some things are more predictable than others) the items should be placed using all space available. For an example see Figure 32. The scenario dimensions we are looking for have to be found in the more impact/less predictable corner.

Before we go on we need to be a little clearer on what is meant here by predictability. On page 229 ("First Data Analysis") we discussed the problem of predicting a possible strike occurring. Recall that the strike as such was highly predictable, but the uncertainty was in when it might happen. This meant that the critical uncertainty is not the strike as such but something like "the speed with which unrest escalates". So do we rank this high or low on the predictability scale? One has to be precise on the question "predictability of what?" Ranking means that we need to be able to bring, if only conceptually, the different candidates back to one common denominator. As we are trying to maximise the range of scenario outcomes the common denominator should be *the potential impact of the critical uncertainty on the client.*

The assessment of the degree of predictability is greatly helped by the specification of scoping outcomes. So in the example one would consider the situation for the client if the strike is tomorrow, compared to the situation that it happens in three years' time. The conclusion may

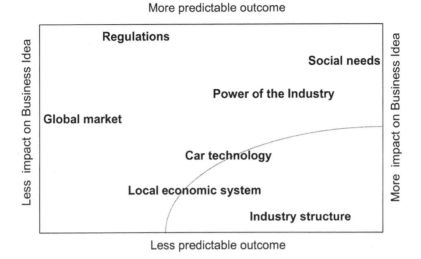

More predictable outcome

Figure 32. *Driving force ranking space*

be that while the impact is significant there is not much difference in terms of the damage done one way or the other, predictability as used here should be scored high. Or you may find that a strike in three years' time is much less serious, e.g. due to new automation in the industry by that time, while a strike tomorrow could bankrupt the company. In that case there is high unpredictability, and this variable becomes a candidate for being a scenario dimension.

Having selected the two most critical uncertainties in this way these are now further specified by working out the scoping outcomes in the horizon year for each one in some more detail. Recall that the scoping outcomes have to be chosen such that they are illustrative of the range of uncertainty in the scenario dimension. These can then be combined in a 2 × 2 matrix as illustrated in Figure 31. This is called the scenario matrix, specifying the essential differences between a set of four scenarios.

The resulting four corners of the scenario matrix pose four questions to the scenario team. In each corner two scoping outcomes of different dimensions are combined to specify a future world. This leads to the four most important questions to ask, e.g. what kind of world would it be in which we have to contend with both high taxes and a fragmented industry structure? Or what sort of conditions could lead to a drop in the price of oil in a recessionary world. It is important for the team to work out these questions in detail to ensure that the understanding is shared. For example, the team can jointly write into each of the four corners a list of keywords that characterise the four worlds. The scenarios in each corner then become the response of the team to these four questions.

The next step is for the scenario team to fill in the detail in each scenario, and to create a story of how the end-state is reached from the current state of affairs, through a series of events, with one event leading to another over time. A storyline over time needs to be developed based on cause-and-effect logic. One way to achieve this is by translating research data into illustrative events, and to record these on event cards, as discussed above under the inductive method. A practical way of developing event cards is by using the scoping outcomes developed earlier during the first data analysis (see page 228). In the deductive method the basic scenario structure has already been decided, and event cards are allocated to one of the four scenarios where they fit most naturally.

A helpful feature of the matrix approach is that the team can now be broken up in subteams each developing one scenario. The matrix makes clear up front the type of future each subteam addresses and what should be left to the other teams. It helps them to focus more. The subteams arrange the cards in time order, to create the storyline, filling in new detail wherever this is helpful to create a satisfactory story.

The more successful the team is in identifying truly *orthogonal scenario dimensions* the better the resulting scenario framework can encapsulate the findings from the scenario research process. This will allow the team to better explain their findings and show new ways in which history and present developments can be interpreted. This will help the client to get on top of the business environment through reframing of traditional mental models, and to test, and if necessary challenge, strategic plans for the future.

The way scenarios are developed deductively, through the selection of key scenario dimensions, helps in avoiding scenarios in the "good/bad mode", but it can still happen. Therefore the same test needs to be made as suggested for the inductive approach. If it is found that the scenarios call up very different value judgements (positive or negative) in the client group it is worthwhile making another iteration with this criterion in mind. All scenarios should reflect worlds in which the client would want to live and to prepare for.

A word of warning. An illusion that the matrix fosters is completeness. "We filled all four corners. We've boxed the future." But the biggest unknowns are those uncertainties the team hasn't even considered, those that are not on the mental map of the group building the scenarios, the uncertainties we have called the unknowables. Unexpected events will happen. This is why organisations need to think about an ongoing action-learning approach to scenarios, instead of one episodic scenario building project. This is where monitoring/early warning systems and iteration become important, and where the organisation engages with its environment on an ongoing basis, and slowly but surely starts noticing the "differences that matter".

The Incremental Method

In situations where scenario-based planning is well established the deductive and inductive methods are the preferred approaches. They offer the best opportunities for generating new thinking as a contribution to the strategic conversation. However, not all client teams are ready for this type of approach. For example, in a situation where scenario-based planning is just being introduced the client team may still have to be convinced that it offers an improvement over the traditional forecasting method, and that it is cost effective. Very often interest in the scenario approach will have been created by means of a "challenge scenario" (see page 270), but there may still be a strong attachment to the shared Business-As-Usual forecast of the business, the "official future". A lot of time will often have been invested in this and once it has been accepted as the agreed plan, people who want to open this up again are not always welcome. This is the world of management as described by Lindblom (page 31) where decision making is a negotiative business, and where people are expected to stick to an agreement. Mavericks are not welcome here.

The scenario team needs to tread very carefully here, if they want to avoid being rejected altogether. In such a case the incremental method may be indicated. This takes the official future as the starting point. The team first tries to identify the major issues and threats that people are concerned about in relation to the official future. Typically these are threats or bottlenecks or, sometimes, looming opportunities that define, by themselves, the logic of a scenario. They then build the scenarios around these, one scenario per issue. The incremental method is sometimes called the "threat approach". Finding flaws in the official future does not normally prove too difficult, as forecasting methods do not force analysts into in-depth analysis of driving forces. Extrapolation will always lead to obvious inconsistencies if it is stretched out far enough into the future (see below under "Phantom Scenarios").

Superficially what the scenario planners are doing may look to the clients as what they will know as "sensitivity testing". However, the scenario planners will make sure that there is a fundamental difference, namely that alternatives will not be conceived as variations in a single business variable, but as variations in underlying driving forces, and that each scenario will be conceived as an internally consistent story on that basis.

The first step in this approach is for the scenario team to analyse carefully the official future scenario. Specifically the team needs to establish the degree to which this can be considered as internally consistent. This requires two specific analytical jobs:

- Trend analysis. In this step the analyst tries to identify trends that can, in the long run, undermine the structure on which the forecast is based, because of the existence of a breaking point or threshold in that trend. They can be surfaced by considering similar events in the past and/or by extrapolating trends, implied in the official future, further out, until they clearly hit such fracture lines.
- Actor logic. In this step the most important stakeholders in the official future are identified, and the forecast is analysed from the perspective of each of these. The question here is whether the forecast is consistent with the logics of the actors in the game.

If the official future violates the requirement of internal consistency in either of these categories, the first alternative scenario will be an adjustment to the official future addressing this problem.

The team then ranks the major issues and threats that are of concern to the client and selects a few that are of strategic importance. For each of these a driving forces analysis is carried out as discussed above under the deductive method. Having identified the structural relationships between these the scenarios then are designed as illustrations of how this structure could drive futures that are different from the official future. The challenge is to surface the logics that point to or may even define the nature of the issues identified. For example, a strategic issue could be triggered by market vs. regulatory logic in which the issue for the company would be market competition on the one hand and political manipulation on the other.

It needs to be remembered that all this remains very much "thinking within the box" and will not lead to any fundamentally new insights. Everything starts from the existing Business-As-Usual mental model and already existing concerns about strategic issues. The incremental method will structure thinking and make the situation mentally more manageable, but scanning the horizon for entirely new developments and opportunities will require the outside-in thinking of one of the other approaches.

Selecting an Appropriate Method

Which approach is appropriate in which situation? In addition to personal style of the facilitator, and time available for the project, diversity of thinking and tolerance for ambiguity in the client group seem to be important. But the ultimate criterion is the purpose of the exercise.

The value of the deductive method, and the matrix approach in particular, is that it has the potential to jog the team's intuition in a way that leads them into scenario territory that they would not otherwise visit. The inductive approach does not do that to the same extent, it allows the team to stay within the comfort of taking one step at a time. The deductive method is more challenging, as it is designed to push the scenarios out towards the edge of the plausible region. This is important because it is there that the group discovers what they don't know yet, where they articulate the questions they are struggling with and become specific on what needs to be researched. If the purpose of the project is to learn more about the situation this is the way to go.

The deductive method is the most analytical, it offers the best opportunity to explore widely in areas where the thinking would not otherwise penetrate, and it has a strong outside-in emphasis. In situations of strong groupthink where thinking outside the box is an important objective of the project the deductive method is indicated. If the client group thinks cohesively, and has difficulty in widening thinking, its more regimented nature helps to force the thinking into new areas.

This makes it suitable for "sense-making" projects. Deductive scenario building, incorporated in an iterative learning process, can potentially make major contributions in long-standing intractable problems. Its unique feature is its combination of (1) integrative analysis across multiple disciplines that scenarios bring, with (2) in-depth research within individual disciplines where the world has stored most of its knowledge.

The deductive method has the potential of leading to new entrepreneurial inventions if it is built into a wider iterative learning process where scenario building alternates with in-depth research into the questions raised in the scenario building. As we discussed earlier there is no successful strategy without original inventions. If the purpose of the scenario project is to develop new strategy this is the approach worth considering.

It also offers a more codified step-by-step approach than the inductive method. If time is at a premium and it becomes necessary for the facilitator to force the pace it has distinct advantages.

On the other hand, if the emphasis is on conversation, exchanging views and building accommodation and consensus the inductive approach is more productive. It is more engaging than the deductive method, when people often find themselves drumming their fingers during the "driving forces" discussion. Up to the moment of excitement when the analysis leads to a new understanding of critical uncertainties the conversation often feels vague, promiscuous, and "so what". Not so in the inductive approach.

A divergent client group, or a group with a high degree of tolerance for ambiguity, often does well with the inductive approach. The method exploits the diversity in the group to the maximum, and enriches the scenarios by providing scope for a wide range of views to be incorporated. Groups that have difficulties compromising and coming to joint conclusions often do well with the inductive method. However, the method, if done well, cannot be forced, and suffers under time restraints.

If the purpose of the scenario project is mainly processual, related to group dynamics and behaviour, the inductive method is indicated. It is engaging and motivating and it brings people's thinking together. On the other hand it does not have a clear-cut end-point or end-product. It can go on for ever.

The incremental method is indicated if the client still needs to be convinced of the worth of the scenario method. In such a case the deductive method may seem daunting and the inductive method too ill-defined. Often a client team has over time developed a shared understanding of the environment, embedded in an official future, and feels an intuitive reluctance to open this up for scrutiny. In this situation the thinking process needs time to evolve. The scenario project becomes a first step in a learning process in which the client team discovers the value of outside-in thinking. In such a case the incremental method is indicated.

Therefore the selection depends on the purpose of the scenario project. If the purpose is analytical, such as making sense of a puzzling situation or developing a new original insight, the deductive method is indicated. If the purpose is associated with people, conversation, engagement, team building, consensus building, the inductive method is superior.

In many cases facilitators use more than one approach. Often client teams started off on the incremental or inductive methods run into time constraints, and switch to the deductive method to finish the job. Or teams working through the incremental or deductive methods may halfway decide to take stock of the range of thinking in the team by doing an inductive scenario exercise. Switching of methodology during the project can enrich the process, and should be considered an option by the facilitator at all times.

An Example, Inductive and Deductive Methods Compared

Interestingly the two methods often lead to the same or similar scenarios. This may be indicative of a strong inherent structure in the situation imposing itself on the thinking of the team. This is illustrated in the following example.

Some time ago a group of senior Canadian public servants and private-sector executives got together to discuss the issue of how to organise and govern successfully in a world of rapid change and increasing interconnection. They decided to adopt the scenario methodology to structure their conversation. After inviting a number of interesting people to discuss the theme with them, they met for a workshop for the purpose of structuring their findings in a few scenarios. The following description is an excerpt from Steve Rosell's account (Rosell 1995).

After an initial introduction an essentially inductive process was adopted to develop a set of scenarios for how the information society might shape the environment for governance over the coming decade. Prior to the workshop, we had worked in smaller groups to identify some of the major certainties and uncertainties in how the environment for governance might evolve. Early in the workshop we reviewed the reports of the small groups and synthesised these.

Then, working individually, we were asked to write snippets, short causal sequences describing how several of those key elements might develop. An example of a snippet: education focuses on information technology skills → surge of young people entering information industries → Canada becomes key player in software. We were encouraged to write the snippets in telegram style. The next step was to break into 3 small groups, which worked to combine the snippets that their members had produced into several longer story-lines. Those were given a name and presented to the plenary session.

We then worked together, in plenary, to organise these bits of story-lines into an initial set of scenarios. Each of the snippets was written on a yellow adhesive Post-it note. The story-lines were constructed by stringing together sequences of these notes. As the story-lines were presented in plenary and then developed into first-cut scenarios the walls of the meeting room soon became covered with large and lengthening streamers, snippets becoming story-lines, becoming scenarios. In that plenary discussion a generally positive scenario began to be developed, built around such story ideas as a wired world, a new economy and the global teenager, along with a largely negative scenario based on unemployment, social unrest and disintegration. There was also a generally positive middle-range scenario that started to emerge around a combination of reconstruction of the social contract, shared transfer of wealth, life-long learning and world institutions for the environment and peacekeeping, while a more negative mid-range story started to emerge around increased polarisation, the lack of shared myths and identity and decreasing legitimacy of opinion leaders in all sectors. At a number of points in this discussion a participant suggested a possible structure to order the stories that were emerging, but none at this stage received general consent. The process of combining and recombining the story-lines and arguing which made the most sense, and which structures to differentiate the scenarios might be most useful, was complex, fractious, generally good-humoured, frustrating, stimulating and often chaotic. The pivotal moment came when one member suddenly saw a new way in which we might structure the scenarios we had been developing: "It seems to me that the starting point of all these stories is that the information society changes the world. Then there are two dimensions that basically define the scenarios. The first is whether we have had economic growth or not, and the second is whether we have structural change or not. So in the first scenario information technology changes the world, we do have economic growth, and we do make structural adjustments. The result is the scenario built on 'Wired World' and 'New Economy'. In the second scenario information technology changes the world, but we don't get economic growth and there is no structural change and the result is a 'Dark Age' scenario. In the third scenario information technology changes the world, we do get economic growth but we don't get structural change, and the result is a 'Social Fragmentation' scenario, disparity increases, the rich get richer and the poor get poorer. And in the fourth scenario information technology changes the world, but we do make structural changes and the result is a very Canadian form of muddling-through."

Amidst the general agreement that greeted this insight there was a sudden spark of recognition among some members. Some weeks earlier three of us had been reviewing the findings of our first several meetings and trying to determine, through essentially a deductive process, what scenarios it might be possible to derive from that complexity of information. That deductive process had begun by noting that in our discussion of the information economy two polar possibilities had been on the table for the development of the economy over the next decade, either:

- we learn how to use the new technologies to their potential, and embark on a new secular boom, or
- the structural changes in the economy produced by the information age produce persisting unemployment and low or no growth (as conventionally measured).

Similarly our discussion of the social and cultural dimensions defined two polar possibilities, either:

- we manage to find a way to construct a new social consensus, appropriate to the information society, that rebuilds social cohesion and renews the social contract, or
- we face continuing and accelerating social fragmentation and disparities, as the realities of the information age undermine our ability to construct a shared perspective.

These two sets of possibilities, while necessarily over-simplified, had illustrated different ways in which the information society could shape the environment for governance over the next decade, through the changes it might produce in our society and economy. The next step in our deductive process was to try to interrelate these two dimensions. We constructed a matrix with society on one axis and economy on the other, to illustrate the possible environments for governance that might result from interplay of such social and economic changes.

But once we had constructed this matrix we did not know what to do with it, and whether there were viable scenarios that could be devised to fill the various cells. So we had put the matrix aside and did not circulate it. Now, as one of the members presented this structure to the workshop, we all were struck by the degree to which the scenarios, which we had constructed through the inductive process of the last days seemed to fit within the matrix that had been developed deductively earlier. Somehow, the inductive and the deductive routes had led us essentially to the same destination. With this striking realisation, and with the basic structure for differentiating the scenarios now agreed, we broke into four syndicates to develop each scenario further.

DEVELOPING THE STORYLINES

With the general scheme of the scenarios now established the team needs to turn its attention to fleshing out the storylines. The ultimate product needs to be a set of scenarios that compellingly transfers to the user the important discoveries the scenario team has made. The stories need to be provocative, memorable, eliciting a rich imagery. The task before the scenario team is to find a way to develop the most interesting and enlightening stories. Scenario planners should feel free to engage their own creative talents to do this as they see fit. Interest and memorability derive from originality, which should have free rein.

A number of points need to be kept in mind though, while this task is being carried out:

- The scenario is a story, a narrative that links historical and present events with hypothetical events taking place in the future. A story needs to have a beginning, a middle and an end. In order to establish plausibility each scenario should be clearly anchored in the past, with the future emerging from the past and the present in a seamless way.
- Each scenario must elicit a *gestalt*, an integrated structure that can be appreciated as one whole rather than as disconnected parts. The basic logic of each scenario should be capable of being expressed in a simple storyline diagram. Similarly the fundamental differences between the scenarios should be equally transparent.
- Internal consistency implies that each story is based on an underlying structural (mostly qualitatively understood) system. Articulating this is facilitated greatly by the use of influence diagrams discussed earlier, as an explanation of the causal train of events in each scenario. A clear influence diagram of the underlying system involved can be extremely helpful in fleshing out the storyline into an internally consistent result.
- Agreed predetermined elements need to be reflected in all scenarios.
- Key variables need to be quantified and leading indicators listed.

Within these limits there is significant room for artistic inspiration in the scenario team. It is often helpful to consult professional storywriters.

The importance of telling the story must not be underestimated. It's in the twists and turns of a written plot that one observes the workings and structural inter-relationships of the driving forces. And it's also in the twists and turns of the plot that one observes most clearly where understanding is lacking and further analysis would be productive, leading to a relevant research agenda (scenario research is as good as the research question inspiring it).

It is advisable to summarise the scenarios in story-maps in which the main events are shown against a timeline from the present to the horizon year. Events can be connected indicating how one event leads to another.

Identifying the Underlying System

Scenarios greatly gain in strength if the underlying driving system is articulated. Having this at their fingertips will allow the scenario team to answer any "why does that happen" questions. There will in general be different driving systems, one for each scenario. Internal consistency depends in the first place on an intuitive feel for an underlying system driving the story. It is advisable to try to articulate it, to make consistency tangible for the storyteller and the audience. The process of articulation can be taken to various stages. The simplest level involves drawing out the driving forces in an influence diagram, showing how forces exercise influence on each other. As a second stage this diagram can be translated into a conceptual systems dynamics diagram, bringing out the dynamic nature of each variable. A further step is quantification. The purpose of quantification cannot be to simulate reality, which is quite impossible in the social systems considered here. But quantification can help in deepening understanding of the essence of the system, illustrating to an audience how the scenario could come about and should therefore be considered plausible.

The following is a series of steps that will help a team to make some progress here:

- Identify the main story strand of the scenario ("what is the scenario in the final analysis really about?").
- Identify the seven (say) most important key variables related to the main story strand. (Remember: a variable is defined as something that can go up or down, it is NOT an event. Check that you can put "an increase in" or "a decrease in" in front of it, and still retain a linguistically meaningful phrase. So GDP is a variable, so is congestion or level of conflict. An "invasion of Iraq" is not. The overthrow of communism is not. These are events and belong in the story–map, not in a systems diagram.)
- Hand-draw graphs showing the behaviour of these seven key variables against time over the scenario period. The X axis in these little graphs is time, going back in history to show historical behaviour and running to the horizon year of the scenario. The Y axis is the value of the key variable. Just indicate qualitatively when you think the variable will go up and when it will go down.
- Work out an influence diagram that explains the behaviour graphed. Link up the seven key variables and add some if needed. For example, an increase in one variable at a particular time can be explained by the decrease of another some time earlier. That indicates a causal relationship that should be represented in the diagram by an arrow.

- If desired, turn the influence diagram into a systems dynamics model using one of the system dynamics software packages that have made this type of work more practicable. Take a stab at quantifying parameters. Don't prevaricate about this. There is no way of doing this scientifically, so use your intuition. Then simulate scenario behaviour. Compare with your hand-drawn graphs. Notice the differences. Explain what you see. Clarify your thinking.
- Retell the scenario story on the basis of this result, using the model as the driving "engine". Bolt on other strands in the story, consistent with the central driving model. Update the story-map (events linked causally), document what you have done.

Both story-map (the "event against time" schematic) and influence diagrams ("variables influencing each other") are complete representations of the scenario world, but looked at from different viewpoints (time and state). However, the influence diagram represents the type of understanding the client ultimately hopes to gain of the situation through the scenario project. It is this understanding that the scenario client takes away as input into an implications analysis that leads to ideas on what to do now.

Naming of the Scenarios

Scenarios can be important to the client in two ways, they represent different visions of the situation at a future point in time and they represent different views on how the world works. If we focus on the vision for the future we tend to become normative about scenarios, some visions we like better than others. Scenario discussions often end up there, as can be seen from the names of many scenarios that represent such visions. In this way the planner emphasises multiple divergent worlds, which is important.

However, the scenarios also represent different views on how underlying driving forces shape the system. In terms of drawing strategic conclusions this is an even more powerful result that the scenarios provide, representing their different logics. While these logics drive towards the end-visions of the scenarios they also operate now. For example, an immediate response to the scenario might be to watch for leading indicators that are suggested by their logics. End-visions are fantasies, while logics operate now, can be researched and tested, and provide a foundation for action.

It is strongly suggested that scenario names are selected on the basis of the underlying logic, rather than the end-vision portrayed. Through "naming for the logics" we help the scenario client to focus where it really helps, namely where action can be taken.

Quantification

Even where the client organisation does not require quantification the scenario team may wish to do some of it on their own accord, as it is a worthwhile discipline to check for internal consistency. We saw how a Systems Dynamics approach can be used to quantify the story. There are other ways of quantification, essentially testing the new scenario logics against traditional quantification models. Experience has shown that it is highly likely that discrepancies will surface. It is important that the scenario team identifies these discrepancies and decides whether or not these become a deliberate part of the storyline. It is almost invariably the case that even the most logical narrative will require some adjustment if numbers are applied to the developments in the storyline. If time and resources can be made available quantification proves useful in most cases.

Actor Analysis

Actor analysis surfaces inconsistencies by confronting the internal logic of the scenarios with our intuitive insights in the logic of the various key actors in the game.

Actors/stakeholders around a strategic issue can be subdivided in a number of categories, as defined in Figure 33. "Players" require our attention on two accounts, (1) they have a stake in the outcome, and will therefore be motivated to act, and (2) they are in a position to influence what will happen, i.e. have some power to act. People (or groups of people) who cannot influence the situation are called "subjects". They are on the receiving end of what happens in the scenarios but don't influence the storyline. Subjects need to be considered as potential coalition builders, through which their power increases and they gradually move over to the category of "players". Referees populate the contextual environment; these are actors who have no stake in the situation and who cannot be influenced by individual players.

In an "actor test" the team first identifies the most important actors in the business environment considered. Most of these will be intuitively obvious, but category lists such as Porter's five forces (see "Competitive Positioning", page 213) offer useful checklists to generate potential candidates. The next step is to classify them according to the categories

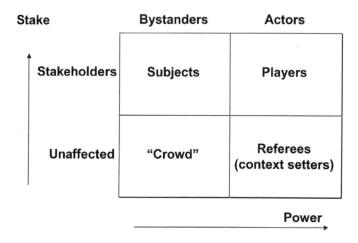

Figure 33. *The actor/stakeholder matrix*

of Figure 33. The team are particularly interested in the category "referees". The task is to test the scenarios against the logic of each of these. The team puts itself in the shoes of each of these actors in turn and, in this role, walks through each of the scenarios, checking whether the detail of the storyline is consistent with the behaviour that might be expected from the actor considered. Almost invariably in this process a point will be reached where the team has to admit that a particular actor will find it very difficult to live in a scenario without taking some action that is not part of the scenario and therefore invalidates it. At this point the team learns something important about the future that would otherwise not have surfaced.

Further actor tests need to be made in the other three boxes, to ensure that no individual actor can logically invalidate the scenarios developed.

Pierre Wack reports an example in his article on the development of scenarios about the future oil price (Wack 1985a), in which testing of first generation oil demand scenarios against the intuitively plausible logic of oil producing countries identified such a possible discontinuity. It was shown that a situation could arise where producing countries would start to question the wisdom of ever-increasing production levels, beyond local capacity to absorb the funds generated. This indicated the need to test strategies against a possible supply crisis, where producers would no longer meet demand, resulting in oil prices shooting up. With more and more money flowing in, this indicated a strong reinforcement

---

Box 12   Stakeholder role play

Step 1

Rank the stakeholders on the basis of their power and interest. Players rank higher than referees. And the latter rank above bystanders.

Step 2

Select the stakeholder that ranks highest, and assign the role to a member of the group. In this way select a role for each member. Allow some time for each group member to consider their role, their interests, their power base and likely attitudes towards developments in the area of interest.

Step 3

Select one of the scenarios. Step together as a group through the scenario, event by event, and consider plausible and likely reactions by the stakeholders at each step. Each stakeholder adds Post-its to the scenario story-map to record important reactions, indicated by their role, which could influence the storyline. Other role players need in turn to consider their reaction to such changes in the storyline, and post new events reflecting their reaction to those changes. Continue until the story is completed.

Step 4

Now sit back and consider whether the scenario storyline still hangs together logically. Consider whether the stakeholder reactions are consistent with the original storyline, or whether there are now clashes in logic. If the latter occurs try to modify the story so that internal consistency is restored.

Step 5

Carry out step 3 for all four scenarios in turn. At this stage people often find that one of the scenarios proves difficult/impossible to reconstruct as an internally consistent story. Feel free to discard one scenario from the set of four on these grounds. Alternatively the group may have to move back further and reconstruct the scenario framework.

---

of the initial decision by the producing countries not to meet all demand. Having identified the possibility and the self-locking nature of such a crisis, the team then analysed its dynamics, and identified the conditions under which it might happen. As we saw, this discovery allowed Shell to prepare themselves for such an eventuality ahead of most of its competitors in the industry.

Actor testing of scenarios is a crucial part of any scenario building process, and should not be skipped.

Use of Experts and "Remarkable People" (RPs)

Apart from carrying out analytical tests as explained above the team can test the scenarios by asking the opinions of other external parties. We introduced the notion of the "remarkable person" earlier in this chapter (page 222). Experts and RPs can be particularly useful in the scenario testing phase. They can look at the preliminary set of scenarios and comment from their perspective on relevance, plausibility and internal consistency.

Such a "validation" step may involve personal discussions or a small half-day workshop involving people who have not participated directly in the scenario development exercise. The draft scenarios should be distributed beforehand so participants can come prepared with comments. The meeting starts with a short presentation/review of the scenarios, followed by a couple of hours or so to discuss the scenarios in turn. This should probe for logic inconsistencies but also allow discussion about specific content items. It can be relatively unstructured and will proceed without much prompting.

Input from people who have not participated in developing the scenarios raises more probing questions than one gets from the original participants who developed the scenarios. This tends to be a simple but highly effective way to make the scenarios more robust. It should be part of every scenario project.

Following the various tests suggested the team reconvenes and reports on learning. Following this decisions are made on what will and what will not be incorporated. They then modify the scenarios accordingly.

Use of Electronic Communications for Scenario Building

Scenario building can make powerful use of electronic communication. Team members do not always have to work in face-to-face meetings, a lot of work can be carried out by a team that is tightly knit together by efficient communication technology. Experience suggests the following points will enable this process to work effectively (Erasmus 1999):

- Diversity (including external people) is strength
- Combine on-line interaction with occasional face-to-face interaction to build trust
- Aim to pull interest rather than push information
- "Fluid" is better than "final", think of things as draft versions
- Use a facilitator to summarise, link discussions, add insights and create focus

- Separate the open, exploratory spaces from the structured, convergent areas
- Use shared knowledge databases
- Archive everything
- Circulate short interim reports to the wider community.

The problem with working from a distance is the issue of attention management. The scenario project will have to compete with other demands for attention in the immediate work environment. In dedicated workshops people can devote all their attention to the project at hand, and influence each other to do so. Considering that the ultimate purpose of scenarios is to find a new unique insight it seems almost inevitable that part of the work will have to be carried out in such dedicated workshops. However, in between workshops a lot of work can be powerfully enhanced by using electronic communications.

NEXT STEPS

In Adaptive Scenario-based Planning

In adaptive scenario-based planning the scenarios are used to "wind-tunnel" (test and develop) strategic options. In this process any consistency weakness will quickly emerge as a major obstacle and the scenarios need to be checked for this. Having come to a satisfactory conclusion the team is then ready to apply the result in the testing of strategic options as identified. We will come back to this in Chapter Thirteen.

In Generative Scenario-based Planning

In generative scenario-based planning the scenarios are not seen as the end-product of the process but as intermediate instruments to guide appropriate research work. As we saw earlier (page 117) the purpose of this iterative approach to scenario-based planning is to develop a new perspective on the situation the organisation finds itself in, with the purpose to come to new and original insights that can serve as the basis of new strategy. Having established the research questions to be tackled the scenarios do not play any further key role, as a new set will be generated at the end of the next iteration. We now turn to the question of how research questions emerge from scenarios and what scenario research entails.

SCENARIO RESEARCH

Most scenario projects include an element of research. The purpose may be, e.g.:

- To increase the level of granularity of the story; which has an impact on the persuasiveness of a scenario is its richness of detail. Hitting upon the right anecdote, the one compelling image is not trivial, but often requires sifting significant volumes of data.
- To increase the depth and dimensionality of driving forces, spelling out exactly what we mean by them. For example, a key driver such as "liberalisation" can be conceptualised in many different ways. The team needs to get beyond a rather vague idea of "freeing up the markets".
- To identify more probable and worked-out dynamics; the dynamics of scenario narratives should delve into a fully plausible nexus of events, patterns and an intricate web of feedback loops that helps the client to understand his situation.

Earlier ("Generative Scenario-based Planning", page 117) we compared generative scenario work with "action learning" where the results of an intervention are compared with what you would expect, based on your prior existing knowledge of the system. Gaps between your expectation and what really happens indicate areas where your understanding of the system is lacking. You now know where to look to improve this understanding. You have generated a research question that can be an effective tool in guiding you in your focused research and learning.

An organisation's understanding of the business environment is such a complex system in which the scenario approach can be used in this way. The scenario planner intervenes in an organisation's strategy by challenging what the organisation thinks about the environment. With scenarios the thinking in the organisation is pushed as far as possible from the Business-As-Usual mental model, to the edge of the plausibility area. The most important result of this is the discovery of what is known and what is not known about the system. What emerges is the strategically appropriate and relevant research agenda. The next step is to research the systemic structures that are inadequately understood (see also Figure 18).

Generative scenario-based planning is about doing a lot of detailed analysis and systemic research and in that way learning about the system driving the relevant business environment. New understanding can only come from deep research. There is no free lunch in scenarios. The crucial moment in generative scenario-based planning is defining the important research questions as precisely as possible. Finding the answer is relatively simple. It involves mostly getting in touch with the relevant experts and RPs. Finding the precise question is the fundamental success factor.

In generative scenario-based planning articulating precise research questions is the purpose of the scenario exercise. Therefore research should mostly *follow* a scenario exercise, not precede it. It is a mistake to expect to do all research before doing the scenarios. Prior research pins down the territory. It is preferable to use the intuitive powers of the group and let the research programme emerge. Iterating between intuition and analysis produces the quickest route to new insights. The project needs to be an emerging "conversation" between intuition and analysis. This is why we talk about generations of scenarios. The first generation scenarios generate the first set of research questions. When these have been answered the newly acquired knowledge has to be integrated by developing the second generation, which in turn generates new and different questions, and so on, until further generations run into diminishing returns.

An Example

The research questions arise mostly while trying to connect the present reality with the stretched-out end-states developed in the 2×2 matrix. Telling that story in some detail is crucially important, because in doing so you discover where you lack understanding of the underlying structure in the situation. For example, consider a recent set of scenarios for a major European airport. The scenario group had chosen as their main dimensions:

- Whether constraints on the level of activity at this airport (which is located in a densely populated area) would persist
- Whether one or more major airline(s) would use it as their main European hub.

This produced three scenarios, as one of the four was considered inconsistent (accommodating a major airline hub within existing constraints). Initially the scenario group did not fill out the scenarios further, and used the three end-states as strategy test conditions. That project was perceived as somewhat less than successful. It is clear that the team at that stage looked at first generation scenarios (or rather end-states) only. It was clear the stories had to be worked out over time. In doing so two major elements emerged as unknowns requiring further study:

- To what extent will the trend towards concentration in the airline industry in Europe persist over the next 20 years?
- To what extent (and at what level) will the hub and spoke system be the most effective way for airlines to make money in the years to come?

These aspects were then analysed thoroughly. In doing so some underpinning structure emerged that allowed the team to understand better what might happen. They found some predetermined elements lurking in this structure that needed to be uncovered to help in the design of strategy. Discovering some systemic features in either or both of these areas constituted a major payout for the project, even though the scenarios were not any longer valid. The team then continued in a second generation round.

The scenario project had allowed the team to avoid wasting time on subjects of secondary importance and highlighted important aspects that needed further work.

So, summarising the discussion so far:

- The purpose of scenarios is to give us an idea of what we don't know and therefore need to research.
- Having learned where our knowledge is lacking, we then have to go and do the research.
- The results of the research have to be incorporated in the next generation scenarios.
- A sound process involves multiple iterations in this way.
- Good projects are measured in months, not days or weeks. Most of the work is systems research.

Scenario planners often stop half-way, developing the scenarios, maybe getting to the right questions, and then failing to carry that through to real new understanding by failing to do the research required. Scenarios alone don't get you there, in as much as just analysis doesn't get you there either. It is the combination, carried out in cycles, that can't fail to lead to the small number of crucial questions, where analysis gives you the key systemic insights. And it is *only* those insights that will lead you to superior strategy.

Generating Research Questions

The action-learning view (see above) is that research questions arise in principle through comparing the actual outcome of an intervention with expectation. Expectations in organisations are embedded in the going orthodoxy, expressing Business-As-Usual thinking. The intervention is creating scenarios, each taking the future to the edge of plausibility. The art of raising research questions therefore involves the confrontation of the scenarios with the Business-As-Usual thinking. Sceptics can play an important role in this. The team should ask them why they think a scenario cannot happen. Then investigate why these reasons are not reflected in the scenarios.

Examples of questions that help in this analysis:

- What is considered as already "in the pipeline"?
- What seems static, but is actually slowly changing?
- What trends are bound to break, e.g. due to saturation?
- What seems really impossible? Why is that?

The questions to the RP (see page 223) are also helpful here:

- What is happening that matters/could matter?
- What is the relevant system to study?
- What is the appropriate level of "granularity" (detail) of observation?
- What are other ways of looking at this?

Research Results

Research results are initially scattered over a wide area, in the form of many relatively unrelated ideas and observations. The team needs to process these by considering how they affect the systemic understanding reached so far. General points to be taken into account:

- The Business Environment is a system. Look for inter-relations in the system, the combinations of the multiple elements that are driving it.
- Look at the current reality and the short term as well as the longer term.
- Pay particular attention to the predetermined elements. Don't rest until as many uncertainties as possible have been turned into predetermineds.
- Find the sensitive points of maximum leverage.

The research phase is always followed by a further scenario building round, during which disparate bits of learning are brought together and integrated in a few storylines.

Let's reiterate the main purpose of the research: to get into the deeper reaches of the "systems iceberg" – being able to identify the truly structural drivers in a given strategic context. And out of that to develop a reframing of one's perspective on the situation, such that it is perceived in a new and original way that leads to new and unique insights. It needs a lot of time, discussion and contemplation. But down there one can find the elements from which the future, in all its uncertainty, can be understood in a new way.

SPECIAL TYPES OF SCENARIOS

The structured approach to scenario construction as discussed here aims at serving the general strategic needs of the organisation. However, from time to time the scenario team may have a number of more limited specific objectives. There is often a need to project a specific message in the organisation (or to management), and scenarios may be an effective way of doing so. Three examples of such specific use of scenarios are discussed here.

"Surprise-free" Scenarios

From time to time a scenario team find they have run ahead of the client and have come up with insights that will be received as too challenging in the organisation. This often happens when the client team are not well experienced in the use of scenarios, or where they do not have much experience with discussion of strategic issues in general. If a client is used to thinking in terms of a one-line future the confrontation with challenging scenarios can be daunting. The introduction of new ideas in scenarios may be particularly difficult if members of the client team have their own strategic agenda and are used to dealing with each other politically in an "advocative" mode.

In such cases it has proven useful to include in the set of scenarios one that represents the common traditional wisdom of the organisation, a scenario that will be recognised by everyone. This is the "surprise-free" scenario, based on a Business-As-Usual world, which can anchor the set of scenarios in the existing belief system of the decision makers. This "link with the old world" serves as a basis for recognition of change and can be helpful as a platform from which to develop the more challenging futures.

"Challenge" Scenarios

Working through a surprise-free scenario may look simple, but it often isn't. What scenario teams often find is that the Business-As-Usual

---

Box 13   Tips for researchers

Chris Ertel, GBN's top researcher, has a few suggestions for scenario researchers that are worth considering:

Think like a journalist
Approach your research in the spirit of a journalist, learning as much as you can as fast as you can without being too concerned about whether you are "covering everything" or not. The goal is not to reach the definitive answer to a question, but to raise the level of understanding as best we can as fast as we can. To succeed, we merely need to know more than we did when we started about the topic at hand.

Use interviews as much as possible
Talking with very knowledgeable people is the most time-effective way to learn a lot about a topic. Still, if you are approaching an issue you know little about, you will want to do just enough reading and scanning in advance to make sure that you are asking good questions. And the most important question in any interview is the last one: "who else should I be talking to about this?"

Focus on lead users/adopters
Most aspects of your scenarios are already happening – somewhere. "Visiting" these worlds (by reading or interviews) is one of the best ways to "see" the futures now.

Focus when doing research, get rid of other tasks
Even if just for an hour at a time. Good research really does require careful thought and minimal distraction. Few people can do good research with the phone ringing and email a-chirping in the background.

Don't forget the 80–20 rule
Research is *never* done until you say it is. It is up to you to decide that it *is* done when you are hitting a clear point of diminishing returns (i.e. when you are working harder and harder to learn less and less new things).

Have fun!
It's a great luxury to learn. Think like a detective. Play with the material. Talk with people who think differently than you do. Go for a walk or a run. Juggle. Keep looking at the question from different angles.

---

outlook is the result of inertia and not of detailed analytical work. As a consequence serious analysis often reveals the inconsistencies in the set of beliefs that together make up the official future. People may be making assumptions in different parts of the business that, if put together, will prove incompatible. Or by carefully considering the underlying structure of the situation the team may develop an understanding of predetermined elements or structure that are violated in the "official future". If this is the case the scenario team needs to make itself heard, and often urgently. A useful technique is to produce just one challenge scenario, which through its strict internal logic exposes the flaws in the conventional wisdom. This mostly takes the form of describing conditions that need to coincide in order to make existing planning assumptions feasible. This will trigger the client team to consider the plausibility of this development or state of affairs. If the scenario team are successful and the client accepts that an alternative view of the environment is urgently required the discussion then needs to move on to the development of a full scenario set as a basis for an evaluation of strategies, policies and plans as currently pursued.

Challenge scenarios generally are useful if the scenario team have made a discovery that is important enough to pass on to the client team as quickly as possible.

"Phantom" Scenarios

A phantom scenario is a further development of the challenge scenario. It is a useful device if the scenario team finds that the client team strongly project ideas that are simply infeasible. Rather than attacking these ideas straight on, or developing a challenge scenario in which the team tries to create a logical alternative framework, it is often more effective to work out the unlikely scenario in which these ideas would play out consistently over time. The aim of the exercise is to make the intellectual authors of these assumptions consider the logical consequences, in order to suggest that these may not be the ideal planning basis.

Chapter Thirteen

Option Planning

The learning loop is not closed until we have addressed the link between new insights and actions. Actions result from decisions taken by people with the power to act. Decisions-to-act are taken under the influence of an avalanche of experiences, interpreted as the consequences of earlier actions. The output of the scenario analysis as such does not cause action, but it influences the learning loop that mediates between experience and action. The scenario work will have effect in various places in the corporate learning loop. For example, it will help the organisation to filter in experiences that would otherwise not have made it to institutional consciousness. It provides additional systemic structure to question long-standing recipes and enhance theories-in-use. It builds coherence and optimism that enables decision making.

In this chapter we will consider the way in which the scenario analysis affects the theories-in-use in the organisation. The scenario planner needs to consider the impact made and think about how this can be optimised. How does decision making take place in the context of a scenario-based planning approach? This is the area of adaptive scenario-based planning.

DEVELOPING STRATEGIC DIRECTION

Scenarios can provide the basics of strategy through addressing questions in two categories:

- The internal perspective; is our organisation equipped to survive and flourish in any of the multiple equally plausible future environments we may be facing (organisational capability)?
- The external perspective; are we developing our business(es) in the right territory, considering the sort of organisation we are and the environment we may encounter (business portfolio)?

The direct application of scenarios for strategy design addresses these questions in four steps:

- Capability review.
- Portfolio review.
- Strategic option generation.
- Strategic option testing.

The dialogue in all these steps is essentially about the ability of the organisation to survive and grow. The issue raised at this point addresses the question whether this organisation is well prepared to face the uncertainties of the future as portrayed in the completed set of scenarios. Remember that the scenarios are not forecasts, none of them will actually happen. But as a set they are a representation of "the sort of thing that could happen" in the outside world. They need to be considered against an equivalent representation of the organisation itself, out of which strategic conclusions emerge. The strategic dialogue requires a language, in which the essence of organisational capability and success can be expressed. As we have seen, the concept of the Business Idea serves this purpose. The Business Idea expresses the basis of the organisation's overall competitive strength and growth principle.

In the chapter "Articulation of the Business Idea" (page 193) we have described how a Business Idea can be developed in a management team, and we have seen how the contextual environment scenarios provide a testbed with which the worth of the Business Idea can be assessed. Opportunities and threats can come from many directions, including societal trends, technological development, political developments, economics, environmental concerns etc. Threats can also arise from competitive imitation. Significant potential developments in these areas need to be reflected in the scenarios. This is why we have suggested using the current Business Idea in the scenario agenda setting exercise. This will ensure relevance of the scenarios in the options analysis that is now to follow.

By running the Business Idea through multiple futures the team discusses whether it will stand up across the range of what might happen and in this way the team acquires an overview of potential threats facing it. This involves them in considering the performance outlook for the Business Idea in each of the scenarios in turn. The team mentally walks through each scenario one by one and decides in each case:

- The extent to which the Business Idea continues to create customer value/cost leadership. Will our system of Distinctive Competencies continue to be socially efficient? Will there be continuing demand for our current offerings, and for any new offerings we are planning to introduce. Will we be able to continue to exploit the Competitive Advantage through the unique activity set we derive from our system of Distinctive Competencies?

- The competitive threat to the Distinctive Competencies system. Will our system of Distinctive Competencies continue to be defensible against competitive onslaught? How can we stop others from just copying what we are doing. How can we continue to protect our systemic uniqueness? What are the continuing barriers to entry in this future?

Having considered these questions for each scenario the management team will develop a view on the overall strength of the organisation, and a conclusion will emerge on the resilience of the Business Idea against the uncertain future.

The discussion then moves to the options this opens to the organisation. If the conclusion is that the Business Idea is weak the team needs to turn its attention to the question of how to make it stronger. This leads to a discussion around the capabilities of the organisation, resulting in the generation of Capability Options. If the conclusion is that the Business Idea is robust and will stand up under a range of futures, the primary task becomes finding ways of extending the range of its exploitation. This leads to the generation of Business Portfolio Options.

A more detailed discussion of important points in these stages of the strategic conversation follows.

Options Categories

The review of the Business Idea against the scenarios may lead the client team to the conclusion that it is strong and capable of standing up robustly against the whole range of futures as we can see them. If the conclusion is positive the basic question then becomes how we can exploit the Business Idea in the future business worlds as portrayed. This requires the development of a portfolio of new optional businesses exploiting the Business Idea in the real world.

Before discussing potential new additions to the business portfolio in the light of the scenarios the management team needs to review its *existing* business portfolio. Are current businesses successful in their own right, or have they become a management distraction? Are they still exploiting the current Business Idea and its Distinctive Competencies?

Or do they have the potential to do so in the future? A systematic analysis would address the following questions:

1. If a Business Unit is directly related to the overall Business Idea its justification needs to be demonstrated through:

   - identification and confirmation of its embedded Distinctive Competencies, and
   - synergy with the rest of the business.

2. If a Business Unit is unrelated to the current Business Idea its justification needs to be based on two criteria:

   - it is successful in its own right, and
   - it offers opportunities for Distinctive Competencies to be integrated into the Business Idea at some future time.

If these conditions are not fulfilled, the business under consideration has no relation to the Business Idea, now and in the future, and is an isolated activity to be judged on its own merits. It does not form part of this analysis.

The next step is to consider new *Portfolio Options*. This discussion can be based on the current portfolio as a starting point. Options to add to that can be found in internal development, joint ventures, acquisitions or mergers. They can be classified under the following generic headings:

1. Inside-out focus (investments in organic growth):

   - Concentrated growth (expansion into similar markets adjacent to those already served).
   - Market development (investments in expansion of market share).
   - Product development (spreading the Business Idea across a wider range of products).

2. Outside-in focus (investments in growth through partnerships, joint ventures, mergers and acquisition):

   - Horizontal integration (expand into adjacent similar markets by mergers and acquisitions).
   - Concentric diversification (expand into different, but closely related markets by mergers and acquisitions).

The other main category of options is the *Capability Options*. These are the raw material from which the new Business Idea has to be created. These are options to develop the capabilities of the organisation, by leveraging Distinctive Competencies the organisation already possesses. The strength of a Business Idea deteriorates over time with the depreciation of their Distinctive Competencies. If the management team decides that the current Business Idea is less than robust it will discuss what needs to be done to protect it against serious threats, while, if possible, developing its upward potential. Through this discussion the management team may start to realise the fundamental weakness of the Business Idea, and the conclusion may be that changes are desirable.

The following generic categorisation of Capability Options can be used to trigger the thoughts of the business managers:

1. Inside-out focus (investments in organic growth):

   - Market development (developing new relational Distinctive Competencies in the market).
   - Product development (developing new generative Distinctive Competencies, leading to new product ideas).
   - Innovation (applying new combinations of Distinctive Competencies, changing the "rules of the commercial game", cost innovation).

2. Outside-in focus (investments in partnerships, joint ventures, mergers and acquisitions):

   - Vertical integration (buying competencies that leverage the existing Business Idea upstream or downstream of current activity).
   - Conglomerate diversification (buying competencies that leverage the Business Idea in new business areas).

It may not always be possible to come up with ideas to redesign the Business Idea towards increased robustness. The conclusion may be that the Business Idea is weak, and that it will be difficult to strengthen it through development of new capabilities. In that case the conclusion may be reached that the portfolio may need to be reduced, and the following options considered:

- Reformulating of existing businesses.
- Concentration, through consolidation, divestment or abandonment.
- Liquidation.

MANAGING THE OPTION SET

Properly developed scenarios prove to be potentially useful triggers for generating ideas in discussions on potential Portfolio and/or Capability Options. The process requires the client team to imagine itself living in each of the scenarios in turn, and asking the question: "What would we want to do if this was how the real world would be developing, what would seem good business opportunities?" As we saw above (see page 59) the process cannot be rushed. This exercise requires a number of discussions in the management team, possibly organised as a series of workshops. Members need to prepare themselves by becoming familiar with the thinking embedded in the scenarios and with the ideas generated by the facilitator trawling throughout the organisation. Chances of success are improved if the meeting is well prepared and facilitated, and the discussion captured on a flipchart.

It has proven useful to organise the discussion at three levels in turn:

1. *At the level of societal value*, addressing the question of what the world at large, and specifically the organisation's stakeholders (including existing and new customers, competitors, employees, shareholders etc.), will need in each specific scenario. Specify for each stakeholder what value changes are involved in the scenario. What are the new bottlenecks in the system? Who is getting squeezed? And what will they want to do about it? Identify for each value change the associated business opportunity. This discussion is crucial to set the appropriate context for option generation, and should not be skipped.

2. *At the level of strategic implications for the organisation.* Useful questions to assist this part of the discussion:

   - What is the degree of overlap between each of the identified opportunities and the Business Idea?
   - What are good things to have?
   - What happens if the organisation does nothing?
   - What happens if the organisation reacts optimally?
   - What can be done now to be prepared?

3. *At the level of strategic options.* As we saw these come in two varieties:

   - Opportunities that can be readily exploited, i.e. portfolio options.
   - Opportunities for further development of the Business Idea, i.e. capability options.

Option Surfacing

One source of ideas is the scenarios themselves, but these are by no means the only source. Original ideas often come from elsewhere. It needs to be recognised that very few of the strategic options pursued by organisations are normally generated in formal management meetings. Specific ideas for Portfolio or Capability Options are continuously created throughout the organisation. The word "option surfacing" often better indicates what management needs to aim for at this stage than "option generation". Most ideas for options grow out of the general formal and informal strategic conversation that takes place in the organisation, both in meeting rooms but also in the corridors and over the lunch table.

Options living in the organisation need to be surfaced. Trawling through the organisation, looking for insights that may already be alive somewhere, is obviously useful. It is normally advisable to assign the job to one of the managers. Business development managers are logical candidates to co-ordinate this job. Otherwise the team needs to appoint one of the managers for this task. The facilitator (as we will designate this person) needs to go around the organisation having in-depth interviews with the business managers to explore ways in which the Business Idea can be further exploited or developed. People seem to need time to think these issues through. Therefore it is advisable for a facilitator to discuss people's ideas one-on-one in individual interviews. It is useful to circulate the above lists of generic option categories to the interviewees in advance, to trigger thinking and help them to articulate any ideas that they may be able to raise in these terms. The lists also serve as triggers during the interview itself. Going around the organisation the facilitator collects all relevant ideas from the managers, ideas already articulated somewhere in the organisation or ideas developed in a generative scenario project. Having gone through the organisation, and having checked back with each interviewee on "second thoughts", the facilitator writes an overview of the options available to the organisation, for feedback to the management team.

Scenarios come into their own if they can penetrate this conversation and help in giving it direction. A process is needed that can bring the discussion deep into the organisation. We discuss the institutional aspects further in Part Four of this book.

Option Creation

At this stage a list of strategic options has been created under two categories:

1. Capability Options (development of Distinctive Competencies), relating to, for example physical assets, legal position, reputation and brand image, human resource, knowledge, process, culture and so on.
2. Portfolio Options (development of business areas), relating to, for example, markets, channels, new product development, pricing, promotion and so on.

Sometimes ideas for renewal may be hard to find inside the organisation. An original invention may be required. This is the territory of generative scenario-based planning (see pages 53 and 117). It requires a wholly different degree of willingness to explore until a new perspective on the business situation emerges. It is based on the assumption that success can only be achieved by being different. Sometimes the old distinctiveness system does not any longer function. Something entirely new has to be generated. The business needs a new and original/unique insight. A new Business Idea needs to be invented.

In this context the notion of leveraging is useful. As we saw under the heading "Building for the Future" (page 87) in Chapter Five the important point to make here is that future distinctiveness cannot be bought, it can only be developed by inventing new ways to leverage existing distinctiveness. The team needs to invent a new way of developing the existing competencies into a new system that can reconnect with the business environment. The new business success formula is not readily available in the consciousness of the management team. The team will need to look outside its usual territory. Earlier we quoted Kauffman (1995) who refers to that space, i.e. the nearby, but poorly understood or articulated possibilities, as "the adjacent possible". Generative scenario-based planning aims at redefining the strategic direction by developing unique, yet articulated insights about the business in this adjacent space. What is needed here is generative scenario-based planning, in which new business environment areas and business configurations are explored in various iterations until a fundamentally new understanding emerges in the mind of the team. This new understanding needs to be of a quality to cause a reframing of the existing distinctiveness in its business environment context, capable of being developed into a new distinctiveness system.

This process is about invention, it cannot be forced. Management will need to take the time to work through the various iterations, alternating scenario integration with analysis of elements of the business environment that need better understanding. This process has to be continued until the new insight emerges. There is no way of predicting when this will happen. On the other hand experience has shown that persistence pays off and provided the project is allowed to run its course the new insight will emerge.

Option Clustering

With options surfacing from many different sources the resulting overall list will contain ideas over a wide range of conceptualisation, from major restructuring to relatively modest actions to address hygiene factors. Before moving on to option evaluation, the management team will want to reformulate possible action options into a manageable number of genuinely strategic options of appropriate weight to ensure a successful future. This can be achieved by clustering ideas together. The approach is similar to the clustering of ideas generated in interviews, see page 182. The clustering criterion is that two ideas belong together, if pursuing one logically requires serious consideration of the other. Each cluster represents an optional strategy and should be given a suitable indicative name, under which it will be evaluated.

OPTION EVALUATION

Having generated a set of ideas for enhancement of the business, and having reached diminishing returns in the creation/surfacing activity, management now needs to start thinking about relative option evaluation. The strategic discussion takes place against the background of limitations and scarce resources. Management need to consider constraints in various categories of resources, including:

- Financial assets
- Physical assets
- Human resources
- Managerial attention.

It is because of these constraints that choices have to be made. Resources will be particularly scarce in the absence of a strong Business Idea, when the ongoing activities do not throw off a big surplus.

Apart from triggering ideas scenarios also provide conditions under which these choices can be tested.

The Traditional Approach

Most managers will not find option evaluation particularly problematic. It will include at least a financial assessment of the value of the option, possibly in terms of "payout time" or "net present value". Traditionally one of the many plausible futures, somewhere in the centre of the field, will be chosen as a "base case". This single line future will be used as the zero line for the calculation of the differential future cash flow of other options under consideration. The option with the highest net present value, or the shortest payout time prima facie seems to be the one to be preferred.

In fact most managers would consider this approach somewhat simplistic, and would be looking for additional dimensions in which the options need to be compared. The more thoughtful manager in addition to financial forecasts would look at three categories of risk that companies need to consider in judging strategy options (Schoemaker 1992):

- Scenario risk. Significant uncertainty that we can articulate in specific terms, and that is portrayed by the scenarios.
- Strategic fit. This concerns the fit with the existing Business Idea of the firm. If there is a high degree of fit the firm may be assumed to be able to judge risk factors. If the fit is poor the company must assume that it is not in a good position to judge where unspecified uncertainty might come from.
- Organisational risk. This considers the risk resulting from the degree of fit between the option and the organisational and cultural characteristics. If a large organisational or cultural change is required in order to realise the option a gap here adds additional risk factors.

These three risk factors are orthogonal, i.e. independent from each other. As a consequence one of them will normally overwhelm the others. For many unconventional options strategic and/or organisational risk may well be much more significant than what we can assess through the scenario exercise. For example, mergers and acquisitions projects between dissimilar partners are normally significantly more risky than indicated by a scenario analysis, simply because the two partners do not understand each other's business sufficiently. These projects often fail as something has been overlooked or implementation produces intractable organisational problems. Scenario analysis to assess risks is only productive if the option falls clearly within the competencies of the organisation.

The Processual Approach

The traditional approach to strategic evaluation expresses a rationalist decision-making frame of mind. The more processually thinking scenario planner will think not only in terms of "choice", but will always be on the look-out for using the evaluation process to improve the set of options on the table. Until commitments have to be made many parameters in the situation will remain open to further enhancement. The instinct of the processual scenario planner is improvement of the options set rather than closure of alternatives, until this becomes absolutely inevitable.

Therefore scenario-based decision making is philosophically different from traditional "rationalist" decision analysis. The latter aims to reason to a point where a proposal can be characterised as either acceptable or unacceptable. The assumption is that there is one ultimate right answer, and the purpose of the analytical work is to get as close as possible to that. The scenario approach is based on the assumption that every proposal has attractive and unattractive aspects, and that there are no absolute criteria to weigh one side against the other. The premise is that the future is uncertain in a fundamental way, and that beyond a certain point no amount of additional analysis will throw any further light on what might be happening. One needs to consider multiple equally plausible futures. And in some futures that we can think of the proposal may work better than in others. Decisions therefore always are compromises, capable of being improved upon at any time.

While specific scenarios generate ideas for specific options, the evaluation of each option needs to be done against the full scenario set. When this evaluation is made management does not know which of the multiple equally plausible futures will develop. The evaluation of options against multiple futures is known as "wind-tunnelling" of strategic options. The metaphor tries to put across the idea of the scenarios being used as test conditions for the assessment of the value of options. No design will be satisfactorily tested until the full range of conditions (the full range of scenarios) has been applied, see Figure 25, page 204. To ensure that option evaluation will be done against the full range of possible futures it is useful to draw up a matrix in which columns designate scenarios, and rows designate optional strategies, and intersection fields are used to score each option against each scenario.

Most work associated with strategic decisions is concerned with redesigning proposals and options such that the upsides are maximised and the downsides are minimised. In the metaphor of the wind-tunnel, scenarios are the test conditions that bring out the strong and weak points of a proposed design. Possible business strategies are the models to

	Ostrich	Lame Duck	Icarus	Flamingos
Sell out	0	0	0	0
Keep ticking over		+	+	++
Short-term investments	-	+	+++	+++
Long-term Investments	---	-	+	+++++

Figure 34. *Scenario/option matrix*

be tested. The purpose is to assess a proposal under a range of conditions that are representative of what could happen. The purpose is not primarily to decide between acceptance and rejection, but to work towards improving the proposal, such that outcomes are as robust as possible over a range of possible futures. This is why it is important for the scenario planner to see all scenarios as equally likely, and therefore equally valuable as test conditions. On the other hand test conditions must be appropriate for the model to be tested and modified. Therefore scenario projects are always customised.

A useful device in the "wind-tunnelling" exercise is the scenario/ option matrix of which Figure 34 is an example. It shows a number of broad optional strategies for a business in South Africa in the later years of apartheid, considered against the "Mont Fleur" scenarios (see page 244). Each of the options under consideration is evaluated for each scenario, and appropriate annotations are made in the boxes in the matrix showing the attractiveness of the option under those scenario conditions. Only a qualitative distinction can be made in the table, using evaluative words, colour codes, shades of grey, or symbols making use of plusses and minuses. The matrix provides a quick overview of the degree of robustness of the options as they are formulated at that point in time. The main purpose of the scenario/option matrix is to instil a discipline to consider options across all scenarios.

One should try to include the "zero" option in the table against which the other options are evaluated. Options do not have an absolute value, only a relative value against other options. As we are moving into the future we will always exercise one of the options, even if it is only the "continue as is" strategy. The relevant question here is whether we would have done better by selecting another option. Option evaluation is always relative. (In the example of Figure 34 the "sell-out" option has been chosen as the zero line. The reason is that its value is independent of which scenario develops. As a consequence evaluations are comparable not only in the vertical direction but also horizontally.)

STAKEHOLDER TESTING OF OPTIONS

A final check takes us on to the playing field in the transactional environment. It evaluates the strategies emerging against the most important stakeholders and actors involved in it. In the same way as options were reviewed across the scenarios a similar exercise is now done across actors/stakeholders.

The matrix in Figure 33 categorises the main actors and stakeholders around a strategic issue. In the testing of strategic options we are particularly interested in the category of actors called "players", who have both interest and power. The most obvious example is direct competitors. They are directly interested in the Business Idea of our organisation, and will consider doing something similar if it proves successful. Options need to be evaluated against the possibility that the Business Idea might become ineffective through imitation by competitors. We discussed this earlier as the devil's advocate question. But other potential claimants have to be considered as well. These may include suppliers, customers, new entrants, employees, the government, financial markets etc. which need to be specifically identified. Will they act deliberately to sabotage or support the strategies the organisation seeks to play out? Once again it is useful to adopt a matrix approach, in this case showing the options against stakeholders, with intersection fields indicating the reaction to be expected from the stakeholders concerned. Figure 35 is an example.

Once again the objective is primarily to attempt to improve the options considered, by making them more robust against possible onslaught by adversarial stakeholders.

In preparation for a discussion in the management team the option/stakeholder matrix needs to be prepared by the facilitator, listing the real and potential key players in the situation associated with each option. These have to be ranked in terms of their potential influence on the

	Government	Pressure groups	Employees	Fin. markets	Customers
Sell out					
Keep ticking over	**++**	**-**	**+++**		**+**
Short-term investments	**++**	**---**	**++++**	**+**	**+**
Long-term investments	**+++**	**----**	**++++**	**-**	**++**

Figure 35. *Option/stakeholder matrix*

organisation. The facilitator needs to concentrate on the most powerful in the list.

The team discussion can be structured by going systematically through the option/stakeholder matrix, evaluating each intersection. For each option/player combination the potential reaction of the players is evaluated, and indicated on a scale from adversarial to supportive. In this way an overview is obtained of the area where further thinking and development is required. The facilitator then addresses the question whether the options that do not seem robust can be made stronger. Once again taking account of the whole portfolio of options while studying the possible improvement of one will help building the list of options gradually into one overall strategic approach.

INTEGRATION OF STRATEGY

The scenario planner, thinking in terms of option development and improvement, aims towards the development of an overall strategy out of all options on the table, which fits within resource constraints. The scenario/option and the option/stakeholder matrices help in guiding this activity. The main purpose of the matrix is not to make a decision on which option is preferred, but to obtain an impression of where work is still required in option development. For example, in Figure 34 a composite option that seems risky in one of the scenarios may do better overall if it is broken down in a number of steps, and only the first step committed to at this stage. The option/stakeholder matrix triggers a similar line of thinking. In this way the scenario planner works through the list until not much further improvement can be made. Some options will prove attractive across all scenarios, some will be less attractive in one, but at an acceptable risk, and some will show an unacceptable risk in one or more of the scenarios.

Once the scenario planner starts working on reducing the downsides of the options on the table these often start to converge, and eventually many can be combined into a small number of more generic strategic options, or strategic directions. The process needs to continue until the scenario planner finds that strategies no longer constitute "lists of things", but have grown into single holistic concepts of a "direction" for the organisation, and a small number of such fundamentally different strategic directions are left for consideration.

Part Four

Institutionalising Scenario-based Planning

OVERVIEW

So far we have discussed scenario-based planning as a series of largely rational conversational events in the life of a management team. In fact many scenario projects are not much more than that. However, as discussed under the heading "Purpose" (page 158) in Chapter Nine, the potential of scenario-based planning extends far beyond that into adaptive or generative Organisational Learning. Aiming for this level has institutional implications that we will discuss in Part Four. We will argue that the full benefits of scenario-based planning can only be realised in an organisation that has adopted scenario thinking as the dominant strategic thinking style. In that case it becomes a cultural phenomenon that co-evolves with the quality of institutional action.

The introduction of scenario-based planning and thinking is a long-term project, not just an isolated decision. The objective is full integration of scenario thinking in the ongoing planning and decision-making processes rather than projects of an episodic nature. This is a significant change process. The literature on change management has interesting things to say to the manager or management team wishing to introduce scenario thinking in the organisation.

Cultural processes are the result of communication and networking. Attention needs to be paid to both the formal and the informal communication processes in the organisation. Culture is heavily influenced by informal communication. In the context of scenario-based planning we are particularly interested in the formal and informal "strategic conversation". It is the part of the conversational process by which people influence each other's thinking about the business, the decision making and the longer-term pattern in institutional action and behaviour.

Culture change works slowly, the introduction of scenario thinking is not something that can be "plugged in" overnight. It is only over a period of time that people in the organisation start to realise that without it they are becoming more and more handicapped playing in the competitive game. Getting to this stage requires persistence and consistency on the part of management.

Chapter Fourteen

The Management of Change

ACTING ON THE SCENARIOS

"Acting on the warnings of scenarios" could be called the minimal rule of scenario-based planning. If you don't do that you are not engaged in scenario-based planning. But it is only the beginning.

In Part One we suggested that the full impact can only be understood if we integrate scenario-based planning in the institutional learning loop, with aspects of perception/reflection, building theories/understanding, and acting on this in the outside world.

In Part Two we saw how scenarios affect perception by putting in place a richer arsenal of concepts embedded in "memories of the future" enhancing what the organisation can recognise as relevant. We studied various cases of organisations recognising in scattered signals from the outside the real meaning of what was going on there, and taking more skilful and prompt action on the basis of that. We also saw how the scenario approach is designed to enrich the internal mental models available to the organisation for more skilfully adapting existing recipes to the needs of the times.

Finally we suggested that scenario thinking has an important processual function in aligning mental models to empower the organisation to take action on the basis of its understanding, and minimise the paralysis that comes with fragmented mental models and consequent lack of cohesion. In this part of the book we will be primarily interested in this action-focused aspect of scenario-based planning.

Adam Kahane suggests four steps to help people link scenarios and action. These can be mapped on to the Kolb learning loop. The four steps are:

1. Live inside the scenario stories. The desired result from this step is for people to learn about, understand and remember the scenarios, and be willing to suspend disbelief and play the scenario game of "living the future in advance". This process of engaging with the stories and imagining being in the scenario worlds produces the virtual equivalent of Kolb's "concrete experiences".
2. Examining the implications of each of the scenarios. The desired result is for the participants to make connections between possible futures for their contextual environment, and the consequences for them and their organisations. This corresponds to "observation and reflection".
3. Drawing conclusions from the scenarios as a set. The result is an integration of the insights obtained from the imaginary scenario journeys, into the participants' mental models, i.e. the "formation of abstract concepts and theories".
4. Planning next steps. The result is agreement on how to move from thought to action, i.e. a process of "testing the implications of theory in new situations".

The integration of thought and action is the fundamental and most difficult part of this cycle. How to do that in an institutional context? Without it there cannot be scenario-based (generative or adaptive) organisational learning.

In Part Three we discussed development of strategy. In Part Four we will discuss both formal and informal aspects of the institutional process that bridges the gap between management's view of strategy and the organisation's ideas on what needs to happen, i.e. what makes an organisation act in a strategic way. We will briefly touch on the important phases of the planning cycle and other possible interventions in the strategic conversation, which turn the thinking phase into learning and adaptation in the organisation. In particular we will discuss the contribution of scenario-based planning in all of these areas.

Scenario-based Planning as an Institutional Process

So far we have discussed scenario-based planning as if it were an individual or small team activity. But the link with action is an institutional process. As Lindblom pointed out (1959) institutional decision making is a polycentric process. Significant decisions relating to strategy normally emerge from contributions from and interaction between many people. Even if the formal power to act is in the hands of one individual or management team the actual decision itself will have been influenced by many others, both inside and outside the organisation. Some of these contributions are formal activities, for example the preparation of a case in favour of a proposed decision, but many more people influence the outcome by participating in the ongoing strategic conversation in the organisation.

The theory of the learning cycle suggests that scenario-based planning can only lead to institutional learning if it affects institutional action and feedback. Institutional action requires a critical mass of consensus and/or compromise on what to do. Scenario-based planning can affect institutional action by contributing to this process of alignment of ideas. Only if it becomes an organisational process of sufficient significance to affect mental models will it play a role in the institutional learning loop and thereby make the organisation a more effective adaptive and/or innovative player in its ever-changing environment (Galer & van der Heijden 1992).

Many management teams initially engage in a scenario-based planning process in order to conceptualise and clarify for themselves an otherwise unstructured area of concern about developments in the outside world. The purpose is making sense of the situation. Management teams that take scenario-based planning seriously can widen their range of vision in this way and possibly gain new and original insights (compare Schrage 2000). In such a case the scenario planner will find that the management team, having spent time and resources on the development of a set of scenarios, will want to take these further into, first, a consideration of strategy and if successful, second, a process of institutional development.

This can be done on an ad hoc basis or it can be formally tackled in the organisation. The latter requires embedding scenario-based planning in a formal process of strategy development, by making it the basis of the corporate planning cycle. If this is done effectively scenario-based planning will influence strategy in the formal decision-making process, but also in a less formal way by becoming part of the general conversation about strategy in the organisation. Views will be heard which otherwise would remain in the background. Weak signals of impending change, which would otherwise go unnoticed, will be picked up and considered. New questions will be asked, triggering new thinking. There will be increased confidence that the organisation is capable of dealing with change. Change and uncertainty are no longer threatening but are understood in context, and therefore experienced as exciting and manageable opportunities for growth and development. Pessimism is turned into optimism, and paralysis into action (see Weick's story on page 36).

Effective institutionalisation will lift scenario-based planning from an intellectual exercise by a group of individuals, following the rationalist paradigm of strategy, to a capability for generative organisational learning and adaptive action, in line with the processual view of strategic management. In this context we can speak of scenario-based planning opening up the organisational mind to the many different possible futures that could arise, and in that way developing more skilful navigation through the business environment.

Planning for Action

Institutional action is planned, even if only informally. Conceptually this planning for action consists of four steps:

- Specification of the present situation.
- Specification of the desired future, understood as one choice among many within an environment that becomes more and more uncertain the further out we look.
- Clarification of the gap between the two to be bridged.
- Development of detailed plans to make the transition from current to desired reality (Figure 36).

Moving the organisation from the present to the desirable future will have to be done within resource constraints imposed on the organisation. Therefore choices have to be made. Strategy is about making choices.

Once the objectives have been set plans to bridge the gap can be made and actions undertaken by the organisation. But even the best-laid plans meet unexpected obstacles. Management need to appraise progress on a continuous basis, and exercise control action if unexpected deviations occur. For this reason objectives need to be expressed such that progress can be measured against them, as an indication whether corrective action is required. What is included in, and what is excluded from, the set of objectives will influence where action will be focused, according to the old adage "what is measured is what you get". It is therefore crucially important that objectives include all areas where strategic initiatives are important. The discussion of the Business Idea (and hygiene factors, see page 172, if applicable) shows management where to look beyond obvious financial targets.

This "making it happen" is not a trivial matter. Many management teams have experienced what is known as an "implementation" problem of how to realise a specified strategy through organisational action. The problem is closely linked up with the rationalist paradigm, in which thinking and action are seen as different consecutive activities. The

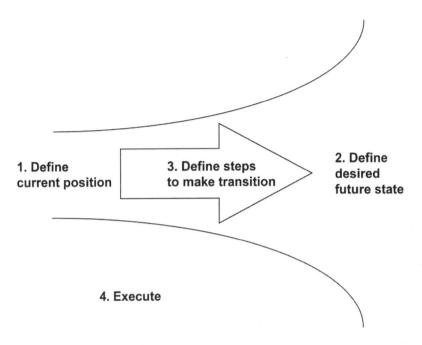

Figure 36. *Creating action*

processual view sees thinking and action as interwoven activities, and "implementation problems" as signals of failure of the whole strategy process. Learning from experience is a fundamental aspect of the processual perspective. The organisation's ability to acknowledge, assess and deal with deviations of actual experience from intentions is seen as directly driving the organisation's learning and adaptation.

An organisation's skill in this respect depends heavily on the interaction between the individuals in it and the degree to which the culture allows ideas to be exchanged and aligned. The skill of an organisation to adapt and innovate will depend on the degree to which deviations are discussable. In a political "blaming" culture, where deviations are interpreted as "error", defensive routines will throw up barriers to exchanging of views. It will take longer for experience to be reflected in corporate action. The more open culture in which deviation from plan is seen as a way of life will perceive weak signals earlier and react more quickly.

In the processual paradigm it is preferable to think in terms of "management of change", which involves both thinking and action rather than "implementation of strategy" which picks them apart. Understanding how scenarios can make an impact on institutional action and thereby become a part of the institutional learning loop can benefit from considering the "management of change" literature.

CONDITIONS FOR SUCCESSFUL CHANGE MANAGEMENT

The formal planning process cannot in itself produce change. More is required. However sophisticated the formal planning processes, most of the decision making takes place through informal contacts in which most of the strategic conversation takes place. Skilful scenario planners will take account of this and attempt to influence action through these channels. In order to study how this can be achieved we need to consider the processes leading to change in organisations.

One perspective on this is based on research by Pettigrew, who identified five conditions required for any planned change and adaptation to take place (Pettigrew & Whipp 1991):

- Awareness in the organisation of the business imperative for change.
- Expression of the strategy in operational and actionable terms.
- Active recognition that people are the asset through which change is created.
- Exercise of leadership to put the "change project" on the agenda, and keep it there.
- Coherence of intention and action among all members of management.

This model shows that scenario-based planning can be a major factor for change. It makes a contribution to the operationalisation of most of these factors. For example, it can:

- Create wide awareness of external imperatives for change.
- Guide formulation of operational plans.
- Enlist the people in the organisation with the power to act.
- Create coherence in management action through development of consensus in the management team.

In addition it can make a contribution at the leadership level, through the defusing of political tension around strategic issues in the organisation.

At various points we will revisit Pettigrew's criteria for successful change management and relate these to the contribution made by scenario-based planning.

Role of Management

Do people really want to learn and change? In the modern world there are more opportunities to learn and, at the same time, more difficulties in doing so:

- Change in organisations requires dissatisfaction with the adequacy of the current situation, anxiety about the consequences, and the psychological security needed to attempt change.
- Learners depend on peer group approval. Learning new ways of doing or valuing may be threatening or rewarding to others and therefore to the learner.
- The recognition of a threat to one's organisation is accompanied by an acutely uncomfortable feeling of vulnerability. One's learned successful habits now appear insufficient to protect the sense of self.
- More information is expected to make learning new answers easier and decision making more decisive. Ironically, just the opposite usually happens. More information about the human condition generally leads to more uncertainty.

So what can management do to foster learning behaviour? Don Michael (1998) suggests the following:

- Open up channels of communication (a recent three-year study by University of Denver's Stephen Erbschloe found that poor communication and political infighting were the no. 1 and no. 2 causes, respectively, for slowing down change at 46 companies setting up Net businesses. Erbschloe says successful companies were able to resolve internal strategy conflicts quickly – Stepanec 1999).
- Tell stories of successful learning behaviour.
- Accept uncertainty and error as part of the learning/control system.
- Use crisis as learning occasions.
- Reduce sense of vulnerability for the learners in the organisation.
- Don't chair, facilitate.
- Reward learning.

Learning appropriate for this world has to do with learning what are the useful questions to ask and learning how to keep on learning since the questions keep changing. There will be no place to settle down, no time to stop asking.

Chapter Fifteen

Planning Process

THE PLANNING CYCLE

Most organisations in their approach to planning and budgeting institutionalise a form of the learning cycle (Part One, page 37). Consider a budget system, which looks one year ahead against which actual performance is compared as results come in during the year. Management tries to make sense of events by discussing the reasons for these differences. This can be compared with the reflection and theory building phases of the learning cycle. On the basis of the explanation of differences from the budget new predictions are made for the coming year and the budget is adjusted. This can be compared with the "planning new steps" stage of the learning cycle. This leads to new actions by the organisation. Results deviating from plan constitute the new experience on which new organisational learning is based.

The formal planning activity is often financially oriented. Money is the primary common measure of performance in organisations. But there are points in the planning cycle where a more fundamental view needs to be taken of what is being done. Most management teams feel the need to base their budgets and plans on a strategy. This is caused by the awareness that there are many more things an organisation could undertake than it has capacity to carry out, and choices have to be made. The discussion about these alternatives is often somewhat informal and many choices are made intuitively. This means that they are not very well explained to others in the organisation, leading to tacit, but significant, differences of view, in the management team and beyond. If these are not resolved the team starts to fragment, resulting in mixed signals to the organisation. As we saw in the previous chapter mixed signals from the top is one of the five conditions that frustrate planned change. Most teams therefore feel the need to take off time to think together about the future. In Part Three we discussed ways to improve the quality of this discussion. The next step is to bring this thinking into the rest of the organisation. Particularly when the conclusion is that significant change is necessary this is an important part of the management process.

The learning cycle view of organisational success emphasises the importance of the link to action in the cognitive processes underlying organisational behaviour. So far we have discussed processes that help thinking in the management group. How does the link to action take place?

HYGIENE FACTORS

Managers are people with institutional "power-to-act". Triggers to action originate in strategic objectives or the need to apply accepted principles of "good practice". The latter are sometimes referred to as hygiene factors, activities that are generally seen as necessary for the proper conduct of organisational and business affairs (see page 172). For example, an organisation requires a good bookkeeping system. Commercial organisations need proper marketing skills. Management needs a system to control expenditure and keep cost under control. A system of internal communications is required. And so on. These are the principles of good management practice that need to be in place if the organisation is to survive at all.

Hygiene factors should be considered in two categories:

- Ensuring sound and efficient business processes.
- Maintaining sound and efficient relationships with all stakeholders.

Stakeholders have expectations and the challenge is not only to identify these, but also to find a balance in terms of what can be delivered. Sound and efficient business processes will establish the company as an efficient going concern.

Knowledge about management hygiene factors is readily available to every manager, codified and documented in textbooks, and taught in management courses. This is not repeated here. Professional managers are expected to be aware of these hygiene factors, and non-performance in these areas is accepted ground for disqualification. They are the necessary minimum conditions to join the game. Organisations that find the necessary hygiene factors lacking have to address these deficiencies immediately, and raise projects to repair the situation as soon as possible.

This book is in the first place about strategy. Strategic management as a discipline assumes that the necessary hygiene factors are in place. If this is not so, then management is well advised to concentrate on establishing these minimum conditions first. You cannot win the race if you haven't got to the starting line first.

FIVE LEVELS OF PLANNING IN A PLANNING CYCLE, OVERVIEW

We can distinguish five stages in the organisational planning cycle, namely strategic planning, masterplanning, project planning, budget planning, and appraisal, see Figure 37.

At the top we find strategic planning, which incorporates the activities as described in Part Three of this book. It involves exploring the future

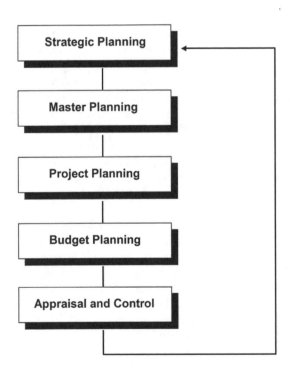

Figure 37. *The five levels of business planning*

and defining and developing it in the form of a Business Idea of the organisation. This involves two stages, generating the Business Idea and then testing it against multiple futures that could develop. As we saw strategic planning can take place at the business and the corporate level. These two levels of strategic planning affect each other. The corporate Business Idea describes competencies the corporate level contributes to the businesses. On the other hand the corporate competencies do not exist in isolation but are to a considerable extent embedded in the businesses. When starting the strategic planning phase from scratch the preferred order is to develop the Business Ideas of the businesses before tackling the corporate level. Being able to put the businesses next to each other and identify commonalities in Distinctive Competencies provides a strong steer towards the shape of the corporate Business Idea.

A useful output of the strategic planning phase is the definition of a set of strategic objectives, defining the main elements of the state of affairs the organisation hopes to achieve over time. Strategic objectives will give a broad indication of the result of the consideration of Portfolio and Capability Options in the management team, and the conclusions reached on which direction to adopt. A strategic objectives statement should never be overly complex. It should reflect the Business Idea for the future, which describes the success formula of the organisation in a limited number of Distinctive Competencies (see page 84).

Actions can range from taking small incremental steps to undertaking major projects. Any operational plan intended to result in action requires a project to make it happen. Some projects are undertaken by individuals, some by groups of people who join forces for the purpose of bringing a bigger strategic project to fruition. In order to organise their actions project managers engage in project planning, intended to convert strategy into action. It concerns the detailed operational planning of the steps in such terms that they are immediately indicative of what individuals need to do.

Very few projects can be planned entirely in isolation. Organisations operate an "infrastructure" which benefits more than one project. Most projects contain elements of planned activities of an infra-structural nature that need to be put together with related actions planned in other projects to create a coherent overall plan that deals with it across the organisation. For this reason organisations, especially large ones, need to engage in "masterplanning", through which the overall coherence of the totality of all project plans is ensured. For example, personnel requirements will need to be aggregated across the organisation in order to create an overall recruitment/training plan. Masterplanning typically results in an overall plan that addresses the total cost/benefit performance of the combined project plans.

Specifically it considers allocation of corporate resources across the whole of the organisation.

Some masterplans may develop into significant projects in their own right. Others may be developed informally, e.g. in a series of meetings between the various project champions involved. Masterplanning is carried out in conjunction with project planning. It can only be done in direct co-operation with project planners, who will be the ultimate users of the outcomes of masterplans.

Having developed the various plans the next task is to express these in a detailed budget. This includes targets for income and expenditure, based on performance assumptions that take account of the projects and masterplans that are being undertaken. The targets are the basis against which actual performance will be measured and assessed later.

In summary, the planning cycle involves the development of strategy (as discussed in Part Three of this book), masterplanning (involving the translation of this into a description of the cross-functional plans), project planning (involving the translation of the strategy into business projects and action steps), budget planning (involving the overall quantification and the setting of targets), and appraisal (looking at actual performance in the light of what was intended in the plans). Ultimately the purpose of all this is to learn from experience such that the organisation becomes more skilful in dealing with change in the business environment. The main purpose of creating a planning system in the organisation is to create a conversational process around these issues, mobilising the totality of the organisational knowledge towards an emerging solution to this complex optimisation problem.

Having overviewed the whole process we will now revisit the various aspects of the corporate planning cycle and consider these in the context of the approach to strategy discussed here, involving scenario-based planning of the Business Idea.

STRATEGIC PLANNING

In Part Three we considered the intellectual processes a management team invokes to develop strategy for the organisation. It involves considering the fit between the Business Idea and scenarios of the future business environment. The strategic planning phase involves analysing and mapping the Business Idea and analysing the relevant environment in a scenario exercise.

As we saw there are two different approaches the management can choose from, adaptive or generative strategy design. Adaptive scenario-based planning aims at selecting available strategic options that will most favourably react to the anticipated future environments. But let us recall the limitations of this process. The possibility/option space of the organisation is constrained by the existing mental models and language of interpretation available to it and its members. Recall how memories of the future shape our attention span. What is not being foreseen cannot be seen when it happens. The choice of frames (defining meaning) and metaphors (which can provoke new images) within an organisation determines what an organisation can both extract and absorb from the environment around it. From time to time the organisation has to move on from the old formula and generative strategising becomes essential.

Management will not normally want to do this thinking in isolation, but instead mobilise the knowledge of the whole organisation. New frames and metaphors have to be developed throughout the organisation. Management will need to set the process in motion by sharing the conclusions of their strategic thinking with the rest of the organisation. They will need to indicate whether the prime strategic thrust is in exploitation of the Business Idea or in the development of it. They will have to indicate in which direction they see these developments taking place in order to maintain overall coherence between the Business Idea and the business environment outlook. A useful way of summarising this is through the formulation of strategic objectives, shared by all members of the management team. This sharing is important. As we saw from Pettigrew's research, one of the main reasons why change programmes derail is lack of coherence resulting from mixed signals from the top.

Scanning

Generative scenario-based planning aims at developing new, unique, yet articulated new insights about the business, making parts of the adjacent space visible. Scenarios are not only helpful when taking specific decisions but they also encourage decision makers to become aware of new signs of change beyond the traditional Business-As-Usual environment. Therefore scenarios have a role to play in scanning the environment for signs of change.

Importantly the identification and monitoring of signposts is not a self-standing activity, but remains embedded in the larger strategic conversation process. Even so, formal scanning systems seem to have a limited lifetime, many systems we know were abandoned again some time after they were introduced, as the activity becomes routine and thereby loses its effectiveness. Living in the adjacent space is hard, the attraction of the comfort of "Business-As-Usual" seems difficult to resist.

Strategic Objectives

All change programmes depend on the human resource for their execution. The organisation needs a set of unified and relatively stable plans of action that can be articulated, communicated, discussed and agreed such that all can subscribe to them and make a contribution where appropriate. These plans will exist at various levels in the corporation, linking strategic purpose with details of operation. Corporate management face a formidable task in maintaining coherence across the whole front. The specification of shared and agreed corporate objectives is the first crucial step in this process.

A complete set of corporate objectives will include the following elements:

- The level of profitability aimed for to keep the Business Idea loop robustly in the growth spiral (what level of profitability will be manifestation of our competitive success?, what level will be required to exploit the growth opportunities the Business Idea will open up for us?)
- Major repairs required in hygiene factors. This may cover ensuring sound and efficient business processes (what are our most important business processes?, where is our performance less than what may be expected from a professional company?, what needs to be done about repairing the situation?) and/or sound and efficient relationships with all important stakeholders (who are our key stakeholders, and how do we need to perform on the interfaces with them to maintain optimal relationships?)
- Adapting and developing the Business Idea (what are the Distinctive Competencies we intend to rely on for our future success?, how will we know that they are in place?)
- Adapting and developing the business portfolio (what portfolio options do we intend to develop in order to exploit our Business Idea, what, how, at what pace?)

A comprehensive set of corporate objectives considers all four categories.

How many objectives should a company pursue? If objectives are to lead to action and results, the set as a whole should become a holistic source of inspiration in the organisation. This requires that the whole set can be seen as one image of the organisation working on its future. It is important to remember that a holistic overview is lost if the number of objectives exceeds around seven to 10. If an organisation has more than this number of "corporate objectives" it is losing the potential enlisting power of this management instrument. Management must also know the limitations to its own attention span. The potential list of objectives is very long. Only a very limited number can be achieved. Prioritising is key.

The four categories above can be used as the basis for developing specific corporate objectives. In each of the four categories management needs to consider how performance will be measured, what will be considered a satisfactory state of affairs to be reached in the future. The organising question here might be: "If, in 10 years' time, the organisation has been a roaring success, how will we know? What are the very few necessary *and* sufficient markers of success?"

In principle the steps involved are the following:

Step 1. Identifying objectives

The management team will first of all think about what is required in each of the four areas and try to discover the implicit objectives. A useful way to think about what is required is to consider why the absence of each objective could not be tolerated. What would we expect to happen if the objective was not met, and how would this undermine the whole operation.

Step 2. Quantifying objectives

The next question to address is how management will know that objectives have been reached. This will require the objective to be expressed in measurable terms. Each qualitative objective may find expression in one or more quantitative targets to be reached.

Quantitative objectives come in two forms:

- Static targets to be achieved independent of time. For example, a management team may aim to maintain a market share of at least 25%.
- Dynamic targets to be reached at a specific point in time. For example, management may specify that logistics costs should have become competitive within one year. Time dependent objectives can be seen as milestones on the way.

Most strategic objectives are difficult to quantify. And those that cannot be quantified are often the most important. Distinctive Competencies may be especially hard to express in numbers, as they are often culture related. For example, the Business Idea may identify the area of customer relations management as an opportunity to develop unique capabilities (a high profile example of this was British Airways' well-known "Putting People First" policy and programmes). In such cases, objectives may have to express inputs rather than results, such as number of employees trained. However, managers should try to express the basic competitive aims of an objective as closely as possible, to ensure that no false impressions are created, based more on hope than reality. Measuring the wrong thing may cause a false mood of complacency, which could be even more dangerous than not having the policy in the first place.

The final test that the right measures have been found is whether measuring performance in these terms will indicate to management whether and to what extent the objectives are met.

Step 3. Considering appropriateness

Following the quantification of the objectives management needs to consider whether the quantified objectives are appropriate. The following questions may help management in considering this point:

- Is the objective realistic, and attainable within the means available?
- Is the objective stretching?

Both criteria are important. An unrealistic target will be ignored in the organisation and become ineffective. On the other hand the target must be stretching if it is to lead to competitive improvement. Care should be taken to find the right balance between the two. Erring on either side would make the exercise less than effective as an institutional device.

Step 4. Assigning responsibility

Finally each of the corporate objectives should become the explicit responsibility of one of the members of the management team. This responsibility involves:

- Ensuring that one or multiple programmes are in place to bridge the gap between the present state of affairs and where we aim to be.
- Ensuring that aims are communicated down the line, discussed and modified, until full buy-in has been achieved.
- Ensuring that objectives are translated into action projects, assigned to individuals or teams.

- Ensuring that resources are made available at the appropriate place and time.
- Measuring progress against target, and taking control action if progress is unsatisfactory.
- Informing the management team if achieving the objective is becoming less than likely.

Developing Objectives in a Management Team

Although the above four tasks can be executed by an individual manager, the resulting set of objectives will need to be discussed in the team, where agreement and "buy-in" needs to occur. Also the result of appraisal activities will need to be considered, before management finalise the set of objectives.

The development of objectives is not a once-and-for-all exercise, but needs to iterate with the development of feasible action plans and the allocation of resources. Initial ideas about objectives may prove unrealistic, or the resources needed to do everything that the management team might find desirable may not be available.

Specifically it is desirable that objectives are developed in conjunction with a first specification of masterplans. This will result in a robust set which carries a realistic relationship to action plans in the company.

MASTERPLANNING

Masterplanning is closely connected with the economic purpose of organisations, which is to bring activities together to exploit economies of scale and scope. Masterplanning is the process of thinking about this, planning it and ultimately exploiting it to the maximum.

Because the Business Idea runs across the whole organisation many of the ideas for change involve various functions and departments in the organisation. Some ideas will meet resource constraints and will have repercussions for the infrastructural needs in the organisation as a whole. As we saw earlier, constraints are normally encountered in infrastructural resources, such as:

- Financial assets
- Physical assets
- Human resources
- Managerial attention.

The organisation needs to establish which resource limitations constrain further development. These limiting resources need to be considered on potential scope for expansion. But expanding a scarce resource requires the investment of resources, often of the same resource. For example, the expansion of the human resource requires recruitment and training, which will temporarily reduce the availability of the human resource for other business. Therefore such constraints require making choices and priority setting. Development needs to be carefully planned. And a limitation in scope for expansion has repercussions for the overall concept of the organisation. All this is co-ordinated across the organisation by means of masterplanning. Masterplans deal with scarce corporate resources required by projects. Interfunctional co-ordination involves two tasks:

- Allocation of the scarce resource across individual projects.
- Planning of expansion of the resource, in a way that balances costs and benefits.

Both aspects involve the individual project planners, who have to be able to make their case in the allocation process, and who have to develop the benefit side of the cost/benefit equation.

Generally a masterplan is a description of the future generation and disposition of scarce central resources, and a plan to reach this future state by deliberate action. It describes the physical state of affairs as it is intended to develop over time in terms of assets, people and resources for the activity concerned with implications across the whole organisation (and beyond). Typical examples include a computer/information systems masterplan, a production/factory masterplan, a human resource masterplan (including recruitment, career development, succession plans and so on), a management development masterplan, etc. Financing needs can only be dealt with at the aggregated level and needs a masterplan. Offices and buildings need to be planned across the departments. The factory layout will depend on more than one project. Relations with suppliers involve overall purchasing considerations, but also logistics, including warehousing, working capital and so on. "Softer" masterplans address less tangible assets, such as creating desirable cultural characteristics across the organisation, in line with the Business Idea.

Some of these responsibilities naturally fit in the mandate of specific departments, and these are the logical candidates to champion the development of the appropriate masterplans. Other masterplans may not be the subject of departmental responsibility and these need special attention from the management team. Departments responsible for physical facilities will often already be familiar with the concept of a masterplan. Laying out a factory, for example, cannot be done in a step-by-step fashion, but must be approached top down from the perspective of a future integrated state of affairs. Thought will have to be given to future expansion and space, and capacity will have to be reserved for that. Most factory managers will have experienced that without enough top-down facilities planning workflow will gradually become unwieldy and work efficiency will be lost. The same applies to departments responsible for logistics, computing and communications, facilities management etc.

While using the Business Idea/scenario approach described here management will become more skilful in articulating change in terms of less tangible resources of the organisation such as its people's skills and culture, brand name, information flows etc. Many of these invisible assets are of an infrastructural nature, involving people and behaviour across the organisation. They often require long lead times to plan. If these are the basic drivers of the Business Idea for the future they will require their own masterplans as much as the more tangible physical manifestations of the organisation.

Therefore masterplans can be characterised as follows:

- They are blueprints describing the future manifestations of a specific shared scarce resource, showing actions designed to develop the resource.
- They can cover both tangible and intangible assets.
- They tend to take a longer-term view of the future, related to the lifespan of the resources considered.

Good masterplanning will manifest the following characteristics:

- It identifies key decision points, and key "milestones" to be reached at specific times in the future.
- It allows communication both vertically and horizontally in the organisation.
- It is a vehicle for delegation from the top.
- It ensures compatibility between the long and the short term.
- It ensures consistency between functional and departmental plans.
- It provides data for budget and cash flow planning purposes.

Masterplans help the organisation in the management of change:

- Comparison with the current state of affairs will provide an overview of additional resources required. Aggregation allows management an overall view of the needs resulting from the totality of the projects under consideration, as a result of which control action can be taken.

• An important aspect of the masterplan is the overview it provides of the way that projects link areas of responsibility across the organisation, allowing people not directly involved in its conception to study and comment. In this way a masterplan is a powerful integrating mechanism in the organisation.

Drawing up masterplans can be organised in various different ways. Management can appoint ad hoc teams to draw up these plans. Alternatively existing organisational units can be asked to take on the task. Some masterplans can be farmed out, particularly those relating to the maintenance of hygiene factors in the organisation. However, masterplans for the development of Distinctive Competence by their nature cannot be left to anyone other than the organisation itself.

Responsibility for development of Distinctive Competencies will often be allocated to functional units while business units will consider development of business areas. However, the masterplan does not only involve this co-ordinating unit. It will be their task to ensure that others involved are consulted and that the final plan has the support of everyone with an interest across the whole organisation.

The project planning and masterplanning activities need to take place in conjunction with each other. A process of iteration is required, in which project plans inform the masterplans, and the other way around. This requires a deliberate approach towards the planning activity. It is normal practice in most organisations to make someone responsible for the overall co-ordination of the total planning activity, which includes ensuring that all appropriate masterplans are considered. If the process is suitably co-ordinated it will be possible to aggregate plans into an overall business plan, as input for discussions with stakeholders.

Scenarios and Masterplanning

Scenario-based planning can play an important direct role in masterplanning. As masterplans tend to be of a long-term nature there will be a lot of uncertainty to be considered in their development. The masterplanner can improve his/her understanding of the potential and uncertainty involved by developing a number of suitably focused scenarios through which masterplans can be tested.

PROJECT PLANNING

Experience has shown that "making it happen" requires the allocation of specific responsibility to teams and individuals. Translating the overall strategy and masterplan into specific projects for identified teams and individuals is a critical success factor in creating change. For this reason we develop the topic in some detail here.

As we saw earlier one of the five essential conditions for change is the linkage of strategy with operations, and the translation of strategy into actionable operational plans. Managers need to be proactive in this area. Developing the strategy is not enough, there should be conscious activity in the organisation to start things moving by operationalising strategy. A useful intervention at this stage is engaging the organisation in conversation about implementation of plans through "implementation workshops". There are many ways of conducting these. Below we discuss one model (based on Figure 36, page 295) that has proven productive in practice at various levels in the organisation.

It is assumed that through strategic planning and masterplanning an overview has been obtained of what needs to be done. The manager responsible needs to take the lead by bringing together a team of implementers in a workshop. It normally helps to appoint a facilitator who is not directly involved in the project. A suitable process for defining and breaking down the projects required involves the following steps:

Step 1. Introduction of the workshop

It has proven important that participants early on get as clear a picture as possible of what is to be expected from the workshop. Operational teams are often not used to discussing strategic issues formally and in depth. Therefore the manager starts the meeting by explaining the objectives:

- To discuss strategic issues as specified by the management team, and options for addressing these.
- To review masterplans in which this group is involved.
- To develop detailed project objectives and action project commitments.

The manager needs to set the scene by making the link with the Business Idea, the strategic objectives developed and the masterplans being prepared. In addition some participants may be asked to prepare presentations on the detail of new masterplans that involve this group.

It is often useful to give a few minutes' air time to all participants to allow them to indicate what issues, from their perspective, they see emerging. Participants should be left free (within time limits) to decide what they wish to bring up.

This process helps in starting the conversation on implementation. The manager can also observe to what extent the issues are shared among the members of the team.

Step 2. Project objectives and key implementation domains

The facilitator then invites the group to discuss the objectives that they as a project group need to pursue. Some proactivity is required here, to avoid vague, not actionable formulation, which would derail the workshop. The facilitator must insist that any objectives are quantified and implementable. The best way of going about this is to start with a free brainstorm on what might have to be included in the list. At this stage no rules apply, and anything goes. The facilitator records on a flipchart. Not only physical and operational, but also financial and human resource objectives are included.

When this activity reaches diminishing returns the facilitator changes tack. At this point specific corporate strategic objectives and masterplans are raised, addressing the question where this group needs to make a contribution. From this the group will generate further ideas on project objectives for them. These are added to the flipchart record.

When no further ideas come forward the facilitator goes back to each stated objective and raises the following questions:

- Is the objective realistic?
- What are the criteria for success, how and when will we know that the objective is fully met?
- Why is *not* meeting this objective unsatisfactory. What would happen if the objective were not met?
- How will we measure that satisfactory progress is being made on the way?
- Who in the group is primarily responsible for ensuring that this objective is reached?

The facilitator needs to keep this process moving, prevarication in the light of uncertainty is the big danger here. Initially this may require that some arbitrary decisions be made. Later on the list will be revisited and further iterations will be made. Participants must be kept fully aware that opportunities will arise later to have another go at this.

Having developed an initial idea of the project objectives the next step is to brainstorm, and then cluster the various activities, required to realise the project. The purpose of clustering here is to come up with implementation domains in which activity can be organised.

Implementation domains largely overlap with organisational units, but new projects often require the identification of domains that are not (yet) the subject of a formal organisational responsibility. The relevant implementation domains are decided by reference to the objectives formulated. Some examples of implementation domains are:

- Relations with authorities
- Relations with customers
- Retail
- Brand development
- Competition
- Facilities management
- Cost reduction
- Plant optimisation
- Human resources development
- Management processes
- Information and information systems.

Developing a list of implementation domains during the workshop is essentially a brainstorming process, with subsequent clustering until a reasonably practical number is achieved, that overlaps with the organisational structure as much as possible.

Step 3. Gap analysis

The next step may take place in subgroups. Each syndicate is allocated one or a few implementation domains, and the job is to develop an understanding of the gap between "where we are" and "where we need to be".

Composition of the syndicates is worth some thought. If possible members have some organisational responsibility for the domain activities. However, it often proves productive to include in each syndicate a person from a different part of the organisation, to perform the function of "devil's advocate".

The steps covered by the groups are the following:

- Revisit project objectives
- Articulate present domain position
- Articulate critical success factors
- Analyse strengths/weaknesses.

First of all project objectives developed in the workshop earlier are made specific for the domain. The question addressed here is: "What domain objectives do we need in order to realise the overall objectives?" The domain objectives must be quite down to earth, and quantified as much as possible.

These are then compared to "where we are at the moment". This leads to understanding of the gap to be bridged, in quantitative terms as appropriate, against the objectives.

Bridging this gap requires consideration of the following two questions:

1. What are the critical success factors (CSFs), of an external or an internal nature, that will determine our ability to bridge the gap? This stage concerns the few developments that must go well. Typically the group is looking for around five CSFs. An example of a typical list of CSFs:

   - Externally: Demand for the product
     Attitude by the authorities
   - Internally: Distribution skills
     Motivated people
     Information system

2. Having thought through what needs to happen we need to ask: "Where does the organisation stand in terms of its ability to deliver? What are the strengths and weaknesses in the CSF areas?".

Both of these questions are addressed in brainstorming mode. The job entails identification and quantification of the gap, and assessment of the organisation's chances and ability to bridge it at some appropriate time in the future.

Following this step it is advisable to review the overall objectives in plenary. The facilitator brings everyone together, and leads a discussion on how the list of overall objectives needs to be modified. At this point the participants have given thought to what is involved in getting there, and this may throw a new and different light on the overall objective as formulated earlier. For example, second thoughts will have come up on the feasibility of some of the objectives. Or new ideas may have come up. A discussion in plenary is useful at this stage to ensure that the set of overall project objectives remains the accepted goal of the entire group.

Step 4. Development of action items

Having formulated the revised organisational objectives the syndicates review their earlier work and redefine the gap. The next step is to list in detail what needs to be done to bridge the gap. The following steps are involved:

- A list of actions is developed by systematically thinking through how the gap will be bridged.
- It has proven useful to remind syndicates specifically to include actions for building organisational capabilities, related to the development of Distinctive Competencies, as these are often overlooked.
- Actions are ordered in terms of priority.
- Syndicates indicate who is the responsible party for each action.

Finally syndicates summarise their findings under the following headings for each implementation domain:

- Domain objectives.
- Present position.
- Critical success factors.
- Actions per objective, including capability building.
- Relative priorities and approximate timing.
- Responsible party per action.

The facilitator collects this from all syndicates for subsequent editing and amalgamation in a report. The workshop breaks up at this point to allow the report to be prepared. The number of domains can be large, each addressing a number of objectives, which in turn each produces a list of actions. Therefore the resulting overview can be substantial and good editing is essential for the next step to progress smoothly.

Step 5. Development of action programme

As soon as the report is available it is circulated to all participants. This is the first time that people see how other syndicates have translated organisational objectives into actions. Following this the workshop reconvenes to discuss the amalgamated result.

First syndicates meet separately to discuss and comment on the actions developed in the other syndicates. Following this the comments are presented in plenary. The resulting discussion can be time consuming. Many alterations are proposed and adopted or rejected. At the end of this discussion the meeting needs to agree on the final set of organisational objectives. This step is crucial for ownership of the whole programme and therefore should not be rushed. The facilitator must ensure there is enough time available for this stage.

When reasonable agreement has been reached the actions, expressed as action subprojects, are written on cards. Each card contains a short title with a verb describing the essence of the action subproject, the approximate timing, together with the party, team or individual, responsible for its execution. It is useful to use different colours for different action parties. Each action item is individually vetted by the action party indicated. These cards are then displayed on a whiteboard in time order.

It is to be expected at this stage that too many action items end up for immediate execution, beyond the capacity of the organisation to cope. The colours show clearly who is overloaded, and how projects can be reallocated over people and over time. The final step is then to move action projects along the time axis until the total programme seems manageable. The new target times are copied on to the action cards.

Step 6. Reporting

The final step is for the facilitator to document the result obtained, indicating who is responsible for which project step, when progress is expected and what are the relative priorities. This final report subsequently becomes the basis for regular project appraisal meetings to assess progress in each subproject, and to adjust in the face of unexpected deviations.

Scenarios and Project Assessment

As in masterplanning, scenarios can play an important part in the development of a project. Large projects need to be considered against the longer-term future, and there will be considerable uncertainty around many key variables. By looking at the range of possible outcomes across a range of possible equally likely futures an indication is obtained of the robustness of the profitability assessment and uncertainty involved in the many aspects of the project. Large projects, which involve the organisation in commitments that are significant in comparison to its overall operation, should always be assessed against multiple futures.

BUDGET PLANNING

Once the organisation has, through masterplanning and project planning, obtained an idea of what it can reasonably hope to achieve it will want to create an overview of what the total plan looks like. There are a number of reasons why a management might want to develop an overall quantified business plan:

- Management needs to maintain overall coherence. For example, it needs to satisfy itself that resources are available for the plans formulated. Specifically they will want to make sure that cash resources are sufficient.
- Management may also want to compile an overall business plan for presentation to outside stakeholders, including shareholders, financiers or funding agencies.
- Another purpose of developing the overall business plan is to define budgets for control purposes across the organisation.

The activity is co-ordinated by the planning co-ordinator and often delegated to the finance/controller function, which collects the results of the deliberations and compiles the overall financial overview.

The activity can be particularly useful if it is part of the overall iterative planning process. The first results may not be quite acceptable to management, if these indicate that the total commitment would stretch the resources beyond what is considered prudent financial policy. In that case management may want to reconsider and postpone some projects that are now seen to be beyond its financial capability. Most budget planning takes place as part of an annual cycle, if only to set budgets and targets for the following year. In such a cyclical process strategic and implementation planning does not start from scratch and planning often boils down to adjusting last year's plans to take account of new developments and information. Therefore the overall plan normally is not too much of a surprise, and iteration proves to be a manageable activity.

APPRAISAL

In the introduction, the planning cycle was compared with the learning cycle (Figure 4). We compared strategic planning with the "building of mental models" stage, and masterplanning and project planning with the "planning new steps" stage. The learning loop is completed by reflection on the experience obtained as a result of the actions undertaken. In the planning cycle this is embodied in the appraisal of the actual performance. This may result in control action to bring things back on track, as articulated in the Business Idea and the associated objectives. In Part One we discussed this under single-loop learning (page 40). Or appraisal may give rise to awareness that the situation has changed enough to put the basic concept of the organisation (its Business Idea) in doubt. In this case the whole strategy concept has to be rethought. This we have called double-loop learning (in which generative scenario-based planning plays a role). See Figure 5, page 41.

Although appraisal goes on constantly at many different levels in the organisation (most intra-organisational interactions imply some level of informal appraisal at a person-to-person level), most organisations also operate a formal institutionalised system of appraisal of business units, and of individual performance appraisal. Actual performance as expressed in measured performance data, mostly generated by the accounts function, is compared with the budget for the same variables. If a significant difference opens up this is an indication that things are not working out as anticipated. An attempt is made to try to explain this difference, and control action may be undertaken, adjusting activity to achieve actuals closer to what was planned.

Appraisal processes are often compared with control feedback loops, where the state of the system is compared with a desired state and control action undertaken if the two deviate. There are a number of problems with this representation:

- In reality there are multiple decision centres deciding on goals. Several feedback loops interact, and sometimes counteract. And actions undertaken often are only a weak reflection of collective goal decisions by such decision centres, reflecting more the unco-ordinated private goals of the people down the line.
- In organisations that are not strongly centrally planned, interpretation and prioritising of goals is ambiguous. In such systems authorities often set goals that are expressions of values, without concrete criteria for error or success.
- Measuring the actual state of affairs is problematic too. Financial and economic variables can be quantitatively measured, but we often lack the conceptual tools to appraise the more value- and culture-based goals set to the organisation.

How can management address these problems?

The Dilemma Between Joint Learning and Accountability

Target setting and appraisal of actuals against these targets are essential parts of the managerial control function. Reasons for doing this are both hierarchical (making people accountable for their actions) and organic (creating organisational learning from experience).

In the accountability mode management looks back and requires people to account for the stewardship of the assets entrusted to them. Performance assessment takes place on the basis of predetermined appraisal categories. It is essentially an individual motivational activity, often officially linked to reward/penalty systems. In this context the relationship between the management and the appraisees is a political one, involving the exercise of power of one over the other. It is done to create and encourage accountability and commitment to the plan, to exercise shareholder responsibility and to inform parties of possible changes in the plans. It is related to solving problems, demonstrating realism in objectives and supporting credibility of the planning process. It is the exercise of single-loop learning, and aims to keep things on a predetermined track. However, focusing on making things happen loses sight of the appropriateness of the track.

Appraisal as part of organisational learning is sometimes called strategic evaluation, or guiding the strategic thinking process. It is double-loop learning, as the strategic goal is up for discussion. It involves a fundamentally different relationship, in which both parties attempt to reflect on and understand deviations, and to adjust mental models accordingly, as a basis of future planning. This can only be successfully done in an atmosphere of openness, in which knowledge about the situation is freely exchanged.

The appraisal activity puts management in a dilemma, between on the one hand emphasising accountability and on the other double-loop learning. Like all other managerial dilemmas this cannot be resolved once and for all but needs to be carefully managed.

To consider how this can be approached it is useful to go back to the concept of the learning loop. The driving forces behind the learning loop are threefold (see Part One, page 39):

- The need to adjust the system's behaviour to deal with external contingencies.
- The need to direct the system towards more favourable environments.
- The need to reorganise the system itself to make it more effective in these functions.

Normally the appraiser does not need to motivate organisational units to pursue these goals on their own accord. There is no pleasure for an organisational unit in underperforming or being pushed about by the competition in an unfavourable business environment. The substantive role of the appraiser relates to the higher hierarchical level imposing constraints on the behaviour of the lower levels to the extent required to create the desirable emergent behaviour of the whole. Creating synergy is the only substantive justification for a higher level imposing itself on the affairs of the units in the organisation. Synergy requires behavioural adjustments on the part of the members of the organisation and to bring this about is the concern of the appraisers.

A legitimate appraisal system requires a clear-cut understanding and expression of synergy in the organisation, in terms of its sources and related rules of the game. Unless the appraiser is specific on this there will be legitimate doubt about their contribution.

An organisation's appraisal system needs to start with consideration of the question of what constitutes the extra value of the overall organisation, over and above what its separate units, operating independently, would create. Examples of corporate synergy include:

- The central know-how pool, constituting the institutionalised memory of business experience.
- The identity of the organisation, associated with emergent behaviour of the whole.
- Reputation, based on history, size and scope.
- Portfolio management and overall optimisation through allocation of scarce resources, such as management, expertise, talent, capital.
- Cohesion and internal trust, leading to commitment.
- Development of "requisite variety" in thinking, to enable the organisation to broaden its perception of the business environment.

There are many synergy issues to be considered when discussing subsidiary behaviour. The underlying common element is to decide in what way belonging to the overall organisation will assist the subsidiary unit in driving its own learning cycle, including dealing with disturbances, finding its own "high ground" and organising for survival and success.

Analysing the appraisal role we inevitably have returned to the definition of the Business Idea of the organisation as a whole. It seems that appraisal effectiveness requires clear-cut answers to the corporate Business Idea question. Unless the overall Business Idea is fully understood it is not possible to define the appropriate appraisal criteria that steer units towards the desired overall behaviour. Unless the organisation has a clear and shared understanding of the Business Idea it is probably better to de-emphasise the accountability aspect of appraisal, and stress its joint learning and problem solving aspect. In the absence of a clear explicit understanding of what units should be accountable for, a general discussion is to be preferred, which leaves room for people's intuition to consider the whole terrain.

Chapter Sixteen

The Informal Strategic Conversation

So far we have discussed the elements of the formal planning activities in an organisation and the contribution made by scenario-based planning, focused on the Business Idea, to this strategic process. However, in many organisations the formal decision-making processes contribute only little to what is ultimately decided. Often the informal "learning" activity is much more important. It consists of unscheduled discussions, debate and conversation about strategic questions that go on continuously in the corridors and canteens at all levels in the organisation. It provides the environment of "good enough" trust in which people can explore ideas freely. They couldn't perform without it.

Embedded scenario thinking lives in this culture. Scenarios provide space. The new language of uncertainty is now not any longer disempowering. There is now "approval" to consider other perspectives. The conversation moves from arguing about, and defending, worldviews to negotiating action through a process of accommodation of alternative views.

Its introduction cannot be a "plug and play" decision by management. Introducing scenario-based planning in an organisation involves more than just introducing a new planning system. It can work only provided that the organisation has achieved the necessary level of sophistication in thinking that is compatible with the sophistication of the tool. Scenario-based planning co-evolves with the quality of strategic thinking in the organisation. Eventually it becomes largely self-organising, but there are some fundamental "rules of the game":

- There should be no premature decision making
- Every participant has permission to consider multiple perspectives and multiple futures

- Proactive attention for major uncertainties is encouraged
- Uncertainties should be stretched to the limit to explore implications
- Unusual conjunctions of events should be explored through development of consistent causal stories
- Unconnected ideas will be processed into a coherent framework, making them cognitively operational, and thereby introducing them in the emerging conversation
- Thinking time is allowed if ideas need to mature.

Like most other cultural characteristics of organisations such a shared thinking style can be a true Distinctive Competence, not easily emulated by competitors. This is the basis of its competitive advantage.

Scenario-based planning involves intervening in the general ad hoc conversation about strategy that takes place among cognitively "networked" people. Weick (1979) has argued that organisations can be interpreted as systems of cognitive loops, created through such interactions of members. As Bougon points out Weick created in this way a dynamic theory of organisational change (Bougon & Komocar 1990). Most theories concerning organisation are of a static nature, based on hierarchy and sources of influence. Change is replacing one steady state with another. For example, in order to implant a new strategic direction the CEO is replaced. However, such change projects are often unsuccessful, organisational behaviour often persists, notwithstanding the hierarchical changes made. It is the nature of conversational systems of loops that the resulting thinking can get locked into either a rigid or a fragmented pattern. It clarifies why patterns of behaviour can be strongly entrenched in organisations. Weick's ideas make it clear that lock-in, created by loops of influence, is a lot more complex than the hierarchical structure might imply. Organisational structure exists in action and interaction. The interaction takes place through conversation, some formal but most of it informal. Conversation leads to action, as illustrated in the learning loop (see Part One). Such systems of interactive loops behave rather differently than static models would imply. Because of the dynamic nature of systems of loops organisations are systems of change, the situation is dynamic, not static.

These systems of loops consist in conversations, which lead to action that changes the organisation, and the associated conversation. Figure 38 summarises this diagrammatically. To intervene in organisations is to intervene in these conversational/influence loops.

Successful organisations contain within their system of loops self-reinforcing feedback loops that drive growth. We have tried to map the essence of this in the Business Idea. Many of the other loops take the form of control feedback loops, which attempt to keep disturbances

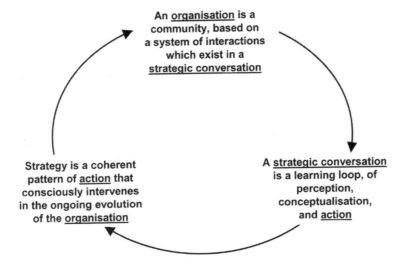

Figure 38. *The art of strategic conversation*

outside the system, in order not to interfere with the growth loop. If this has been operating successfully for some time the defence loops may become strongly entrenched. This often leads to the denial of signals of change, disabling the organisation from perceiving threats to its successful Business Idea. As we quoted Miller in the introduction, "nothing fails like success". It is in recognition of this danger that management may wish to broaden the field of vision of the organisation, by introducing scenario-based planning. A project of this nature benefits from awareness of the dynamic system of loops, involving both formal and informal processes of strategic conversation.

SCENARIOS AND THE INFORMAL EXCHANGE OF VIEWS

So what can management do to develop the level of sophistication of the strategic thinking culture?

First of all the formal part of the strategic conversation can be mapped out along scenario-based planning lines, including such activities as:

- Processes, systems, methods
- Explicit and implicit processes and topics
- Key meetings, decision points
- Budgeting, project evaluation

- Strategy reviews
- Cost-cutting exercises
- Product, capital, and market decision points.

Normally it is within management's power to ensure that scenario thinking is introduced in each of these activities and events. Management can require communications to take account of a scenario view of the business environment. In this way the organisation will become used to thinking in terms of multiple equally plausible futures, and incorporate scenarios in the day-to-day conversation, as shorthand to convey multiple business futures.

With scenarios introduced at appropriate points in the ongoing strategic conversation, they will gradually start to serve the following functions:

- Strategic conversation tools
- Awareness raisers
- Question raisers
- Conceptualisation tools and elements of language.

Eventually scenarios become the expression of the "meaning context" of organisational knowledge. Assigning meaning is the big challenge of knowledge management. The problem arises from the fact that organisations (and the world in general) partitions knowledge in disciplines, while strategically meaningful knowledge is always multi-disciplinary. The scenario methodology offers a way to meaningfully connect disciplinary knowledge, embedded in databases and experts, with cross-disciplinary strategy and organisational success.

Knowledge management preaches that human skills, expertise, and relationships are the most precious resources in an organisation. Knowledge managers may want to pay attention to the scenario method as an effective way for mobilising these.

Scenarios and the Corporate Language

If a set of scenarios is widely disseminated in an organisation they tend to become part of the corporate language. A well-chosen name becomes the shorthand for communicating a complex image of a particular future. In the conversation there is no need to go into detail, the other party knows what the scenario name stands for. This process can be assisted by the choice of *effective* names that need to be at the same time:

- Short (not more than two or three words)
- Descriptive of the essence of the scenario
- Memorable.

A good example of effective scenario names are the "flying" or "bird" names of the Mont Fleur scenarios mentioned in Part Three (page 241). "Ostrich", "Lame Duck", "Icarus" and "Flight of the Flamingos" call up images that clearly and efficiently characterise the nature of the story involved. Experienced scenario planners devote serious attention to the choice of good scenario names.

Once the scenarios have entered the corporate language they start having a major influence on corporate strategic thinking by triggering multiple equally plausible futures in conversations about strategy. This constitutes a major evolution in the thinking process in the organisation, from an episodic activity of trying to find the "one right answer" to an ongoing activity of trying to steer the organisation closer to a robust "high ground", where it will be less vulnerable to whatever business environment comes about. Scenario storylines have proven to be one of the most effective devices for mentally organising a large area of seemingly unrelated data. A set of corporate scenarios makes people in the organisation share a wider set of models with which events can be interpreted. This means that a wider range of events will be seen. For examples, see Chapter Eight (page 131).

An organisation that has reached this stage will see focused scenario projects emerge throughout the organisation, whenever a group of people are confronting a difficult or puzzling situation. Managers, people in charge of projects or masterplans, even appraisers will reach for the scenario planning tool to enhance their effectiveness. It will become apparent that a short and sharp scenario project, executed in a matter of days, or even hours if necessary, although not ideal, is nevertheless a lot more useful than looking at one projection. Eventually scenario-based planning will pervade all five levels of planning. It will no longer be seen as a management technique or tool, it will become a natural way of thinking about the future. Scenarios will provide new interpretations of what is going on in the environment, open new perspectives, and help the conversation as memorable thinking aids. And by developing understanding they will reduce anxiety about the future.

Institutional Process

But in order to function in this way scenarios need to be institutionalised. The degree of institutionalisation will depend on the situation in the organisation, its structure, its culture, and its experience with the scenario-based planning methodology. Various models can be distinguished:

- Scenario-based planning by planners on behalf of a management team.
- Scenario-based planning as a tool for management team discussion on corporate development.
- Scenarios as a tool used by management to influence the organisational agenda.
- Scenarios as a language to facilitate institutional discussion on corporate development.

Scenario-based planning typically starts in the management team as an aid to thinking and strategy development, as described in Part Three. If they become understood as instruments in the design of strategy they will quickly be adopted as tools for communicating strategic direction and objectives down the line. In a scenario-based planning culture it is impossible to discuss strategy without bringing in the various futures this has been based on.

Initially scenarios will be passed on to the organisation in presentations, and in written form. Scenario presentation, by top managers or their planners, is an important part of most scenario-based planning processes, and the next section discusses some aspects of this. The transfer of scenarios into the organisation can be improved by engaging teams down the line in strategic workshops in which they consider the strategic implications for them of the set of scenarios as developed by top management. Examples of such workshops are discussed below.

The final proof that scenario-based planning has arrived is when acceptance is such that corporate management incorporates it in the formal communication processes about strategy. Ultimately the most effective way to ensure institutional effectiveness of the scenario process is for management to make the scenarios part of the ongoing formal decision-making process. An example is given on page 9 where management required any project submitted for approval to be evaluated and justified on the basis of the going set of scenarios. It is a simple but powerful way to ensure that everyone pays attention to what is in the scenarios. The locking-in of scenario-based planning is completed when management realise the extent to which scenarios have come to influence decision making across the organisation, and consequently become deeply interested in their content. Once this state of affairs has been reached management will find that the organisation has acquired a powerful new management approach through which they can ensure that important themes are on the agenda, whenever decisions are made down the line in the organisation. A simple "rule of the game" of this nature firmly seals the scenarios in the strategic conversation, and provides a new degree of strategic integration between management and operations. Management can now afford to loosen the direct strategic control it exercises over organisational units.

Scenario Presentations

To become fully effective scenarios must become part of the language used in the organisation for discussing strategic questions. Depending on how far scenario-based planning has been embedded in the organisation the scenario team needs to undertake a few tasks in preparation for this "rolling out" process:

- Quantification of the scenarios to make them useful down the line, e.g. as input to project appraisal (as we saw on page 261, quantification can be useful for other purposes).
- Development of presentation, e.g. writing a scenario book, development of audio/visual media etc.
- Organising the institutional discussion process, through presentations, meetings, workshops, documentation etc.
- Institutionalising scenarios in the "rules of the game" of the formal decision-making process.

There are many ways in which scenarios can be publicised in the organisation. Most companies print a booklet with the scenarios as developed by the scenario team. GM used cartoons accompanied by audio tapes to convey the stories. Stentor used a series of vignettes. Another organisation used newspapers set in the future to communicate with staff and engage them in thinking about the future. Others just rely on presentations and videos/CD-ROMs – creative, colourful and attractive – as well as traditional reports. Modern technology provides multiple options in the form of inter/intranets, multimedia etc. reinforcing personal presentation. Whatever the medium used, there are a number of points of "good practice" in presenting scenarios that are worth keeping in mind. Scenarios can be characterised at many different levels, which all have a role in the organisational strategic conversation, and therefore need to be presented and discussed. The following is a list of representations from the simplest to the most complex:

- A symbolic icon
- A scenario name
- An end-state description
- Key events (what the story "is about")
- A story summary
- The main story strands
- Time behaviour of key variables
- Systemic representations
- A story–map
- An internally consistent story.

The first and foremost need is to engage the audience. This depends to a large extent on how "true" the story rings. In that respect the scenario presenter can learn from the courtroom analogy of good storytelling (Bennett & Feldman 1981, Hastie *et al.* 2002). This triggers some suggestions for scenario presenters, worth considering, such as:

- There is no basis for distinguishing true from false stories just on the properties of the narrative. The truth value of a scenario is related to how good a story is being told. A bad story is not easily believed, a good story is considered more plausible.
- Evidence proves a good story. Evidence in story order is believed more than just facts. (Evidence is nothing more than still another narrative.)
- Proof consists of a narrative connected to generally accepted beliefs, through more specific narratives, in a hierarchical ordering.
- Good stories have:
  - A readily identifiable central action. Everything is related to the central action, nothing sticks out on its own.
  - A context that provides a full and easy/natural explanation of why the central action happened and why the actors behaved as they did. Without that the story is ambiguous and unconvincing.
- In summary: contributors to truth value include:
  - The plausibility of the main narrative.
  - The number of elements in the narrative that are anchored.
  - Logical relationships between the evidence and the storyline detail.
  - Validity of the general beliefs in which the narratives are anchored.

The scenario structure

Reading/listening to and absorbing a number of different stories in a row is cognitively a demanding task. If the scenario presenter wants the audience to internalise a set of scenarios it is important that a cognitive framework is provided first, such that the listener can "place" each scenario and avoid confusion between one and the other. A number of examples for such frameworks were discussed in Part Three, pages 244, 246, 247. A popular approach places the scenarios in a 2×2 matrix, in which the scenarios are distinguished by reference to the two most impactful dimensions used to delineate the storylines. Following from this the scenario presenter may want to consider providing further help to the audience, including:

- Providing an overview of all scenarios and their differences as a road map for the audience.
- Explaining the logic of branching points, i.e. why these scenarios and not others.
- Rooting each story in history, i.e. showing logical cause-and-effect development from history to the present and on into the future.
- Highlighting the driving forces behind each scenario, in their systemic interaction.
- Summarising cause/effect logic of each scenario in simple logic diagrams.
- Selecting effective names for all scenarios.
- Minimising the use of text, and maximising the use of images, to emphasise the holistic character of the scenarios.

The following example of effective scenario presentation refers to the driving forces of liberalisation and cohesion/fragmentation in society. Figure 39 shows the way in which the two scenarios were summarised in one diagram. This showed in one simple context the most crucial elements of the analysis by the scenario team:

- The central role of liberalisation.
- The distinguishing contrasts of opportunity/threat and hope/fear.
- The distinguishing contrast between reinforcing feedback (growth) and stabilising feedback dynamics in the system presented.
- All this illustrated in the two evocative scenario names, New Frontiers and Barricades.

Once internalised this representation of the scenario structure is not easily forgotten.

The scenario presentation

The task of the presenter is to embed the scenarios in the memories of the audience. Many experienced scenario presenters like to tell the

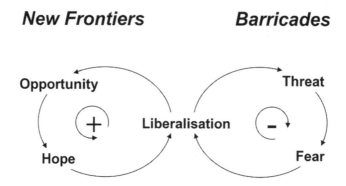

Figure 39. *Two scenarios about societal development*

stories in the past tense, i.e. from the perspective of an observer living in the end-state and looking back. We are quite used to making sense of past realities by telling stories as if all causal connections are known. This distinguishes histories from stories about the present, which we accept as a buzzing mess where we do not know causal relations (yet). A scenario in the past tense will feel like history being told, making it more credible.

The question is how complex stories can most effectively be presented in media such that they stick in the mind of the audience. A few approaches that scenario presenters have found useful over the years include:

- *Metaphors.* Compare the scenario story to a generally known phenomenon, if possible found in nature. Scenario names often are metaphoric, and this can obviously be exploited in the presentation.
- *Anecdotes.* Any logic structure can be humanised and personalised. Think like a novelist, i.e. think what the story is; *not* the issue, the story. Use narrative flow. Issues come later.
- *Repetition.* Tell essentially the same story a few times. Change the characters and the dialogue; change the setting; change the bells and whistles. But tell the same story.
- *Aphorisms.* Make up a few quotable sentences per scenario. Say them frequently.

In Part Three (page 264) we discussed the use of electronic media by scenario teams. Electronic communications have been used a lot in

---

Box 14   Suggestions to presenters by Donella Meadows (2001):

- Be concise. The public's attention is fleeting, come quickly to the argument.
- Be clear. Use everyday language, be specific, not abstract, use lots of easily imaginable examples, be sure the words make pictures in people's minds (the pictures that you want).
- Use three quarters of the time for evidence. Tell stories, give statistics, show impact.
- Use hooks to the news. People need to know why what they are about to hear is important. Daily news is important to them.
- Write an interesting lead.
- Avoid tone mistakes. Do not speak in a condescending, apologetic, defensive tone. Always have at least a hint of something positive.
- Tell it through people. Human beings are much more intrested in other human beings.
- Be humble. No human being knows much about anything. Say what you can say, with the appropriate degree of certainty, and no more.

---

scenario communication. The experience has been that communication "in the adjacent space" loses a lot in this relatively "narrow bandwidth" mode, compared to person-to-person communications. Recall that the scenario roll-out process in an organisation is not a matter of senders and receivers, but of making the stories start a life of their own in active conversation. However, for those who would otherwise not be reached directly the new media can be invaluable. The electronic communication offers the opportunity to engage a large number of people in scenario development across time and space.

The electronic media also have a powerful supporting role. Support materials, booklets, templates, reading etc., are never too much. Scenario-based planning is rational, but it is not entirely common sense. Operational managers, who never thought more than three months ahead, naturally take time to "get it" when hearing about scenario-based planning for the first time, and support materials help a lot.

In addition there is a need to experiment with new approaches to keep scenario development fresh and new, especially if individuals are involved in a series of scenario exercises over time. The new media can make an important contribution here.

Finally, presentations can only be decided upon when we know why they are being given. There are no general rules, only "tricks of the trade". Options should be evaluated on their effectiveness to reach the goal you have set for the presentation.

Scenario Workshops

However professionally the presentation of the scenarios is approached, there is a limit to what a passive audience can absorb in a lecture-type presentation. For a more effective process of transfer it is preferable to get the audience actively involved.

Scenarios can be highly effective as a basis for running strategy workshops. A typical model brings a team of managers together for a 24-hour period for a facilitated discussion. The discussion starts over dinner, with a short overview presentation of the scenarios and a free-ranging discussion of strategic implications. The following day the team meets to work this out more formally. This can be done by creating a situation in which they are made to retrace some of the steps in the thinking process of the scenario team. Alternatively the audience can be invited to work through each scenario by considering strategic implications.

Retracing the Scenario Building Process

The challenge here is to make the audience build their own scenarios, but at the same time make sure that they do this in the context of the conclusions reached by the management team. The essence of the thinking of management has to be transferred, but there must be enough room for the workshop audience to experiment themselves. An effective way to do this is by using the "event card" methodology developed by David Mason (page 237). In preparation the scenario team captures each scenario storyline in a series of illustrative events. These are transferred on to cards, one per event, giving a short description of the event and the timing in the scenario story. Typically one scenario might be reasonably highlighted by a series of 20 to 30 event cards. Altogether a scenario set might produce some 100 cards. The presenter hands over the cards in one pile in random order to the workshop audience. The task is to lay out the cards along a timeline, so as to create a number of logical scenarios. The workshop should be provided with plenty of empty event cards, and the audience should be invited to produce their own, as required to complete the storylines. They should be specifically encouraged to fill in local detail by creating events that make the scenarios particularly relevant to their own specific business situation.

In order to create a well-rounded workshop it is advisable to divide the group into a number of subgroups, and ask each to perform the task separately. When finished they are invited to present their results to each other. To round off the occasion the scenario presenter then explains how the management team organised the events in scenarios, and shows how this represents current understanding of driving force dynamics. The work in the syndicates will have prepared the audience and created a "need to know" which makes the final presentation a more effective transfer of knowledge. Having struggled with the events themselves the audience will be particularly interested in the way simple causal loop models can be brought to bear to organise events into storylines. Experience has shown that this is a powerful way of making scenario stories stick in the mind of the audience.

Implications Workshops

This type of workshop is modelled on the option planning activity as explained in Part Three, page 273. Here the scenario presentation takes place in a conventional lecture style, but the audience is invited afterwards to consider strategic implications by articulating strategic options that are indicated by the developments as discussed in the scenarios. This activity again best takes place in small syndicates, and is organised in two steps:

Step 1. Option generation by scenario

Each of the syndicates is allocated one of the scenarios. The task is to think through strategic options indicated by the developments in the scenario. This is in itself a two-step activity, in which the group first translates the scenario into terms that are relevant to their own specific business situation, and then consider how they would wish to react to such a train of events.

Step 2. Option evaluation across all scenarios

Following this the syndicates meet in plenary to create an overall list of strategic options generated by all syndicates. The next step is to cluster these options using Post-its in the by now familiar way, and to create a small number of generic strategies to be carried further. Each syndicate is allocated one or two of these, and the task is to evaluate the optional strategy across the scenarios. The first task is to consider the performance of the optional strategy in each of the scenarios. This is followed by a discussion of how the strategy could be made more robust across all futures considered. For example, the team may try to build in optional decision points in the future.

The last part of the task is to consider what signals should be followed in the environment to ensure that when the time for subsequent decisions arrives a better idea has been developed on where the business environment is heading.

One should not have exaggerated expectations of the outcomes of these types of workshops in terms of new strategy. This is not their primary objective, which remains to transfer the scenarios as effectively as possible. The discussion on strategic options is intended to focus the attention on the scenario futures, and to make the audience actively involved in them. It is important that the scenario presenter explains this sufficiently up front, such that expectations for the workshop remain realistic.

TREATING ORGANISATIONAL LEARNING PROBLEMS

An organisation that has scenario-based planning culturally embedded in its strategic conversation has developed a learning capability, in terms of the learning loop model as discussed in Part One. Specifically it has developed the following institutional capabilities:

- Increased institutional perception and awareness of the business environment through an enriched shared mental model, based on multiple scenarios functioning as institutional "memories of the future".
- Increased ability to make sense of a wider range of events based on this mental model.
- Acquired a rich language in which views can be discussed, compared and integrated.
- Enhanced action capability by addressing "management of change" issues (page 291), particularly dealing with learning disabilities and motivation.

As we saw in Part One (see "Learning Pathologies", page 45), the first task of managing organisational learning is to manage the dilemma between differentiation and integration, to avoid the dangers of the extremes of either fragmentation or groupthink in the organisation. Like any genuine dilemma, it cannot be resolved, it requires constant management. What can management do if it comes to the conclusion that the situation is out of balance, and requires correction?

Increasing Integration

Management may come to the conclusion that there is not enough integration in the organisation's strategic thinking. Symptoms include a lack of strategic discussion in the management team, a lack of a shared sense of direction, a lack of co-ordination in decision making, too much "us and them" feeling among factions in the organisation, a lack of openness, a political orientation in the way groups interact, manifesting itself in defensive routines, strategic implementation problems, generally people or groups "doing their own thing" without taking account of others, and so on. Under these circumstances management needs first of all to increase the "quantity" of strategic conversation. This can be done by creating conversational events during which people are brought together and encouraged to discuss strategy. These can range from small ad hoc affairs to large well-prepared gatherings.

Both top-down and bottom-up information exchange are important in the integration process. In the top-down mode management informs the organisation of the results of their strategic deliberations. A popular vehicle for this is the printed "mission statement", which management formulates to summarise conclusions reached as a result of the strategic thinking process they have gone through. Not all mission statements are equally valuable. Only those that are based on a strategic thinking process like the one described in this book can be considered worthwhile. A somewhat less formal way to achieve the same result is in the form of a confidential letter by the CEO to the organisation. Documents of this nature are expressions of the strategic objectives management have formulated, preferably following a quality strategic conversation process (see page 305).

On the other hand management may wish to communicate on strategic objectives in a two-way communication mode, in which the organisation is invited to participate in the development of the strategic objectives. Information meetings may be organised in which various levels of management interact with their reports on strategy and where dialogue is encouraged. Meetings of this sort are often organised as part of the planning cycle, for example as part of the strategic appraisal process.

Organising the bottom-up process is not a trivial matter. Because of hierarchical relationships good bottom-up strategic dialogue is not common. A special effort may be required from management to engage the organisation in such processes. An example of such a discussion is the Strategy Evaluation Session.

The Strategic Evaluation Session

The Strategic Evaluation Session is a relatively modest effort, in which top management engages in a dialogue about specific businesses with the business managers involved. In order to minimise barriers in the conversation a number of "rules of the game" need to be agreed in advance:

- The meeting is basically an interaction between the CEO and the business manager, with intermediate levels present, if desired.
- Initiative for the meeting may come from either the CEO or the business manager.
- Length of the meeting is typically half a day.
- The business manager refrains from advocating preferred lines of action, projects or expenditures.
- The CEO refrains from making decisions or suggesting particular lines of action.
- An initial presentation is made by the business manager, not by intermediate management layers.
- There are no formal minutes, only copies of presentation material are distributed.
- The participating group is kept small, maximum say 10 people.

The agenda of the meeting would typically include items under the following headings:

- The business environment scenarios
- The competitive position
- The Business Idea
- Optional strategies open to the business.

The purpose of the meeting is to increase understanding by the CEO of the business details, and by the business managers of overall strategy at the top. It is important that the process does not develop into a bureaucratic "rain dance". Documentation needs to be kept to a minimum, and any hand-out prepared by the business manager needs to be limited to one page only.

Increasing Differentiation

On the other hand, management may come to the conclusions that there is too much groupthink, and not enough "requisite variety" in ideas in the organisation. As we saw this can be a particularly dangerous state of affairs, as it leads to the organisation closing its mind unwittingly to processes of change in the environment, and thereby failing to adapt in time. It becomes important that the organisation starts putting increasing value on divergent views. An atmosphere needs to be created in which exploration and experimentation in the margin are encouraged. Management needs to reduce the top-down part of the strategic dialogue, and let the bottom–up process dominate. Clear signals are required from the top that the "maverick" view is valued. Tolerance for error needs to be increased, error should become a positive investment in the future, not a mistake to be punished.

In situations that are locked-in a clear signal from management may be required. This can take an organisational form, such as a reorganisation or reallocation of responsibilities. The purpose is to shake up the organisation and give a signal: "Things are changing, new ideas are rewarded."

Scenario-based planning can be particularly powerful in helping the organisation to increase its field of vision. In analogy with the model of "memories of the future" (see page 133) management needs to increase the number of different futures which play an active role in the strategic conversation. Scenarios can be seen as the memories of the future of the organisation. Just as a wider range of memories of the future helps the individual to see and perceive more of what happens around him, so can the organisation use a wider range of shared images of the future to spread its attention wider.

This mode of scenario-based planning relies heavily on outside impulses. The main purpose is to get the organisation to move outside its existing thinking box, and this can only be triggered externally. In this case management will want to pay particular attention to the introduction of appropriate "remarkable people" who have the capability to move the thinking on (see page 222). The introduction of these new ideas may be organised through a process known as an Innovation Search.

The Innovation Search

When a large number of people need to be involved in opening up the thinking, management can organise an Innovation Search. These are events in which up to 50 people can participate. The purpose is to develop ideas for future development of the business. Events of this nature need to be carefully prepared. The first step is to decide a list of focus areas in which the group will brainstorm. The organisers need to search widely to come up with as many candidate focus areas as they can. In consultation with management this list is prioritised and the top-ranking four or five are selected. This is the maximum that one workshop can deal with.

Participants need to prepare themselves for such a meeting by prereading. A folder of "stretching" material is prepared, containing articles from the literature with innovative ideas, and sent around in advance for people to read. The purpose is to get the thinking away from the conventional. Organisers need not be too careful with the quantity of material included, there is an advantage in sending more material than people can be expected to absorb. A degree of information overload will help in getting out of traditional "thinking boxes".

The setting within which the meeting takes place is important. This will need to be away from the workplace so that interruptions are minimised. The environment presented by the meeting room needs to point towards the purpose of the meeting, which is to come up with innovative ideas. The seating arrangement in the room should be visibly different from a usual meeting room. The atmosphere is informal, dress is casual. Participants are permanently reminded of the discussion topics by means of posters on the wall summarising each topic area in some visible way. An overall facilitator reminds participants frequently why they are there, and encourages them to write down any idea that comes up on an idea sheet, blank copies of which are made available to participants in large quantities. To emphasise the importance of idea generation the idea sheets are given a distinct appearance, using preprinting and colour.

During the meeting each of the focus areas is visited one by one. Approximately half a day is spent on each. The discussion is opened by a presentation discussing the relevance of the area to the organisation. This is done by someone from the organisation itself. This is followed with a presentation on how the topic area is seen from outside the organisation. This presentation needs to be prepared by an outside speaker, who is not part of the circle within which people in the organisation normally discuss the topic. Plenty of time needs to be allowed for discussion. The overall facilitator urges participants to continuously think about novel ways in which the organisation could improve and innovate its activities in the topic area. Breaks need to be scheduled frequently to allow participants to move around and discuss ideas with others one-to-one or in smaller groups of their choice. Participants are reminded to write down any ideas, however immature, on the idea sheets. These are collected frequently and the ideas are entered into a computer database in the backroom. Printouts are distributed at various times during the sessions to trigger further ideas. In true brainstorming style no quality judgements are made at this stage.

The meeting can be organised as an idea generation exercise only, as input to management consideration of strategy. It is important that participants are made aware of this in advance. People come to meetings expecting results or a "conclusion", and if instead the meeting ends without closure they will feel dissatisfied. In this case advance expectation management by the organisers is important to avoid disappointment and switch-off. In addition it is advisable to distribute a report after the meeting containing the ideas generated, hierarchically ordered in appropriate clusters, as a manifestation of what has been achieved.

If it is considered that the culture requires a more formal closure before the meeting breaks up participants may be asked to rank ideas. Usually a considerable number will have been generated and these need to be clustered first. Generally there is no time to cluster in plenary. Therefore clustering needs to be done in the backroom continuously as the ideas come in. Appropriate database software is a significant success factor in this process.

In a final step the facilitator may suggest that the group indicates action parties who will champion the specific innovation areas, at least until these have been incorporated as a strategic option in the company's strategy process.

PERSEVERANCE

We have been discussing a cultural phenomenon that cannot be implanted or turned around quickly. The scenario-based planning approach to institutional learning will stick in organisations if the requisite locking-in loops have been put in place among its networked people. In most cases for this to happen assumptions and values have to change. This takes time, and until this is the case management needs to continue to actively promote it. This is not a "get-rich quick" scheme for organisational development, effort must be sustained over time if the full benefits are to emerge. Making an organisation adaptable requires perseverance. However, for organisations interested in survival and self-development the rewards are fundamental, including:

- An organisation aware of its identity, in terms of its purpose, Business Idea, strategy and objectives.
- An organisation alert to change in its business environment and capable of reading signals of structural change early.

- An organisation making sense of rapid change in its environment and its own relation to that, and thereby being confident enough to look at the future in terms of opportunities rather than threats.
- An organisation coming to timely conclusions on specific actions to take.
- An organisation adapting more quickly and effectively to a changing environment than its competitors.

As this culture pervades throughout the organisation it will affect and alter the nature of the many links in the organisational system of cognitive loops. It will become all-pervasive. The high degree of adaptation skill required by the organisation will have become a systemic phenomenon, manifesting itself in all its strategy and decision making, independent of the particular individuals involved. For this reason it will be difficult to "prove" direct links between any specific scenario project and any specific strategy pursued. As Andre Benard (ex-Shell managing director) put it, "We are trying to make people think". There is no other way to develop better strategy. As this involves organisational culture it cannot be easily copied, and for this reason will be the source of genuine Competitive Advantage and organisational success. Or to quote Arie de Geus (ex-planning co-ordinator at Shell): "The ability to learn faster than your competitors may be the only sustainable advantage".

Conclusion

Organisations are systems of individuals linked together through a network of interconnections, largely based on conversation within a framework of rules and tacit assumptions. Organisations can be interpreted as complex adaptive systems, existing in cognitive loops, internally and through its environment, therefore subject to continuous change. These loops over time develop more and more complex mediating processes that intervene between external forces and behaviour. At higher levels of complexity these mediating processes become more independent and autonomous and more determinative of behaviour. Most of our organisational models are quite inadequate to make any reliable predictions of this. Much of the pattern of reactions to events that organisations display can be interpreted only after the event, in terms of "emergent strategy".

Generally managers do not accept that all organisational behaviour is emergent, they tend to believe in investing energy in trying to make the organisation more skilful in reacting to environmental input. A useful way of thinking about organisational behaviour is by the notion of organisational learning. Not all organisational behaviour can be learned. Fortunately in a competitive world one does not need to be perfect. If the organisation can react a little faster than its competitors to environmental impulses, seeing dangers and opportunities a little earlier, then it has a preferential position in the battle for survival. This idea makes managers highly interested in the processes of decision making in their organisation.

The starting point of our study of organisational behaviour has been the network of interconnecting conversations that make up the organisation. The exchange of ideas between individuals about the organisation in its environment is expressed in language. And the language of organisations is rational. People try to explain their point of view in terms of a rational argument. A rational argument carries weight.

This is why strategy is a discipline based on rationality. However, most managers realise that in an uncertain world skilful process is equally, if not more, important. And having paid due attention to rationality and process they realise that what happens nevertheless often feels like a "throw of the dice", and that one requires a lot of luck for survival. We have paid attention to all these perspectives on the managerial task. But the central theme throughout this book has been the importance of the strategic conversation, as the underlying mechanism in which organisations come into being and give shape to their actions.

We have concluded that strategic navigation by organisations through the world is based on making a fundamental distinction between the environment and the organisational self. Organisational learning is interpreted as the attempt to improve the fit between these two. The quality of the conversation can be focused more effectively on strategic navigation if the available language includes simple and ready concepts in which the self and the environment can be expressed in its essence. So we have spent time trying to consider such concepts. As we are ultimately considering questions of survival we have expressed the organisational self in terms of its "success formula". We have considered what elements need to be included in corporate success. This has led us to the concept of the Business Idea as a valid and sufficient characterisation of the organisation in the conversation about fit with the environment. An important aspect in this is the notion of uniqueness vis-à-vis competitors. Success is closely related to having something unique to offer. We have discussed how a management team can go about articulating the Business Idea for their own organisation.

We then moved on to the question of the characterisation of the environment. We have considered that this needs to be capable of looking into the future, which has led us to the question of how to deal with uncertainty. We have concluded that if there is uncertainty there is more than one feasible future, and we have introduced scenario-based planning, which uses a set of different but equally plausible futures, as a suitable way to characterise the environment and understand the uncertainty. We have discussed practical ways in which the environment can be captured in a set of scenarios.

This has led us to the problem of organisational perception. So far the discussion has been entirely based on rationality. If rationality was the whole story one sufficiently intelligent and knowledgeable person could do the thinking on behalf of the entire organisation. However, no person (or organisation) has a complete and perfect model of the situation to work with, therefore we have considered mechanisms by which organisations filter events in or out. This has led us to consideration of organisational cognitive processes, and how organisational learning takes place. We have identified two major flaws in these processes that require active management intervention, aiming for organisational mental capabilities that are to a degree contradictory. First of all the organisation needs differentiation in thinking, it needs to incorporate a wide range of different views to perceive, make sense of and react to what is happening over a wide range in the environment. But organisational learning also requires joint experiences that can only derive from joint action. Joint action requires integration of views. Here we have entered the realm of organisational process intervention. The individual, however intelligent and knowledgeable, can no longer do all the thinking. The organisation needs to consider the contribution of all individuals in it, and the effect of their interactions on strategy.

The first concern of management is to manage the dilemma between differentiation and integration in the organisation. At both sides of this continuum lurk pathologies, in the form of either organisational fragmentation or groupthink, both threatening survival. True dilemmas cannot be resolved, they need continuous management. This is the first task of a management who want to make their organisation more skilful in organisational learning. It requires management attention for the effectiveness of the strategic conversation in the organisation, both its formal and its informal parts. Management needs to identify intervention opportunities to steer away from organisational pathologies and towards creating effective organisational behaviour.

The institutional discipline of scenario-based planning offers approaches to management to do this effectively. It provides the organisation with concepts such as the Business Idea and the environmental scenarios, which become powerful elements in the organisational learning process. Multiple perspectives and differentiation in thinking is a fundamental part of the scenario approach. They become institutional concepts and language objects, used by the members of the organisation to make their strategic conversation more skilful and meaningful. In this way they enter institutional memory, and make the organisation more aware of what is going on outside, in a way that allows it to understand the meaning of signals and impulses. Shared concepts and stories then allow it to share conclusions, and therefore react faster. This richer arsenal of shared concepts becomes embedded in the language and culture, and in this way influences and mobilises the learning skills of the organisation as a whole.

This cultural aspect suggests that creating a learning organisation is not "plug and play", but requires a high degree of perseverance on the part of management and the organisation. The various practical implementation tools discussed in this book are not difficult; what is difficult and takes time, energy and persistence is to stick with them until they have become part of the corporate culture, as part of the "way we do things over here". This is only to be expected. "Cheap and easy" success is a contradiction in terms. A simple formula that would seem to work quickly would be copied by everyone, become a hygiene factor and lose its competitive power.

Strategic success cannot come cheap and easy. If there is one element essential to success it is being able to develop new and unique insights about the world. Without this no strategy can succeed. An original invention does not come easy, it needs a lot of time, discussion and contemplation. The strategic conversation in the organisation is the basis of its ability to gain such original insights. It can be powerfully supported by the two modes of scenario-based planning we have discussed, the adaptive approach aiming for continuous and fluid adaptation to the ongoing changes in the business environment, and the generative approach aiming for fundamental reinvention of the organisation's formula for success.

We are dealing with a complex cultural phenomenon, which can be turned around only slowly with a lot of energy and perseverance. But once you're there and have gained sight of the structure and predetermined elements of the situation, yes, it is possible to "see" the future, and your own unique position in it.

References

Allen, J., Fairtlough, G. & Heinzen, B. (2002), *The Power of the Tale: Using Narratives for Organisational Success*, John Wiley & Sons, Ltd, Chichester

Amara, R. & Lipinsky, A.J. (1983), *Business Planning for an Uncertain Future, Scenarios and Strategies*, Pergamon Press, New York

Argyrus, C. & Schon, D. (1978), *Organizational Learning: A Theory of Action Perspective*, Addison Wesley, Reading, MA

Ashby, W.R. (1983), Self-regulation and requisite variety, in Emery, F.E. (ed), *Systems Thinking*, Penguin, New York

Bandler, R. & Grinder, J. (1982), *Reframing, Neuro-linguistic Programming and the Transformation of Meaning*, Real People Press, Moab, Utah

Bateson, G.W. (1967), *Mind and Nature*, Dutton, New York

Bateson, G.W. (1972), *Steps to an Ecology of Mind*, Ballantine, New York

Benard, A. (1980), World oil and cold reality, *Harvard Business Review*, Nov–Dec 1980, 91–101

Bennett, W.L. & Feldman, M.S. (1981), *Reconstruction Reality in the Courtroom*, Tavistock, London

Bougon, M.G. & Komocar, J.M. (1990), Directing strategic change, a dynamic holistic approach, in Huff, A.S. (ed), *Mapping Strategic Thought*, John Wiley & Sons, Ltd, Chichester

BP Statistical Review, The British Petroleum Company Plc, Britannia House, 1 Finsbury Circus, London EC2M 7BA

Brand, S. (1999), *The Clock of the Long Now, Time and Responsibility*, Basic Books, New York

Buzzell, R.D. & Gale, B.T. (1987), *The PIMS Principles, Linking Strategy to Performance*, The Free Press, New York

Checkland, P. (1981), *Systems Thinking, Systems Practice*, John Wiley & Sons, Ltd, Chichester

Christensen, C.M. (1997), *The Innovator's Dilemma, When New Technologies Cause Great Firms to Fail*, Harvard Business School Press, Boston, MA

De Geus, A.P. (1988), Planning as learning, *Harvard Business Review*, vol 66, no 2, 70–74

Douglas, M. (1986), *How Institutions Think*, Syracuse University Press, New York

Eden, C. (1987), Problem solving/finishing, in Jackson, M. & Keys, P. (eds), *New Direction in Management Sciences*, Gower, Aldershot

Eden, C. (1992), Strategic management as a social process, *Journal of Management Studies*, vol 29, 799–811

Eden, C. & Ackermann, F. (1998), *Making Strategy, the Journey of Strategic Management*, Sage, London

Einhorn, H.J. & Hogarth, R.M. (1982), Prediction, diagnosis and causal thinking in forecasting, *Journal of Forecasting*, 22–36

Emery, F.E. & Trist, E.L. (1965), The causal texture of organisational environments, *Human Relations*, vol 18, 21–32

Erasmus, D. (1999), *Mastering Information Management, a Common Language for Strategy*, Financial Times, London

Freeman, S. (1984), *Strategic Management*, Pitman, London

Galer, G. & van der Heijden, K. (1992), The learning organisation, how planners create organisational learning, *Information Systems for Strategic Advantage*, vol 10, no 6, 5–12

Gerstner, L.V. (2002), *Who Says that Elephants Can't Dance*, HarperCollins, New York

Goold, M., Campbell, A. & Alexander, M. (1994), *Corporate Level Strategy, Creating Value in the Multi-business Company*, John Wiley & Sons, Inc, New York

Goold, M. & Quinn, J.J. (1990), *Strategic Control, Milestones for Long Term Performance*, Hutchinson, London

Grant, R.M. (1991), The resource-based theory of competitive advantage, *California Management Review*, vol 23, Spring 1991, 114–135

Haeckel, S.H. (1999), *Adaptive Enterprise: Creating and Leading Sense-and-Respond Organizations*, Harvard Business School Press

Hamel, G. (2000), *Leading the Revolution*, Harvard Business School Press, Boston, MA

Harris, P.L. (2000), *The Work of the Imagination*, Blackwell Publishing, Oxford

Hart, S. & Banbury, C. (1994), How strategy-making processes can make a difference, *Strategic Management Journal*, vol 15, 251–269

Hastie, R., Penrod, S.D. & Pennington, N. (2002), *Inside the Jury*, The Lawbook Exchange Ltd

Ingvar, D. (1985), Memories of the future, an essay on the temporal organisation of conscious awareness, *Human Neuro-biology*, 1985/4, 127–136

Janis, I. & Mann, L. (1977) *Decision Making: A Psychological Analysis of Conflict Choice and Commitment*, Free Press, New York

Johnson, G. & Scholes, K. (2002), *Exploring Corporate Strategy* (6th ed), Financial Times Prentice Hall, London

Kahane, A. (1992a), Scenarios for energy, sustainable world versus global mercantilism, *Long Range Planning*, vol 25, no 4, 38–46

Kahane, A. (1992b), The Mont Fleur Scenarios, *Weekly Mail and The Guardian Weekly*, Bellville, SA

Kahn, H. & Wiener, A. (1967), *The Year 2000*, Macmillan, New York

Kauffman, S. (1995) *At Home in the Universe: The Search for the Laws of Complexity*, Viking, London

Kay, J. (1993), The structure of strategy, *Business Strategy Review*, vol 4, no 2, 17–37

Kelly, K. (1994), *Out of Control: The Rise of Neo-biological Civilization*, Addison Wesley, Reading, MA

Kemeny, J., Goodman, M. & Karash, R. (1994), Starting with storytelling, in Senge, P. *et al.* (eds), *The Fifth Discipline Fieldbook*, Doubleday Currency, New York

Kirkland, R.I. (1987), L.C. van Wachum, Royal Dutch/Shell, *Fortune*, 3 August 1987, vol 116, 28

Kolb, D. & Rubin, I.M. (1991), *Organizational Behavior, an Experiential Approach*, Prentice Hall, Englewood Cliffs, NJ

Lewin, K. (1935), A Dynamic Theory of Personality, *Selected Papers*, McGraw-Hill, New York

Lindblom, C.E. (1959), The science of muddling through, *Public Administration Review*, vol 19, 79–88

Lorenz, C. (1993), Avoiding the IBM trap, *Financial Times*, 15 October 1993, 18

Marsh, B. & van der Heijden, K. (1993), System thinking and business strategy, *Systems Thinking in Action Conferences*, 8 November 1993, Boston, MA

Martin, P. (1997), Look out, it's behind you, *Financial Times*, 15 May 1997, London

Meadows, D. (2001), Dancing with systems, *Whole Earth*, #106, Winter 2001, 58–63

Michael, D.N. (1973), *On Learning to Plan and Planning to Learn*, Jossey-Bass, San Francisco, CA

Michael, D.N. (1998), *Barriers and Bridges to Learning in a Turbulent Human Ecology*, vol 2, no 2, Presearch series, GBN, Emeryville, CA

Miller, D. (1993), The architecture of simplicity, *Academy of Management Review*, vol 18, no 1, 116–138

Miller, G.A. (1956), The magical number seven, plus or minus two, some limits on our capability for processing information, *Psychology Review*, vol 63, no 2, 81–96

Mintzberg, H. (1979), Patterns in strategy formation, *Management Science*, 1979

Mintzberg, H. (1990), The design school, reconsidering the basic premises of strategic management, *Strategic Management Journal*, vol 11, 171–195

Mintzberg, H. (1994), *The Rise and Fall of Strategic Planning*, Prentice Hall, Hemel Hempstead

Mintzberg, H. & Waters, J. (1985), Of strategies, deliberate and emergent, *Strategic Management Journal*, vol 6, 257–272

Mohr, L.B. (1982), *Explaining Organizational Behaviour, the Limits and Possibilities of Theory and Research*, Jossey-Bass, San Francisco

Morgan, G. (1986), *Images of Organisation*, Sage Publications, Beverly Hills, CA

Normann, R. (1977), *Management for Growth*, John Wiley & Sons, Ltd, Chichester

Normann, R. (1984), *Service Management, Strategy and Leadership in Service Businesses*, John Wiley & Sons, Ltd, Chichester

Normann, R. (2001), *Reframing Business, When the Map Changes the Landscape*, John Wiley & Sons, Ltd

Normann, R. & Ramirez, R. (1994), *From Value Chain to Value Constellation, Designing Interactive Strategy*, John Wiley & Sons, Ltd, Chichester

Perkins, D.N., Allen, R. & Hafner, J. (1983), Differences in Everyday Reasoning, in Maxwell, W. (ed), *Thinking: The Frontier Expands*, Erlbaum, Hillsdale, NJ

Pettigrew, A. & Whipp, R. (1991), *Managing Change for Competitive Success*, Blackwell, Oxford

Porter, M.E. (1980), *Competitive Strategy, Techniques for Analyzing Industries and Competitors*, The Free Press, New York

Porter, M.E. (1985), *Competitive Advantage, Creating and Sustaining Superior Performance*, The Free Press, New York

Quinn, J.B. (1980), *Strategies for Change, Logical Incrementalism*, Irwin, Homewood, IL

Quinn, L.L. & Mason, D.H. (1994), How digital uses scenarios to rethink the present, *Planning Review*, vol 22, no 6, 14–17

Ramirez, R. & Wallin, J. (2000), *Prime Movers, Define your Business or Have Someone Define it Against You*, John Wiley & Sons, Ltd, Chichester

Rosell, S.A. (1995), *Changing Maps, Governing in a World of Rapid Change*, Carleton University Press, Ottawa

Rumelhart, D.E. (1980), Schemata, the building blocks of cognitions, in Spiro, R.J., Bruce, B.C. & Rewer, W.F. (eds), *Theoretical Issues in Reading Comprehension*, Erlbaum, Hillsdale, NJ

Rumelt, R.P. (1987), Theory, strategy and entrepreneurship, in Teece, D.J. (ed), *The Competitive Challenge*, Ballinger, Cambridge, MA

Rumelt, R.P., Schendel, D. & Teece, D.J. (1991), Strategic management and economics, *Strategic Management Journal*, vol 12, 5–29

Schein, E. (1992), *Organizational Culture and Leadership*, 2nd edition, Jossey Bass, San Francisco, CA

Schoemaker, P. (1992), How to link strategic vision to core capabilities, *Sloan Management Review*, vol 34, no 1, 67–81

Schoemaker, P. & van der Heijden, K. (1992), Integrating scenarios into strategic planning at Royal Dutch/Shell, *Planning Review*, vol 20, no 3

Schrage, M. (2000), *Serious Play, How the World's Best Companies Simulate to Innovate*, Harvard Business School Press, Boston, MA

Schwartz, P. (1991), *The Art of the Long View*, Doubleday Currency, New York

Schwartz, P. (1992), Composing a plot for your scenario, *Planning Review*, vol 20, no 3, 4–9

Schwartz, P. & Gibb, B. (1999), *When Good Companies Do Bad Things, Responsibility and Risk in an Age of Globalization*, John Wiley & Sons, Inc, New York

Selznick, P. (1957), *Leadership in Administration*, Harper and Row, reissued in 1984 by University of California Press, Berkeley, CA

Senge, P. (1990), *The Fifth Discipline*, Doubleday, New York

Simon, H.A. (1971), Designing organizations for an information-rich world, in Greenberged, M. (ed), *Computers, Communications and the Public Interest*, pp 40–41, The Johns Hopkins Press, Baltimore

Simon, H.A. (1979), *Models of Thought*, Yale University Press, New Haven

Smith, G.N. & Brown, P.B. (1986), *Sweat Equity, What It Really Takes to Build America's Best Small Companies – By The Guys Who Did It*, Simon and Schuster, New York

Stepanec, M. (1999), How fast is net fast, *Businessweek Online*, Nov 1, 1999 issue

Stern, W. (1906), *Person and Sache*, Verlag von Johann Ambrosius Barth, Leipzig

Teece, D.J. (1986), Firm boundaries, technological innovation and strategic management, in Thomas, L.G. (ed), *The Economics of Strategic Planning*, Lexington Books, Lexington, MA

van der Heijden, K. (1993), Strategic vision at work, discussing strategic vision in management teams, in Hendry, J. & Johnson, G. (eds), *Strategic Thinking, Leadership and the Management of Change*, John Wiley & Sons, Ltd, Chichester

van der Heijden, K. (1994), Probabilistic planning and scenario planning, in Wright, G. & Ayton, P. (eds), *Subjective Probability*, John Wiley & Sons, Ltd, Chichester

van der Heijden, K., Bradfield, R., Burt, G., Cairns, G. & Wright, G. (2002), *The Sixth Sense, Accelerating Organisational Learning with Scenarios*, John Wiley & Sons, Ltd, Chichester

Vickers, G. (1965), *The Art of Judgment*, Chapman and Hall, London

Vygotsky, L.S. (1986), *Thought and Language*, MIT Press, MA

Wack, P. (1985a), Scenarios, uncharted waters ahead, *Harvard Business Review*, Sep–Oct 1985, 73–90

Wack, P. (1985b), Scenarios, shooting the rapids, *Harvard Business Review*, Nov–Dec 1985, 131–142

Weick, K.E. (1979), *The Social Psychology of Organizing*, Addison Wesley, Reading, MA

Weick, K.E. (1990), Cartographic myths in organizations, in Huff, A.S. (ed), *Mapping Strategic Thought*, John Wiley & Sons, Ltd, Chichester

Whittington, R. (1993), *What Is Strategy and Does it Matter?* Routledge, London

Index

Index

Index compiled by Annette Musker